Bra[illegible]

2005

# Event
## & PARTY
### RESOURCE GUIDE

bravoportland.com

A comprehensive guide featuring over 400 venues and services for oregon and sw washington

mary lou burton

**Bravo!® Publications, Inc.**
**P.O. Box 1647**
**Lake Oswego, Oregon 97035**
**503.675.1380, 800.988.9887; Fax 503.675.1204**
**bravoportland.com**

*This resource guide is comprised of paid advertisements. Although advertisers must meet a quality level of standards to be featured in this guide, Bravo! Publications, Inc. cannot and does not guarantee or take responsibility for services provided by said advertisers. No affiliation exists between Bravo! Publications, Inc. and any advertiser featured. Every reasonable effort has been made to provide the most accurate and up-to-date information. The copyright of each individual vendor page is held by that vendor, and has been used with permission by that vendor. Any questions regarding content on the individual vendor pages should be directed to the vendor directly. We assume no responsibility for errors, inaccuracies, or misrepresentations by any of the vendors listed in this publication.*



Printed in the United States of America

ISBN #1-884471-35-8

# TABLE OF CONTENTS

## ENTERTAINMENT – BANDS ........................................269-282



## ENTERTAINMENT – CONSULTANTS ...........................283-288



## ENTERTAINMENT – DISC JOCKEYS ...........................289-296



## ENTERTAINMENT – MUSICIANS ...............................297-302

## EVENT DESIGN & PRODUCTION ..................................303-304



## EVENT PLANNERS ..................................................305-314



## EVENT PROFESSIONAL ORGANIZATIONS ......................315-334



## EVENTS & FESTIVALS ..............................................335-338

# ACKNOWLEDGEMENTS

This Guide would not have been possible without the hard work, dedication, and endless hours from the following people:

**Publisher**
Mary Lou Burton

**Account Managers**
Denise Hall
Tracy Martin
Jennifer Maust
Carinne McCulloch

**Production Manager**
Amy Drews

**Production Assistant**
Katalin Linder

**Web Design**
Amy Drews

**Trade Show**
Denise Hall
Tracy Martin
Carinne McCulloch

**Office Assistant**
Olga Zaytsev

**Public Relations**
Terri Wheeler

**Special Projects**
Helen Kern

**Database Design/Online Registration**
Denise Hall
Margaret Chapman

**Prepress & Printing**
Lynx - *Salem, Oregon*
*www.lynxgroup.com*

COVER
**Cover Design**
Amy Drews

**Mary Lou Burton**

All great things begin with only a single thought. On her honeymoon, with the planning of her huge Italian wedding still fresh in mind, she and husband, John, relished in the thought of having a single resource to use when planning such an important event. Turning that into reality, Mary Lou and friend Marion Clifton crafted the first Bravo! Publications Wedding Resource Guide in 1990 with an Apple IIe and a single-sheet bubble-jet printer. By 1994, the idea was taken a step further into publishing the first Event Resource Guide to hit the Oregon and Southwest Washington market. Mary Lou is proud to announce the birth of yet a third resource aimed at another unanswered market starving for attention. The Family Resource Guide marked its debut in April 2002.

Life is never quiet at the Burton household. Graced with husband and best friend, John, for over 15 years, and four wonderful children: Alex, Nick, Will and Greta, Mary Lou is no stranger to the need for an organized, simple way to entertain, educate, and care for her family. She dedicates her life to acting with intention: if it is going to bring a smile upon a sad face, light the fire within a soul, or illuminate a cloudy path, she will find the time and energy to accomplish it. Admired and respected within the event industry, Mary Lou finds her ability to persevere both personally and professionally in the inspiration and support of her husband. "It would all still be just an idea without his positive 'can do' attitude," says Mary Lou.

**Carinne McCulloch**

After several years in the recreation industry and a previous client of Bravo! herself, Carinne now is the company's veteran at nine years and counting! A graduate of Oregon State University, she takes her Beaver football seriously, while experiencing the many ups and downs of "game day." She and her husband, Derek, are enjoying life from a child's perspective with their daughters Hailey, 5, and Aiden, 2.

**Amy Drews**

Amy joined the Bravo! team seven years ago as Production Manager and Web Designer after graduating from Valparaiso University with a degree in Communications. When not renovating their 1920s bungalow or trying to train their dog, Madi, she and husband, Jason, can be found training for their next ultra marathon, trail running, skiing, cooking, oil painting and spending time with family and friends.

**Tracy Martin**

Tracy joined Bravo! six years ago as an Account and Show Manager, planning and managing the Bravo! Showcase. She and husband, Darin, are enjoying their sons Grayson and Austin. Tracy expects the coming years to be filled with soccer games, muddy footprints, pet snakes and all kinds of surprises stored as keepsakes in those jean pockets!

### Helen Kern

In charge of Bravo! Human Relations for the past five years, Helen is not only Mary Lou's mother but a mother to all of us as well. There isn't a day that goes by where the grapefruit, fresh flowers or tasty treats aren't topped with a beautiful smile and a lot of love. Her inspiration, parenting advice (as a mother of nine herself), and charisma are all integral to the morale here at the office.

### Jennifer Maust

Jen joined the Bravo! team five years ago as a Marketing Manager. She obtained her Bachelor of Science degree from Portland State University in 1997. Jen added home owner to her resume, and when not busy designing, decorating or landscaping, most would expect to find her biking, traveling and in the company of good friends.

### Denise Hall

Denise is beginning her third year working at Bravo! After teaching elementary school for many years, she occasionally fills in as a substitute teacher to keep her license current. She spends her free time looking for new athletic adventures and trying to convince her friends to join her. She also enjoys reading and her monthly book club. She and her husband, Tom, are busy with house projects and are waiting for their new puppy, Penny, to join them and older sister Abby.

### Katalin Linder

Katalin joined Bravo! in June 2003 as a production assistant after graduating from the University of Oregon with a degree in Journalism and Public Relations. She spends her free time reading, working out and looking for new projects and inspirations as an amateur photographer. Katalin loves to travel and makes frequent trips to Missoula, Montana to visit her boyfriend, Kyle, of five years and their golden retriever, Dudley.

### Alison Gullion

Alison left Bravo! in August 2002 to pursue a lifelong goal, and rejoined the team in November of 2003 to help Bravo! achieve another. In the spring of 2004, she graduated with her Masters in Counseling and simultaneously played an integral role in Bravo!'s first annual Showcase of the Hospitality and Meeting industry in Orlando, FL. She has spent a lifetime enjoying outdoor sports and recognizes passion, perspective, and fun as essential elements in her life. "We work hard to play hard!"

### Olga Zaytsev

Olga joined Bravo! in May 2004 to assist with the Bravo! Showcases and special projects. She recently graduated high school at the age of 16, and plans on attending PCC in January 2005. When she's not working, she can be found at the gym, shopping for the latest fashions, going to church and spending quality time with her boyfriend.

# SPREAD THE WORD!

## We need your help

To continue to supply this Guide to you at no charge we rely on you, the reader, to let the businesses and services in this book know that you heard about them through the *Bravo! Event and Party Resource Guide*. Our featured businesses will recognize the Bravo! name.

## Pass it on to a friend

Before they walk away with your copy, let them know they can fill out the order form on page 21 or visit bravoportland.com to receive their own complimentary copy.

## Say You Saw It In Bravo!

Every business or service needs to track where their business is coming from. By letting them know you are using one of the *Bravo!® Resource Guides*, you not only ensure that Bravo!® will be available for meeting and event planners in the future, but you also let the businesses or services know where you heard of them.

**Visit our Web site:**
**www.bravoportland.com**

# ORDER FORM

Pass this form onto a friend

***I would like to order the***

## Bravo! Event & Party Resource Guide

***The Guide is free to pre-qualified meeting planners***

❒ *Portland • Vancouver • Salem '05 Edition*

❒ *Greater Puget Sound '05 Edition*

**To receive your Guide, please fill out the information below and mailor fax to Bravo!**

**Name:** ______________________________

**Title:** ______________________________

**Company Name:** ______________________________

**Address:** ______________________________

**Mail Stop:** ______________________________

**City:** ______________ **State:** ________ **Zip:** ________

**Phone:** ______________ **Fax:** ______________

**E-mail:** ______________________________

**Type of Business:** ______________________________

**What type of events do you plan?**
*(Circle all that apply)*

- Conferences
- Conventions
- Fundraisers
- Golf Tourneys
- Holiday Parties
- Meetings
- Parties
- Picnics
- Retreats
- Seminars
- Special Events
- Trade Shows
- Other:

**Number of attendees you plan for**
*(Circle all that apply)*

- 1-50
- 51-100
- 101-250
- 251-500
- 501-1,000
- Over 1,000

***Send order to:*** **Bravo! Publications, Inc.**
P.O. Box 1647 • Lake Oswego, OR 97035
(503) 675-1380, (800) 988-9887; Fax (503) 675-1204; E-mail: info@bravoportland.com
www.bravoportland.com

**Great Ideas for your:**
Company Picnics, Holiday Parties, Auctions, Meetings & Seminars, Team Building Events

# Wednesday, October 19th, 2005

## Noon –6pm • Oregon Convention Center

*Fill out this form to receive an invitation.*

**Name:** ______________________________

**Title:** ______________________________

**Company Name:** ______________________________

**Address:** ______________________________

**Mail Stop:** ______________________________

**City:** ______________ **State:** ________ **Zip:** ________

**Phone:** ______________ **Fax:** ______________

**E-mail:** ______________________________

**Type of business:** ______________________________

**What type of events do you plan?**
*(Check all boxes that apply)*
- C–Conventions
- F–Fundraisers
- G–Golf Tourneys
- X–Holiday Parties
- M–Meetings
- S–Seminars
- N–Conferences
- T–Parties
- P–Picnics
- W–Trade Shows
- R–Retreats
- E–Special Events
- O–Other Functions

**Number of attendees you plan for**
*(Check all boxes that apply)*
- 1–50
- 51–100
- 101–250
- 251–500
- 501–1,000
- Over 1,000

***Send RSVP to:*** **Bravo! Publications, Inc.**
P.O. Box 1647 • Lake Oswego, Oregon 97035
(503) 675-1380, (800) 988-9887; Fax (503) 675-1204; Web site: www.tradeshows.com

# BRAVO!® RESOURCE GUIDES

## When you want information, not glossy ads—you want Bravo!

Bravo! Publications is proud to offer five regional *Resource Guides* for planning meetings, events, weddings and family activities. Each of the Guides featured on this and the following page is filled with important information and details about the area's finest businesses and services providers, and is presented in easy-to-read, resumé style formats, alphabetically, by category. Designed to be user-friendly, each of these Guides truly are your planning *Resource*!

### Greater Puget Sound
### *Event Resource Guide*

*Venues, Attractions & Activities, Audience Participation, Ad Specialties, Corporate Gifts & Awards, Food & Beverage Services, Accommodations, and more...*

**The 2005 Edition features 674 pages** of easy-to-read, resumé-style write-ups on area businesses and service providers, listings of area Banquet and Event Sites, how-to's, check lists, and all the helpful hints you've come to expect from Bravo!

**Suggested Retail: $11.95**

### Greater Puget Sound
### *Bridal Resource Guide*

*Churches, Chapels, Banquet & Reception Sites, Caterers, Florists, Photographers, Videographers, Invitations, Bridal Attire, Tuxedo Rentals, Bridal Registry, Favors, Accessories, Consultants and more...*

**The 2005 Edition features 672 pages** of easy-to-read, resumé-style write-ups on area businesses and service providers, listings of area Banquet and Reception Sites, how-to's, check lists, and all the helpful hints you've come to expect from Bravo! Available January 9, 2004

**Suggested Retail: $9.95**

**TO ORDER CALL 888-832-7286**

**Bravo! Family Resource & Activity Guide**

Oregon and Southwest Washington

Activities and Attractions, Camps, Clothing Stores, Family Activities, Music and Arts, Toy and Learning Stores and more...

352 pages area businesses and service providers, how-to's, articles, camp/education listings and valuable coupons make this an indispensable guide for moms, dads, grandparents and teachers alike.

Available throughout the Portland/Vancouver metro area.

**Bravo! Event & Party Resource Guide**

Oregon and Southwest Washington

Venues, Accommodations, Audience Participation, Gifts & Promotional Items, Food & Beverage, Rental Services and more...

The 2005 Edition features 528 pages

of easy-to-read, resumé-style write-ups on area businesses and service providers, listings of Banquet and Event Sites, how-to's, checklists and all the helpful hints.

Complimentary to pre-qualified Meeting and Event Planners.

**Bravo! Wedding Resource Guide**

Oregon and Southwest Washington

Churches, Chapels, Banquet & Reception Sites, Caterers, Florists, Photographers, Videographers, Invitations, Bridal Attire, Tuxedo Rentals, Bridal Registry and more...

The 2005 Edition features 640 pages of easy-to-read, resumé-style write-ups on area businesses and service providers, listings of banquet and reception sites, how-to's, check lists and all the helpful hints!

Suggested Retail: $9.95

**TO ORDER CALL 503-675-1380**

# BRAVOPORTLAND.COM

## *If you like our Guide... you'll love our Web pages*

- **Search by area, capacity and type of service**
  You'll be able to search our site for the type of product or service you need. Find all downtown facilities that will accommodate more than 500 guests or a gift basket company that will deliver to Beaverton.
- **The Guide is online**
  Every client in the book is listed on the Web site with location, phone number, contact and type of business or service. Client pages can be found online as well, with the same easy-to-read format.
- **Links to event services and facilities**
  Many of our client pages have direct links to their home pages with more details and photos of their facility or service. You can get more detailed information or communicate with many of these services easily online or through e-mail.
- **Guestbook and order form**
  We'd love to hear from you. Sign-in to our guest book and let us know what you like about the Bravo! products or services. You can order any of our products online.

# OTHER BRAVO! WEB SITES:

bravowedding.com • bravofamily.com
bravoevent.com • bravotradeshows.com

### Bravo! Web sites:

- **Easy to use.**
- Feature all the **detailed information** you're used to seeing in your Bravo! Event Resource Guide.
- Have their own **search engine** so you can find things easily by category.
- Features **Guestbooks** and **Order forms.**
- Have a comprehensive **Calendar of Events** that will let you know when and where the next meeting planning trade shows, wedding or family events will be taking place.

### The Bravo! Event, Family and Wedding Web sites...

grow and change weekly, so be sure to browse them often to see what's new.

# INTRODUCTION & HOW TO USE THIS GUIDE

The objective of the *Bravo!® Event & Party Resource Guide* is to help planners of any experience level reference information from facilities, caterers, florists, entertainers, etc. Businesses and services are listed in the book based on merit and not just the amount of money they have paid for an advertisement. Small businesses are portrayed in the same light as their counterparts. Information has to be complete, reliable, and factual, including important details like deposits, cancellation terms, and cost.

The *Bravo!® Event & Party Resource Guide* was created by popular demand! Many meeting and event planners were using the *Bravo!® Wedding Guide* as a resource for its many facilities and services. Bravo! Publications published the first Bridal Guide in 1990, and its popularity among brides has made it a number-one seller. Meeting and event planners found the information listed in the Guide invaluable to finding a specific location that met their needs, including information like capacity, price, sleeping rooms, etc.

In creating the *Bravo!® Event & Party Resource Guide,* we worked with professional meeting and event planners and vendors in the industry to offer information and helpful hints based on years of knowledge and experience in the industry.

In addition to the *Bravo! Resource Guides* and *Organizers®,* we also produce events throughout the year for meeting and event planners to attend, where planners receive information and ideas directly from the businesses and services in the Guides. Your attendance in supporting these events will help us to continue to provide quality products and services. For dates of upcoming Bravo! shows and events, check out our Web site at: **www.bravoportland.com or bravotradeshows.com.**

## IMPORTANT NOTE!

It's important to make sure you mention to the businesses or services that you selected them from the Bravo!® Event & Party Resource Guide. This will help us continue to provide this Guide complimentary.

# PROFESSIONAL GUIDANCE EASES EVENT PLANNING

*by Steve DeAngelo, President, DeAngelo's Catering & Events*

As a caterer and event professional, I am continually amazed at the amount of resources that are available to us as planners. Not only does the quality of resources in the marketplace seem to increase, so does the quality. Add the combinations of event components and the results are endless. Achieving the most for your event dollar is a key focus in our planning strategies.

Projects of all sizes deserve decisions that revolve around concept development as well as conclusions. Challenging your client about the scope and objective of their event will give the planner immediate direction as well as define the events parameters. Venue, group size, and purpose as well as restrictions, permits and special guest needs will help build the events personality. Planners today easily spend $25 to $500 per guest for events, add destination travel and management and budgets can grow or exceed $500 per guest. By creating a budget outline to achieve the clients desired impact and results of the event will give further direction to the planner.

Food, beverages, floral décor and rentals many times become the foundation of the event. Beyond these basics there are a myriad of other services available. Examples of the following will enhance and create a memorable experience for your guests. Consider transportation and parking alternatives, security, entertainment, interactive games, team building exercises, demonstrations, guest list management and virtual offices to name a few. Beyond the initial event components, consider lighting, sound, audio / visual, staging, trussing, electronic or on site registration, additional restrooms, themed breaks, refreshments and break out sessions. Keynote speakers, theme décor, buffet treatments, specialty linens, seating alternatives, chair covers, special effects, balloon art, props, confetti canons, wind dancers ceiling and wall treatments, costumed staff, greeters, coat check areas as well as valet are all popular with attendees.

Focusing on the guest is a key in special event planning. Remember special guest needs, such as handicapped accessibility. Audience demographics as well as ethnic and religious belief when planning menus will be much appreciated. Many caterers offer gluten, whey or sugar free menu items as well as vegan, vegetarian, kosher, ethnic and macrobiotic foods.

Legal issues surrounding special events are also necessary to consider also. Many events require noise variances, vehicle access permits, propane or natural gas permits, special public assemblage permits, site plan reviews, and parking, street or lane closures. Depending on your events location, city, county, state, health department and liquor permits may also be needed.

Protect your guest's best interest and safety by considering terrorism threats, evacuation procedures, fire exits, police, medical and fire access routes and availability. With large scale events, ask vendors for proof of insurance or request to named insured on their policy.

When enlisting professionals for your event planning needs ask for references, interview event producers, ask for a tour of the facility, letters from previous clients are helpful as well. Ensure as the planner you are comfortable with all of the elements and details. Does the company have a green policy statement or earth friendly awareness?

When hiring catering, insist on licensed and insured companies. Ask for copies of the health departments most recent inspection report. Ask how food is transported to the event; consider the proximity of the kitchen to the event site.

Allow realistic timelines to hire event providers. Many large scale events are planned as far as three years out, while smaller scale events might be turned around in as little as two weeks. At any rate, the more time allowed for preplanning, the better overall event you will produce. Hiring professionals again will ensure your success on your client's behalf. A site manager or responsible individual or firm will assure the expectations of the client are met.

The weather and Mother Nature can always play havoc with events, especially here in the Pacific Northwest. Canopied entry points, shuttle transportation, as well as doormen to assist with ingress/egress all can add to guest convenience and comfort.

Communication within the event team is crucial. Cell phones and radios can solve a crisis in a matter of moments. Debriefing will only help the planner plan better events, notes regarding traffic within the event, food quantities, areas that may be improved upon are all useful tools to help complete your project professionally.

*Steve DeAngelo is the president of DeAngelo's Catering and Events (see page 326), a twenty one year old company. To learn more about the services DeAngelo's provides visit their website@ www.cateringbydeangelos.com*

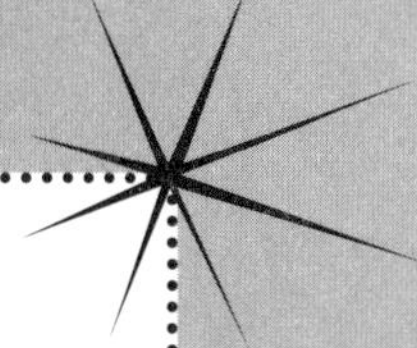

# Planning a Meeting or Event

BravoPortland.com

Planning a Meeting or Event

# TYPES OF EVENTS & WHERE TO START

## MANY TYPES OF EVENTS

- Conventions
- Holiday Parties
- Seminars
- Tours
- Groundbreakings
- Grand Openings
- Festivals
- Concerts
- Trade Shows
- Sporting Events
- Fund-raisers
- Product Announcements
- Anniversaries
- Picnics
- Sales Meetings
- Carnivals/Fairs

## PURPOSE OF EVENTS AND MEETINGS

Corporations are planning more events and special meetings and they have become a big part of the companies overall marketing budget. The reason being that it is more difficult to motivate and attract attention with just a regular in-house memo, announcement or traditional meeting.

## BENEFITS OF A WELL-PLANNED EVENT

- More sales, higher profits and employees take ownership of ideas
- Media attention and free publicity
- Target marketing
- Education
- Employee incentives
- Name recognition
- Good will in the community
- Product loyalty
- Problem-solving
- Networking

## PLAN...PLAN...PLAN

Ask professional meeting planners how to ensure a successful event or meeting and they will say, "pay close attention to the logistics and details and plan...plan... plan...ahead so that when the day of the event comes, all the good planning will kick into gear, and you can take care of the 'surprises' that Murphy brings to the event!"

## DETAILS

When meeting and event arrangements work well, the attendees have no idea of the details that went into the planning. But, when arrangements aren't right, everyone is aware of the details that needed to be handled and weren't! Whether it's too few chairs or faulty audiovisual equipment, everyone's attention will be focused on the one who planned the event and how things could have been organized and handled better!

## ASKING QUESTIONS

Whether it's for yourself, a corporation, a non-profit convention, or other clients, when planning a meeting or an event, you need to start with the basic questions, and from there you will get your event off to a good start. Without the solid foundation of knowing your meeting goals and attendees' expectations, you have no way of determining if your event was successful.

So, before you can get into the nuts and bolts of planning a great meeting or event, you need to ask lots of questions!

On the following pages we offer you the basic questions to ask to start your planning.

## DO YOUR HOMEWORK!!!

# WHY, WHAT & WHO



## WHY? THE PURPOSE...

Why are you, your client, or your boss wanting to have a meeting or event? Whatever the occasion, you, as the planner, need to know WHY! Ask questions!

- Is it for a celebration?
- An annual convention?
- New product introduction?
- A sales meeting?
- Retirement or anniversary party?
- Employee motivation?
- To educate?
- Allow for networking?

## WHAT? THE OBJECTIVE...

Along with the WHY is WHAT are the objectives of the event? Is the objective to thank employees for a hard year at work or to provide recognition for some special people or individuals? Is your objective to promote good feelings within the company or to the general public? Is this an event that has many audiences or just one? How do you want your audience to feel when this event is over? Do you want them to buy your products, feel pride in working for an outstanding company, or learn new techniques to make their jobs more productive?

## DETERMINE YOUR OBJECTIVES

The meeting may have multiple objectives...keeping within a budget is one of them, along with keeping the planning time to a minimum. What kind of a retirement party can I realistically plan with $1,000 and two weeks notice?

## WHO? PROFILE THE AUDIENCE...

Determining objectives of your meeting is an important first step because meeting programs are designed from these objectives to bring about the results desired. In order to measure your success, you need to determine goals and objectives, then create a meeting that provides the results you want.

Who will be your attendees, speakers, sponsors, etc? These are all the different audiences with whom you will be working. You need to have a profile of who they are, where they are coming from, and how old they are. Are they couples? Do any have disabilities? Will any attendees be international? Do they speak English? The more you know about your participants, the more success you will have meeting their expectations!

## AMERICANS WITH DISABILITIES ACT (ADA)

The Americans with Disabilities Act (ADA), passed into law in 1991, guarantees protection for disabled persons in the area of public accommodations. The meeting planner is legally responsible to make certain all effort has been made to comply with the ADA; know the individual needs of attendees. In compliance with ADA, it is very important to ask your attendees if anyone has disability-related needs. A follow-up call should be made to determine specific needs of attendees, and by clearly communicating these needs to the facility, you have established the intent to comply with ADA. Contact the ADA Portland office or your facility to get detailed regulations.

# CHECKLIST, PROFILE & SCHEDULING

## PLANNING CHECKLIST

It is helpful to develop a Planning Checklist for your event or meeting; this allows you to jump into the planning and delegating without trying to "re-invent" the wheel with a plain notepad. You can even assign each category to the qualified attendees.

- Profile the audience
- Determine the needs
- Site selection
- Budget
- Publicity plan
- Work plan or work flow
- Registration, invitations, programs
- Staffing
- On-site coordination
- Evaluation and accounting

## WHAT ARE YOUR NEEDS FOR THIS EVENT?

Make a list of what you think will be your immediate need. Will you need a facility, or can you do it at your own location, home, or business? Will you need to arrange transportation? Air or ground? Will you include food and hotel lodging for your event guests? Will you need meeting rooms and function space? Will you need audiovisual equipment? Will you need printed materials, signage, extra staff?

## SUB-CATEGORY QUESTIONS

These are general questions, but this is the beginning of a needs list. From this general list you will naturally develop your sub-category of questions including: site selection criteria, room rates, bus or shuttle, etc. And then the fun begins....negotiating what you want!!

## DETERMINING YOUR SCHEDULE OF EVENTS

Determining the "schedule" of an event needs to start in the initial planning stages! Changes and more changes will occur, but having a sense of timing for the various aspects of a two-hour meeting, a one-day seminar, or a five-day conference will help set the groundwork for selecting the site and vendors. Decide what "TYPES" of activities your group will be involved in during your meeting or event. For example: business portions, social portions, recreation free time, exhibits, etc. Begin to map out a schedule of events.

## SCHEDULE OF EVENTS (SAMPLE)

DATE: ____________________

| TIME | EVENT | LOCATION | NUMBERS | SETUP |
|---|---|---|---|---|
| 8–9 a.m. | Registration | TBD | 300 | Flow<br>See Diagram |
| 9–10 a.m. | Breakfast | TBD | 300 | Rounds |
| 10 a.m.-Noon | General Session | TBD | 300 | Theatre Style |
| Noon–1 p.m. | Lunch | Off Property | N/A | N/A |
| 1–3 p.m. | Workshops<br>A<br>B<br>C | TBD<br>TBD<br>TBD<br>TBD | 300<br>100<br>100<br>100 | Classroom<br>Classroom<br>Classroom<br>Classroom |

# BUDGET

## PREPARING A BUDGET

Preparing a budget is critical to effective meeting or event management. The budget provides you with the control and accountability of all meeting revenues and expenses. Your meeting objectives will influence both the revenues and the expenses of the program. Whatever the goal, it is important to document everything you commit to spending so you know at any time where you stand financially. A well-developed financial plan is a tool to guide the planner in making decisions and identifying priorities throughout the event.

## REVENUE

There are two concerns in creating a budget: revenue and expenses. Revenue is determined if you are going to expect income. How will it be generated? Registration fees, exhibitor fees, sponsorships, individual event fees, concession fees, are all ways money is brought in. How much income will you expect to receive in each category?

## EXPENSES

After determining your NEEDS PROFILE and your SCHEDULE OF EVENTS, you can develop a list of expenses involved or anticipated with each item. Don't forget the costs of administration, phone, mailings, faxes, staff, and supplies, in other words, your overhead. Experience helps in this process, but if you are a novice, you can do some research with vendors to determine reasonable estimates at this stage.

## GOOD PLANNING AND BUDGETING

Good planning results in meeting your objectives. During the budget portion of planning, you need to determine what your financial goals are as well. Determine what the group expects to gain. Should the meeting make money, lose money, or break even? If the group wants to make a profit, the amount or percentage should be determined in this initial stage.

## BUDGET WORKSHEET (SAMPLE)

### BUDGET WORKSHEET

Meeting Name ____________________

Meeting Date ____________________ Division/Cost Center ____________

Name of Person Responsible for Meeting ____________________

**HOTEL**

Sleeping rooms $ ____________
*($___/night + ___% tax= $___x___ room nights)* __
Meeting room rental $ ____________
Audiovisual charges $ ____________
TOTAL: $ ____________

**MEALS/FUNCTIONS**

Breakfast $ ____________
Breaks $____________
Lunch $____________
Receptions $____________
Entertainment $____________
Recreation $____________
TOTAL: $____________

# THE PLANNING & TIMELINE PROCESS

## MANAGING THE DETAILS

This is what meeting and event planners are famous for and everyone has tools to help them be successful. Everyone develops his or her own style and methods, but generally detail management includes these elements:

- TASKS...determine the tasks needed to be completed to ensure a successful event
- ORDER....determine the order in which these tasks need to be completed
- DEADLINE...determine the time in which they need to be completed
- DELEGATE... determine if, and to whom, they can be delegated. This is where you'll hear those magic words: **TIMETABLES, WORKPLANS AND CHECKLISTS**

## THREE-PART TIMELINE

One simple way to begin managing your information is to break your timeline into three parts:

1. PRE-EVENT or MEETING
2. ON-SITE
3. POST-EVENT or MEETING

You can then add the functional sub-categories under each part like event design, speaker recruitment, marketing and promotion, registration, site selection, etc. Determine what needs to be accomplished during each phase.

# MANAGEMENT TIMELINE

## (SAMPLE TIMELINE)

### 12-18 MONTHS BEFORE THE EVENT

Suggest program and "needs" list subjects

Define audiences

Determine needs

Draft theme/title

Determine pricing

Establish program budget

Select dates

Conduct site inspections

Book meeting, banquet, and sleeping room space

### 9-12 MONTHS BEFORE THE EVENT

Determine speakers

Determine agenda: business and social

Contact speakers

Contract transportation: ground and air

Coordinate facility needs

Send "save the date" mailings to audiences

Solicit exhibits and sponsors

*Management Timeline continued...*

## 6-9 MONTHS BEFORE THE EVENT

Review program needs

Review audiovisual needs

Review and refine budget

Select catering and event menus and themes

Communicate with vendors

Establish registration procedure

Design registration materials

***and so on...***

## USING A WORKPLAN

Once you have determined the tasks, give them a deadline and delegate. Responsibilities may be assigned to individuals, groups, committees, or suppliers, such as hotels, caterers, etc. Even if you are the ONLY person working on your event, suppliers or vendors do have a place in your delegation timeline. They need to get back to you in a timely way that works for you; you need to get signed contracts and guarantees back to them. Through the WORKPLAN you can manage the details.

## WORKPLAN (SAMPLE)

| WORK ELEMENT | DEADLINE | ASSIGNED TO |
|---|---|---|
| PROGRAM: | | |
| Theme design | Oct. 1 | Smith/Jones |
| Draft agenda | Nov. 5 | Staff |
| Determine speakers | Nov. 15 | Smith/Staff |
| BUDGET: | | |
| Draft budget | Oct. 1 | Meyer/Staff |
| Setup ledgers | Dec. 1 | Smith/Accounting |

# SITE SELECTION

## SELECTING THE SITE

Decision time...if you have done your homework, you will be armed with information that will help you make good decisions about your site selection. Once your needs are identified, you must match them with the sites that can handle them. Determine the geographic location that best suits your event...the United States, the West Coast, the Northwest, Oregon, Portland, Downtown Portland. These are all decisions that determine from whom to request proposals.

## RESOURCES TO SELECT THE SITE

You can call upon many resources to help you determine the best location for your event. Once you have narrowed the possibilities, you will be ready to make some comparisons and decide. Use the expertise of travel agents, Convention and Visitors Bureaus, Chambers of Commerce, professional planners–anyone that you feel understands your needs. ***This publication gives you a good comparison of local meeting and event facilities in the Portland, Salem, Vancouver and outlying areas.***

## MEETING PROFILE

Develop specifications and requirements for your meeting. This is sometimes referred to as a "Meeting Profile." This will be the natural outcome of your Needs List. It may be as simple as, "I need a room and meals for 30 people on this date, at this time." It might include preferred dates, number of sleeping rooms, meeting rooms, types of food functions, range of acceptable rates, exhibit requirements, and special needs of your group. The more information you can provide, the better chance you have of getting what you want. Many groups provide a detailed history of their event or meeting and the monetary value it has to a property. The profile becomes a request to all sites you choose to bid on your business. Once bids begin to come in, the planner can begin the evaluation and elimination process. After selecting an appropriate number to consider–and that number is up to you–it is recommended that you conduct site inspections.

## SITE INSPECTION

A site inspection is the best time to ask questions and get a good look at what each facility has to offer. It will be important for you to identify the property that can best meet your space requirements and the level of service you will need. Request references from groups with similar attendance and requirements, then contact them.

# NEGOTIATION

## NEGOTIATION AND CONTRACTS

Facility negotiations sound serious, but they don't have to be intimidating. These are important conversations because negotiations build relationships, which will lead to contracts. Contracts are serious business and when you, as a planner, enter into a contract, you want to be sure you have all the knowledge and information you need. Keep in mind that negotiable items and practices vary between areas of the country, so what may be standard procedure on the East Coast is not necessarily the same on the West Coast.

## HOMEWORK PAYS OFF!

Before you begin negotiating, you need some tools! If you have done your homework (refer to the first section), you'll be set! You need your meeting profile or prospectus, a history of your meeting or event, the value of your meeting to the facility (your budget), and a profile of your group. If you know your requirements, they will dictate the specific items you can negotiate.

## NEGOTIATIONS SHOULD BE WIN-WIN

Don't get bogged down in sleeping room rates! Rates are only one item that can be negotiated. The list of negotiable items may be as long as you want ...it never hurts to ask! But, in order to have a successful meeting, negotiations should be a win-win process. For example, if you get the hotel to provide complimentary meeting room space, but in order to afford this, the hotel cuts back on service staff for your meeting...who wins?

## CONTRACTS

The most important things to remember are that contracts should be written with an equal amount of risk for both parties, and that all your discussions are put into writing so there will be no confusion when it's time for your event.

# VENDOR SELECTION

## WORKING WITH VENDORS

Facilities are not the only vendors you will be working with to put on meetings and events. You will communicate with many different suppliers of services. Good planners realize that vendors have their own needs as they relate to your event. You need to select vendors on criteria that you develop for your event. XYZ bus company may have the most modern and comfortable equipment available, but if they are late, or their drivers are rude, they might cause more problems than the shiny buses are worth!

## BE SURE TO CHECK REFERENCES

Take every bit as much care in selecting a caterer, transportation company, or a dance band as you do in selecting a site for your event. Unless you have worked with the same vendors over and over again (personnel does change), make sure you check references and ask for bids for their service. Good vendors know how to make planners look good...and good vendors want and deserve repeat business!

## USING THE BRAVO! EVENT RESOURCE GUIDE

This Resource Guide is an invaluable resource of goods and services. Everything from caterers to musicians is listed in an easy-to-read format that allows you to make informed "apples to apples" comparisons of hundreds of products and services. You can count on reliable information and reliable references, as each business is screened before being listed in the Guide. Also included are helpful hints on checking references, protecting your deposits, securing dates, and more.

# ADMINISTRATIVE NEEDS

## DAILY TASKS

In conjunction with site and vendor selection, you, as the planner, will also attend to the daily administration tasks necessary to put on an event or meeting. Administration is where communication with your audiences will take place.

## COMMUNICATING WITH YOUR AUDIENCE

This is where you will determine appropriate mailing lists and how to handle RSVP's or registrations. How will the mailing happen? Volunteers or mailing houses? Create the graphics and coordinate the printing of all your written materials as early as possible. This is your promotion and publicity for your event. If staff or volunteers are needed, start recruiting them early.

## DEVELOPING A SMOOTH SYSTEM

The administration portions of the task list and budget usually include registration, name badges, financial record keeping, database, and computer work. Developing a smooth system that allows checks and balances along the way will help you feel confident that the paperwork is getting handled. A lot of meeting planning is telephone and paper work! The development of clear instructions to the registrants in all your materials will save time and money throughout the meeting process!

## GOOD COMMUNICATION

Good communication with your attendees is only half of the successful meeting equation, the other half is good communication with your selected vendors. This means ordering the food and beverages, the room blocks, the room setup, the flowers and the awards! Hopefully, you have selected a great team, and they are supporting you all the way! But they are not mind readers...let them know in writing, in diagrams, charts, and phone calls what you expect–what you are planning, what you need, and when you need it. Lack of information and lack of feeling for the big picture are two of the biggest problems in planning an event. You, as the planner, want to get a timely response from your vendors, and they want to get direction from you.

## STAFFING ASSISTANCE

For a large event or trade show, extra staffing and assistance is going to be necessary. There are companies and coordinators that can even deal with the entire registration for your event–handling reservations, organization name badges and staffing. Refer to "Meeting and Event Planners" section of this Guide. Also, there are staffing companies that can offer assistance on a temporary, as needed basis; data entry of names, greeters, setup help. The benefit of these companies is that the company you hire from assumes all the liability of the employee, you just pay an hourly wage. You can find these type of businesses in the "Staffing and Employment Services" section of this Guide.

# PROMOTION

## SELL THE AUDIENCE ON ATTENDING THE EVENT

Will they come? Even if this is the 100th annual conference, your attendees have to be sold on attending. Even if this is the biggest awards banquet in the history of your company, the employees have to be motivated to come. As the planner, you are in charge of making sure your event is marketed to the right audience. They need to know where, what, when, and how to sign up!

## MARKETING TOOLS

You have many tools available to you for marketing your event. Some obvious options include direct mail, in-house newsletters, press releases, paid advertising, billboards, bus sides, invitations and word of mouth. Don't rely on what has worked before–things change, people change. Good programs and reasons to attend will always be your best tools.

## PUBLIC RELATIONS/PRESS RELEASE

Refer to the "Advertising and Media" section of this Guide for local media (newspapers, radio, and television) addresses and phone numbers. Listed below is information about writing the different types of releases:

## MEDIA ALERT (SAMPLE)

WHAT: Press Conference

WHEN: Wednesday, December 17, 2003–10:00 a.m.

WHERE: Convention Center, 455 Grand Ave.

WHO: Greta Burton, President, Meeting Planners

TOPIC: Oregon's largest convention coming to town

ADDITIONAL INFORMATION: Press pass available. Photo opportunity. Meeting Planners is the largest meeting planner association in the country.

## PRESS RELEASE (SAMPLE)

The press release starts the same as the "media alert," then expands upon the what, when, where, who, and topic. Bold the key information throughout the copy.

## CALENDAR ITEM (SAMPLE)

WHAT: Cajun Cooking Seminar

WHEN: Thursday, November 18, 2004–10:00 a.m.

WHERE: Cajun Restaurant, 252 Pacific Road

WHO: Hailey Rose, Chef, Cajun Restaurant

COST: $16 per person, senior citizens $8

REGISTRATION: Space limited to 25 people. Pre-registration is required. Registration deadline is November 12, 2004.

ADDITIONAL INFORMATION: Hailey Rose is a world-renowned Cajun Chef, who is sharing her secrets to preparing the hottest food in town.

The calendar continues expanding upon the what, when, where, who and cost. Bold the key information throughout the copy.

# ON-SITE & MEETING SURVIVAL SUPPLIES
# THE BIG DAY...
# BIG AFTERNOON... BIG WEEK...

## THE BIG DAY!

Whether your event is a lunch or a major exposition, the Big Day always arrives! Your good planning will determine just how BIG that day will be. If you have met your deadlines, used your timelines, checked off your checklists, verified menus, orders, schedules, and agendas, you will be ready for the last-minute disasters!!

## PRE-CONFERENCE MEETINGS

It is a good idea to plan rehearsals, run-throughs, and team meetings. Conference planners often have pre-conference meetings where all the players are in attendance: the food and beverage managers, the audiovisual people, the registration supervisors, the transportation providers, the off-site providers. This is when the last-minute changes are noted, the lines of communication are finalized, and the team is energized for a successful meeting or event!

## THE PLANNER IS THE RINGMASTER

On-site is not the place to be determining agenda, policy, or making arrangements. On-site is reacting to the unexpected situations that arise, no matter how good your planning. On-site is maintaining balance as the months, weeks, and days of preparation kick into gear and the event unfolds. The planner is the ringmaster as the acts perform. What happens backstage will most often go unnoticed if good planning has taken place!

## TRUST THE TEAM

Delegate as many tasks as possible so you, as the organizer, can attend to the event and troubleshoot. If you are stuck at a registration desk when the lights go out on the main speaker, who's going to get the wheels moving to fix the problems? When the buffet lines are out in the street, who's going to get another serving station set up? Circulate and be everywhere, but don't be in anyone's way. The team has a job to do. They're there to support you and work together to make the event a success. TRUST THE TEAM you have assembled. They are the cast and crew of your production!

# MEETING SURVIVAL SUPPLIES

- ❒ File boxes
- ❒ Date and number stamps
- ❒ Stationery and envelopes
- ❒ Computer and computer supplies (disks, etc.)
- ❒ Pens, pencils, markers (multicolor)
- ❒ Staplers and staples
- ❒ Tape (single and double-faced), duct tape
- ❒ Clips, rubber bands, scissors, rulers
- ❒ Toolbox (hammer, screwdriver, assortment of nails)
- ❒ First aid kit
- ❒ Extension cords
- ❒ Colored dots, file folders, labels
- ❒ Flashlight
- ❒ Emergency numbers (messenger services, all-night copy center, etc.)
- ❒ Local telephone book
- ❒ Cash boxes
- ❒ Message pads
- ❒ Extra name badges, place cards, card stock, ribbons
- ❒ Local tourist information, maps, restaurant guides
- ❒ Three-hole and single punches
- ❒ Hand calculator
- ❒ Chalk and eraser, pointer
- ❒ Projector bulb, batteries, carousel tray
- ❒ Cellular phone
- ❒ Packing knife
- ❒ Measuring tape
- ❒ Spot remover
- ❒ Cassette tape and recorder
- ❒ Camera, film
- ❒ Typing whiteout
- ❒ Sewing kit
- ❒ Throat lozenges
- ❒ Stopwatch
- ❒ Fishing line or cable ties
- ❒ Breath mints
- ❒ Other:
- ❒ Other:
- ❒ Other:

# POST MEETING OR EVENT

## FINAL WRAP-UP

The event is over, but the work is not. For many meeting and event planners the final wrap-up is the biggest struggle. Not only have you ended months of preparation, now you have to finalize the billings, check the invoices, distribute the monies, etc. The wrap-up may not be fun, but it is crucial.

## START THE PROCESS IN THE BEGINNING

Good planners start this final process long before they get on-site. They plan with their vendors how they will verify services during the event, when payments will be due, and what kind of documentation will need to be completed in order to take care of matters in a timely way.

## THINGS TO MAKE THIS STEP EASIER

Ask to get all function bills the day of the event so you can verify their accuracy while things are still fresh in your mind. When verifying charges, ask yourself:

- Were you charged for the correct number of people?
- Are there any charges you cannot identify?
- Are there charges you did not anticipate?

## DAILY DIARY

Make a daily diary notation of things that worked and didn't work, notes for next year, and things to remember. Write it down or it won't be remembered. Follow-up should include making arrangements in advance to have materials returned or disposed of.

## THANK-YOU NOTES

Determine who will receive thank-you notes. Verify addresses, spelling of names, facility, and vendor contacts. Make a note of those people who were especially helpful to you or your attendees!

## MEETING WRAP-UP

Schedule a wrap-up meeting in advance with the facility's major department heads, or for small events, your contact. The purpose of this meeting is to find out how well EVERYONE performed, and what could be done differently in the future. This is also a time to ascertain whether you provided the facility and other vendors with appropriate information and instructions. Did you schedule enough time for activities on the agenda? Did you guarantee enough meals within the deadline? Should you have ordered another bar?

## FEEDBACK

While you are evaluating, make sure you ask the attendees what they thought of the event, the facility, and the program? Do they have ideas or suggestions for next year? Their feedback can be one of the most important tools to help you plan the next event. Take time before the event to design questions that will initiate answers and help you plan future events.

## REWARD YOURSELF!

Last, but not least...reward yourself! Many planners make this their first task of the meeting or event. They plan what they will do after the BIG DAY. Whether it is a bubble bath or an island cruise, plan something for yourself–you've done a great job and you deserve it!

# SPONSORSHIP

## HISTORY OF SPONSORSHIP

Sponsorships came about as a good way to finance community events. Large companies were able to generate product awareness, target marketing ad, a good sense in the community as well as receiving a tax break for sponsoring such events. This tradition of philanthropy is one of the oldest forms of corporate social responsibility where companies build stronger communities in which they do business in.

## CREATING FINANCE

Almost every event begins with a budget. The shorter you are on budget, the more you must creatively finance. One excellent way to stretch your dollars is to obtain a co-sponsor. When planning your event, seek out another organization or company who is not a competitor, but would likely benefit from exposure to your audience.

## SPONSORSHIP PARTICIPATION MAY INCLUDE:

- Share in the cost of the event
- Donate their service
- Advertise the event to their employees or customers
- Include your business at their next event

Terms of co-sponsorship may vary greatly.

## YOUR PARTICIPATION MAY INCLUDE:

- Include their name and logo in all event advertising
- Promote them at the event themselves
- Include some of their literature in the next mailing to your customers
- Give them the mailing list from your event
- To follow through on what was promised. Keep samples and photos of sponsor acknowledgements and send a thank-you following the event.

## PROMOTIONAL ADVERTISING

Always ask if there is extra promotional support that can go along with any dollars spent, it can help stretch your budget. For example if a radio schedule is purchased, ask if you can be the sponsor of the morning news broadcast "This message brought to you by.....", then have your commercial run in conjunction with that announce-ment.

## REMEMBER

- Select your co-sponsors wisely. The affiliation with a sponsor will impact the image of the event.
- Always put your arrangements in writing.
- Promotional coupons at their stores for the event.
- Confirm, confirm, confirm. This is the event planners mantra.

This type of teamwork often leads to very positive, ongoing alliance, making it one of the most exciting aspects of event planning. If the event is a win-win for both and the event is reoccurring, you may have an annual sponsor and funding or promotion for your event.

# ORGANIZING A GOLF TOURNAMENT

Planning a golf tournament is a fun way to raise dollars. Golf is also a recreational sport that can promote team building. There are many forms of golf activities:

- Retreat break
- Fund-raiser
- Reunions
- Team building
- Employee motivation
- and pure recreation

There are fun forms of golf for even those with little experience. Scramble golf is where a team of four all play the same ball—each gets a chance to hit. This is a fun, fast way for a large group of experienced and not so experienced golfers to have fun! Try to book golf tournaments early in the morning or late in the day during hot summer months.

Consult your golf courses in "Recreation, Attractions & Sports" section of this Guide for more detailed information about coordinating a golf tournament.

## ADMINISTRATION/ GOAL SETTING

- Planning, objectives, action plan, budget setting
- Event planning, layout of event
- Tournament calendar
- Mailing list, timelines, committee assignments
- Logo design, brochure design
- Sponsorship packages, sales
- Signage, prizes, auction
- Award Ceremony

## COMMITTEE FUNCTIONS/ A GOOD WORKING COMMITTEE IS A MUST

- Securing local clubs for the tournaments
- Developing a calendar for planning the event
- Establishing and obtaining prizes
- Planning additional fund raising activities such as auctions and raffles
- Solicitation of sponsors and "thank you's" after the tournament is held
- Arranging publicity and promotion participation
- Provisions for proper records, including accounting, contestant entries, etc.
- Notifying the committees of all meetings

## SPONSORSHIP DEVELOPMENT

- Design packages
- Solicitation, sales, contact list
- Pro/Am packages

## SUB-COMMITTEES

- Sponsorship committee: secures sponsors
- Publicity committee: news releases, media exposure
- Prize committee: set and obtain tournament prizes and tee gifts

## VOLUNTEERS

- Contact charities to help with parties, day of event registration, etc.

## FORMAT FOR DAYS OF PLAY

- Sponsor contests, putting contest, hole-in-ones
- Layout signage
- Tournament play, format of day's play
- Catering services
- Awards, auction

# PLANNING A SKI DAY

1. Contact the ski resort and determine the details: dates, times, ski packages available, and prices. (Refer to "Recreation, Attractions & Sports" section of this Guide for more information about ski resorts.)
2. Determine if you need transportation. Check with the ski resort to see if they can provide this service. If they do not, refer to the "Transportation" section of this Guide for transportation ideas.
3. Publicize the ski trip with flyers, posters, and announcements (E-mail, newsletter, etc.). Information should include: dates, package prices, a contact person, transportation pickup points, and where to sign up for the trip.
4. Set a time frame in which to collect all sign-up sheets and fees. It is recommended to get all information at least a few days before the ski trip.
5. After the sign-up sheets and fees are collected, contact the ski resort to place the ticket order. This reservation must be received to confirm the number of lift tickets, lessons and abilities, rental equipment needed, and beginner packages.
6. Arrange to pick up tickets in advance to save the group time waiting in line. Always treat tickets as though they are money.

# DAY OF THE SKI EVENT

**Arrive early**:
Schedule your morning departure time early enough to accommodate common delays in boarding the bus and traveling to the mountain. Drive time to Mount Hood from the Portland area is roughly one-and-a-half hours. The best arrival time for a ski day is between 8–8:30 a.m.

**The bus**:
Let all participants know where the bus will be parked and post the group name on the windshield. The bus will be your best base of operation and storage place. Designate a loading and unloading crew and devise a simple system to identify skis.

**Safety:**
Trail maps are available at the ticket office for distribution; familiarize the participants with locations of important facilities (restrooms, ski patrol, guest services desk, etc.). Make sure everyone knows the departure time and have a checklist of all people on the bus to avoid leaving people behind.

# PLANNING A CLASS REUNION

At one time or another in your life you will face the challenge of going to your class reunion. There is nothing more uncomfortable than a poorly planned function, but if you don't lend a hand or ideas, then you can't complain. As the leader or as a team member, class reunions can be fun to coordinate. Here are some helpful hints if you find yourself involved:

- Recruit your team members.
- Track down your classmates and mailing addresses (work with the school to get alumni information).
- Join classmates.com to send the latest information for free via email.
- Send a questionnaire to classmates to ask what they would like to see happen at the reunion.
- Establish your own web site for the reunion.
- Begin finalizing major details (when, where, what, budget, etc.).
- Organize lodging accommodations/group rates for out-of-towners.
- Print invitations or flyers. See if the school has a newsletter or booklet that is sent to alumni and can include information about your class reunion in it.
- Have a team party to address and stamp invitations.
- Begin compiling "Where We Are Now" booklet.
- Determine if RSVP response is enough to cover expenses.
- Plan fund raising event (if necessary).
- Contact classmates who have not responded.
- Finalize menu and entertainment selections.
- Inform caterers and other vendors of final attendance estimates.
- Think of fun decorating ideas like what was popular during your high school years (Psychedelic '60s, Flower children '70s, etc.).
- Name tags with an old graduation photo on badge (the yearbook is a great source) is a fun way to remember who is who.
- Hire temporary employees to check-in classmates and guests on-site.
- Develop fun ways for spouses to become involved and meet others.
- Ice Breaker Ideas: slide show presentations of classmates – ask classmates to mail current photos and include in the presentation with music from the era.; Jeopardy – ask questions such as "who was President," top 10 movies, favorite TV show," giving a prize to the classmate with the most correct answers.
- Make plans to stay in touch with team members. Have a "before the event" congratulations party.
- Decide who will be in charge of the next reunion. Instruct everyone to notify that person if their address changes at any time before the next reunion.

# ADVERTISING & MARKETING

**The many choices of advertising vehicles:** There are hundreds of choices of where to spend your advertising dollars if there are any. Radio, direct mail, newsprint, magazines, television, billboards, etc. There may be a proven medium that has always been used by your company, or you may be faced with making the confusing decision yourself. Advertising agencies and consultants can be helpful in exploring the many options available and the results that may be achieved, they can also help in target marketing your customer.

**Create the marketing plan and set the goals:**

- Critique last year's promotion by reviewing the invitations and brochures.
- Determine your target market in a brainstorming session.
- Gather examples of outstanding ideas and printed pieces you have seen that grab the reader's attention (keep an ongoing library of ideas year-round).

**Pick a theme and create a campaign:**

- Search for a relevant theme within your organization. Professional companies can help you develop ideas (refer to this section and Event Services in this Guide).
- Decide the key components to your campaign: posters, mailers, teasers, promotional gifts, giveaways, invitations, paid advertising, media contacts and press releases, etc.

**Plan your activity schedule over a six-month period of time:**

- Order ad specialties/giveaways, invitations and teasers no later than six weeks before the event.
- Mail teasers four to six weeks prior to event (some meeting planners mail immediately following that year's event, so attendees will save the date)
- Mail invitations three to four weeks prior to event.
- Write a press release at least two weeks prior to the event, and target media alerts for two days prior (after sending a press release, a follow-up phone call to answer any questions can be effective).

**Check the design at the post office before printing:** Make sure your design is within postal requirements before completing project. Rules are always changing, and it is important to keep up to date.

**Bulk Mail:** Bulk mail can save dollars when mailing high volume campaigns or invitations. You will need a bulk mail permit or you can buy bulk mail stamps, or the mail house can inkjet the info on your piece. Remember with bulk mail you are not guarateed a quick delivery. Mail that is addressed incorrectly will not be returned to you, unless you type "address correction requested" on the piece. If you plan on sorting your own bulk mail it can be a long process, the post office offers seminars on bulk mail. A mail house is the best investment in this case; it can cost you more in your own time, than if you hired a professional mail house.

**Post Card can save you dollars:** If printing a post card to save postage dollars, make sure it does not exceed 6" by 4" or it will not qualify for the post card rate. Check the post card rates at the post office.

**Tracking your results:** The best way to know if advertising is working or not for your company is to track results. It can be as simple as asking "how did you hear about this event?". Keep a list at the phone specifying all the ways you received your rsvps or sales. This list should include all forms of advertising: yellow pages, newspaper, direct mail, word-of-mouth.

# Notes

# Accommodations – Portland Hotels

Accommodations – Portland Hotels

# ACCOMMODATIONS

**Room Rates**: Rates are available in several categories. Be sure to know which ones you qualify for: commercial rates, corporate rates, government rates. Rack rates are common rates that hotels provide. Rack rate is the facility's standard, pre-established guest room rate and is never considered or accepted by groups.

**What determines group rates?** Group rates are determined by group size. Definition of the group size might vary or other factors may affect the rate you receive. Rates for sleeping rooms are determined in several ways:

- **Time of year:** "Peak" season, hotels can demand higher rates.

  Shoulder seasons and off-season rates are usually your best buy.

- **Number of rooms required:** Groups with large numbers are in a better position to negotiate lower room rates.

- **Arrival and departure patterns:** Business hotels tend to have high occupancy mid-week and lower occupancy over the weekend. The opposite is true at resorts.

- **Future business:** If you are, or may be, a repeat customer, you may get more favorable rates.

**Be prepared with past history:** If the meeting was held at the same place in years past, be sure to know the history and past negotiations. You will be able to negotiate better knowing your previous room block, pickup rate of rooms, and dollars generated by the hotel.

**Last minute bookings:** Be flexible with the details of the meeting or event to negotiate best rates. You may not be able to get everything you need but by changing the starting or ending time of your meeting to accommodate another meeting, then you may receive a greater concession on rental fees. Also, the hotel is anxious to fill up any last-minute open space.

**Off-season can offer great benefits:** Most properties offer a 25-50% discount in what they call off-season and shoulder season.

**Americans With Disabilities Act (ADA)**: This law passed in 1992 requires public buildings (convention centers, hotels, restaurants, etc.) to meet minimum standards making their facilities accessible to individuals with disabilities. Expect facilities to comply. It is the planner's responsibility to find out what auxiliary aids are available in the facilities they use. Although it may not be readily apparent, nearly every group has at least one person with a disability. Ensuring barrier-free accommodations for disabled people goes beyond inspecting for wheelchair ramps. Keep other attendee needs in mind, such as hearing and visually impaired guests and people with special dietary needs (insulin dependent diabetics may need refrigerators in their rooms).

**Amenities provided by hotels**: Complimentary items provided by a facility for guests may include toilet articles, writing supplies, bathrobes, or fruit baskets. Some planners say that in-room coffee is one of the best amenities. It is reasonable to ask for extra towels for health club use, or for quick delivery of forgotten items, such as razors, toothbrushes, or hair dryers. Find out before if these supplies are available. Concierge services and business centers are valuable to your guests. Don't be afraid to ask for the extras: an extra room for every block of ten rooms, complimentary use of hotel limousine for VIP pickups. Free breakfast for staff.

**Tipping:** A tip or gratuity is given to an individual at the time the service is provided. Personnel that most frequently receive this type of gratuity are doormen, bell staff, waitstaff, and housemaids or room attendants. If these tips are meeting or event related keep a detailed record, because they need to be accounted for in the budget.

# EMBASSY SUITES PORTLAND DOWNTOWN

*319 S.W. Pine Street • Portland, Oregon 97204*
*Contact: Sales Department (503) 279-9000; Fax (503) 220-0206*
*Web site: www.embassyportland.com*



## Description of Hotel

Portland's luxury all-suite hotel. On February 8, 1912, Portland enjoyed its first formal look at a hotel that would become the center of social life in the Rose City: The Multnomah Hotel, with its marble stairways, crystal chandeliers and grand ballrooms. The careful restoration in 1997 of this magnificent building has brought the hotel back to its original grandeur, including all modern added touches event planners and travelers expect to find in a great hotel.

## Location

The Embassy Suites is located at Third and Pine Streets in the heart of downtown's business and cultural district, just steps from restaurants, nightspots and shopping.

## Special Packages

The Embassy Suites has several unique packages including Suite Romance and New Year's Eve.

## Other Amenities

All 276 two-room suites have wet bar, microwave, refrigerator, three phone lines with computer jacks and voice mail, video checkout, irons, ironing boards, hair dryers, coffee makers and make-up mirrors. All guests can enjoy a complimentary full cooked-to-order breakfast and a two-hour manager's reception nightly. The fitness center offers exercise equipment, indoor swimming pool, whirlpool, and sauna. Adjacent to the lobby is Salon Nyla, an Aveda Concept Salon and Day Spa.

The Embassy Suites has over 22,000 square feet of meeting space including the Queen Marie Ballroom, an elegant restoration of the hotel's original ballroom. The Embassy Suites' dedication to offering unmatched service assures planners of memorable events at the hotel.

## Special Services

There are 404 covered parking spaces in the hotel's private garage just across the street. Valet and self-parking are available.

**See page 93 under Banquet, Meeting & Event Sites.**

EMBASSY SUITES®

# Portland—Washington Square

*9000 S.W. Washington Square Road*
*Tigard, Oregon 97223*
*Contact: Charles Holt*
*Phone: 503-644-4000; Fax: 503-526-1929; www.embassysuitestigard.com*

## Description of Hotel

The luxurious Embassy Suites Hotel Portland—Washington Square is Oregon's premier all-suite property featuring 354 beautifully appointed suites, each with separate living room and bedroom. Suites overlook the cascading waterfalls of our nine-story tropical atrium and Crossroads Restaurant, which features the finest in Northwest cuisine. The comfort of home awaits your attendees while staying at Embassy Suites; your guests will enjoy our complimentary, full cooked-to-order breakfast and evening Manager's Reception daily. From board meetings to annual conferences, our hotel is perfect for your every occasion.

## Location, Location, Location

Location means everything for your special events, and Embassy Suites is right where you need us. Located in the heart of Washington County and adjacent to Portland's RedTail Golf Course, Embassy Suites is where you will want to be. Washington Square Mall is also adjacent to the hotel, and we are minutes from Oregon's most prestigious wine country—found right here in Washington County. All highway arterials are easily accessible to our hotel offering you close proximity to downtown Portland, Beaverton, Tigard and Lake Oswego.

## Meeting and Banquet Facilities

The conference center at Embassy Suites is ideal for your special occasion; our reputation for attention to detail and customer satisfaction assures you the perfect event. We proudly offer:

- 15,000 square feet of meeting space
- 15 rooms to accommodate groups of 10–800 guests
- conference suites: ideal for small board meetings
- in-house audiovisual company available for your every need
- ample free parking for guests and attendees of your event
- high-speed Internet access

## Suite Accommodations/Amenities

- 354 beautifully furnished suites
- refrigerator, microwave and coffee maker in each suite
- complimentary, full cooked-to-order breakfast
- complimentary Manager's Reception: cocktails, beverages and snacks
- complimentary newspaper delivered to your suite daily
- indoor pool, jacuzzi and sauna open 24 hours
- complimentary use of onsite fitness facility
- telephones featuring voice mail and data ports
- high-speed Internet access
- complimentary parking
- business services available
- hair dryers, irons and ironing boards in all suites
- full-service restaurant and lounge open daily

*50 S.W. Morrison Street*
*Portland, Oregon 97204-3390*
*Contact: Sales Department*
*(503) 484-0255; Fax (503) 484-1414*
*E-mail: fourpoints.fppdx@starwoodhotels.com*
*Web site: fourpoints.com/portlanddowntown*



## Description of Hotel

Four Points Sheraton offers gorgeous views of the Willamette River and Portland's downtown skyline. Featuring 140 guest rooms, including one suite, we offer contemporary accommodations with the warmth and personality of an intimate European Inn. Working with nearby river boats and other facilities, we are the perfect combination for comfort, fun and a successful event.

## Location

A downtown waterfront hotel located on the corner of Southwest Naito Parkway and Morrison Street, on the MAX light-rail line, we offer easy accessibility from all the major freeways. Walk to parks, river, marina, shopping, Saturday Market, Pioneer Square, Pioneer Place and the World Trade Center. Cultural attractions in the area include the Portland Art Museum, Portland Center for the Performing Arts, Arlene Schnitzer Concert Hall, Keller Auditorium and the Oregon History Center. The Oregon Museum of Science and Industry (OMSI) with the USS Blueback submarine is just across the Willamette River.

## Guest Rooms and Amenities

All guest rooms are equipped with:

- Four Points Comfort Beds in our newly renovated rooms
- Complimentary in-room high speed Internet access
- Color television with remote; pay per view movies and games
- Two telephones, one with a data port
- Iron and ironing board, coffee maker

## We Also Offer

- On-site parking
- Pet friendly
- Non-smoking Riverview restaurant and lounge, including room service
- Special floors for nonsmoking guests; 90% of guestrooms are non-smoking
- Complimentary use of adjacent health club
- Complimentary weekday newspaper
- Wireless Internet access throughout property

## Meeting Space

- **The Riverside Restaurant:** We offer riverview dining in our newly renovated restaurant and bar. Dinner parties and other social gatherings are welcomed into the relaxed atmosphere overlooking Waterfront Park and the Willamette River—all with the finest dining and most reasonable prices in the area.
- **The Hawthorne Room:** 180 square feet in our riverview board room located within The Riverside Club seats ten comfortably for an all-day meeting, lunch or dinner
- **The Columbia Room:** At 576 square feet, our second-floor meeting room serves as a great gathering place. Whether you're meeting business associates or friends and family, this room will suit your needs. Our Sales and Catering Office will be happy to assist with any special requests. We are flexible and at your service.

**Enjoy Four Points Sheraton Portland Downtown**
**"Where downtown meets the river"**

# THE GOVERNOR HOTEL

*S.W. 11th at Alder • Portland, Oregon 97205*
*(503) 224-3400 or (800) 554-3456; Fax (503) 224-9426*
*E-mail: sales@govhotel.com; Web site: www.govhotel.com*

## Rich in History

Listed on the National Register of Historic Places, The Governor Hotel is an architectural beauty with a striking exterior of terra cotta and white brick. The Hotel, built in 1909, has been completely restored to its original grandeur. With a lobby styled in Italian Renaissance design, The Governor takes your breath away from the very first step.

## Location, Location, Location

In the heart of the city center, this turn-of-the-century luxury hotel offers convenience to and from the airport, proximity to the financial, retail, historic and arts districts, ease of access to city attractions, including our new Portland streetcar service, and a safe, quiet neighborhood in which to dine, shop and relax.

## Meeting Facilities and Services

Offering 24,000 square feet for meetings and banquets, The Governor Hotel's West Wing is unique in size and presentation. Twelve elegantly crafted, historically rich rooms offer space for intimate meetings of six to elegant dinners for 600. Rooms such as the new Heritage Ballroom, the Grand Ballroom, the Renaissance Room, and the Library begin to describe the ambiance and feel of the former 1923 Elk's Lodge, which is also found on the National Register of Historic Places.

Event services are provided by Jake's Catering at The Governor. Audiovisual in-house support is available along with a full-service business center for last-minute needs.

## Guest Rooms and Suites

The Governor features 100 handsomely appointed and newly refurbished rooms, including 24 suites. Some suites feature jet spa baths. Several include fireplaces or terraces with dramatic views of the sparkling skyline. The Governor offers the charm and style of a boutique hotel with the utmost in gracious, personalized service, including 24-hour room service, twice-daily maid service with turndown, complete concierge services, as well as complimentary shoe shine, newspaper, and morning coffee served in the lobby. There are private bars, voice mail, computer and fax ports, wireless Internet, irons and ironing boards, and coffeemakers in all rooms. For a nominal fee, fitness-minded guests may enjoy privileges at the hotel's on-site, adult-only athletic club. Group rates are available. Please call the Hotel Sales Office for information and details (503) 241-2102.

**PORTLAND DOWNTOWN/ CONVENTION CENTER**

*1441 N.E. 2nd Ave*
*Portland, Oregon 97232*
*Contact: Kellie Ohlfs,*
*503-233-2401; Fax 503-238-7016*
*Executive Meetings and Events Manager*
*E-mail: kohlfs@hiportland.com*
*www.holiday-inn.com/hiprtldwtn*

---

## Location:

The Holiday Inn Portland-Downtown/Convention Center offers easy access from I-5 and I-84 and is just 20 minutes from Portland's International Airport. The hotel is four blocks from the Oregon Convention Center and only two blocks from the Rose Quarter and Memorial Coliseum. The Holiday Inn is located in "Fareless Square" with access to the MAX Light Rail where passengers can easily explore downtown Portland's incredible shopping, museums, galleries and restaurants. The Lloyd Center Mall (Oregon's largest shopping mall) is located just seven blocks from the hotel and features an eight screen cinema and indoor ice skating rink.

## Hotel Amenities:

- 239 spacious newly remodeled guest rooms featuring coffee makers, hairdryers, iron and ironing boards, deluxe size work desks, microwaves and refrigerators
- Complimentary parking
- Complimentary airport shuttle
- Free wireless high speed internet access and free local phone calls
- On-site restaurant, lounge and room service
- Indoor heated pool and spa December 2004
- 24 hour business center
- State-of-the-art fitness center
- Over 3,000 sq. ft. of meeting and banquet space seating groups from 10 to 200
- Additional 6,000 sq. ft. conference center opening December 2004

## Attractions:

- Rose Garden Area – 2 blocks
- Oregon Convention Center – 4 blocks
- Willamette River and the East Esplanade walking path – 4 blocks
- Lloyd Center Shopping Mall – 7 blocks
- Oregon Museum of Science and Industry – 1 mile
- Chinese Gardens – 1 mile
- Saturday Market – 1 mile
- Oregon Zoo – 6 miles

# MALLORY HOTEL

*729 S.W. 15th Avenue • Portland, Oregon 97205*
*Contact: Ginny Gardea, Director of Sales and Marketing*
*E-mail: ginnygardea@malloryhotel.com*
*503-223-6311, 800-228-8657*
*Fax 503-223-0522*
*www.malloryhotel.com*

---

*Classic...Charming...Elegant...Affordable*
Built in 1912, the Mallory is Portland's premier uptown hotel. This classic and architecturally significant boutique hotel offers traditional décor and ambiance. Located uptown on the corner of S.W. 15th and Yamhill, adjacent to the MAX light rail, the Mallory is ideally situated within walking distance of downtown and the trendy Northwest and Pearl districts. Guests enjoy complimentary continental breakfast and free parking.

## Honeymoon Packages

Unique Bridal Suite complete with round, mirrored bed. Packages available.

## Guest Rooms and Suites

130 deluxe guest rooms, including 13 suites. With every overnight stay guests enjoy complimentary continental breakfast, free parking, the newspaper delivered to the room each morning, complimentary high speed wireless Internet access, HBO and pay per-view movies. Local calls are complimentary and check-out is always at 1 pm. Other amenities include in-room refrigerators, safes, iron and ironing board. Group and corporate rates are available.

## Banquet and Meeting Facilities

With 1,782 square feet of meeting and banquet space this is the ideal location for any event. The Mallory is well noted for superb dining and classic service, pairing the benefits of tradition with modern features such as complimentary high speed wireless internet access and top of the line audio-visual equipment.
**The Crystal Room:** Accommodates up to 85 for plated meal service or 100 for receptions and meetings. The high paneled ceilings are intricately detailed with gold gilding, and the crystal chandeliers mirrored by the back wall give this room its name.
**The Garden Room:** Accommodates up to 26 for plated meal service or 35 for receptions and meetings.
**The Executive Room:** Accommodates up to 16 for plated meal service or 24 for receptions.

**Room and Catering Pricing:** $9.95 to $35.95 per person for catered meals plus 17% gratuity. Room fees may apply depending upon food and beverage purchase.
Audiovisual: Equipment is available–fees vary, please inquire.
Parking and Ground Transportation: Mallory Park Garage is across the street and is complimentary for overnight guests and guests attending functions at the hotel. MAX light rail is adjacent to the hotel on Yamhill Street.
**Other Amenities:** Pet friendly, fitness center

# RiverPlace Hotel

1510 SW Harbor Way • Portland, Oregon 97201-5105 • 503.228.3233 hotel
503.295.6167 sales & catering • sales@riverplacehotel.com
www.riverplacehotel.com

## Description of Hotel

Our unique location, natural beauties and waterfront resort provide our guests with a range of possibilities. RiverPlace Hotel is an urban getaway, known for providing the ultimate in personalized service. From intimate to corporate stay-overs, RiverPlace Hotel is sure to cater to your every need.

## Location

RiverPlace Hotel is located in downtown Portland along the Willamette River, overlooking the RiverPlace Marina and adjacent to Tom McCall Park. This unique European style hotel is ideal for business travelers, corporate functions and special events. Our doors open onto the popular RiverPlace waterfront within walking distance of storefronts, RiverPlace Athletic Club, galleries and restaurants.

## Guest Room Accommodations

RiverPlace Hotel has 84 elegantly appointed guest rooms. Take advantage of our grand suite, fireplace suites or one of our deluxe guest rooms for the finest accommodations in Portland.

- **Grand Suite:** features include a large living room, dining room, wet bar, marble wood-burning fireplace and a guest bath off the living room. The master bedroom has a king-size bed, walk-in closet and jetted soaking tub.
- **Fireplace Suites (5):** a combination of a private living room and private bedroom with a king-size bed, wood-burning fireplaces, wet bars and oversized whirlpool tubs.
- **Parlor Suites (18):** king-size beds and separate living rooms
- **Junior Suites (11):** oversized rooms perfect for business travelers
- **Deluxe Rooms (39):** king-size or two double beds
- **Condominiums (10):** located adjacent to the hotel, these beautiful condominiums include balconies, wood-burning fireplaces, washers and dryers, separate living and dining rooms, queen-size hide-a-beds and fully equipped kitchens.

## Amenities Included with Guest Rooms

This European-style hotel offers discounted rates for corporate travelers and groups. Guest rooms are spacious and comfortable with numerous amenities available such as:

- Choice of Newspapers
- Continental Breakfast
- Concierge Services
- Shoe Shine
- Evening Turn Down
- Down Feather Beds
- Alaska Airlines Mileage
- RiverPlace Athletic Club
- Bose® Radio/ CD Players
- High Speed Wireless Internet
- Business Services
- Japanese Paper and Tea Service
- Lucere Restaurant and Bar

***and Conference Center—***
***Portland Airport/I-205***
*11707 N.E. Airport Way*
*Portland, Oregon 97220-1075*
*(503) 252-7500; (800) 222-2244*
*Sales:(503) 252-5800*
*or portland205@shiloinns.com*
***Web site: www.shiloinns.com***
*Business Hours: Mon–Fri 8am–5:30pm;*
*Sat by appointment*

## Description of Hotel

This beautiful property offers spacious accommodations and wonderful family dining. An indoor heated pool, a spa, steam room and fitness center are open 24 hours a day to delight any guest. Free shuttle to Portland Airport.

## Guest Room Amenities

Children under 12 stay free at Shilo Inns with an adult. Enjoy free Showtime. All rooms come with a microwave, refrigerator, hair dryer and first run movies and entertainment.

## Location

The Portland Airport Shilo Inn is located 2.5 miles from Portland International Airport, just off I-205 on Airport Way (Exit 24 or 24B).

## Meeting Space

Accommodates up to 400 people for banquets; 250 people for receptions. Full service catering to meet your needs.

## Other Amenities

- Complimentary Barista Brunch, espresso, fresh French pastries
- Kids under 12 stay FREE with an adult
- 24-hour indoor pool, Jacuzzi, sauna, steam room and exercise room
- Complimentary airport shuttle
- Complimentary parking for overnight guests
- Park & Fly available
- Complimentary local calls, dual lines, featuring voice mail and data ports
- Short stature accessibility kits available
- Free high speed Internet access

## Reservations

Call toll free 1-800-222-2244 or visit our Web site for online pictures, information and reservations at www.shiloinns.com.

Sweetbrier
Inn & Suites

*7125 S.W. Nyberg Road (Exit 289 off I-5)*
*Tualatin, Oregon 97062*
*Contact: Sales and Catering Office*
*(503) 692-5800, (800) 551-9167*
*Fax (503) 404-1950*
*www.Sweetbrier.com; Office Hours: Mon–Fri 7:30am–5:30pm; Sat 9am–1pm*

## Location

The Sweetbrier Inn is a two story "country inn" located only 10 minutes south of downtown Portland. Our beautifully landscaped grounds create a true picture of Oregon's beauty. The accessibility style and personalized service of the Sweetbrier Inn & Suites makes us an ideal choice for your event.

## Accommodations

Our 131 newly remodeled guestrooms and executive suites provide a high level of warmth and comfort. Some of our standard amenities include: complimentary continental breakfast and *USA Today*, laundry facilities, free local phone calls, in-room coffee makers, touch tone phones with dataport capabilities, 24-hour fitness center and heated outdoor pool. Our executive suites feature oversized work stations, refrigerator, microwave, separate living room and patio, two televisions and iron with ironing board, making it ideal for an extended stay. AAA rated–Three Diamond.

## Dining and Entertainment

Award-winning cuisine awaits you at the Sweetbrier Restaurant and Jazz Bar. Open daily for breakfast, lunch and dinner. Our chefs' creations appeal to all tastes. Join us for our Champagne Sunday Brunch or relax Wednesday through Saturday to the live sounds of Portland's premier jazz artists.

## Convention and Corporate Pricing

Special rates and services are available for group bookings. Contact our sales staff for current prices.

## Meeting and Banquet Facilities

The Sweetbrier Inn & Suites offers 4,000 square feet of meeting space that can accommodate up to 400 guests. Let our professional sales and catering staff help plan your next important meeting, reception or reunion. More specific information on catering and meeting facility is available upon request.

**See page 151 under Banquet, Meeting & Event Sites.**

# Notes

# Accommodations – Extended Stay Hotels

BravoPortland.com

**PORTLAND DOWNTOWN/ CONVENTION CENTER**

*1441 N.E. 2nd Ave*
*Portland, Oregon 97232*
*Contact: Kellie Ohlfs,*
*Executive Meetings and Events Manager*
*E-mail: kohlfs@hiportland.com*
*www.holiday-inn.com/hiprtldwtn*

---

## Location:

The Holiday Inn Portland-Downtown/Convention Center offers easy access from I-5 and I-84 and is just 20 minutes from Portland's International Airport. The hotel is four blocks from the Oregon Convention Center and only two blocks from the Rose Quarter and Memorial Coliseum. The Holiday Inn is located in "Fareless Square" with access to the MAX Light Rail where passengers can easily explore downtown Portland's incredible shopping, museums, galleries and restaurants. The Lloyd Center Mall (Oregon's largest shopping mall) is located just seven blocks from the hotel and features an eight screen cinema and indoor ice skating rink.

## Hotel Amenities:

- 239 spacious newly remodeled guest rooms featuring coffee makers, hairdryers, iron and ironing boards, deluxe size work desks, microwaves and refrigerators
- Complimentary parking
- Complimentary airport shuttle
- Free wireless high speed internet access and free local phone calls
- On-site restaurant, lounge and room service
- Indoor heated pool and spa December 2004
- 24 hour business center
- State-of-the-art fitness center
- Over 3,000 sq. ft. of meeting and banquet space seating groups from 10 to 200
- Additional 6,000 sq. ft. conference center opening December 2004

## Attractions:

- Rose Garden Area – 2 blocks
- Oregon Convention Center – 4 blocks
- Willamette River and the East Esplanade walking path – 4 blocks
- Lloyd Center Shopping Mall – 7 blocks
- Oregon Museum of Science and Industry – 1 mile
- Chinese Gardens – 1 mile
- Saturday Market – 1 mile
- Oregon Zoo – 6 miles
- Japanese Gardens – 6 miles
- Multnomah Falls – 30 miles

# OXFORD SUITES

*www.oxfordsuites.com*

## OXFORD SUITES
## JANTZEN BEACH

*12226 N. Jantzen Drive*
*Portland, Oregon 97217*
*(503) 283-3030*
*(503) 735-1661 fax*
*(800) 548-7848*

---

## Where Elegance and Affordability Meet

The Oxford Suites at Jantzen Beach offers guests the opportunity to experience "suite life" at an affordable price. Suites range from Business Suites and Family Suites to Presidential Suites, all for the price of a regular hotel room. In addition to spacious accommodations, guests will enjoy a complimentary Hot Country Breakfast Buffet daily as well as an evening reception with delectable hors d'oeuvres and beverages.

## Location

The Oxford Suites is located at Jantzen Beach, famous landmark on the Columbia River at the south end of the Interstate Bridge. Easy access to Interstate 5 provides a quick trip to the Portland International Airport, the MAX station, or downtown Portland. Nearby shopping at the Jantzen Beach SuperCenter will keep guests entertained, as well as the many fine restaurants within walking distance.

## Suite Amenities

- 200 guest suites with separate living areas including sleeper sofa
- King or two queen beds available
- Refrigerator, microwave and coffee maker in every suite
- High speed Internet access
- Entertainment Center with VCR

## Hotel Amenities

- Complimentary Full Hot Country Breakfast Buffet daily
- Complimentary Evening Reception with hors d'oeuvres and beverages daily
- Complimentary airport shuttle
- Complimentary Business Center with PC, printer, fax, copier and high speed Internet
- Indoor swimming pool, Jacuzzi, steam and sauna
- Complimentary use of onsite fitness facility
- Free parking

## Banquet and Meeting Facilities

1,200 square feet of conference space is available for your meeting and event needs. With one primary meeting room, your guests will have an intimate environment and avoid the distraction of competing with other conventions or groups. Our dedicated staff with work in tandem with you to create the perfect event.

# Notes

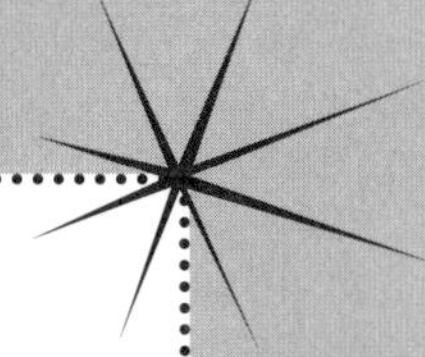

Audiovisual & Communication Services

Audiovisual

&

Communication

Services

BravoPortland.com

# AUDIOVISUAL & COMMUNICATION SERVICES

Planning for audiovisual equipment, lighting and staging for your meeting or event is very important. Exciting new technologies like interactive computer use, live video enhancement of speakers and teleconferencing have arrived, but the budgets that have arrived with them are steep. The type of audiovisual support you will need for your meeting or event may be simple or more complex. Be sure to review all your options.

**Think ahead to what your audiovisual needs will be:**

- Get a list of the speakers' needs well in advance of your event and schedule a rehearsal. You will avoid last-minute and rush labor charges this way.
- Give speakers a chance to rehearse with equipment.
- Test equipment immediately prior to beginning of the event.
- Have spare bulbs and extra extension cords on hand.
- Having a technician available to attend to your needs throughout the meeting may be your best insurance policy.
- Many facilities have in-house equipment (check availability and working condition).
- Remember that poor-quality audiovisual equipment can ruin a meeting.

**To maximize your audiovisual budget, try the following:**

- **Reserve equipment early** so you have what you need from a reputable company. If you have never worked with the company, ask for references and check them. This is an important part of the meeting.
- **Negotiate all costs.** Package deals are good for you and the rental companies. If they know your needs and have your timelines, it will be cost effective.
- **Put your agreements in writing.** If one company is not able to meet your needs, look at other companies until your needs are met.
- **Write all instructions.** Include agendas and room layouts so your vendors know exactly what you expect. This will eliminate surprises or the need for mind reading.
- **Save yourself headaches.** If you are too busy doing the many other jobs needed for a meeting, seek out and use experienced production managers and technicians to oversee the audiovisual portions of your event.
- **Barter goods and services with your rental companies.** They may want to advertise in your publications, exhibit at your trade show, or acquire leads from your attendees.
- **Guaranteed performance is often a policy of audiovisual companies.** They will compensate clients for rental costs in the event of equipment failure. Even better, many will provide on-site back-up.

**Checkout the audiovisual equipment:** Many facilities have their own in-house audiovisual department. Ask if any audiovisual equipment is included in your room charge, then be sure to check out the quality and age of the equipment. Most facilities only provide a podium and microphone, so you will need to rent additional equipment from a qualified audiovisual rental company.

# BEARCOM

## *Two-Way Radio Rental*

*Contact: Janell Albarghouthi*
*3605 S.E. 21st Avenue • Portland, Oregon 97202*
*(503) 232-5600; Fax (503) 232-5601*
*Nationwide toll free 888-371-2327*
*E-mail: Janell.albarghouthi@bearcom.com*
*Web site: www.bearcom.com*

### Rental Program

For the times when you need daily, weekly, or monthly use of 2-way radio equipment, BearCom Rental is the answer. With the nation's largest fleet of equipment and the support of our experienced communications engineers, we can exceed your expectations.

### Expert Assistance and Support

Along with reliable, quality equipment, you'll get something extra: BearCom's team of experts. We'll listen to your needs and design a system that meets your exact requirements to help your special event or project run smoothly, safely and profitably.

### Service Provided

24-hour on-call service and support; our nationwide offices to assist you whenever your next event may be; free programming on our private carrier frequencies or on yours; delivery and pick-up available for a nominal fee. On-site demos available at no charge to determine the requirements per location.

### Rental Equipment

BearCom's current inventory consists of over 20,000 portable and mobile radios and a large number of Nextel phones and cellular phones are available.

### Equipment

- Portable and Mobile Radios
- Nextel 2-way/Cellular Combination
- Cellular Phones
- Pagers
- Trunking Radios
- Repeaters
- Base Stations

### Accessories

- Earpieces
- Surveillance Kits
- Spare Batteries
- Speaker Microphones
- Radio Chargers
- Double-Muff Headsets
- Lightweight Headsets
- Carrying Cases

# FocalPoint Digital

*11516 S.W. Oak Creek Drive • Portland, Oregon 97219*
*503-245-5300 (voice) • 503-245-3250 (fax)*
*steve@focalpointdigital.com • www.focalpointdigital.com*

***Image is everything***

---

Specializing in state of the art video projector rentals for discriminating corporate and private event planners.

**Rental Services:** **FocalPoint Digital** provides rental projector services utilizing JVC D-ILA, Sanyo LCD and Sharp DLP technologies because they truly embody our goal of producing vastly superior graphic and video images for corporate and private events. From PowerPoint presentations to life-like High Definition video, JVC D-ILA delivers the best combination of brightness, resolution, contrast and color available anywhere. For the event planner on a budget, our Sanyo LCD projectors represent the best value and enhanced flexibility solution available in an otherwise commodity rental marketplace. Sharp DLP technology brings great picture quality to a new level of convenience. When only the very best will do, call **FocalPoint Digital.** We are poised to take any computer or video production feed from the client, extract every nuance of information and display it on 6 ft. to 30 ft. wide screens, front or rear, with uncompromising clarity and visual impact. We also rent a wide variety of screens, plasma panels and audio support equipment.

**Technology:** JVC D-ILA (Direct Drive Image Light Amplifier) proprietary projector technology delivers what conventional LCD and DLP designs only promise. Current JVC D-ILA projectors lead the competition in creating the standard for High Definition images. With the highest pixel density in the industry, D-ILA packs 1.4 million pixels onto a 0.9" chip at a resolution of 1365 X 1024 (SXGA3) combined with a record 93% fill factor (less space between pixels). These statistics only begin to explain why D-ILA based projectors produce the least pixilated, most film-like image available. Our Sanyo LCD 1100 to 7700 lumen projectors maximize the industry's brightness/high value proposition, making difficult placement or high ambient light conditions easy to overcome. For smaller applications or that road warrior on the go, try our 5.8 pound, cost effective Sharp DLP 1500 and 2000 lumen units.

**Client Benefits:** Our company motto, ***Image is everything*** has become an axiom that says as much about our clients as the quality of the image itself. When communicating your special message, the back row should not be having difficulty reading the details, nor should the front row be subjected to a highly pixilated, artificial looking image. Better projection equipment is not a luxury. It is a reflection of the clients' reputation.

**Inventory:** **FocalPoint Digital** is Portland's largest video projector rental company. We rent 1,000-15,000 ANSI lumen projectors in a variety of lens configurations for the most demanding applications. From small breakout rooms to large-venue or outdoor scenarios (utilizing our proprietary "screen tunnels"), **FocalPoint Digital** has you covered.

**References:** **FocalPoint Digital** has provided video projectors to organizations such as Adidas, AT&T Wireless, Fluke, Hewlett Packard, Intel, National Meeting Company, Nike, Oregon Dental Association, Oregon Public Broadcasting, Oregon and Washington Restaurant Associations, Sun Microsystems, The Oregon Symphony, West Coast Event Productions, Wells Fargo and many others across the US and Canada.

**Rates:** Daily projector rental rates are based on projector type, lumen output (brightness), number of rental days and whether the client is retail (end user) or wholesale (i.e. production company). Please call for specific details and projector availability. Video technician assistance is required on some projectors at current daily rates. Screens and audio support are also available.

**Contact Us:** **FocalPoint Digital** typically schedules events up to six months in advance and will work with your event planning staff to select the most appropriate equipment within your budgetary guidelines. Our experienced video technicians will gladly provide an estimate. Please call 503-245-5300 and ask for Steve Smith.

## Hollywood Lighting Services

5251 S.E. McLoughlin Blvd
Portland, Oregon 97202-4836
503-232-9001 800-826-9881
Production Contact: Dwayne Thomas
Rentals Contact: Greg Eggen
Sales Contact: Dixon Soracco
email production@hollywoodlighting.biz
website www.hollywoodlighting.biz

---

**Trust Hollywood Lighting Services for:** Corporate Meetings, Product Rollouts, and Conferences — Weddings, Galas, Auctions, and Parties — Tradeshows and Exhibitions — Concerts and Theatrical Productions — Sporting Events, Grand Openings, and Special Events of all types.

**The Experience You Need:** Hollywood Lighting Services has set the standard for great lighting in the Pacific Northwest and beyond for over 55 years. We're proud to say "we've lit everything from microchips to 18 wheelers, from tennis shoes to haute couture, from dog shows to the Dalai Llama. We provide lighting for staged events from ballet to opera to theatre, and concerts from Pavarotti to Everclear."

**Technology You Can Trust:** We create lighting for over 300 events each year, with the majority of the design coming from our in-house creative department, and 99% of the equipment from our warehouses. We use only the best gear, including automated fixtures and consoles from Martin, Vari*Lite, and High End Systems, the safest rigging products from Thomas and CM, and industry standard conventional fixtures and dimming from ETC, Altman, and Leprecon.

**Superior Service, The Creative Approach:** Lighting Production is not just about equipment....anyone can rent you a light! What sets Hollywood Lighting apart is our passion for creativity, problem solving, and exceptional service! We strive to find meaningful ways to add value and quality to your event's objectives. Do you want to motivate your team at your next meeting? Transform a plain-jane space into an elegant gala? Or do you simply want to drive a visual theme? By utilizing our talented staff of in-house lighting design professionals with decades of event experience, you get a creative team that is committed to helping you achieve your lighting dreams! Here are a few comments from our valued clients:

*"THANK YOU! I'm sure you've heard by now, but we won both Best Presentation as well as Best Vendor, which speaks to how well we reached the audience during the event... in a nutshell, our goal was to 'steal' the show, and we did just that!"*

– Shirley Turner, Intel SBS Conference, Los Angeles

*"It was a pleasure to work with your crew. I was VERY impressed with their work ethic, professionalism and in making the lighting as perfect as the conditions would allow. No matter what from beginning until the very end your crew continued to try for 'Perfect Perfection' and did whatever it took to get it!"*

– Wayne Southard, WWE Production Manager, WWE Fan Axxess, Seattle

*"Great working with you....thanks for making my event look so good!"*

– Marciano Agabon, Portland Monthly Launch Party

**Some of our clients include:**

Nike, Columbia Sportswear, Intel, Microsoft, In Focus, Hewlett Packard, Rose Festival, Nordstrom, Classic Wines Auction, Smirnoff Brands, Portland Trailblazers, adidas America, OMSI, Wagner Edstrom, M Financial Group, KGW-TV, Freightliner, Land Rover, Audi, Pendelton, Fluke Digital, ReMax, Nautilus, ESPN, VH1, Animal Planet, Comcast Cable, Luis Palau, Standard Insurance, Spirit Mountain Casino, Clark Amphitheatre, TriMet, Oregon Zoo, Oregon Ballet, and many others.

# PDX AUDIO

*P.O. Box 92065 • Portland, Oregon 97292-2065*
*Contact: Dave Grafe*
*Office: (503) 284-2727   Mobile: (503) 807-4595*
*E-mail: info@pdxaudio.com   Web site: www.pdxaudio.com*

---

**OUTSTANDING SOUND SYSTEMS**
**SUPERB TECHNICAL SUPPORT**
**TOTAL PRODUCTION SOLUTIONS**

**CUSTOMER SERVICE**
**COMES FIRST**

Our depth of experience and our unwavering commitment to excellence are at your service, assuring courteous and professional production assistance for every event, no matter how large or how small.

**IF WE CAN'T DO THE JOB RIGHT**
**WE KNOW SOMEONE WHO CAN.**

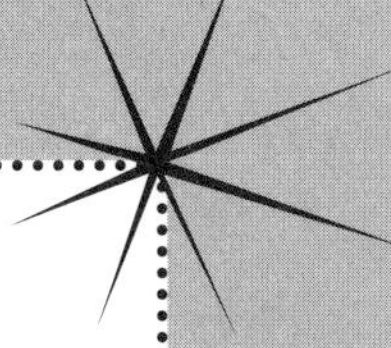

# Banquet, Meeting & Event Sites

BravoPortland.com

# BANQUET, MEETING & EVENT SITES

- **Begin looking for your banquet or meeting site immediately:** As soon as the event date is decided upon, the first decision that needs to be made is where the event or meeting will be held. Some hotels and facilities will book one to three years in advance, depending on the time of year and size of the event. It is not uncommon for a large convention to be booked five years in advance.
- **Visit the location:** When you narrow down the options of sites available, it is always a good idea to look at the room in person before you reserve it or send the deposit. The look and setup of the room or location will make a difference for the type of event. Also, the room setup will determine the room layout, which is essential to the rest of the planning.
- **Visit your site with vendors:** A site inspection of the facility is important, and you might consider also bringing your vendors for a site visit. These visits can answer questions for caterers, decorators and musicians about parking and unloading, lighting, electrical requirements and permitted work areas.
- **Most common room layouts:**
  - Banquet Seating
  - Classroom Style
  - Conference Style
  - Hollow Square
  - Theatre Style
  - U-Shape
- **Be honest about your budget:** Do not be afraid to tell the facility coordinator or event planner what your budget is. This important information can be used as a guideline that can save time and effort on everyone's part. Make sure to work as a team with your facility staff because they will be the ones that will help create a successful event for you. They can also offer time and budget-saving ideas based on their experience.
- **Deposits are important:** Remember that when you reserve a facility, a deposit is usually required to confirm the date. Do not count on a verbal commitment, everything needs to be confirmed in writing. Facility staff can frequently change, so verbal commitments may be forgotten.
- **Find out what equipment is available at the facility:** (audiovisual, staging, tables and chairs). Find out what you can get at no charge, as well as the quality and quantity of the various equipment. If you are planning to use the equipment, make sure it is reserved in writing. The day of the event, thoroughly check the equipment to make sure it is in working order.
- **In-house audiovisual departments:** Many hotels have their own in-house audiovisual department. Ask if audiovisual equipment in is included in your room charge, then be sure to check out the quality and age of the equipment. If the facility has an in-house specialists they usually know the rooms well, and can help with the most effective room setup and equipment needs. Most facilities only provide a podium and microphone, so you will need to rent additional equipment from a qualified audiovisual rental company. Remember: poor quality audiovisual equipment can ruin a meeting.

*606 15th Street • Oregon City, Oregon 97045*
*(503) 722-9400; Fax (503) 722-5377; www.abernethycenter.com*
*Business Hours: Mon–Fri 9am–5pm; by appointment*

---

**Capacity:** indoors: 320 banquet, 500 concert, 250 classroom; outdoors: 300+
**Price Range:** varies according to event; please call for information
**Catering:** full service, in-house catering only
**Types of Events:** We have complete indoor and outdoor facilities for all of your events, including but by no means limited to: weddings, receptions, corporate meetings and banquets, fundraisers, sit-down dinners, trade shows, retreats, seminars, reunions, auctions, weddings and receptions.

## Availability and Terms

Every attempt will be made to accommodate your event no matter when it is booked; however, we do recommend early reservations. A deposit is required at the time of booking.

## Description of Facility and Services

**Seating:** table and chair setup is included in the site rental
**Servers:** provided with catering service
**Bar facilities:** available through Abernethy Center
**Dance floor:** included in the site rental
**Linens:** available through Abernethy Center
**China:** provided with catering service
**A/V:** Bose® surround sound system, 9x12 ft. screen and LCD projector, DVD, VCR and CD players, and wireless microphones available (indoor only)
**Equipment:** podium and staging available
**Setup/Cleanup:** included in the site rental
**Parking:** 125 free parking spaces; additional free street parking
**ADA:** fully accessible

### *"At Abernethy Center, we create experiences, not events.™"*

Welcome to *The Complete Event Facility.* Indoors or out, we have it all!

**The Gardens ~**
Whether you choose a sunny, summer day or an elegant evening, Abernethy Center has the facility and staff to satisfy your event needs.

**The Ballroom ~**
Muted color tones and classic chandeliers, bathed in natural lighting from expansive windows, create a warm ambiance suitable for intimate affairs or extravagant galas.

# *The Adrianna Hill Grand Ballroom*

*An Enchanting Place of Celebration*

*918 S.W. Yamhill • Second Floor • Portland, Oregon 97205*
*Contact: Philip or Linda Sword (503) 227-6285 • Shown by appointment only*
*E-mail: info@adriannaballroom.com; Web Site: www.adriannaballroom.com*

**Capacity:** 80 to 300 guests
**Price Range:** fully inclusive packages, charges vary
**Catering:** full service in-house catering and beverage service only
**Type of Events:** corporate and private celebrations, holiday parties, wedding ceremonies and receptions, concerts, dances, fundraisers, reunions, proms, and auctions.

## Availability and Terms

A deposit is required to confirm your date at one of the most unique facilities in Downtown Portland. Early reservations suggested.

## Description of Facility and Services

**Packages include:** Victorian ballroom decor, all table and chairs, dressing room for artists, Roman columns, ambient lighting, reception tables and coat racks.
**Event staff and OLCC Licensed bartenders:** included in package costs
**Bar facilities:** full bar services provided in-house (host, no-host or combination)
**Dance floor:** hardwood floors perfect for dancing; bands and DJs welcome
**Silverware, china, glassware and linens in your choice of colors:** included in package costs
**Cleanup:** included in package costs
**Parking:** across the street at 10th Avenue and Yamhill Street - City Center Smart Park
**Gratuity/service charge:** included in package costs

## VICTORIAN GRAND BALLROOM

The Adrianna Hill Grand Ballroom is an elegant 8,000-square-foot Victorian ballroom with a beautifully restored hardwood floor, suspended "U" shaped balcony, 55 foot-long stage backed by a high cathedral-style wall, large ornate brass chandeliers and 35-foot high beamed and vaulted ceiling. Built in 1901, this storybook setting with distinctive architecture has been recently refurbished. Elaborate Old World designs along the sculpted balcony are highlighted by white lights and tulle. Large gold framed mirrors, elegant artwork, antique-style foyer furniture, statuary, specialty lighting and decorative floral further enhance this unique setting. No additional decoration needed. We are proud to offer you a treasured and unforgettable experience in this nonsmoking environment.

# *Albertina's*

*The Shops at Albertina Kerr*

*424 N.E. 22nd Avenue*
*Portland, Oregon 97232*
*503.231.3909*
*www.albertinakerr.org*

---

**Capacity:** up to 200 for receptions; 90 for formal dinners
**Price Range:** varies according to event and menu; please call for information
**Catering:** full service, in-house catering
**Types of Events:** weddings and receptions, anniversaries, retirement parties, birthdays, family reunions, holiday functions, rehearsal dinners, business meetings, showers, brunches, luncheons, hors d'oeuvres and formal dinners.

## Availability and Terms

Albertina's offers four beautifully appointed rooms and two garden patios that can accommodate up to 200 guests in the summer and 150 guests in the winter. We suggest you reserve early to ensure availability. A $500 deposit will secure your date. Let our catering coordinator help plan your special day. Call 503-231-3909 for an appointment.

## Description of Facility and Services

**Servers:** all servers, hostess/host are provided by Albertina's
**Bar facilities:** champagne, wine, beer service; bartenders and servers provided
**Dance floor:** dance floor available upon request; ample electrical hookups
**Linens:** cloth tablecloths and skirting for service tables and paper napkins included for receptions; individual tablecloths and cloth napkins included with formal sit down events
**China, glassware and silver service:** provided by Albertina's
**Decorations:** beautiful fresh floral arrangements are provided for service tables, fireplace mantels and more in colors of your choice; please discuss your decorating ideas with Albertina's catering coordinator
**Cleanup:** provided
**Parking:** on-site parking as well as free street parking
**ADA:** accessible

## CHARMING HISTORIC SETTING FOR ALL SPECIAL OCCASIONS

Listed on the National Register of Historic Places and a Portland landmark, the stately, three story Georgian-style Old Kerr Nursery is conveniently located barely a mile from downtown Portland. Renovated in 1981 and refurbished in 2001, the Nursery is equally beautiful inside and out. The charming, home-like building and garden patios are the perfect setting for your special occasion. Experience the history of the Nursery building and the gracious attention to detail provided by Albertina's dedicated volunteer staff. Albertina's, one of The Shops at Albertina Kerr, is operated as a nonprofit business with all proceeds donated to Albertina Kerr Centers, whose programs provide services for children and youth at risk, families in need and individuals with disabilities.

**Capacity:** 300 people

**Price Range:** full course sit-down dinners or buffet style $40 Friday or Sunday, $40 Saturday during the day, $50 Saturday evening; plus 18% gratuity. Weddings are also available at the Lake Oswego location, same prices!
Business lunches: $20 plus 18% gratuity; business dinners: $30 plus 18% gratuity.

**Catering:** full-service in-house and off location catering

**Types of Events:** individual rooms for conferences, seminars, private meetings, large group luncheons, holiday parties, celebration dinners; from small intimate events up to 300, weddings and rehearsal dinners

## Availability and Terms

Reservations should be made as soon as possible to ensure availability. A deposit is required at the time of booking. Half the deposit is refundable if cancellations are made at least nine months prior to your event. **No** cost for using the facility, bartending services, linens, flowers, and candles, valet parking and classic piano.

## Description of Facility and Services

**Seating:** table and chairs provided for up to 300

**Servers:** provided with catering services

**Bar facilities:** full-service bar with bartender provided; host/no host; liquor provided according to OLCC regulations

**Dance floor:** available

**Linens:** cloth tablecloths and napkins provided in cream color

**China and glassware:** fine china and glassware

**Cleanup:** provided by Amadeus at the Fernwood, no cost.

**Decorations:** early decorating available; fresh flowers for guest tables provided by Amadeus; please discuss ideas with Kristina

**Parking:** ample free parking; valet service; **ADA:** disabled access available

## ROMANCE OVERLOOKING THE WILLAMETTE RIVER

Amadeus at the Fernwood is the perfect setting for an annual, monthly or quarterly function; or dinner for two. You and your guests will enjoy fine continental dining in a wonderful old mansion on two wooded acres, filled with antiques, fireplaces, crystal chandeliers, candlelight and fresh flowers, overlooking the Willamette River. We offer a full bar with a wide variety of Oregon and international wines, outdoor dining and wedding ceremonies on our patio is available. Piano music is also included.

**SUNSET DINNER SPECIAL:** Tue–Sun • 5–6:30pm • $9.95

# Ambridge Event Center

*300 NE Multnomah St.*
*Portland, Oregon 97232*
*website: www.ambridgeevents.com*
*email: info@ambridgeevents.com*
*phone: 503.239.9921*
*Business Hours: Mon–Fri 8am–5pm*

**Capacity:** Twelve private rooms totaling more than 20,000 sq. ft. of premium event space, including our Ambridge Rose Ballroom. We can accommodate group sizes from seven guests conference style, to 700 in a standing reception.
**Price Range:** Prices vary according to size of group and selection of service.
**Location:** Conveniently located in the heart of Portland near Interstate 5 and Interstate 84 bordered by the Oregon Convention Center and the Rose Quarter.
**Catering:** Full in house service, or choose from our preferred caterers.
**Types of Events:** Meetings, conferences, seminars, banquets, fundraisers, auctions, holiday parties, wedding ceremonies and receptions, proms, graduations, special celebrations.

## Availability and Terms

Reserve early for desired dates. Use our online request form to inquire about available space. A deposit and signed contract will confirm your space. Our Account Executives will be happy to assist you with our current event policies.

## Description of Facility and Services

**Seating:** Tables and chairs provided.
**Servers:** Provided in formal attire.
**Bar Facilities:** Full-service professional bar.
**Dance floor:** Original hardwood dance floor in our Ambridge Rose Ballroom and Portable parquet dance floor available; electrical hook ups for a band or DJ.
**Linens, napkins, china, glassware, and service items:** White linen tablecloths, napkins provided with catering.
**Cleanup:** Included in catering costs.
**Audio Visual:** High speed internet available in all rooms. In-house state of the art equipment. Prices vary based on needs.
**Parking:** Ample parking for clients plus MAX light-rail stops at our door.
**ADA:** Main and mall levels fully comply.

## FIRST STOP FOR EVENTS

Ambridge Event Center has crafted an unequalled reputation for personalized service that uniquely complements events like yours. Grown in the tradition of hospitality, the Ambridge Event Center takes its name for a perfect, old fashioned rose that thrives here in Portland. We are independent, privately owned and operated. For over 14 years, we have successfully hosted Corporate Events, Seminars, Workshops, Training Classes, Trade Shows, Company Retreats, Special Events, Proms, and much more. Remember, your event is as important to us as it is to you. Call and schedule a tour today!

*309 S.W. Broadway at Oak Street*
*Portland, Oregon 97205*
*Contact: Sales (503) 295-4100;*
*Fax (503) 471-3921*
*Office Hours: Mon–Fri 8am–6pm;*
*Available other times by appointment*
*E-mail: sales@bensonhotel.com*
*Web site: www.bensonhotel.com*

**Capacity:** a number of rooms available that will accommodate 10 to 600
**Catering:** full-service, in-house catering
**Types of Events:** 16,000 square feet of meeting space for breakfasts, luncheons, breakouts, receptions, dinners, fundraisers, social functions and meetings

## Availability and Terms

Make reservations as early as possible, especially for the holidays. A deposit may be required. Please call the sales department for details.

## Description of Facility and Services

**Seating:** variety of seating options available up to 400; tables and chairs provided
**Servers:** all servers and support staff included as needed
**Bar facilities:** full bar service; we provide all beverages, bartenders, and servers
**Linens and napkins:** linens provided
**China and glassware:** fine china and glassware available for your use
**Decorations:** we will be happy to discuss your ideas and needs; candles, mirrored tiles
**Cleanup:** handled by the staff
**Audiovisual:** complete audiovisual needs arranged by catering department; high-speed internet access available in all meeting rooms
**Equipment:** podium, easels and risers are available; on-site audiovisual company
**Parking:** ample parking near the hotel; cost varies according to time of day; valet parking available
**ADA:** handicap accessibility and facilities in all areas

## PORTLAND'S GRAND HOTEL

The Benson has long been known throughout the world for its elegance and fine service. Since 1912 The Benson Hotel has provided excellent service for the business community, entertainers and politicians. We offer traditional hospitality, and we pay attention to every detail to ensure our customers' satisfaction, may your event be for 10 or 600 people.

## GREENWOOD INN & SUITES

*S.W. Allen Boulevard at Highway 217*
*Beaverton, Oregon*
*(503) 643-7444*
*Office Hours: Mon–Fri 8am–5pm*
*And by appointment*
*Web site: www.greenwoodinn.com*

---

**Capacity:** 10 to 800 people
**Price Range:** room rentals and setup fees usually waived when meal minimums are met. Ranges: Breakfast $8 to $12; Lunch $10 to $16; Dinner $18 to $32; Reception $10 to $30
**Catering:** full service in-house catering
**Types of Events:** conferences, seminars, conventions, award luncheons and dinners, receptions and retreats

### Availability and Terms

The Greenwood Inn & Suites has nine private rooms accommodating a variety of group sizes. Advance reservations of two to six months are recommended. Also available is our Grand Suite for your special VIP events.

### Description of Facility and Services

**Seating:** various setup styles available
**Servers:** setup, full service, tear down
**Bar facilities:** host/no-host bars available; hotel supplies all liquor and bartender
**Dance floor:** spacious dance floor available
**Linens and napkins:** cloth linens available in a wide variety of colors at no additional cost
**China and glassware:** included in the cost of food and beverage
**Decorations:** limited decorative items provided at no additional charge. Elaborate theme events can also be arranged by our professional staff.
**Cleanup:** handled by The Greenwood Inn & Suites at no additional cost with normal usage
**Audiovisual:** complete in-house sound system; remote controlled, programmable lighting, and video capabilities; wide range of rental equipment available upon request
**Equipment:** lectern, whiteboards, easels, and risers available at no charge
**Parking:** ample free parking
**ADA:** meets all standards; all meeting rooms on ground level

### OVER 25 YEARS OF EXCELLENT SERVICE

The Best Western Greenwood Inn & Suites offers a resort-like atmosphere with a convenient location for you and your attendees. From rooms for your out-of-town guests to complete event and meeting planning services, we are here for you. It is our pleasure to be a part of your special event.

# Bossanova Ballroom

722 East Burnside
Portland, Oregon 97214
**Phone:** 503.233.7855
**Fax:** 503.445.7797
**Visit:** www.bossanovapdx.com
**Email:** booking@bossanovapdx.com

**Capacity:** 200 seated, 600+ cocktail
**Price Range:** Please contact Bossanova for information
**Catering:** Select your favorite caterer; in-house catering is not available
**Types of Events:** Live music shows, weddings, corporate events, private parties

## Availability and Terms

Contact Bossanova for availability. A 50% deposit is due to book event date, fully refundable if event is cancelled 30 days prior to date of event.

## Description of Facility and Services

**Seating:** Limited number of tables and chairs provided with rental
**Servers:** Provided by caterer or yourself
**China and glassware:** Can be negotiated with rental
**Linens:** Can be negotiated with rental
**Set up/clean up:** provided by client or caterer for catered events
**Bar facilities:** Full-service bar and bar staff provided exclusively by Bossanova; fully licensed and insured facility
**Dance floor:** yes
**ADA:** Limited accessibility

## PORTLAND'S BEST KEPT SECRET

From the moment you walk in to the Bossanova Ballroom you can feel the refined ambiance of a classic, turn-of-the-century social club turned hip, urban, and exclusive. It is a truly unique and versatile place to host your next big event; bringing the elegant, art-deco stylings of an old-world Freemason's Lodge/Dance Hall into the 21st century with state-of-the-art lighting and sound systems. The dance floor is hand-crafted and from imported Brazilian Cherry, and offers a beautiful, red-velvet curtained stage that is dynamic and flexible to accommodate a wide variety of live talent. The double-height ballroom boasts 25 foot ceilings with a view from the Mezzanine level above, which features an antique Billiards Room with five full-size tables and a separate, rentable private lounge. The entire venue can be easily sectioned off to accommodate an intimate setting for groups of 20-600+. We offer you the freedom to hand-select all of the people and services that will help you truly personalize your event. Our professional and courteous staff is completely committed to putting forth the extra effort to ensure that your event will exceed all of your expectations.

**Shown by appointment only**

# BRIDGEPORT BREWING COMPANY

*1313 N.W. Marshall Street • Portland, Oregon 97209*
*Contact: Manager of Special Events (503) 241-7179 ext. 210; Fax (503) 241-0625*
*Hours: Mon–Thurs 11:30am–11pm; Fri–Sat 11:30am–midnight; Sun 1pm–9pm*
*Web site: www.bridgeportbrew.com*

BRIDGEPORT ALES

---

**Capacity:** Two event rooms with total capacity of up to 150 people
**Price Range:** varies depending on group size, time, and day of event
**Catering:** Varied menu including assorted appetizers, salads, entrees and hand-crafted pizzas
**Types of Events:** Business meetings, holiday parties, project celebrations, reunions, receptions; great for both daytime and evening events

## Availability and Terms

BridgePort will undergo a facility remodel and renovation beginning in January 2005, to be completed over the course of the year. During the time of our renovation, event space will be unavailable for booking. Please consider us for future celebrations. Our unique and beautiful facility will be a great setting for your next event.

## Description of Facility and Services

**Seating:** tables and chairs provided for your group; arranged as requested
**Servers:** friendly, professional staff included
**Bar facilities:** up to six handcrafted ales ranging from our bright and hoppy India Pale Ale to our Heritage Blue Heron Ale; local wines, juice, sodas, fine coffee and teas are also available
**Dance floor:** accommodates DJ or band setup; electrical outlets available
**Linens and napkins:** napkins provided; linen can be arranged upon guest request
**China and glassware:** china provided by client; glassware provided by BridgePort
**Decorations:** please discuss decorating ideas with the Manager of Special Events; early access available with prior arrangement
**Cleanup:** included in room rental
**Audiovisual:** equipment available upon request
**Equipment:** any equipment needs arranged on request
**Parking:** limited street parking; complimentary evening parking offered in lot across street; daytime parking can be arranged upon request
**ADA:** yes, within the limitations of a historic building; elevator accessible

## HISTORIC LOCATION—RELAXED ATMOSPHERE

BridgePort is Oregon's oldest Craft Brewery, located in Portland's historic Pearl District. Exposed brick and timber beams, combined with the fresh aroma of microbrewed ales and homemade pizza, create a cozy pub atmosphere. All of our ales are handcrafted; our kitchen adheres to the same standard of quality that made our beers regionally famous. Uniquely Northwest, BridgePort (an entirely nonsmoking brewpub) is comfortable for meetings, social gatherings, and weddings. View or tour the brewery to see how the famous BridgePort Ales are made.

# CH2M HILL ALUMNI CENTER AT OSU

*204 CH2M HILL Alumni Center • Corvallis, Oregon 97331*
*Contact: Reservations Department (541) 737-2351; Toll free (877) 305-3759*
*Fax (541) 737-3481; Office Hours: Mon–Fri 8am–5pm;*
*E-mail: osualum@oregonstate.edu; Web site: http://alumni.oregonstate.edu/center/*

---

**Capacity:** **Cascade Ballroom:** 7,000 sq. ft.; **Willamette Room:** 1,600 sq. ft.; **conference rooms:** 680 sq.ft., 940 sq. ft.; **lounge:** 730 sq. ft.; **library:** 550 sq. ft.
**Price Range:** $50 to $1,395 per room
**Catering:** list of approved caterers provided
**Types of Events**: conferences, meetings, banquets, receptions, weddings, and parties

### Availability and Terms

We reserve rooms up to three years in advance and more, with some restrictions. A 30% deposit is due at time of booking, with the balance due 30 days prior to the event.

### Description of Facility and Services

**Seating:** tables and chairs included in rental cost
**Servers:** provided through caterer
**Bar facilities:** provided through caterer
**Linens and napkins:** white linens included in rental cost
**China and glassware:** provided through caterer
**Audiovisual:** podium, slide projector, overhead projector included in room rental
**Equipment:** risers and staging provided
**Parking:** visitor parking available
**ADA:** fully accessible

## EXPERIENCE THE UNIVERSITY DIFFERENCE

Take your event back to campus at the CH2M HILL Alumni Center at Oregon State University. This beautiful 45,000 square foot facility contains a variety of board and conference rooms, banquet and dining rooms, vendor and display space as well as an elegant lounge and living room area. The facility can host groups up to 1,000. All rooms feature multimedia presentation systems and teleconference capabilities.

The Center has a wide variety of indoor and outdoor spaces to accommodate everything from large regional, national and international conferences, to smaller local meetings, banquets, and receptions. Located in the heart of the Oregon State University campus, clients have access to the intellectual capital of OSU faculty and a multitude of University resources. Activities abound on campus including PAC-10 sporting events, concerts, world-renowned speakers, art exhibits, theater productions and films. Corvallis and the Alumni Center are centrally located in Oregon and an ideal place to host meetings and conferences. Those seeking quality and affordability need look no further. Call the CH2M HILL Alumni Center and let our event coordinators and staff ensure a successful conference! Mention this ad when booking your event, and receive a complimentary VIP Suite rental (*subject to availability).

*5700 S.W. Terwilliger Boulevard • Portland, Oregon 97239*
*(503) 246-6963*
*Business Hours: Mon–Fri 11:30am–10pm; Sat 5–10pm; Sun 5–9pm*

**Capacity:** 20 to 200 people
**Price Range:** please call for current prices
**Catering:** in-house
**Types of Events:** business meetings, retirement, award banquets, holiday parties, Bar/Bat Mitzvahs, rehearsal dinners, cocktail receptions and memorial services

## Availability and Terms

Entire restaurant can be reserved for private functions on Saturdays and Sundays until 3:30 p.m. During business hours, semi-private dining areas are available for lunch, cocktail and dinner events. Group dining reservations are secured with a deposit.

## Description of Facility and Services

**Seating:** View tables are available on all levels of the restaurant. Linens are provided and special color requests can be accommodated at no additional charge.
**Servers:** Prices include staffing. A 19% gratuity is added to all food and beverage sales
**Bar facilities:** Full or limited bar service is available
**Equipment:** Audiovisual equipment, dance floor, podium, microphone, etc. available at additional charge
**Linens:** tablecloths and napkins available in many colors at no additional charge
**China and glassware:** white china; clear glassware
**Decorations:** Assistance with floral, cake and music arrangements are available. Schedule early decorating - no confetti, please
**Parking:** complimentary valet service
**ADA:** limited handicap accessibility; restroom for disable on entrance floor

## Special Services

Manager will be available to direct staff and provide personal attention to ensure your event's success. We offer an extensive wine list and can special order wines and champagnes. Dietary requests can be accommodated.

## SPECTACULAR VIEWS!

There is nothing like a spectacular view to enhance a delicious dining experience. For those in quest of a seamless blend of sumptuous cuisine, impeccable service, and exceptional atmosphere, Chart House is the perfect venue.

Situated in Southwest Hills, Chart House imports a sense of subtle elegance and is distinctive for its picture windows overlooking Mt. Hood, Mt. St. Helens, the Willamette River and downtown Portland. The seafood and steaks are as impressive as the views, and the menu changes daily with fresh fish options joining menu staples like macadamia crusted mahi mahi, seared ahi tuna, and a fantastic slow-roasted prime rib.

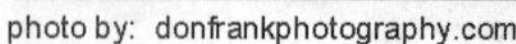

photo by: donfrankphotography.com

# The Chelsea Ballroom

## at Arnegards

*tours by appointment*

*Ninth and SE Hawthorne*
*1510 SE Ninth*
*Portland, Oregon • 97214*
*(503) 236 - 2759*
*www.chelseaballroom.com*

**Capacity:** 240 Seated, 350+ Reception style. The Chelsea Ballroom, with its large stage, will hold 300 guests. The Grace Ballroom can accommodate 96. Our Meeting Room holds 24 people.

**Price Range:** Prices vary according to number of people and date of event, please call for details. Discounts available to non-profit organizations.

**Catering:** Choose from our list of preferred caterers.

**Types of Events:** Banquets, meetings and seminars, dances and proms, concerts, wine tastings, reunions, holiday and retirement parties, luncheons, dinners, private cocktail parties, wedding ceremonies and receptions, rehearsal dinners.

### Availability and Terms

To ensure reserving the date you want, plan to make your reservations six to nine months in advance. A 50% deposit is due at the time of booking to confirm your date.

### Description of Facility

Convenient Southeast Portland location just two minutes from downtown, our ballrooms feature hardwood floors, round tables and chairs for 240 people and banquet tables.

**Bar facilities:** The bar is located off the Chelsea Ballroom, staffing provided by your caterer.

**Dance floors:** The Chelsea Ballroom has a maple dance floor with a capacity of 300. The Grace ballroom has an oak dance floor with a capacity of 96.

**Servers, linens and china:** Provided by caterer.

**Decorations:** The facility is well decorated with mirrors and artwork. Please discuss your decorating ideas with our event coordinator.

**Cleanup:** Provided by your caterer.

**Parking:** On-site for 10-15 cars as well as plenty of free street parking.

### HISTORIC 1920s BALLROOM

Conveniently located just across the Hawthorne bridge in Southeast Portland in a beautiful 1920's historic building, the Chelsea and Grace Ballrooms feature 14' high ceilings, decorative woodwork, chandeliers, lighted ceiling fans and great acoustics. The Grace Ballroom (capacity 96), is perfect for your company function, holiday party, banquet or reception. The larger Chelsea Ballroom will comfortably hold up to 300 people and is a wonderful location for receptions, dances and other large events. Our Meeting Room, holding 24 people, is available for smaller functions and can be rented on an hourly basis. We'd love to talk with you about your event – feel free to call anytime to schedule a tour of the Chelsea Ballroom.

RESORT

*1777 N.W. 44th Street*
*Lincoln City, Oregon 97367*
*Contact: Steve Chrisman*
*(541) 996-5925, (888) CHINOOK ext. 5925*
*stevec@chinookwindsgaming.com • www.chinookwindscasino.com*
*Business Hours: 8am–6pm; messages taken 24 hours*

**Capacity:** groups from 20 to 2,000; over 44,000 square feet total; main room, 20,000 square feet accommodating 1,610 theater-style and 1,120 sit-down; eight rooms with 3,000+ square feet; five rooms, 550+ square feet; additional showroom space available: 15,000 square feet, theatre seating for 1,400 or 60 trade show booths (depending on setup)
**Price Range:** prices vary depending on menu selection and size of event
**Catering:** Full-service, in-house catering
**Types of Events:** any type of function: 20 to 2,000 people; dinners, receptions, trade shows, conventions, meetings, fundraisers, seminars, conferences, weddings, reunions; breakout rooms available

## Availability and Terms

We encourage you to book early to ensure availability.

## Description of Facility and Services

**Seating:** various styles for up to 1200
**Servers:** provided by Chinook Winds
**Bar facilities:** full-service bar and bartender
**Dance floor:** in-house floor can be rented
**Linens:** provided; variety of colors to choose from at a minimal charge
**China:** provided; variety to choose from
**Decorations:** various themes to choose from
**Audio/Visual:** complete equipment available upon request
**Parking:** abundant free parking and valet service, free hotel shuttles
**ADA:** meets all ADA requirements

## Special Services

Our 4-star chef and professional staff work to produce a magnificent event that your company will be proud of. Other amenities include full-service Business Center, childcare, arcade, ocean view, buffet, deli, private gaming tournaments, golf and wedding packages, fine dining.

### FLEXIBLE MEETING SPACES

The newest resort on the Oregon coast, Chinook Winds Casino and Convention Center overlooks the picturesque Pacific Ocean and offers over 44,000 square feet of meeting space. The recent acquisition of the adjacent 247 room oceanfront hotel (formerly Shilo) makes us an even more spectacular location. Our host of services provide for a wide range of needs and afford the meeting planner creativity and flexibility with their event. The main conference area opens to 20,000 sq. ft. of carpeted meeting space. The ample room can be divided into as many as six rooms of over 3,000 sq. ft. each. Also available are three meeting/breakout rooms and a full-service Business Center. An additional 15,000 sq. ft. is available in the showroom to accommodate trade shows or theatre style seating for up to 1,400. All these options add up to 44,000 sq. ft.! Just minutes from great golf, outlet shopping and nature's impressive splendors, let us make your next event fresh and exciting while you watch your attendance rise. We don't just say *It's Better At The Beach,* we prove it.

# COOPER SPUR MOUNTAIN RESORT

*10755 Cooper Spur Road • Mt. Hood, Oregon 97041*
*(541) 352-6692, (800) ski-hood*
*www.cooperspur.com*

---

**Capacity:** groups of up to 70, or take your event outdoors
**Price Range:** moderate to customized events; please inquire
**Catering:** in-house catering only; cabins include kitchenettes; log home has full kitchen
**Types of Events:** business meetings, team building, conferences, seminars, retreats, weddings, social gatherings, buffet, sit-down, cocktails, overnight lodging, skiing, hiking, snowshoeing

## Availability and Terms

Advanced bookings are encouraged. Deposits required with payment due in full upon arrival.

## Description of Facility and Services

**Seating:** provided to accommodate group size
**Servers:** provided
**Bar facilities:** full-service bar available
**Audiovisual:** full selection of audiovisual services available; please inquire for pricing
**Parking:** ample complimentary parking available
**ADA:** fully applies

## Social Services:

Cooper Spur Mountain Resort is a mountain lodge and meeting center on the north side of Mt. Hood, featuring log cabins, lodge condo suites, hotel rooms, a log home, restaurant and lounge, Alpine ski area, Nordic Center with cross country trails, tennis court, spa facility with a deck, four hot tubs and two massage therapy rooms. Cooper Spur Mountain Resort facilitates business meetings, team building sessions and recreational pursuits, as well as family vacations. It is located on 775 acres of private forest land, a 1,400 acre US Forest Service permit area, all surrounded by the Mt. Hood National Forest. The cabins and lodge structures portray a simple elegance and invite you to come and stay. Our cabins and log home provide the perfect place to meet and retreat. Intimate and private yet fully supported by the Cooper Spur meeting planner and restaurant staff.

## MT. HOOD MEADOWS SKI RESORT

Cooper Spur Mountain Resort is located just 12 miles from Mt. Hood Meadows Ski Resort. Guests of Cooper Spur ski for just $25. Group rates are also available for lessons and rental equipment.

The Best Value Under The Sun.™

# DAYS INN CITY CENTER

*1414 S.W. Sixth Avenue • Portland, Oregon 97201*
*Contact: Sales Department*
*(503) 484-0255 or (800) 899-0248; Fax (503) 274-7325*
*E-mail: daysinn.inpdx@starwoodhotels.com*
*Web site: www.the.daysinn.com/portland05313*

---

**Capacity:** we offer three rooms and one suite to accommodate up to 200 people; seasonal outdoor space up to 400 people
**Catering:** in-house catering available
**Price Range:** varies depending on menu and type of event
**Types of Events:** breakfast meetings, brunches, lunches, business meetings, seminars, dinners, banquets, weddings, wedding receptions, any social or business gathering

## Availability and Terms

Days Inn City Center recommends that you make your reservation for space as early as possible, particularly for our outdoor pool and pavilion area.

## Description of Facility and Services

**Seating:** tables and chairs provided; banquet, round and classroom tables available
**Servers:** staff included in catering cost
**Bar facilities:** full beverage service available
**Linens and napkins:** an extensive array of colors available at no extra charge
**China and glassware:** white china and stemmed glassware
**Decorations:** mirrored tiles, votive candles, bud vases, silk plants, themed decor available
**Audiovisual:** available upon request
**Equipment:** podiums, risers and staging available
**Cleanup:** provided by hotel staff
**Parking:** on-site, subject to availability
**ADA:** accessible

## Special Services

Days Inn City Center features 173 newly renovated guest rooms, including one suite. Your guests will enjoy our "heart of downtown" location and other amenities including on-site parking, complimentary daily newspaper delivered to your door, data ports, and pay-per-view movies and games in each room. Our heated outdoor pool is available seasonally, and an adjacent Health Club is available complimentary to all guests. Group rates are available for 10 or more rooms.

## IN THE HEART OF DOWNTOWN PORTLAND

Plan your event in our flexible meeting space and banquet facilities. We will cater to the needs of your guests while you focus on the business at hand. *We are truly at your service!*

# DESCHUTES COUNTY FAIR & EXPO CENTER

*3800 S.W. Airport Way • Redmond, Oregon 97756*
*Contact: Roxia Thornton Todoroff, Director of Sales (866) 800-EXPO, (541) 548-2711*
*Fax (541)923-1652; Office hours: Mon–Fri 8am-5pm*
*E-mail: roxiat@deschutes.org; Web site: www.expo.deschutes.org*

---

**Capacity:** Northwest Premiere Convention & Exhibition Facility: Event Center, 40,000 sq. ft. arena floor, 28, 250 sq. ft. concourse, concert seating up to 7,500, arena seating up to 4,000, 274 trade show booth space. Three Sister Conference Center & High Desert Activity Center: meeting rooms total 46,420 sq. ft. divisible into fourteen individual rooms, ceiling height is 14'. Three main halls can accommodate 1,200 – 1,600 theatre style.

**Price range:** Please call for current rates.

**Catering:** Exclusive on-site catering is provided by C&D Event Management, ensuring exceptional quality and a dedication to excellence.

**Types of Events:** conventions, trade shows, meetings, banquets, weddings, receptions, performances, concerts and sporting events

## Availability and Terms

Please call for available dates. A 20% deposit is required to contract space with full prepayment 60 days prior to event date. Guarantees seven days prior to event with final guarantee 72 hours in advance.

## Description of Facility and Services

**Seating:** tables and chairs available
**Servers:** provided by C&D Event Management
**Bar facilities:** provided by C & D Event Management
**Linens and napkins:** provided by C&D Event Management
**China and glassware:** provided by C&D Event Management
**Cleanup:** provided by staff
**Trade Show Services:** A perimeter road gives easy access to the back of each building with 14' roll-up doors for easy load in/load out. All buildings are climate controlled with built-in sound systems; conference center features power, telephone and data port connections in floor on 20 ft. squares.
**Banquet & Conference Services:** equipment, classroom, banquet tables and chairs, staging, podium, house sound and microphones available
**Lodging:** assistance with lodging through CVB and Visitor's Association
**Parking:** parking for over 4,000 with direct access to Conference & Event Center; additional 100 acres of parking for Expo Center
**ADA:** fully accessible; meets all ADA requirements

We really can do it all and are eager to share what we know will exceed your expectations.

## HAYDEN ISLAND COMPLEX

©Adams & Faith

*Jantzen Beach*
*909 N. Hayden Island Drive*
*Portland, OR 97217*
*(503) 283-4466*

*Columbia River*
*1401 N. Hayden Island Drive*
*Portland, OR 97217*
*(503) 283-2111*

*Contact: Sales and Catering Office*
*Office Hours: Mon-Fri 8am-5pm*

---

**Capacity:** up to 1,400 for sit-down events; combined total of over 55,000 square feet of space
**Price Range:** price will vary depending on type of event and menu selection
**Catering:** full service in-house catering provided by the hotel exclusively
**Types of Events:** receptions, luncheon and dinner affairs, meetings, seminars, conventions, reunions, corporate retreats; any special event!

### Availability and Terms

Our hotels feature many meeting rooms to accommodate groups of all sizes. It is suggested that reservations be made as soon as possible. Please call the Sales and Catering office for details.

### Description of Facility and Services

**Seating:** tables and chairs provided by the hotel
**Servers:** staff included in catering costs
**Bar facilities:** full beverage service; hotel provides all beer, wine and liquor
**Dance floor:** ample size available at no additional charge
**Linens and napkins:** an extensive array to select from at no additional charge
**China and glassware:** white china; stemmed glassware included
**Cleanup:** provided by hotel staff
**Decorations:** silk plants, mirror tiles, candle votives, theme enhancements
**Audiovisual:** in-house audiovisual provided by Presentation Services
**Equipment:** podium, risers, and staging provided at no additional charge
**Parking:** ample, complimentary parking; **ADA:** accessible

### Special Services

The Doubletree Hotels Jantzen Beach and Columbia River offer deluxe guest rooms with in-room coffee makers, irons and ironing boards. For the business traveler, each room has a large desk with data port phones and no telephone access charge. Fitness room, business center, tennis courts, pool and spa are also available.

### BEAUTIFUL RIVERFRONT LOCATION
### PROFESSIONAL AND QUALITY SERVICE

Our hotels feature many spacious meeting rooms, several of which have floor to ceiling windows overlooking the beautiful Columbia River. Our reputation for extraordinary cuisine and exceptional service, makes us the ideal location for your next event! We are located directly off I-5 just 10 minutes from downtown and the airport, making us convenient for all guests. Spectacular cuisine abounds with casual dining in the Coffee Garden or Jantzen Beach Café and formal dining in the Hayden Island Steak House or Brickstones Restaurants. Docking is available for all Portland area riverboats as well as spacious patios for riverside events. Jantzen Beach is also home to Portland's largest hotel ballroom!

# DOUBLETREE®

## HOTEL & EXECUTIVE MEETING CENTER

PORTLAND • LLOYD CENTER

*1000 N.E. Multnomah • Portland, Oregon 97232*
*Contact: Catering Office (503) 331-4952*
*Business Hours: Mon–Fri 8am–5pm*

**Capacity:** four ballrooms seating up to 1,100; 17,000-square-foot exhibit hall accommodates 120 8'x10' exhibit booths; 8,500 sq. ft., IACC approved Executive Meeting Center
**Price Range:** price will vary depending on type of event and menu selection
**Catering:** full-service in-house catering provided by the hotel exclusively
**Types of Events:** light hors d'oeuvre receptions to elegant luncheon and dinner affairs, weddings, meetings, seminars, conventions, holiday parties, kosher events, etc.

### Availability and Terms

The DoubleTree Hotel & Executive Meeting Center Portland • Lloyd Center offers four separate newly redesigned ballrooms to accommodate any size event. Our 9,100 sq. ft. Lloyd Center Ballroom is one of Portland's finest. Divide it up into five sections or open it up as one large room; its flexibility is amazing.

### Description of Facility and Services

**Seating:** rounds, u-shape, classroom, conference or theater
**Servers:** staff included in catering costs
**Bar facilities:** full beverage service available; DoubleTree Hotel & Executive Meeting Center Portland • Lloyd Center to provide all alcohol
**Dance floor:** available at no additional charge
**Linens and napkins:** your choice of house linen colors
**China and glassware:** white china; stemmed glassware
**Cleanup:** included in price
**Audiovisual and meeting equipment**: in-house audiovisual company; podium, risers and staging available; dedicated T-1 line for meeting space; all meeting rooms hardwired with CAT 5e; wireless connectivity in all public space
**Parking:** parking for over 550 cars
**ADA:** accessible

### Special Services

The DoubleTree Hotel Portland • Lloyd Center offers concierge services as well as a business center to meet all your business and meeting needs. We offer special group rates on our 476 beautifully appointed guest rooms.

### LET US TAKE CARE OF THE DETAILS

Choose the DoubleTree Hotel & Executive Meeting Center • Lloyd Center. Our professional catering coordinators can accommodate all your planning needs. From menu planning to room decor and design, our experienced and friendly staff are specially trained to take the stress and pressure out of planning your event. Our convenient location and ample parking make attending your special event easy for your guests. Our Pacific Northwest Ballroom, with beautiful window-views of the outdoor pool and patio area, provides the perfect setting to make your event memorable.

## at the Eastmoreland Golf Course

*2425 S.E. Bybee Boulevard*
*Portland, Oregon 97202* Clark
*Contact: ~~Jerilyn Walker~~, Events Coordinator*
*(503) 775-5910; Fax (503) 775-6349*
*Web site: www.eastmorelandgrill.com*
*Office Hours: 9am–5pm*

---

**Capacity:** 125 for a sit-down dinner; 175 for a reception
**Price Range:** price varies depending on the season
**Catering:** full-service catering available in-house
**Types of Events:** cocktails and hors d'oeuvres, buffet, sit-down dinners, luncheons, breakfast, barbecues and business meetings

### Availability and Terms

The Eastmoreland Grill encourages your reservations up to one year in advance. A deposit is required and is nonrefundable. Half-payment is required 30 days in advance, with the remaining half payable on the day of the event.

### Description of Facility and Services

**Seating:** tables and chairs provided
**Servers:** full staff available; a gratuity will be added to food and beverage purchases
**Bar facilities:** full-service bar and staff bartender provided upon request; host/no-host; liquor, beer, and wine
**Dance floor:** we can provide a dance floor on a rental basis
**Linens and napkins:** cloth tablecloths and napkins available in some colors
**China and glassware:** white china; glassware in plastic or glass, as required
**Decorations:** our catering manager will discuss with you and help develop your decoration plans
**Cleanup:** cleanup provided
**Audiovisual and meeting equipment:** arrangements can be made to accommodate
**Parking:** large parking lot with overflow area
**ADA:** fully complies

### GRACIOUS STYLE OVERLOOKING LUSH GREENS

The lush, beautiful greens of the Eastmoreland Golf Course are the setting for our gorgeous new Tudor-style clubhouse. The banquet room overlooks the tenth tee and has a large, gracious veranda for outdoor entertaining. Winter events are equally blessed with a handsome fireplace where guests love to gather. Our staff has extensive experience in corporate events, anniversaries, weddings, birthdays, and reunions, and we will create a personal menu exactly to your specifications. A telephone call to our staff will start you on your way to a carefree and beautiful event.

## ECOTRUST CONFERENCE CENTER

***In the Jean Vollum Natural Capital Center***

*721 N.W. Ninth Avenue, 2nd Floor, Portland, Oregon 97209*

*(503) 227-6225 • www.ecotrust.org • events@ecotrust.org*

---

**Capacity:** 10 to 130; 2nd floor conference room, 1,800 sq. ft.; 3rd floor outdoor terrace, 2,200 sq. ft.

**Price Range:** Rates for non-profit and for-profit organizations vary depending on size of event.

**Catering:** Preferred caterer's list provided upon request. Hosting kitchen attached to conference center.

**Types of Events:** Workshops, seminars, lectures, board meetings, fund raisers, receptions, weddings, movie house

### Availability and Terms

The Conference Center is available year-round, Monday through Saturday, 7am–10pm. The 3rd floor terrace is available during the summer months Monday through Friday, 5–10pm, Saturdays 8am–10pm.

### Description of Facility and Services

**Seating:** Herman Miller 2x5 rectangular tables (40 total) and chairs (150 total)

**Servers:** Upon request with preferred caterers

**Linens and napkins:** Provided by caterers

**China and glassware:** Provided by caterers

**Audiovisual:** The Conference Center provides a state-of-the-art, fully-equipped A/V system: microphones; powerpoint, slide, and overhead projectors; DVD, CD, VCR; flip charts and white boards, all included in the rental.

**Cleanup:** Provided by caterers and the Natural Capital Center

**Parking:** Ample street parking and public parking lots very close to the building; two hour visitor parking available in Natural Capital Center parking lot

**ADA:** Yes

### "THE UN-CONVENTIONAL CONVENTION CENTER"

The Ecotrust Conference Center is located on the 2nd floor of the newly renovated Jean Vollum Natural Capital Center. Originally built in 1895, the three-story warehouse has been transformed into a landmark for green building and the conservation economy. Strategically situated in the heart of Portland's Pearl District, the Natural Capital Center is the perfect location for your next gathering.

# EMBASSY SUITES PORTLAND DOWNTOWN

EMBASSY SUITES HOTELS®

*319 S.W. Pine Street • Portland, Oregon 97204*
*Contact: Lisa Going-Green (503) 279-9000 ext. 6166; Fax (503) 220-0206*
*Web site: www.embassyportland.com*

---

**Capacity:** Colonel Lindberg: 2,905 square feet, 220 banquet, 300 meeting; Queen Marie: 2,240 square feet, 150 banquet, 234 meeting
**Price Range:** please inquire
**Catering:** in-house catering
**Types of Events:** meetings, banquets, wedding receptions, trade shows

## Availability and Terms

Two elegant ballrooms, seven smaller rooms and 20 conference suites. Most rooms have windows and are decorated in the classic style of the Multnomah Hotel with all the amenities of an Embassy Suites. Direct billing with approved credit application.

## Description of Facility and Services

**Seating:** tables and chairs for up to 220 in largest room
**Servers:** professional service staff available
**Bar facilities:** hotel provides liquor and bartenders; corkage charge of $15 per bottle of wine brought in
**Dance floor:** available with electrical hookups
**Linens and napkins:** several colors available at no charge
**Decorations:** check with hotel staff representative
**Cleanup:** provided by hotel
**Audiovisual:** on-site; DSL lines in all meeting rooms
**Equipment:** staging, podiums, risers and flip charts on site
**Parking:** 404 covered parking spaces; valet and self parking available
**ADA:** all facilities handicapped accessible

## Special Services

276 guest suites, full cooked-to-order breakfast, manager's reception. Full sales and catering staff to assist in event arrangements.

## FLEXIBLE MEETING SPACE IN MAGNIFICENT SURROUNDINGS

The Multnomah Hotel, originally built in 1912, has been restored to its original grandeur and is now the Embassy Suites Portland Downtown. The original grand ballroom of the hotel has been magnificently restored and is part of over 22,000 square feet of flexible meeting and banquet space. The largest room can do banquets up to 220, meetings up to 300 and 25 exhibit booths. The hotel's 20 conference suites are perfect for small board meetings or hospitality suites.

# EVERGREEN AVIATION MUSEUM

*500 N.E. Captain Michael King Smith Way, off Hwy. 18*
*McMinnville, Oregon 97128*
*Contact: Kristin Russell*
*(503) 434-4023; Fax: (503) 434-4188*
*Business Hours: Daily 9am–5pm*
*Web: www.sprucegoose.org; E-mail: events@sprucegoose.org*

---

**Capacity:** up to 3,000 people (reception) and 1,000 people (sit-down)
**Price Range:** varies according to rental space and size of group; please call for specific information
**Catering:** no in-house catering; offer recommended catering list
**Types of Events:** social or business meetings, reunions, receptions, holiday parties, auctions, theme events and weddings

## Availability and Terms

Reserve as early as possible for your desired date. Short-term notice events are available, space-permitting. A 25% deposit is required to reserve the date and the space.

## Description of Facility and Services

**Seating:** tables and chairs available
**Bar facilities:** provided by caterer
**Servers:** provided by caterer
**Dance floor:** available
**Linens:** white linen tablecloths included, colored linens are an additional cost
**China:** provided by caterer
**Equipment:** podium, portable speaker system, tables, chairs, stage and unique airline seats
**Cleanup:** courtesy of Evergreen Aviation Museum and caterers
**Parking:** ample parking available in adjacent parking lot for free
**ADA:** accessible

## Special Services

An experienced event coordinator is on site for every event. Volunteer docents are available for gallery tours. A variety of rental spaces are offered within the gallery, in the theater, on the patio or in the oak grove.

## AWE-INSPIRING ENVIRONMENT

Our patrons experience the joy of celebrating momentous occasions and unique events in an awe-inspiring environment. Being surrounded by vintage and one-of-a-kind aircraft, including Howard Hughes's "Spruce Goose" and the SR-71 "Blackbird," makes every event in this 121,000 sq. ft. structure an experience of a lifetime.

## FAMILY FUN CENTER & BULLWINKLE'S RESTAURANT

*29111 SW Town Center Loop W., Wilsonville, Oregon 97070*
*Contact: Group Sales (503) 685-5000 ext. 21*
*Email group@fun-center.com Fax: (503) 685-9694*
*OPEN YEAR ROUND*
*Web site: www.fun-center.com*

---

**Capacity:** 10 to 350 people in meeting areas; 2,000 capacity in amusement park
**Price Range:** $18 to $35 per person
**Catering:** in-house catering
**Types of Events:** Corporate meetings, seminars, company picnics, trade shows, wedding receptions, social functions, birthday parties, team parties and more.

### Availability and Terms

Reservations should be made as soon as possible to ensure availability. The park is open year-round. A non-refundable deposit is required at the time of booking.

### Description of Facility and Services

**Seating:** indoor: tables and chairs provided for up to 350 people. Smaller meeting rooms are available
**Servers:** provided by Bullwinkle's Restaurant
**Linens & Napkins:** provided by Bullwinkle's
**Audiovisual and Equipment:** available upon request
**Cleanup:** included in price
**Parking:** plenty of parking
**ADA:** meets all standards; meeting rooms are on ground level

**ADULTS DESERVE TO HAVE FUN TOO!**

CONVENTION & PERFORMING ARTS CENTER

*715 Quince Street • Florence, Oregon 97439*
*(541) 997-1994, (888) 968-4086*
*Fax (541) 902-0991; Web site: www.eventcenter.org*

---

**Capacity:** up to 500; seven meeting rooms totaling 8,000 square feet and a 457-seat proscenium theater for general session; total facility is 21,000 square feet.
**Price Range:** varies according to rental space; please call for specific price information
**Catering:** full-service in-house and off-premise catering available
**Type of Events:** conferences, meetings, trade shows, banquets, receptions, weddings, parties, concerts, theater and more

## Availability and Terms

Florence Events Center offers 8,000 square feet of meeting space. The flat-floor area divides into five rooms. Two additional meeting rooms, the Board Room and Green Room, are available as well as the 457-seat theater for general session or additional break-out.

## Description of Facility and Services

**Seating:** various setup styles available
**Servers:** caterer to provide
**Bar facilities:** host/no-host bars available; caterer supplies all liquor and bartender
**Linens and napkins:** linens available to match your decor/theme
**China and glassware:** included in cost of food and beverage
**Dance floor:** dance floor available upon request at standard rental rate; electrical hookup for bands or disc jockey available
**Decorations:** creative theme events may be arranged
**Cleanup:** fees vary
**Equipment:** variety of booth sizes including pipe and drape, podium, easels and risers available
**Audiovisual:** complete inventory for flat floor and theater
**Parking:** complimentary off-street parking
**ADA:** meets standards; all meeting rooms are on ground level; special needs accommodated

## WHERE THE ADVENTURE AWAITS

Located on the beautiful central Oregon coast, with easy access from highways 101 and 126, the Florence Events Center is an ideal location for seminars, conferences, receptions, parties, trade shows, art exhibits and weddings. The center can easily accommodate up to 500 people. Unique to the Oregon coast is our 8,000 square foot meeting space and 457-seat theater in the historical coastal community of Florence. Please call for an information packet or visit our web site.

**The adventure of Florence awaits, experience it for yourself...**

Helvetia, Oregon
Contact: Melinda 503-547-9046
www.gardenvineyards.com



**Capacity:** Small intimate parties to grand events of 500 or more
**Price Range:** Varies based on size and style of celebration, call for details
**Catering:** In-house
**Types of Events:** High-style social events including weddings and associated pre-wedding parties; executive level multi-course luncheons and dinners; corporate parties and events.

## Availability and Terms

Call for current availability, a deposit is required to reserve your date.

## Description of Facilities and Services

**Seating:** Entire estate including interior of villa and gardens are designed and appointed for grand entertaining. Abundant outdoor and garden furniture as well as comfortable height walls and steps for sitting.
**Servers:** All types of service presentations are available.
**Bar facilities:** Full bar available. Garden Vineyards wine is served at all events.
**Floral arrangements:** Our gardens provide the flowers and foliage for some of Portland's premier event floral designers. We can work with your floral designer to provide material for display or you can simply allow the gardens to provide the floral design themselves.
**Music:** We can accommodate a wide variety of music options, ranging from a selection of your favorite CDs playing throughout the villa, terraces and gardens to live band performances.
**Dance floor:** Permanent dance floor.
**Tenting:** Permanent weather-proof awning structures.
**Linens and napkins:** Many options available.
**China and glassware:** Many options available.
**Cleanup:** Completed by staff.
**Parking:** Valet service is provided for all events.
**ADA:** Accessible.

## Special Amenities and Services

Garden Vineyards wines, Pinot Noir and Pinot Gris. Private hotel style suite quarters for wedding party preparations. Permanent gazeboes and other garden seating and structures. Permanent outdoor sound system, weatherproof awnings and landscape lighting.

## A Grand Celebration Venue

Just 15 miles from downtown Portland or in the heart of Tuscany? A Grand Italian Villa perched atop a hillside vineyard. Gardens showcasing the most beautiful flower, the garden rose. Wine grown on-site and produced by one of Oregon's premier wine makers, Peter Rosback.

The gated entry, the vineyard, the acres of lawn, the expansive view of the valley, the gourmet cuisine and the villa itself, create a grandness of scale your guests will never forget. The intimate details like an ancient birdbath hidden amongst lavender and foxglove, the carefulness of a staff member or the beauty of a single perfect rose are the small things that you will always remember.

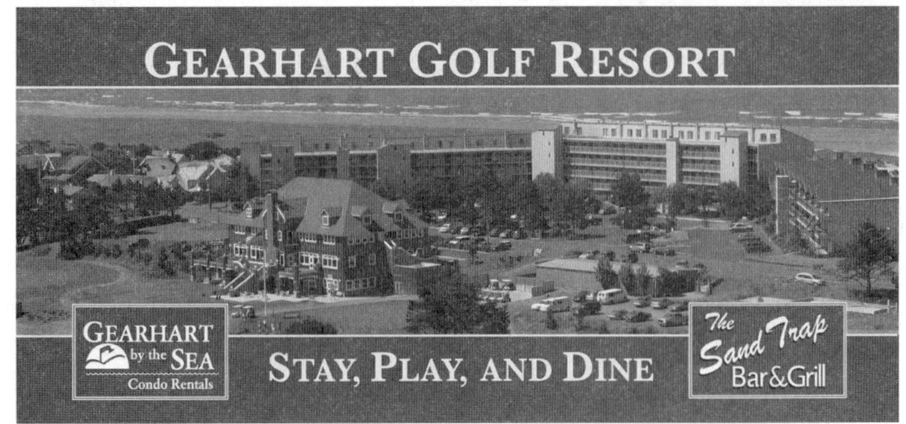


*1157 N. Marion • Gearhart, Oregon 97138*
*Contact: Tami Gandy 1-800-547-0115; Fax: 503-738-0881; gearhartgolfresort.com*

---

**Capacity:** Up to 300 receptions, 180 seated
**Price Range:** Varies depending on event
**Catering:** indoor/outdoor full service catering tailored to your event
**Types of Events:** weddings, receptions, reunions, meetings, and corporate events

## Availability and Terms

Reservations are to be made in advance. A deposit of 25% is required 30 days prior to event or upon reservation.

## Description of Facility and Services

**Seating:** tables and chairs provided
**Servers:** professional and friendly staff provided
**Bar facilities:** yes
**Linens and napkins:** provided
**China and glassware:** provided
**Audiovisual and meeting equipment:** available upon request
**Cleanup:** provided
**Parking:** plenty of off-street parking available
**ADA:** yes
**Guest Rooms:** 92

## A FAMILY BEACH TRADITION SINCE 1892

Gearhart Golf Resort provides the perfect backdrop for weddings, reunions, corporate retreats, meetings, or anyone looking to experience the magic of a coastal getaway. From our spacious one and two-bedroom condo suites equipped with fireplaces, indoor pool, and just moments away from miles of beach, Gearhart By The Sea is meant for relaxation.

The newly remodeled Sandtrap Bar and Grill offers a wide variety of northwest cuisine, daily fresh seafood or mouthwatering steaks and pastas. From casual breakfast and lunch to romantic candlelight dinners you will be able to enjoy elegant dining in a casual atmosphere.

Test your golf on the Nnorthwest's oldest links course. With an upgraded course layout, Gearhart Golf Links provides year-round playability as well as pleasure for both the weekend golfer and low handicappers.

*4200 S.W. Mercantile Drive*
*Lake Oswego, Oregon 97035*
*(503) 635-1313*
*Hours: Mon–Fri 11am–9:30pm; Saturday 4pm–9:30pm*

---

**Capacity:** private room can accommodate up to 80 people
**Price Range:** room is free of charge with the purchase of food or beverages
**Catering:** in-house catering on-site
**Types of Events:** seminars, meetings, group luncheons, holiday parties, celebrations of all kinds

## Availability and Terms

Every attempt will be made to accommodate your event no matter when it is booked; however, reservations should be made as soon as possible to ensure availability.

## Description of Facility and Services

**Seating:** tables and chairs provided
**Servers:** provided
**Bar facilities:** beer and wine
**Linens and napkins:** burgundy linens provided
**Decorations:** table decorations are permissible
**Clean up:** provided with a $50 refundable deposit
**Parking:** free parking on-site
**Audiovisual:** TV and VCR available free of charge
**ADA:** in full compliance

## Special Services

Our private banquet room, located conveniently in Lake Oswego, will accommodate 64 to 80 people and includes audiovisual equipment available to use for any event.

All items on our menu are available for take out or delivery. A minimum order is required for free delivery. Delivery minimum amount depends on location of delivery. Please call for further details.

## A GREAT GATHERING PLACE WITH GOURMET FOOD

Choose from our extensive gourmet menu. Select your favorite Gourmet Stuft Combination or create your own pizza featuring our dough made fresh daily using high-glutten, unbleached wheat flour, hand thrown to create a delicious bread-like crust. Add your choice of 23 toppings! Help yourself to a fresh selection of garden vegetables, delicious dressings and assorted garnishing from our salad bar. Other menu features include "Hot Gourmet Stuft" sandwiches, deli sandwiches, calzoni, soups and "Texas Style" chili.

# THE GROTTO CONFERENCE CENTER

*Contact: Gayle Diehl*
*Sandy Boulevard at N.E. 85th Avenue*
*Portland, Oregon 97294*
*(503) 254-7371; Fax (503) 254-7948*
*Web site: www.thegrotto.org E-mail: volunteer@thegrotto.org*
*Business Hours: 9am–5pm Mon–Fri; Appointments recommended*

---

**Capacity:** 5 to 225 depending on room selection and setup
**Price Range:** varies; please call for price schedule; complete meeting packages available
**Catering:** exclusively by Rafati's Elegance in Catering, we will assist with your selection of the perfect menu for your event. From continental breakfasts to casual or formal receptions, all events are customized to reflect the needs of your organization. Rafati's offers personalized menu planning in all price ranges.
**Types of Events:** corporate meetings, conferences, seminars, Board meetings, retreats, receptions, banquets, rehearsal dinners, wedding receptions, holiday parties, and fund-raising events

## Availability and Terms

The Grotto has three well-appointed rooms available. Hours for The Grotto Conference Center are 8am–10pm. Early booking is suggested. A refundable deposit is required at the time of booking. Client must provide liability insurance.

## Description of Facility and Services:

**Seating:** provided; table and chair setup included in room rental
**Servers:** provided by Rafati's Elegance in Catering
**Bar facilities:** provided by Rafati's Elegance in Catering; fully licensed
**Linens, china and glassware:** china, glassware and silverware included; arrange for linens with Rafati's
**Cleanup:** cleaning fee applies
**Decorations:** you must remove all items you brought in; early access to decorate by prior arrangement; no tape, nails, tacks, staples, or confetti
**Audio visual:** sound system, 4100 Lumen Video Data Projection System with VCR/VHS/DVD Player, microphones, and screens available on request; all other with prior arrangement; extra charge applies
**Equipment:** available with prior arrangement
**Parking:** ample free parking
**ADA**: fully accessible

## Special Services

The Grotto's experienced event planners can assist with all aspects of planning your event. Creative menus, attention to detail, and excellent service will make your event memorable for all your guests. A Grotto staff person is on hand during your entire event to offer assistance. Holiday party packages are available throughout the Christmas Festival of Lights. Group tours, guided or informal, of the upper level gardens can be arranged in advance for an extra charge.

## A PEACEFUL PLACE FOR SPECIAL EVENTS

The Grotto is a peaceful 62 acre retreat located just minutes from downtown and the Portland International Airport. Set among towering firs, colorful rhododendrons and other native Pacific Northwest flora, The Grotto Conference Center provides a unique setting for meetings, conferences, and gala events.

*8187 S.W. Tualatin-Sherwood Road*
*Tualatin, Oregon 97062*
*Contact: Jennie Bernard (503) 691-9111; Fax (503) 691-9112*
*E-mail: Catering@Haydensgrill.com*
*Business Hours: Mon–Fri 8am–5pm*

---

**Capacity:** Boardroom up to 18; Small Lakefront Room: up to 40; Hayden Room: up to 65; Century Room: up to 65; Large Lakefront Room: up to 150; outdoors up to 500; **Off-premise:** unlimited

**Price Range:** rooms from $25-$600; pricing is negotiable with qualified food purchase; a $10 discount applies to each room booked at the Century Hotel. Breakfast starts at $5.50, lunch at $12.95 and dinner at $18.95

**Catering:** extensive catering services; both in-house and off-premise catering available; fun menus and decorative décor will accompany both our in-house and off-premise catering

**Types of Events:** perfect for rehearsal dinners and receptions

## Availability and Terms

Hayden's Lakefront Grill has four rooms from 320 sq. ft. up to 1,400 sq. ft. Rooms require a deposit prior to events and we are flexible with date changes.

## Description of Facility and Services

**Seating:** provided; all types of seating arrangements available
**Servers:** provided by Hayden's
**Bar facilities:** provided; fully licensed
**Dance floor:** available to rent
**Linens and napkins:** choose your own colors at no extra charge
**Decorations:** simple table decor provided at no charge; decorating may take place two hours prior to your event
**China and glassware:** bone china provided
**Cleanup:** provided by Hayden's
**Parking:** available
**ADA:** yes

## Special Services

We can assist you in all of your party needs. We offer groups rates for $89 at the Century Hotel, located next to Hayden's Lakefront Grill.

## Off-Premise Catering

We offer off-premise catering as well as in-house catering. We can handle any group size from 20 on up to 5,000. Not the average catering company, known locally for our great reputation, our off-premise catering will "wow" any guests that you may be trying to impress. Give us a call at (503) 691-9111.

## CHARMING LAKEFRONT SETTING

Hayden's Grill and the Century Hotel are unique to Tualatin. Locally owned, we are located in the heart of Tualatin on the Lake of the Commons, right off I-5. Hayden's Grill is the place to take your date to the prom as well as the place to take your kids for our fun environment. We offer many options for meetings, receptions, weddings, rehearsal dinners and more. For more information, check us out at Haydensgrill.com and take a virtual tour!

# THE HEATHMAN LODGE

*7801 N.E. Greenwood Drive • Vancouver, Washington 98662*
*Contact: Sales Office (360) 254-3100 or (888) 475-3100*
*Business Hours: Mon–Fri 8am–5pm, Sat 10am–2pm*

---

**Capacity:** up to 300 people; 4,500 total square feet of meeting/private dining space
**Price Range:** please inquire
**Catering:** full-service, upscale catering provided by Hudsons Restaurant
**Types of Events:** business meetings, seminars, retreats, award luncheons, dinners, weddings, receptions and trade shows

## Availability and Terms

The Lodge offers 4,500 square feet of meeting and private dining space. The ballroom is divisible into three rooms, each with pre-function space. Two additional meeting rooms are available as well.

## Description of Facility and Services

**Seating:** various setup styles available
**Bar facilities:** host/no-host bars available; hotel supplies all liquor and bartender
**Dance floor:** up to 21'x21' complimentary
**Linens:** assorted colors available at no charge
**China and glassware:** included in cost of food and beverage
**Decorations:** limited decorative items available at no additional charge; creative theme events can be arranged
**Audiovisual:** onsite AV services, built in LCD projector in the ballroom
**Cleanup:** handled by hotel at no additional charge
**Parking:** over 280 spaces complimentary
**ADA:** meets all standards; any special needs accommodated upon request

## Special Services

A night in one of the 121 guest rooms or 21 suites is a truly memorable experience. Old-world craftsmanship is evident in stretched leather lampshades and hand-crafted mirrors and frames. Hickory and pine furnishings lend comfort to the surroundings.

The Heathman Lodge is Vancouver, Washington's full-service upscale hotel. An unexpected urban retreat, the Lodge offers travelers and locals from the Portland/Vancouver area a blend of heart-felt service, business amenities and rustic, mountain lodge comfort.

Inspired by authentic Pacific Northwest decor and cuisine, the Lodge provides each guest a calm refuge and a memorable experience.

## Where Business Meets Pleasure

The Heathman Lodge is bringing more value to our business level including: complimentary reception Monday–Thursday evenings, personal office caddies in each room, VIP turndown service, upgraded personal amenities and complimentary high speed Internet access.

**HAND-HEWN HOSPITALITY**
***"DISCOVER THE AFFORDABLE NW EXPERIENCE"***

**We invite you to take a virtual tour at www.heathmanlodge.com**

# HEATHMAN PRIVATE DINING

*1001 S.W. Broadway at Salmon Street • Portland, Oregon 97205*
*Contact: Catering (503) 790-7126; Web site: www.Heathmanhotel.com*

---

**Capacity:** 300 people reception; 200 people seated
**Price Range:** varies depending on type of event and menu selection
**Catering:** full-service in-house and off-premise catering available
**Types of Events:** sit-down meals, buffets, receptions, meetings and rehearsal dinners

## Availability and Terms

You may reserve one of our eight private rooms, or the entire mezzanine for larger receptions. Please contact the catering office for details.

## Description of Facility and Services

**Seating**: tables and chairs provided
**Servers:** provided, with 19% service charge
**Bar facilities:** full-service bar with bartenders available for your event; The Heathman supplies the liquor, beer and wine
**Dance floor:** available
**Linens and napkins:** variety of linen selections available
**China and glassware:** fine china, silver and crystal supplied
**High Speed Internet:** available in all rooms
**Audio Visual:** prices vary based on needs
**Parking:** parking available; price varies
**ADA:** fully accessible

## OUR GOAL IS TO INDULGE YOU

Walk through the doors into the most elegant and romantic atmosphere in Portland. Located in the heart of the arts and culture district of downtown Portland, the historic Heathman Hotel will exceed your highest expectations. Enjoy the stylish, warm ambiance of one of our eight private dining rooms. Adorned with silk wall coverings, classic wood shutters, topiary plants or even a fire-lit room , each room has its own distinct character. The ambiance is perfectly matched by our staff. Dedicated personally to your event, our goal is to indulge you! Enjoy the cuisine of Chef Philippe Boulout, winner of the James Beard Award as the Best Chef in the Northwest. Chef Boulout maintains his reputation as a culinary star. For a rehearsal dinner, wedding reception, or special event—relax and let The Heathman worry about the details.

*Helvetia, Oregon*
*Contact: Stuart & Melinda Wilson*
*503-789-6221*

**Capacity:** 1,000 or more.
**Price Range:** $15,000 per-day for facilities only (two day minimum).
**Catering:** Required in-house. Not included in facility price.
**Types of Events:** Lavish parties of your choosing.

## Availability and Terms

Call for availability and viewing. A 50% deposit is required to reserve.

## Description of Facility and Services

**Seating:** Not provided.
**Servers:** Provided with in-house catering.
**Bar Facilities:** Not included in facility rental. Provided with required in-house catering at extra cost.
**Linens and Napkins:** Not included in facilities rental. Provided with required in-house catering.
**China and Glassware:** Not included in facilities rental. Provided with required in-house catering.
**Parking:** Valet parking required. Not included in facility price.
**ADA:** Accessible

## SECLUDED AND BREATHTAKINGLY BEAUTIFUL

100 beautifully landscaped acres designed by *landscape architect*, Ed Ceccacci. Fifteen years and fifteen million dollars to create. Award-winning building designs include a covered pool house, largest private conservatory on the West coast, gorgeous classic barn with finished loft, carriage house with finished apartment, lake, covered bridge, tennis court and pavilion, numerous flower gardens and wide expanses of manicured lawns. This is a working farm. Sustainable farming practices employed – chemical free 5,000 apple trees. Organic vegetable and fruit gardens. Quiet, private, secluded and breathtakingly beautiful.

# Helvetia Valley Adventures

*Contact: Susan Adkins, with Class Act Event Coordinators*
*for booking information and a complimentary tour:*
*503.295.7890 • classact@open.org*
*Web site: hvadventures.com*
*Hillsboro, Oregon*

---

**Capacity:** up to 800 people
**Price Range:** please inquire
**Catering:** contact us about our preferred caterer list
**Types of Events:** corporate picnics and events, family reunions and parties, outdoor barbecues, and theme parties

## Availability and Terms

The Farm is a private event site and is available for you on weekends, July through September. Other dates and times are possible by special arrangement.

## Description of Facility and Services

**Seating:** tables and chairs can be rented
**Cleanup:** provided by venue
**Parking:** private parking for up to 800

## PRIVATE PLAYLAND IN THE OREGON COUNTRY

Roloff U-Pick Farms, home of Helvetia Valley Adventures, is a special, private playland, perfect for hosting corporate picnics and events, family reunions, outdoor barbecues and theme parties. Located in the country just outside Hillsboro, there is lots of exciting fun for "kids" of all ages. Events are held for the purpose of promoting Roloff Farms Produce.

**The Adventure Includes:**

-An Old West Town & Underground Secret

-A Medieval Castle

-A Three Story Tree House

-A Pirate Ship docked at the Lagoon

-And so much more!

Come experience Helvetia Valley Adventures for your next special event.

***"If you are looking for a place for family-oriented events, there is nowhere else like it in the country…By far the best outing we have ever had!"***

– Bob Gregg, CEO, Unicru

## Portland Airport

*12048 N.E. Airport Way • Portland, Oregon 97220*
*Contact: Terrie Ward (503) 255-8600; Fax (503) 255-8998*
*Business Hours: Mon–Fri 8am–5pm*

---

**Capacity:** four meeting rooms totaling 2,100 square feet accommodating 10 to 100
**Catering:** full-service catering provided exclusively by hotel
**Price Range:** price will be determined by event and menu selection
**Types of Events:** business meetings, seminars, receptions, breakfast, lunch and dinner

### Availability and Terms

Reservations should be made as early as possible to ensure availability. A $200 deposit is required upon booking with remainder due in full 72 hours prior to event (unless credit has been established). Cancellation of 30 days notice is required.

### Description of Facility and Services

**Seating:** tables and chairs provided
**Servers:** included in price
**Bar facilities:** full beverage service available; provided by hotel only
**Linens and napkins:** wide selection available at no charge
**China and glassware:** provided
**Audiovisual:** high-speed Internet access; full range AV equipment available at additional cost
**Equipment:** additional equipment available for an extra charge
**Cleanup:** provided by staff
**Parking:** complimentary parking available
**ADA:** yes

### Special Services

We offer a special group rate with a booking of 10 or more guest rooms per night.

### FOUR STAR SERVICE AT A THREE STAR PRICE

Our professional and courteous sales staff can handle all facets of your business meeting or special event, from guest accommodations, meeting room/banquet space and catering services. The Hilton Garden Inn—Portland Airport is a beautiful four-story hotel that provides all the amenities you need. Our signature pavilion provides a bright and welcome feeling to all guests. Our staff is trained to give personal, courteous and timely service to all guests, from a business meeting of 10 to that special dinner of 100. Make your next event a memorable one at the Hilton Garden Inn—Portland Airport, where we provide four star service at a three star price!

*25425 S.W. 95th Avenue Wilsonville, Oregon 97070*
*Catering Department (503) 682-2211*
*www.holidayinnwilsonville.com*

---

**Capacity:** 10 to 700; 11,000 square feet of meeting space
**Price Range:** please ask our catering specialists for current menu prices
**Catering:** full-service in-house catering
**Types of Events:** meetings, reunions, conventions, receptions, auctions and weddings

## Availability and Terms

Reservations should be made as early as possible. Our catering specialists will be happy to assist you with our current event policies.

## Description of Facility and Services

**Seating:** tables and chairs for 550
**Servers:** staff included in catering costs; gratuity will be added to final bill
**Bar facilities:** full-service bar available
**Dance floor:** available at minimum charge
**Linens and napkins:** white linen tablecloths, napkins; special colors additional charge
**China and glassware:** white china and stemmed glassware
**Decorations:** silk flower arrangements, mirrors, oil candles, ficus trees
**Audiovisual:** 24-foot screen with In-Focus projection system and videoconferencing
**Equipment:** available upon request
**Cleanup:** provided by the Holiday Inn
**Parking:** ample free parking available
**ADA:** banquet rooms and Atrium fully accessible; elevator to guest rooms; nine ADA compliant guestrooms

## Special Services

The Holiday Inn Wilsonville, Oregon offers 170 spacious, comfortable guestrooms, including Executive Level accommodations. Other amenities include a full-service business center, indoor pool, whirlpool, fitness center, Garlic Onion Ristorante and Cheerful Sports Bar.

### OUR LOCATION IS IDEAL

The Holiday Inn is located in Wilsonville, Oregon only 15 minutes south of downtown Portland and 25 minutes from Salem. Just off of I-5 and 205, easy access makes the Holiday Inn Wilsonville the perfect location for your attendees.

# holocene{lounge}

> 1001 se morrison street, portland

>>> 503/239-7639
>>>> www.holocene.org
>>>>> events@holocene.org

---

**Capacity:** Up to 300, depending on the event.
**Price Range:** Reasonable. Pricing depends on night of the week and menu selections.
**Catering:** In-house. Outside catering is welcome, too.
**Types of Events:** Two large, airy rooms (4,000 sq.ft. total) are available for cocktail parties, receptions, anniversary parties, holiday parties, fundraisers, corporate events, daytime meetings, theme parties, screenings, lectures and photo shoots.

## Availability and Terms:

Call early (2-6 months or more) to ensure availability. The venue is sometimes available on shorter notice. Reservation requires a signed contract and deposit of 25% of the quoted cost.

## Description of Facilities and Services:

**Seating:** Various seating arrangements offered.
**Servers:** Professional service staff is available for all events.
**Bar Facilities:** Full liquor bar, house specialty cocktails, domestic and imported beers and wines, along with coffee, tea and non-alcoholic beverages. The main facility is non-smoking, with a separate smoking room available.
**Linens:** Styles available to suit the event.
**China and Glassware:** Provided.
**Audio/visual:** In-house full live band/DJ systems available for rent. Film and slide projectors available for rent. Call for prices.
**Internet:** Broadband wired and Wi-Fi wireless service available.
**Cleanup:** Included in price.
**Parking:** Plenty of easy street parking. Valet service available.
**ADA:** Entire space is accessible.

Holocene is a gorgeous, airy space with a comfortable and clean urban esthetic – located seconds across the Morrison bridge from downtown. Multiple rooms and modular furnishings let us adapt Holocene to suit your plans perfectly. We serve delicious, well-priced food, beautifully presented. Our bar makes amazing and absolutely unique cocktails. And our staff is famously sweet, attentive and charming.

Holocene operates year-round as a restaurant, lounge and performance venue, but can be reserved for private events any day of the week with good advance notice. Holocene can be reserved with less notice for times we're normally shut - including many Mondays and Tuesdays, and most daytime hours. Please drop us an email or give us a ring with any inquiries.

*102 Oak Avenue • Hood River, Oregon 97031*
***Reservations** (800) 386-1859*
***Sales** (503) 473-7594*
*E-mail: kate@hoodriverhotel.com*
*Web site: www.hoodriverhotel.com*

**Capacity:** 5 to 200 guests
**Price Range:** price varies according to room and time of year; call for proposal
**Catering:** full-service in-house catering and off-premise catering
**Types of Events:** banquets, receptions, parties, retreats, meetings, and seminars

## Availability and Terms

Hood River Hotel's banquet room can accommodate up to 200 people. Additional areas are available for groups of 20 or fewer. We suggest that you book early to ensure availability. A deposit is required at time of booking to secure your date with the balance due 72 hours in advance of your event.

## Description of Facility and Services

**Seating:** tables and chairs for up to 200 people
**Servers and cleanup:** included in catering cost
**Bar facilities:** full liquor service from Pasquale's Ristorante and Wine Cellar Bar; bartender included in price quote; extensive selection of wines and champagnes
**Dance floor:** accommodates up to 55 people
**Linens and napkins:** cloth linens available in a variety of colors
**China and glassware:** traditional pattern; assorted glassware
**Decorations:** floral supplies available upon request; early decorating by prior arrangement; some restrictions apply
**Audiovisual and meeting equipment:** arrangements can be made to accommodate
**Parking:** on-street and designated off-site parking
**ADA:** fully accessible
- Free high-speed Internet

## Special Services

Pasquale's Ristorante, offering breakfast, lunch, and dinner, specializes in fine Mediterranean and Pacific Northwest cuisine with menu items from seafood to pasta. After dinner, enjoy a cappuccino or cocktail by the fireplace. Pasquale's is the perfect place to relax after a day's adventure.

## EUROPEAN-STYLE CHARM

This charming European-style 1913 hotel offers 41 rooms and is listed on the National Register of Historic Places. Conveniently located in the heart of historic downtown Hood River and the Columbia River Gorge National Scenic Area, our banquet facility offers a unique location for your special event. Decorated in a wine cellar theme, our banquet room offers a full bar and the finest Mediterranean and Northwest cuisine in the Columbia Gorge. Our warm European charm and friendly staff will ensure an event you and your guests will remember forever.

*1108 East Marina Way*
*Hood River, Oregon 97031*
*Contact: Sales and Catering*
*(541) 386-2200 or (800) 828-7873*
*Business Hours: Mon–Sat 8am–5pm;*
*Sundays and evenings by appointment*
*E-mail: sales@hoodriverinn.com*
*Web site: www.hoodriverinn.com*

---

**Capacity:** seven banquet rooms can accommodate up to 300 for reception; 250 for sit-down; 149 guest rooms
**Price Range:** prices vary depending on menu selection and size of event
**Catering:** in-house and off-site, indoor and outdoor
**Types of Events:** meetings, seminars, receptions, sit-down, buffets, barbecues, or any custom event

## Availability and Terms

Hood River Inn has seven banquet rooms and outdoor riverside space that will accommodate up to 300 people. We suggest that you book as far in advance as possible to ensure availability. A $500 deposit is due at time of booking with the balance due the day of your event.

## Description of Facility and Services

**Seating:** tables and chairs for up to 300 people
**Servers:** included in catering cost
**Bar facilities:** full-service bar and liability provided by Hood River Inn
**Dance floor:** 24′x24′ dance floor; electrical hookups available
**Linens and napkins:** cloth linens available in many colors at no additional charge
**China and glassware:** bone china; assorted glassware
**Decorations:** limited supplies available; early decorating allowed, subject to availability
**Cleanup:** included in catering costs
**Audiovisual:** all audiovisual needs will be accommodated
**Equipment:** all meeting equipment requirements will be accommodated
**Parking:** ample free parking
**ADA:** fully accessible

## Special Services

- The Best Western Hood River Inn has 142 guest rooms and 7 suites available.
- Our professional staff is prepared to assist you in every detail of your event.

## FUN AND ADVENTURE AWAIT

The Hood River Inn combines excellent service and hospitality with one of America's most scenic locations—the Columbia River Gorge. Situated on the shores of the majestic Columbia River, our professional staff will ensure you a successful and enjoyable event.

# Inn At Spanish Head

RESORT HOTEL

*4009 S.W. Highway 101*
*Lincoln City, Oregon 97367*

*Contact: Tonya Weaver (541) 994-1617 or 800-452-8127 Fax (541) 996-4089*
*Web site: www.SpanishHead.com; E-mail: tonya@spanishhead.com*
*Business/Office Hours: Mon–Fri 8:30am–5pm, or call for appointment*

---

**Capacity:** meeting and banquet facilities up to 200 reception; 150 seated
**Price Range:** meeting room prices vary depending on menu selection and size of event—menu customized to please; room rates vary by season and days of week
**Catering:** full-service in-house catering
**Types of Events:** all occasions—meetings, conferences, seminars, retreats, workshops, weddings, receptions, seasonal outdoor beach activities

## Availability and Terms

Reservations recommended three to six months in advance; secured with contract and lodging deposit. Direct billing available upon approval. Thirty days cancellation notice required.

## Description of Facility and Services

**Seating:** tables and chairs for up to 200
**Servers:** set-up, full service, tear down
**Bar facilities:** host/no-host bars available; hotel provides liquor and bartender
**Dance floor:** available at an additional charge; electrical outlets available
**Linens:** cloth linens and napkins provided in an array of colors
**China:** china and glassware provided
**Audiovisual:** complete AV equipment available; high-speed Internet access available in all meeting rooms; wireless Internet connections in all guest rooms
**Equipment:** podium, white boards, easels available; other items can be obtained
**Cleanup:** included
**Parking:** free valet parking; ample free self-parking in private lot
**ADA:** Meeting and public spaces accessible; guest rooms not wheelchair accessible
**Special Services:** 125 guest rooms (bedroom units, studios and suites), heated outdoor pool, oceanview spa, exercise room, saunas, easy beach access with seven miles of beach to comb footsteps from our door. We are a non-smoking facility. Our professional staff will assist you to plan local activities, entertainment, teambuilding activities and relaxation to ensure every event is a resounding success.

## INSPIRATIONAL ALL-OCEANFRONT MEETING AND GUEST ROOMS

Built to take your breath away, the Inn at Spanish Head Resort Hotel nestles into the bluffs in Lincoln City on the Oregon Coast. Recently remodeled, we offer 125 stylish oceanfront guest rooms, most with balconies to enjoy the sights and sounds of the sea. Our five oceanfront meeting rooms feature floor-to-ceiling windows and over 3,800 square feet of meeting space. Two meeting rooms open directly to poolside and the beach, offering opportunities for salmon bakes, poolside receptions and bonfires. Our gracious service, excellent catering, accessibility and spectacular setting are perfect to inspire or reward achievements, or to celebrate any event.

# JAKE'S CATERING

A T T H E

# GOVERNOR

H O T E L

*611 S.W. 10th Street*
*Portland, Oregon 97205*
*(503) 241-2125; Fax (503) 220-1849*
*Web site: www.JakesCatering.com*

**Capacity:** 600 reception; 450 sit-down dinner
**Price Range:** $32 to $50
**Catering:** Jake's Catering is the exclusive caterer for The Governor Hotel; off-premise catering available
**Types of Events:** from stand-up cocktail/appetizer receptions to fabulous buffet presentations to complete sit-down dinners for groups and gatherings of all sizes

## Availability and Terms

Our Italian Renaissance style rooms offer variety and flexibility for groups of 20 to 600. The majestic Ballroom, Renaissance Room, Fireside Room, Library, and eight additional rooms gracefully complement the charm of The Governor Hotel. We require a 50% deposit to confirm your event and payment in full 72 hours prior to event for estimated charges.

## Description of Facility and Services

**Seating:** tables and chairs for up to 450
**Servers:** all servers included as hotel service
**Bar facilities:** full-service bar and bartender
**Linens and napkins:** cloth napkins and linens provided in a variety of colors
**China and glassware:** fine china and glassware provided
**Decorations:** please inquire about specific decoration ideas and needs
**Audiovisual and meeting equipment:** available upon request
**Parking and ADA:** ample parking available near hotel; full ADA compliance

## Jake's Catering...A Tradition

Jake's Catering at The Governor Hotel is a part of the McCormick & Schmick Restaurant Group and "Jake's Famous Crawfish." Jake's is one of the most respected dining institutions in the Portland area, and Jake's Catering at The Governor Hotel upholds this prestigious reputation.

Known for offering extensive Pacific Northwest menu selection, including fresh seafood, pasta, poultry and prime cut steaks, Jake's Catering at The Governor Hotel has the flexibility and talent to cater to your needs.

## CLASSIC ELEGANCE AND SERVICE

Listed on the National Register of Historic Places, The Governor Hotel is an architectural beauty. Built in 1909 and renovated in 1992, the hotel has been completely restored to its original grandeur. The original design and ornate craftsmanship of the grand banquet space area were preserved in the original Italian Renaissance styling. The room's chandeliers, high vaulted ceilings, marble floors, and black-walnut woodwork and walls are truly unique.

**See page 215 under Catering Services**

## JAX BAR & RESTAURANT

*826 S.W. Second Avenue*
*Portland, Oregon*
*(503) 228-9128*
*www.jaxbar.com*

**Capacity:** **Rooftop:** 175 seated and 300 reception style; **Dining/Banquet Room:** 75 seated and 125 reception style

**Price Range:** Varies with menu selection. Please log onto www.jaxbar.com for further information.

**Catering:** Full service in house. Extensive fresh menus made custom to your needs and budget. Family style, full service or buffet.

**Types of Events:** Full sit down dining or cocktail receptions, rehearsal dinners, weddings/receptions, reunions, company parties, birthdays, graduations parties, meetings and presentations, wine tasting, Tupperware, bachelor/ bachelorette parties, toy parties, holiday events, book signings and board game parties.

### Availability and Terms

Indoor venue is available year round on any day or evening. A food and beverage minimum of $275 is waived with minimum amount spent. Our outdoor Rooftop venue is very popular and can be booked for private events June thru October. A $1,000 non-refundable deposit must be paid upon booking and all balances paid the day of the event. An 18% service charge is added to all events. Most major credit cards accepted, however, we do not except American Express.

### Description of Facility and Services

**Seating:** Tables and chairs provided for up to 140 on the Rooftop. Tables and chairs provided for up to 50 in the Dining Room.
**Servers:** Full staff available
**Bar facilities:** Full service bar and staff bartender(s) available.
**Dance floor:** Available upon request with an additional rental fee.
**Linens and Napkins:** Provided for up to 100 on the Rooftop and up to 50 in the Dining Room.
**China:** Provided for up to 150
**Decorations:** Table mirrors and candles provided for up to 22 tables. Other decoration is permissible with approval.
**Audiovisual:** 60" Big Screen TV and DVD Player available upon request.
**Equipment:** Rooftop Bar, band canopies and bistro lighting provided at no charge.
**Cleanup:** Included
**Parking:** Street parking, close proximity to SmartPark Lots
**ADA:** Yes

### ELEGANCE AND AFFORDABILITY... YOU CAN HAVE IT ALL AT !

Every event is unique and we are happy to customize to your specific needs. Our event coordinators are on site every day and can answer any questions you might have. Drop in any time to view our two very special venues.

15450 S.W. Millikan Way in Beaverton
(503) 626-MEET (6338); Web site: www.kingstad.com

---

**Capacity:** largest room accommodates up to 300 people; 14 event spaces; 24,000 net square feet total
**Price Range:** varies according to event size and menu selection; Complete Event Packages available
**Catering:** full-service catering
**Types of Events:** weddings, receptions, rehearsal dinners, luncheons, dinners, meetings, conferences

## Availability and Terms

Reservations should be made as early as possible to ensure availability. A nonrefundable deposit of 25% of expected expenditures is required to confirm your date. Payment in full is due the day of your function. All major credit cards accepted.

## Description of Facility and Services

**Seating:** various seating arrangements offered
**Servers:** appropriate service staff provided with catering service
**Bar facilities:** alcoholic beverages allowed; coffee, tea, and beverage service
**Linens and napkins:** cloth tablecloths and napkins
**China and glassware:** off-white china; variety of glassware
**Dance floor:** slate tile and wood floors ideal for dancing
**Cleanup:** provided by Kingstad Meeting Centers
**Technology equipment:** video projectors, VCR and monitor, DVD players, built-in sound systems, computer projection equipment, ISDN lines, video conferencing
**Parking:** free
**ADA:** yes

## Special Services

Kingstad Center for Meetings and Events can custom-design your event to meet a wide range of tastes and budgets.

Kingstad Center for Meetings and Events offers full-service facilities that specialize in providing event space for groups of 300 or less. Every aspect of our service and facilities have been designed to help make your event memorable and easy to plan.

# Kruger's Farm

*(503) 621-3489*
*17100 NW Sauvie Island Road • Portland, Oregon*
*www.krugersfarm.com, FarmerDon@KrugersFarmMarket.com*

***Located just 20 minutes from downtown Portland on beautiful Sauvie Island.***

**Capacity:** events of all sizes from 10 to 1,000
**Price Range:** $100–$1,500
**Catering:** We have on-site catering available from our grill or you may pick the licensed caterer of your choice to cater an event at the farm.
**Types of Events:** weddings, receptions, BBQs, dinners, corporate events, picnics, parties

## Availability and Terms:

Event spaces at the farm include the gazebo and flower garden lawn, oak tree area and many other open spaces around the property. All of our spaces are outdoors and available from May through the end of October.

## Description of Facility and Services:

**Seating:** provided by caterer
**Servers:** provided by caterer
**Bar facilities:** provided by caterer
**Linens and napkins:** provided by caterer
**Parking:** ample free parking

**About the Farm:** Kruger's Farm is located just 20 minutes from downtown Portland on beautiful Sauvie Island. The farm is a 100-acre working farm with berries and other regional crops. We operate a large farm store that is open from 9am–8pm daily from May through October.

**Charlton House:** The Charlton House is a historic 1903 farm house located on the hill overlooking the farm. The Charlton House lawn is the perfect spot for intimate *al fresco* dinners for as many as 50 people.

**Corn Maze:** Our ten-acre corn maze is available from September 1 through the end of October for private events and rentals. Include a hayride to our pumpkin field, a fresh caramel apple, mini-donuts, hot cider and a visit to our grill and make your event a real celebration of fall.

***Fall Fun – Pumpkins, Corn Maze, Hot Cider & Fresh Caramel Apples***

*21160 N.E. Blue Lake Road • Fairview, Oregon 97024*
*(503) 667-3483 • Email: metroparks@metro.dst.or.us*

---

**Capacity:** Indoors: theatre-style seating for 150, sit-down dinner up to 90; Outdoor Garden: up to 250
**Price Range:** Varies according to time of year and day of week
**Catering:** Executive caterers list or potluck
**Type of Events:** Including, but not limited to, weddings, receptions, corporate functions, private parties and meetings.

## Availability and Terms

Early reservations are recommended, particularly for summer months. Deposits are required.

## Description of Facility and Services

- Seating: Tables and chairs available
- Servers: Available through caterer
- Linens, china and glassware: available through caterer
- Covered patio
- Picture windows with lake view
- Parking: On-site, private parking
- ADA: Accessible and plenty of handicapped parking

## TAKE TIME OUT TO TAKE CARE OF BUSINESS

Sometimes just getting away from the hustle and bustle of the office can get your employees thinking in new directions. The newly updated Lake House at Blue Lake Park offers a tranquil setting with natural beauty just 10 minutes from Portland International Airport and 20 minutes from downtown Portland.

*24377 N.E. Airport Road*
*Aurora, Oregon 97002*
*503-678-GOLF (4653)*
*Contact: Katie Crossett, Event Coordinator*
*503-678-4723*
*www.langdonfarms.com*

---

Langdon Farms Golf Course is conveniently located 20 minutes south of Portland off I-5. The course is situated on several acres of pristine greens designed from the former farmland of the Langdon Family. This tranquil setting is ideal for the elegant dinner or casual reception. The staff at Langdon is relentless to please and will go the extra mile to make your event a success. Whether your event is outside or in, your guests will delight in the serenity and splendor of the surroundings.

**Capacity:** Space for up to 500 people depending on type of event; inside and outside facilities available
**Price Range:** Price varies according to menu selection – contact Event Coordinator
**Catering:** full-service, in-house catering
**Types of Events:** Sit-down and buffet dinners, cocktails and hors d'oeuvers, wine tastings, breakfast, lunch and dinner meetings, corporate parties, corporate golf tournaments, fund-raisers, barbeques

## Availability and Terms

Reservations can be made anytime, but it is recommended that they be made at least six months in advance. A deposit is required to hold reservation date.

## Description of Facility and Services:

**Seating:** All table and chairs provided
**Servers:** Fully trained and licensed professional servers
**Bar facilities:** Full-service bar and licensed bartender(s) provided; full selections of liquor, beer, wine and champagne
**Dance floor**: Available to rent
**Linens and napkins:** Provided
**China and glassware:** Provided
**Cleanup:** Included
**Decorations:** Please check with catering representative
**Parking:** Ample FREE parking
**ADA:** Fully accessible

## PUBLIC WELCOME

Langdon Farms Golf Club is open to the public and is the only golf club in Northwest Oregon that has an all exclusive Nike Golf Shop.

**See page 354 under Golf Courses & Tournaments.**

# LEWIS RIVER GOLF COURSE

*3209 Lewis River Road*
*Woodland, Washington 98674*
*360-225-8566 or 800-341-9426*
*Visit us on the web at www.lewisrivergolf.com*

---

**Capacity:** North Fork Great Room-160; Great Room Deck-90; Bar and Grill-70; Riverside Patio-400.
**Price Range:** varies depending on event
**Catering:** full service in-house
**Types of Events:** conferences, banquets, fund raising banquets, auctions, holiday parties, indoor/outdoor weddings, receptions and rehearsal dinners

## Availability and Terms

A $500 deposit is required to reserve your date.

## Description of Facility and Services

**Seating:** tables and chairs provided
**Servers:** full staff included in catering cost
**Bar facilities:** full service, portable bar available
**Dance floor:** hardwood floor with electrical hook-ups
**Linen and napkins:** included in set-up fee; many colors to choose from
**China and glassware:** white china and stemware included in set up
**Clean up:** included in set-up charge
**Equipment:** sound system, cordless mic, projection screen, easels, podium and TV/VCR
**Parking:** on-site
**ADA:** fully accessible

## SERENE SETTING FOR YOUR NEXT EVENT

Lewis River Golf Course is tucked away along one of the most scenic stretches on the Lewis River. The Northwest Lodge Clubhouse featuring log and river rock accents and hand forged iron, combined with a serene setting makes Lewis River Golf Course the perfect choice for your special event.

**www.lewisrivergolf.com**

# MARYLHURST UNIVERSITY CENTER FOR CAMPUS EVENTS

*17600 Pacific Hwy (HWY 43)*
*Marylhurst, Oregon 97036-0261*
*Contact: Campus Events*
*(503) 697-8730; Fax (503) 636-9526*
*Business Hours: Mon–Fri 9am–4pm*
*E-mail: campusevents@marylhurst.edu*
*website: www.marylhurst.edu*

---

**Capacity:** 1-500 guests; overnight lodging for up to 75
**Price Range:** please call for current prices
**Catering:** not available in-house
**Types of Events:** seminars, retreats, meetings, weddings

## Availability and Terms

Marylhurst University Center for Campus Events has 11 meeting rooms of various sizes and capacities for up to 500 guests. Weddings may be booked in our 325-seat chapel. Overnight lodging is available in dorm-style setting for 75 guests.

## Description of Facility and Services

**Public transportation:** Tri-Met Public Transportation (busline) to main campus entrance.
**Lodging:** clean, simple, dorm-style guest rooms that include towels and bedding (no private restrooms)
**Seating:** various styles to include classroom, theater, conference, etc.
**Servers:** provided by caterer
**Cleanup:** provided by Marylhurst staff
**Audiovisual:** whiteboards, overhead projectors, slide projectors; please call for current prices on additional AV equipment
**Office equipment:** fax and copy machine available at bookstore
**Parking:** ample free parking available; no RV overnight parking
**ADA:** fully accessible

## MARYLHURST UNIVERSITY RETREAT CENTER

Marylhurst University is situated on a century-old campus of 63 acres of rolling lawns, surrounded by deep-wooded ravines and nestled in a bend of the Willamette River. The University is located 30 minutes from downtown Portland, 20 minutes from the Portland Airport, 1.5 hours from beautiful Oregon beaches and majestic Mount Hood. Within 5 minutes drive time, the area offers fine restaurants, shopping and special events. The Retreat Center is the perfect setting for an out-of-the-way retreat that is minutes from a major metropolitan area.

## McMENAMINS GRAND LODGE

*3505 Pacific Avenue • Forest Grove, Oregon 97116*
*Contact: Group Sales (503) 992-9530*
*Web site: www.mcmenamins.com; E-mail: salesgl@mcmenamins.com*
*Business Hours: Mon–Fri 9am–5pm; weekends by appointment*

---

**Capacity:** up to 150 people indoors; 1,000+ outdoors
**Price Range:** food and beverage minimum varies based on size of room and time of day
**Catering:** in-house catering only
**Types of Events:** This former Masonic Lodge turned historic hotel is ideal for meetings, seminars, weddings, receptions, retreats, banquets and holiday parties.

### Availability and Terms

Welcoming spaces for gatherings include sun-filled meeting rooms that anchor each end of the main lodge, the endlessly adaptable Children's Cottage, and the ornate Compass Room Theater, in addition to outdoor spaces perfect for meetings, parties and receptions. Reserve your space as early as possible to ensure availability. Deposit required. Please contact our sales staff for details.

### Description of Facility and Services

**Seating:** tables and chairs arranged to fit your needs
**Servers:** staff included in price; 18% gratuity added to the bill
**Bar facilities:** full-service bar featuring McMenamins ales, wines and spirits
**Dance floor:** wood floor in Compass Room
**Linens and napkins:** linens include a wide variety of colors; no charge
**China and glassware:** all china and glassware included
**Cleanup:** included in price
**Decorations:** please discuss with our sales coordinators
**Parking:** plenty of free parking
**ADA:** specific banquet facilities and guest rooms are accessible

### Special Services

The historic Grand Lodge has 77 overnight rooms, the Ironwork Grill and the Yardhouse Pub, pool and snooker table, gardens, massage, Aveda spa, specialty bars, wine tasting room, art and history. Revive meeting attendees with a quick round of disc golf on the 10-hole course or take a dip in the garden-enclosed outdoor soaking pool.

### HISTORIC COLONIAL IDEAL GETAWAY

This brick-and-columned wonder rests majestically on 13 acres just east of Forest Grove. Accommodations are of the European style with private marble bathrooms located down the hall. A congenial atmosphere is encouraged by the lodge's common spaces: overstuffed couches, artwork, music, roaring fires and full bars can be found around every corner. The airy first-floor pub serves delicious lunches and dinners daily and is open for breakfast on the weekends. Call the Group Sales Office for a complete catering packet.

# THE MELODY BALLROOM

*615 S.E. Alder • Portland, Oregon 97214*
*Contact: Kathleen Kaad (503) 232-2759; Fax (503) 232-0702*
*E-mail: mballroom@Qwest.net*
*www.themelodyballroom.com*
*Business Hours: Tue–Sat 10am–4pm or by appointment*

---

**Capacity:** two rooms, up to 1,100 people; used separately, 300 and 800 people
**Price Range:** varies, please call
**Catering:** in-house catering and beverage services only
**Types of Events:** sit-down, buffet, theme, cocktails and hors d'oeuvres

## Availability and Terms

The Melody Ballroom requires a room rental fee as a deposit to reserve your date. Reservations are accepted one year or more in advance. Catering cost must be paid one week prior to the event.

## Description of Facility and Services

**Seating:** tables and chairs provided as needed
**Servers:** staff included in catering costs; gratuity on food and beverage
**Bar facilities:** full-service bar provided; host/no-host; liquor, beer, and wine
**Dance floor:** 30'x30'; 300 capacity; two large stages; can accommodate full touring bands
**Linens and napkins:** cloth and linen tablecloths and napkins; limited colors
**China and glassware:** china and clear glassware
**Decorations:** few limitations; we can provide fresh flowers and limited decorating accessories
**Cleanup:** included in catering cost
**Audiovisual:** equipment available upon request
**Equipment:** podium, easels, and risers available; all other by prior arrangement
**Parking:** free street parking
**ADA:** wheelchair accessible and fully air conditioned

## Special Services

The Melody Ballroom rents on a per day basis, giving our clients the flexibility for decorating and music set up at your convenience. Our event coordinators will be happy to help you plan and execute your event to perfection…just ask.

## EXTRAORDINARY FOOD AND FRIENDLY SERVICE WILL MAKE YOUR EVENT A SUCCESS!

The Melody Ballroom is a unique, historic facility, owned and operated by a professional chef. Our philosophy is to say "Yes!" and to make your event truly individual. We work with diverse menus and styles—even your favorite recipes! Our caring staff provides friendly service that will make your guests feel as if they were in your own home.

*2236 S.E. Belmont • Portland, Oregon 97214 • (503) 297-9635 ext. 111*

---

**Capacity:** Up to 80 people for sit down dinner; up to 120 for reception inside and out
**Catering:** Exclusively by Salvador Molly's Catering
**Price Range:** Negotiable rate varies according to day of week and size of event.
Type of Events: Including but not limited to weddings, receptions, corporate functions, private parties, and meetings

### Availability and Terms

Space available for lunch and dinner events any day of the week. Deposits are required.

### Description of Facility and Services

**Seating:** Limited quantity of tables and chairs available
**Servers:** Available through caterer
**Bar Facilities:** Available through caterer
**Decorations:** Our on-site staff can assist with décor needs
**Clean-up:** Handled by caterer
**Parking:** On street neighborhood
**ADA:** Accessible

## MOLLY'S LOFT ON BELMONT

If you're looking for a new space for a corporate function, wedding, or private celebration, check out Molly's Loft on Belmont. Located at 2236 SE Belmont, this one-of-a-kind contemporary event space offers unique spaces, surfaces and lighting that can easily adapt to many distinctive décor options.The newly remodeled loft-like environment features large windows allowing for lots of natural light. Our experienced event and catering staff can assist you with all of your event planning needs.

# MONTGOMERY PARK

*2701 N.W. Vaughn Street*
*Portland, Oregon 97210*
*Contact: Chuck Thomas, Event Coordinator (503) 224-6958*
*E-mail: cthomas@naitoproperties.com*
*Office Hours: Mon–Fri 8am–5pm*

---

**Capacity:** 15 to 800 people (up to 400 seated, 800 standing); 12,100 square feet
**Price Range:** $95 to $3,400
**Catering:** approved caterers: Food In Bloom, Catering At Its Best, DeAngelo's Catering, Elephants Catering, Premiere Catering, Salvador Molly's, Hurley's for Catering
**Types of Events:** meetings, receptions, trade shows, buffets, corporate events, business parties, fundraisers

## Availability and Terms

Montgomery Park has a large banquet facility, a beautiful atrium and two meeting rooms. Deposits are required. Book up to one year in advance. Available hours are 7am to midnight.

## Description of Facility and Services

**Seating:** tables and chairs provided (one setup included in room cost)
**Servers:** provided by caterer
**Bar facilities:** bar services and liquor provided by caterer
**Dance floor:** dance floor in the Atrium accommodates 500+ people with electrical hookup for bands or disc jockeys available
**Linens, china and glassware:** provided by caterer
**Decorations:** no helium balloons or tape; table decorations must be obtained from caterer, florist, or other source
**Cleanup:** you must remove all materials you bring in; some or all of your deposit may be kept for damage or extra labor for cleanup
**Equipment:** podium, easel, flip chart, whiteboard, overhead projector
**Parking:** 2,200 free spaces available on weekends and evenings

## Special Services

An event coordinator, security or maintenance personnel may be available depending on the time of the event.

## SOARING ATRIUM AND MODERN DECOR

Montgomery Park, a beautifully renovated historic building, features a 135-foot soaring atrium, a light airy atmosphere, and a contemporary black-and-white decor. It is an impressive site for your function. Montgomery Park is located in Northwest Portland at the bottom of the northwest hills, providing a beautiful setting for your special event.

# MT. HOOD MEADOWS SKI RESORT

*Marketing and Sales Department*
*1975 S.W. First Avenue, Suite M*
*Portland, Oregon 97201*

*Contact: Karen Lite*
*(503) 287-5438, (800) SKI-HOOD*
*Business Hours:*
*Mon–Fri 8am–4:30pm;*
*evenings by appointment*
*E-mail: klite@skihood.com*

*Photography by Steve Wanke*

**Capacity:** up to 800 people; on-hill capacity much greater
**Price Range:** $200 to $1,200 room-rental charge; discounts available with catering
**Catering:** full-service catering available
**Types of Events:** meetings, conferences, sit-down, buffet, cocktails and hors d'oeuvres, receptions, hillside picnics, summer or winter outdoor barbecues, ski events

## Availability and Terms

Please make reservations as early as possible to guarantee your date; however, we will make every effort to accommodate reservations on short notice. A deposit is required upon booking your reservation, with the remaining balance due 10 days prior to the event. Rates vary depending on group/room size—call for the room that best fits your needs. Room discounts available with catering.

## Description of Facility and Services

**Seating:** tables and chairs provided
**Servers:** friendly staff included
**Bar facilities:** full-service bars available
**Decorations:** by prior arrangement; table pieces at additional cost
**Cleanup:** provided by Meadows
**Audiovisual:** equipment available upon request; please inquire for pricing
**Activities:** skiing, snowboarding, cross-country skiing, snowshoeing, hiking, horse shoes and volleyball
**Parking:** ample parking available; Sno-Park permit required during the winter months
**ADA:** fully complied

## Special Services

Our staff has extensive experience in corporate events. Our professional banquet and catering department offers an array of delicious menu items as well as conference and meeting audiovisual equipment. We also offer group rates on lift tickets, rental equipment, group lessons and custom clinics. We can also arrange for luxury coach transportation to the mountain.

## LODGING

Cooper Spur Mountain Resort, a mountain lodging property and restaurant located 12 miles from Mt. Hood Meadows Ski Resort, provides the perfect atmosphere for your next special event or company retreat.

**Visit us on the Web: www.skihood.com • www.cooperspur.com**

**See page 403 under Recreation, Attractions & Sports.**

*211 Tumwater Drive*
*Oregon City, Oregon 97045*
*Contact: Judi Isbell*
*(503) 655-5574; Fax (503) 655-0035*
*Web site: www.orcity.com/museum*

---

**Capacity:** up to 299
**Price Range:** please call for current prices
**Catering:** choose from our list of caterers or by special arrangement of your preferred caterer
**Types of Events:** receptions, seminars, banquets

### Availability and Terms

Deposit required.

### Description of Facility and Services

**Seating:** round tables, banquet tables, and chairs provided
**Servers:** provided by caterer
**Bar facilities**: provided caterer, additional insurance needed
**Dance floor:** hardwoods throughout
**Linen and napkins:** provided by caterer
**China and glassware:** provided by caterer
**Equipment:** AV equipment and a podium is available
**Parking:** 48 spaces on site, additional on street
**ADA:** meets all ADA requirements

## OVERLOOKING HISTORIC WILLAMETTE FALLS

The Museum of the Oregon Territory is an impressive building perched on a basalt cliff overlooking historic Willamette Falls. Among our many cherished heritage treasurers is the plat map of San Francisco, filed here in 1850 because Oregon City was the site of the only federal courthouse in the Northwest.

The Museum's third floor features a unique new meeting facility with dramatic 360-degree views, plenty of easy parking, and a capacity of up to 299. Tumwater, the Indian word for waterfall, commemorates this historic location which for centuries has been the crossroads of communication, trading, commerce and travel.

A museum tour, guided or informal, is an entertainment option for guests who utilize the meeting facility

# OAKS PARK HISTORIC DANCE PAVILION

***at Oaks Park***

*Portland, Oregon 97202*
*Contact: Catering (503) 238-6622*
*Fax (503) 236-9143*
*Web site: www.oakspark.com*
*Business Hours: Mon–Fri 8am–5pm*

**Capacity:** dance pavilion with formal seating for 275; festival setup with dancing for 500; outdoor gazebo area for 1,000

**Price Range:** will be determined by event, specific menu choices, and services

**Catering:** our in-house catering menus are individually designed to suit your own taste, personality, and style. Our goal is to give you exactly what you want. If you are using an outside caterer, we will charge you a fee of 20% of their final bill.

**Types of Events:** full-line catering, buffet, hors d'oeuvres, and specialty menus

## Availability and Terms

Our indoor facility is available for bookings on any day or evening. Our outdoor gazebo and grounds are extremely popular; please don't hesitate to call and inquire. A deposit of $250 is required on the day of booking.

## Description of Facility and Services

**Seating:** we can formally seat 275 people

**Servers:** we can provide any equipment necessary and the personnel to guarantee your event will run smoothly and at a level of service you expect

**Bar facilities:** Oaks Park Association provides liquor at the liability of the renter; it is Oaks Park's policy to provide a staff bartender

**Dance floor:** 99′x54′ dance floor with a capacity for 400 people

**Linens and napkins:** all colors of linen and cloth napkins and tablecloths available for an additional cost

**Decorations:** we enjoy your personal style—and offer the bonus of fanciful historic carousel horses

**Audiovisual:** available upon request

**Equipment:** podium, easel, and risers available

**Parking:** ample free parking

**ADA:** fully complies

## A PEACEFUL, TRANQUIL SETTING

Join us at our historic riverside park on the Willamette River and let us create a perfect day or evening event for you and your guests. Our facility is ideal for seminars, retreats, corporate dinners, retirement and holiday parties. Children's Christmas parties are a specialty. It is our policy to work with you and offer exemplary step-by-step service all during the event, allowing you to relax and enjoy the party.

**See page 405 under Recreation, Attractions & Sports.**

*1945 S.E. Water Avenue • Portland, Oregon 97214*
*Contact: Event Sales Office (503) 797-4671*
*Tours by appointment • www.omsi.edu*

## WHERE YOU CAN DO MORE THAN MINGLE!

**Capacity:** up to 2,500 reception-style and 250 for a banquet or meeting
**Price Range:** please call for estimates on rental fees and catering, or visit www.omsi.edu
**Catering:** exclusive, full-service in-house catering provided by Aramark Corporation; creative menus are based on budget requirements and/or type of food and beverages requested. Menus and catering guidelines can be found on our website.
**Types of Events:** meetings, banquets, holiday parties, corporate events, or galas; receptions set among the exhibits as well as sit-down breakfasts, luncheons and dinners; most areas offer a fabulous view of the Willamette River and downtown city skyline.

### Availability and Terms

Reservations should be made as soon as possible to ensure availability. A 50% nonrefundable deposit of rental charges is due upon signing an agreement. The balance is due five days before your event. Events held among exhibits typically begin after regular museum hours.

### Description of Facility and Services

**Facility rental:** Located on the east bank of the Willamette River, OMSI's view provides a spectacular setting for any event. Five exhibit halls with more than 200 hands-on exhibits and two theaters entertain and educate your guests. Space is available to suit any event, from meeting rooms and an auditorium for daytime meetings to an outdoor courtyard for picnics.
**Bar facilities and servers:** provided by Aramark Corporation
**Linens and china:** a variety of linens, china and tableware to suit any event
**Dance floor:** OMSI's dining room is ideal for dancing; additional dance floors may be rented from an outside source.
**Equipment:** tables and chairs in current inventory are available for use at no additional charge. Any equipment that OMSI does not have can be rented at an additional cost.
**Parking:** 800 spaces available free of charge.
**ADA:** meets all ADA requirements.
**Special Services:** Our experienced event coordinators will assist you with planning virtually every aspect of your event. Creative menus, outstanding service and close attention to detail will provide you with a magnificent event your guests will remember.

### Event Enhancements

Add to your party with a feature or private show in the Omnimax Theater and Harry C. Kendall Planetarium. Try a wild ride on our motion simulator or hop aboard the USS Blueback Submarine for a personalized tour. We encourage live musical entertainment during after-hours events and would be happy to assist you with arrangements.

**See page 406 under Recreation, Attractions & Sports.**

# Oregon City Golf Club at Lone Oak

*20124 S. Beavercreek Road*
*Oregon City, Oregon 97045*
*Contact: Rose Holden (503) 518-1038 or Vicki Haak (503) 913-6694*
*Business Hours: Mon–Sun 8am–6pm*
*E-mail: rose@ocgolfclub.com or vickie@ocgolfclub.com*
*www.ocgolfclub.com*

---

**Capacity:** 125 seated; 160 standing; can accommodate additional guests depending on season
**Price Range:** prices will vary depending on event
**Catering:** we work with an approved list of caterers or your caterer
**Types of Events:** meetings, seminars, retirements, private parties, tournaments, birthdays, graduations, wedding receptions, bridal showers, baby showers, celebrations of life

## Availability and Terms

We suggest that you reserve as early as possible but we are sometimes able to accommodate parties on short notice. A deposit is required to secure your date.

## Description of Facility and Services

**Seating:** round or adjustable tables with double padded white chairs for 125+ guests
**Bar facilities:** host or no-host; beer, wine, champagne available; bartenders provided; compliance with all local and state liquor laws; liquor liability provided
**Dance floor:** available with electrical for band or DJ
**Linens:** linens available; a variety of colors available from caterer for an additional cost
**China and glassware:** available through caterer
**Cleanup:** provided by Oregon City Golf Club
**Decorations:** we'll be happy to discuss your specific needs
**Parking:** free parking
**ADA:** yes

## Special Services

Our event coordinator will work with you in planning and executing all details, to make your event a total success.

## SOCIAL EVENTS TO TOURNAMENTS

Oregon City Golf Club was built in 1922 and is the third oldest public golf course in the State of Oregon still in operation. With our newly remodeled clubhouse and banquet facility, we can handle all of your social events and tournament needs.

**See page 354 under Golf Courses & Tournaments.**

*2820 S.E. Ferry Slip Road*
*Newport, Oregon 97365*
*Contact: Events Office (541) 867-3474 ext. 5216*
*Fax (541) 867-6846*
*Business Hours: summer 9am–6pm; winter 10am–5pm*
*E-mail: carrie.baldwin@aquarium.org;*
*Web site: www.aquarium.org*

---

**Capacity:** 15-120 seated, 30-1,000+ reception/dinner throughout exhibit galleries
**Price Range:** please call for specific price and catering information
**Catering:** exclusive full-service catering available
**Types of Events:** elegant sit-down dinners, progressive dinners throughout the galleries, barbecues, buffets, wedding receptions, holiday parties, corporate functions, etc.

## Availability and Terms

The lobby, overlooking an estuary (2,140 square feet) with vaulted ceilings and bay windows, is perfect for elegant sit-down dinners and receptions. Four indoor galleries provide opportunities for strolling buffets and cocktail parties. The Sandy Shores gallery (1,360 square feet) features exhibits including leopard sharks, skates and sea pens. A touch pool in the Rocky Shores gallery (1,051 square feet) permits guests to gently handle tide pool animals. The Coastal Waters gallery (1,125 square feet) features our largest indoor exhibit, a wall-to-wall salmon and sturgeon display. Moon jellies and sea nettles are also focal points in the Coastal Waters gallery. Slide presentations or lectures can be held in the US West Theater (1,037 square feet).

The Oregon Coast Aquarium is available for booking year-round. All exhibits are open for after-hours events. A 20% deposit is required upon booking, with balance due within two weeks of event.

## Description of Facility and Services

**Seating:** tables and chairs provided
**Servers:** approved list of caterers provided upon request
**Bar facilities:** full-service bar available/OLCC regulated
**Dance floor:** provided upon request; 110-volt hookups available
**Linens:** linen tablecloths and napkins available in assorted colors at no cost
**China and glassware:** white china and stemmed glassware provided
**Decorations:** all decorations must be approved in advance
**Audiovisual and equipment:** available upon request
**Cleanup:** provided
**Parking:** ample free parking
**ADA:** yes

## IMMERSE YOURSELF— OREGON COAST AQUARIUM

The Oregon Coast Aquarium offers the perfect setting for your special event. Experience Passages of the Deep, an underwater adventure leading you on a journey through shark filled waters—all in the safety of a 200-foot acrylic walkway nestled deep beneath our Oregon sea. Adjacent to the exhibit is an elegant banquet space (1,175 sq.ft.) with a large viewing window that looks back into the spectacular exhibit, and a viewing deck overlooking the picturesque Yaquina Bay.

# PARADIGM CONFERENCE CENTER

---

**Capacity:** up to 290 seating indoors or outdoors.
**Price Range:** varies depending on time of event and services.
**Catering:** award winning in-house caterer. International cuisine available. Ask about our sunny barbecue party.
**Types of Events:** conferences, seminars, retreats, trade shows, banquets, auctions, fundraisers, parties, award dinners and anniversaries.

## Availability and Terms

A deposit is required. Please call for more information; corporate accounts welcomed.

## Description of Facility and Services

**Seating:** tables and chairs provided for up to 290.
**Servers:** all parking, service and support staff included at no charge.
**Bar facilities:** full bar, premium pours, extensive selection of beer, wine and champagne; Bartender and bar setup included at no charge.
**Dance floor:** indoors and outdoors included at no charge; DJ and musician hookups.
**China and glassware:** we offer a variety of china and service ware options.
**Linens and napkins:** included at no charge.
**Decorations:** we offer a variety of decorating options.
**Audiovisual:** state-of-the-art capabilities.
**Equipment:** podium, risers and staging available.
**Cleanup:** set-up, breakdown and cleaning provided by Paradigm staff.
**Parking:** ample free parking.
**ADA:** yes.

## SHIFT TO EXCELLENCE

Just 15 minutes south of downtown, discover your new meeting venue. A state-of-the-art facility disguised as a turn-of-the-century estate.

If your people can't think outside of the box when they are here, it is time for shock therapy. When your analytical mind is agog, just look out the windows or better yet, stroll among the trees or sit by one of the waterfalls. If ever there were a venue that promotes relaxation and sets the stage for getting your people to "shift to excellence," this is it!

Don't be fooled by the marble foyer, the crystal chandeliers or lodge-sized fireplace. We are serious about seeing that you have a successful, stress-free meeting. Our staff will help you plan the event and we will take care of the details. Call today for a tour!

*627 S.W. Washington • Portland, Oregon 97205*
*Contact: Conference Services (503) 412-6309*
*www.pazzoristorante.com • www.vintageplaza.com*
*Business Hours: Mon–Fri 9am–5pm*

---

**Capacity:** 8 to 100 in a variety of set-up configurations to suit your meeting needs
**Price Range:** varies with menu selection, call for details
**Catering:** full-service in-house and off-premise catering from Pazzo Ristorante
**Types of Events:** board meetings, conferences, trainings, breakfasts, lunches, post-meeting cocktail receptions

## Availability and Terms

The Hotel Vintage Plaza has meeting space available to accommodate functions of many sizes. Our meeting rooms are located on the second floor and display the same European ambience seen throughout the hotel lobby, restaurant, and guest rooms. Also available is the Pazzo Cellar, which has the capacity for seating up to 69 guests, 80 for a reception. The Pazzoria bakery can accommodate up to 25 people for an evening event. We encourage you to reserve as soon as possible to secure your desired date. A deposit is required to confirm your space.

## Description of Facility and Services

**Seating:** up to 100
**Servers:** serving attendants available; 25% gratuity
**Audio Visual:** provided by Phoenix Audio Visual
**Bar facilities:** full-service bar with liquor, beer, and wine provided
**Linens and napkins:** linens available in ivory; specialty colors available upon request
**China and glassware:** white china; sheer-rim wine glasses and flute champagne glasses available
**Cleanup:** included in catering charges
**Parking:** valet parking available (limited availability)
**ADA:** yes
**Guest rooms:** Hotel Vintage Plaza has 107 guest rooms and suites; each evening the hotel serves an Oregon Wine Reception in the lobby; call (503) 228-1212 for details

## THE PERFECT EUROPEAN-STYLE FACILITY

From the warm and friendly greetings of the doorman to the pampering from our wait staff, our guests experience personalized and efficient service. Pazzo Ristorante offers exquisite food that embraces the warmth of Italian cuisine. You may have a spontaneous meeting in the living room of your Townhouse Suite and then relax with a glass of wine in our lovely lobby during our evening wine reception. Plan your next event at the Hotel Vintage Plaza. You will quickly see why our guests return again and again once they discover we are one of Portland's most comfortable places to hold an event.

# PERSIMMON COUNTRY CLUB

*500 S.E. Butler Road • Gresham, Oregon 97080*
*Contact: Catering Department (503-) 667-7500*
*Fax: 503-667-3885; Web site: www.persimmoncc.com*

**Capacity:** Persimmon offers indoor and outdoor venues which are able to accommodate groups of 10-300+.

**Price Range:** Price range varies. Please inquire for more specific information.

**Catering:** A variety of menus are available, ranging from casual to elegant faire. Catering is provided in-house through the acclaimed Persimmon Grille.

**Types of Events:** With over 4,200 square feet of meeting and event space, with both indoor and outdoor venues, we are able to facilitate golf outings and tournaments, business meetings, corporate outings, networking functions, seminars, fundraisers, retreats, parties, rehearsal dinners, receptions and weddings.

## Availability and Terms

Please inquire for availability. Advanced reservation encouraged. Event bookings are confirmed with a deposit and signed agreement.

## Description of Facility and Services:

**Seating:** Tables and chairs are provided with event booking.

**Servers:** Banquet staff are included in the cost of catering.

**Bar Facilities:** Full service, licensed bar services are available.

**Dance Floor:** A parquet dance floor is available with adjacent electrical outlets for DJ or band setup. (Additional fees may apply.)

**China and Glassware:** China and glassware services are included with your event booking.

**Linen and Napkins:** White or ivory linens and napkins are included with your event booking. Special colors may be requested with advanced notice.

**Decorations:** The client is responsible for decoration. Modest centerpiece décor is available through Persimmon.

**Cleanup:** Basic setup and cleanup are provided courtesy of Persimmon.

**Audiovisual:** Audiovisual services may be provided by Persimmon at an additional cost.

**Parking:** Onsite guest parking is available at no charge.

**ADA:** Compliant

**Priceless luxury...Pristine views...Persimmon Country Club...the Perfect Setting.**

At Persimmon you will discover the atmosphere of a fine country club, one that ensures your event will be a memorable affair. Your guests will enjoy spectacular views of Mt. Hood, Adams, St. Helens and our own impressive 18-hole championship golf course. With over 4,200 square feet of event space, we are able to accommodate groups of 10-300+. Whatever your particular needs may be, we are certain you will find Persimmon Country Club to be the ideal setting for your event. Schedule your visit today. We are but a mere 20 minutes from the heart of downtown.

*3229 N.W. Pittock Drive*
*Portland, Oregon 97210*
*(503) 823-3623; Fax (503) 823-3619*
*www.pittockmansion.com*

© Portland Oregon Visitors Association



**Capacity:** reception 250; seated dining for 50
**Price Range:** very reasonable; please call to discuss your needs
**Catering:** a list of recommended caterers is offered
**Types of Events:** receptions, dinners, and presentations for businesses and non-profit organizations

## Availability and Terms

The Mansion is available only in the evenings and only to organized community or business groups. A $200 deposit will hold your date.

## Description of Facility and Services

**Seating:** tables and chairs for up to 50
**Servers:** provided by caterer
**Bar facilities:** provided by caterer
**Linens:** provided by caterer
**China and glassware:** provided by caterer
**Decorations:** Pittock Mansion is fully decorated with beautiful antiques and offers interesting self-guided tours
**Equipment:** podium
**Parking:** ample free parking
**ADA:** largely compliant

## Special Services

An experienced event coordinator is available throughout the evening to help your event run smoothly. A grand piano is available in the beautiful French Renaissance living room.

## AN INCOMPARABLE EXPERIENCE AWAITS

Enjoy the magnificent splendor of Portland's Pittock Mansion during your next evening event. Located five minutes from downtown, this beautifully restored 16,000-square-foot French chateauesque mansion offers an incomparable experience of architectural delight, beautiful antiques, fine art and natural beauty with truly inspiring views.

Imagine enjoying the truly unique blend of history, beauty and romance Pittock Mansion offers for your entertaining pleasure.

# PORTLAND ART MUSEUM

*1219 S.W. Park Avenue*
*Portland, Oregon 97205-2486*
*Contact: Patti Nemer, Event Sales Manager*
*(503) 276-4291*
*patti.nemer@pam.org*
*www.portlandartmuseum.org*

---

Situated in the heart of Portland's Park Blocks, the Portland Art Museum offers unique and magnificent rooms—including the Whitsell Auditorium, the Sunken Ballroom, the Grand Ballroom, a formal boardroom, large foyers, and the outdoor sculpture courtyard—for any kind of gathering. Arrangements can be made to view current exhibition or gallery tours in conjunction with your event.

**Capacity:** The Grand Ballroom will accommodate 560 for a seated dinner; all other rooms vary – please call for information.

**Price Range:** Prices vary according to room; please call for details.

**Catering:** In-house caterer.

**Types of Events:** Every imaginable possibility— from business meetings, seminars, training sessions and fundraisers, to holiday parties, elegant receptions, full dress balls, weddings, and more.

## Availability and Terms

Reserve your room up to one year in advance. A deposit confirms your reservation. Liability insurance and nominal security fee are required.

## Description of Facility and Services

**Seating:** tables and chairs available: choose from a variety of floor plans.
**Servers:** available through caterer.
**Dance floor:** hardwood dance floors available.
**Bar service:** available through caterer.
**Decorations:** elegant facilities need little decoration.
**Parking:** available on street or in several nearby lots.
**ADA:** accessible.

**Reserve the Portland Art Museum for a truly artful affair!**

# PORTLAND CENTER FOR THE PERFORMING ARTS

*1111 S.W. Broadway • Portland, Oregon 97205*
*Contact: Booking & Sales Department (503) 248-4335*
*E-mail: judy@pcpa.com; Web site: www.pcpa.com*

---

**Capacity:** Arlene Schnitzer Concert Hall: theater—2,776 seats, lobby—up to 400; Keller Auditorium: theater—2,992 seats, lobby—up to 500; Newmark Theatre—880 seats; Dolores Winningstad Theatre—292 seats; New Theatre Building lobby—up to 800; Brunish Hall—up to 200
**Price Range:** determined by event
**Catering:** on-site: inOvations in Catering and several others; list of approved caterers available upon request
**Types of Events:** performances, meetings, conferences, seminars, lectures, receptions, sit-down dinners, weddings, galas, trade shows

## Availability and Terms

Terms and conditions vary with each event.

## Description of Facility and Services

**Seating:** 250 banquet chairs available at $2.50 each; tables available at $8 each; caterer provides additional tables
**Bar facilities:** caterer provides bar and liquor
**Linens and China:** caterer provides
**Decorations:** no helium balloons, nails, tape, glue, open flames
**Audiovisual:** available from local providers
**Equipment:** lectern, risers, staging available as needed
**Cleanup:** provided at no additional charge
**Parking:** available in one of several adjacent parking lots and garages
**ADA:** meets ADA requirements; special listening systems in all theaters as well as handicapped seating

## Special Services

A professional staff, excellent in-house and approved caterers, all four theaters complete with both light and sound equipment, as well as dressing rooms and backstage areas.

## DISTINCTIVE VENUES FOR BUSINESS AND SOCIAL EVENTS

Located in the heart of downtown Portland and the Cultural District, PCPA's four distinctive performance venues and three beautifully-designed lobby spaces are equipped to meet the needs of business and social events alike. With fully-equipped stages and professional IATSE stage crew, PCPA staff will guarantee a successful event every time! The Arlene Schnitzer Concert Hall's elegant and ornate Rococo-style Grand Lobby is the perfect setting for weddings, dinner parties and galas; in the New Theatre Building's Rotunda Lobby, situated beneath the beautiful and sparkling Spectral Light Dome, any social event will fit perfectly. With Main Street Plaza and its unique ornamental paving situated between the concert hall and New Theatre Building, a special "courtyard" can be created for guests to wander through—a delightful treat on a summer evening.

**See page 336 under Events & Festivals,
and page 407 under Recreation, Attractions & Sports.**

Portland Spirit

Willamette Star

Crystal Dolphin

110 SE Caruthers Portland, OR 97214
503-224-3900 • 800-224-3901
E-mail: sales@portlandspirit.com • www.portlandspirit.com

---

The fleet of the Portland Spirit will provide a unique, memorable experience for your next event. Portland Spirit cruises are ideal for entertaining guests for corporate events, reunions, conventions, weddings and more. Cruise with us for a breakfast or luncheon meeting, anniversary party, or gala holiday event. Our knowledgeable sales staff and professional event planners will handle all the details, making your planning process easy and stress-free!
**Price Range:** prices vary – please inquire
**Catering:** in-house, food minimums apply

## Portland Spirit

Our flagship yacht combines a classic nautical experience with a fine-dining atmosphere. One-deck rentals, private charters of the entire vessel and public group reservations are available. Two levels are fully enclosed and climate controlled, each with a grand piano. The Columbia Deck has a built-in marble dance floor and open air viewing deck.
**Capacity:** up to 540 guests
**Seating:** tables and chairs for 340 plus outside seating

## Willamette Star

Elegance and style has been custom built into the Willamette Star, from its solid cherry wood interior to brass accents and plush carpeting. The Willamette Star has two enclosed, temperature-controlled levels, two outdoor viewing decks, piano and a sound system.
**Capacity:** up to 144 guests
**Seating:** tables and chairs for 100 plus outside and bar seating

## Crystal Dolphin

This sleek and luxurious vessel provides a bright, contemporary setting for any event. The Crystal Dolphin features three fully enclosed and climate controlled levels, a grand piano, outdoor viewing decks and sound system
**Capacity:** up to 120 guests
**Seating:** tables and chairs for 50 plus outside and lounge seating

## Description of Vessel Services and Facilities

**Linens:** linen tablecloths and napkins provided
**China:** house china and glassware provided
**Servers:** included with food and bar service
**Bar facilities:** full service bar, liquor, bartenders and liability insurance
**Cleanup:** provided; **Parking:** commercial and street parking available
**ADA:** limited with assistance; please call for more information

**See page 182 under Boats & Trains.**

# RED LION HOTEL®

**CONVENTION CENTER**
*1021 N.E. Grand Avenue • Portland, Oregon 97232*
*Contact: Sales and Catering Office*
*(503) 235-2100 Fax (503) 235-0396*
*E-mail: lacy.buswell.gaha.biz;*
*Web site: www.redlion.com*

---

**Capacity:** ***Ballroom:*** up to 300; ***Windows Sky Room:*** up to 200; ***Terrace:*** up to 100 people
**Price Range:** varies with menu selections
**Catering:** full-service in-house catering
**Types of Events:**meetings and conventions, breakfasts, luncheons, dinners, receptions, themed events, retirement and anniversary parties, and any special event.

## Availability and Terms

The recently redecorated Grand Ballroom can accommodate up to 300 guests. However, the Ballroom can also be separated into four rooms or combinations to comfortably seat smaller events. Windows Sky Room with floor-to-ceiling windows offers a spectacular view of downtown Portland. Adjacent to Windows, we offer our open-air Terrace, perfect for a ceremony or reception. All banquet facilities are located on the top floor of the Red Lion Hotel. A deposit is required to reserve space.

## Description of Facility and Services

**Seating:** tables and chairs provided
**Bar facilities:** full beverage services are available; hotel provides all alcoholic beverages
**Dance floor:** dance floor, electrical hookups and staging are available at an additional charge
**China and glassware:** white china and stemmed glassware
**Linens:** table cloths, cloth napkins, and skirting are available complimentary with all catered events at the hotel
**Entertainment, props and decorations:** mirrored table tiles and lush silk plants are provided by the hotel. Other entertainment, props or decorations available for additional charges.
**Cleanup:** provided by banquet staff
**Parking:** the hotel provides a parking garage, subject to availability, at a minimal charge
**ADA:** yes

## Special Services

The Red Lion Hotel Portland—Convention Center offers 174 renovated guest rooms, including in-room coffee, refrigerators, iron/board, hairdryers, data ports, voicemail, wireless Internet access, cable television with premium channels, Pay Per View and Nintendo. The hotel also has two recently renovated deluxe jacuzzi suites. The Red Lion is a full-service hotel with a restaurant, lounge, room service, fitness center, business center and guest laundry. The hotel is ideally located just off I-5 at Exit 302A, directly across from the Oregon Convention Center, and within easy walking distance of the Rose Garden Area, Memorial Coliseum and Lloyd Center Mall. The Red Lion is also adjacent to the MAX light rail with free transportation to downtown and to Portland International Airport at a minimal charge.

## ELEGANCE AND SPECTACULAR CITY VIEW

Our flexible 6,000 square feet of meeting and function space will provide your group with an ideal setting for business meetings, conferences, social functions or receptions. Windows Sky Room, located on the sixth floor, offers your guests a panoramic view of the Portland area.

Ask our staff about Guest Awards, the Red Lion loyalty program, offering points for every eligible dollar charged to your room.

# The Reed Opera House

DOWNTOWN SALEM

*189 Liberty Street NE • Salem, Oregon 97301*
*Phone: (503) 391-4481; Fax: (503) 391-4482*
*Web site: www.reedoperahouse.com • E-mail: rogeryost@earthlink.net*
*Business Hours: Mon-Fri 10am–3:30pm*

---

**Capacity:** Trinity Ballroom, 296 seated at tables/chairs. Cyrus Reed Ballroom: 80-96 seated tables/chairs, 150 theater style.
**Price Range:** Varies by day of week: Trinity $1,200-$1,750; Reed $400-$750.
**Catering:** Reed Catering is official caterer; families may self-cater with kitchen fee.
**Types of Events:** Weddings, proms, reunions, banquets, holiday parties, bar mitzvah, bat mitzvah, quinciñeras, trade shows, anniversaries, celebrations, seminars

## Availability and Terms:

A $500 deposit is required to hold the Trinity Ballroom; $200 to reserve the Reed. Balance is due 30 days before event. Refundable cleaning/security deposit required. Rooms are available from 9am until midnight; Sundays from 2:30 pm-midnight.

## Description of Facility and Services:

**Trinity Ballroom:** High ceilings and brick walls. Elegant chandeliers and indirect lighting are on dimmer switches. Tall, arched windows offer dramatic views of state capitol and Downtown Salem's Historic District. All new carpeting. Included in rental fee: 35-5′ round tables, cake table, rectangular 6′ and 8′ tables, 296 chairs, 5′ bar. Setup. Cleaning.
**Servers:** Client must arrange for OLCC licensed server and/or provide proof of liquor liability insurance naming Reed Opera House as an additional insured.
**Dance Floor:** New 24′x24′ Bamboo hardwood floor. Electrical for DJ.
**Decorating:** Discuss options with Reed hospitality staff. Client may access room day before event at no additional cost if room is not booked for another event.
**ADA:** Freight and passenger elevator access to event space.
**Security:** Reed Opera House provides on-site staff security during each event.
**Parking:** Free on-street parking or in large public parking structures nearby.

## THE HISTORIC REED OPERA HOUSE

The Reed Opera House has been the centerpiece of Salem's cultural life since it was constructed in 1870. Its 4,500 s/f Trinity Ballroom was completely remodeled in 2004 by owner Roger Yost, who more recently has restored the building's missing exterior architectural features and modernized both freight and passenger elevators.

# THE RESERVE

## VINEYARDS AND GOLF CLUB

*4805 S.W. 229th Avenue*
*Aloha, Oregon 97007*

*Contact: Jennifer Stensgaard*
*(503) 259-2010 • Web site: www.reservegolf.com*

---

**Capacity:** Harvest Room, 150; Private DiningRoom, 20; Board Room, 12; Vintage Room Deck, 80 (limited availability); three possible tent sites
**Catering:** in-house catering only
**Types of Events:** golf tournament functions, meetings, receptions, banquets

### Availability and Terms

A $1,000 deposit is required and will be applied to the final bill. Deposit is fully refundable with 90-day notice of cancellation.

### Description of Facility and Services

**Seating:** tables and chairs provided as needed
**Servers:** provided as needed
**Bar facilities:** The Reserve provides liquor; outside wine can be brought in with a corkage fee
**Linens:** white provided; other colors must be rented by guest
**China and glassware:** provided
**Decorations:** please inquire about club specifications; no rice, birdseed, confetti, etc.
**Audiovisual:** TV/VCR combo, overhead projector and screen, podium with lapel microphone
**Equipment:** all must be rented by guest with Reserve approval
**Cleanup:** provided by The Reserve
**Parking:** available for 375
**ADA:** all ADA accessible

### Special Services

Nestled amongst the grapevines of Oregon's fabulous wine country is a magnificent new celebration of golf and pleasure. Our championship courses are ready to host your tournament, as well as provide the utmost "challenge" to the avid golfer. In our spectacular 40,000-square-foot clubhouse, where no detail has been overlooked, we have numerous locations to host your variety of events. The Vintage Room restaurant features the finest in Northwest cuisine inspired from our regionally influenced wine list. Just as a "reserve" label distinguishes a premium wine, The Reserve Vineyards and Golf Club provides the premium event experience.

**See page 355 under Golf Courses & Tournaments.**

# THE RESORT AT THE MOUNTAIN

*68010 East Fairway Avenue*
*Welches, Oregon 97067 (at the western base of Mount Hood, just one hour from downtown Portland)*
*(503) 622-3101; (800) 669-ROOM*
*sales@theresort.com web: www.theresort.com*

**Capacity:** 18,000 square feet including our 7,040 sq ft ballroom and 3,200 sq ft tent; groups of up to 700 in any one of our 13 meeting rooms
**Price Range:** moderate to customized events; please inquire
**Catering:** in-house catering only
**Types of Events:** business meetings and conferences, themed galas, banquets, reunions, retreats, golf outings and weddings

**Availability and Terms**
Advance bookings are encouraged. Deposits required.

## Description of Facility and Services

**Seating:** provided to accommodate group size; up to 700
**Servers:** provided by The Resort
**Bar facilities:** provided by The Resort
**Dance floor:** available for a rental charge
**Linens:** provided complimentary; speciality linens also available
**China:** fine china and all glassware provided
**Decorations:** prior approval must be obtained by Conference Services; onsite decorating services available
**Audiovisual:** well-equipped with in-house audiovisual; equipment and technicians; T-1 high-speed Internet access in all meeting rooms including tent
**Equipment:** all necessary meeting/convention equipment provided.
**Parking:** ample complimentary parking
**ADA:** fully complies

## Special Services

The Resort at The Mountain offers 160 luxury guest rooms, including suites and golf villas. Our sales and catering staff are known for their creativity, flexibility and desire to assist in coordinating a flawless event.

**The Resort at The Mountain** offers the spirit of Scotland in the Highlands of Mount Hood. It's the perfect location for events, meetings or conferences. In addition to one of the most beautiful 27-hole golf courses in the Northwest, The Resort at The Mountain offers restaurants, lounges, shops, Scottish artifacts and decor, croquet and lawn bowling, a fitness center, Jacuzzi, pool (seasonal), tennis courts, and a mountain of other activities such as fly fishing on the Salmon River, miles of nearby hiking trails and skiing on Mount Hood just 20 minutes away.

# RHEINLANDER
## GERMAN RESTAURANT

*5035 N.E. Sandy Boulevard*
*Portland, Oregon 97213*
*Contact: Banquet Manager (503) 288-5503*
*Business Hours: Mon–Fri 9am–5pm*

---

**Capacity:** 20 to 85 people; 100 people for stand-up
**Price Range:** please call for current prices, customized menus available
**Catering:** full in-house catering; call for information regarding outside catering
**Types of Events:** sit-down dinners, hors d'oeuvres, rehearsal dinners, wedding receptions, anniversaries, birthdays, holiday parties, retirements, luncheons, meetings, seminars and corporate functions

### Availability and Terms
Our beautiful banquet rooms can accommodate up to 100 people. We recommend reserving a room as soon as possible, but welcome you on short notice—space permitting! We require a deposit which is applied to the balance.

### Description of Facility and Services
**Seating:** round or rectangular tables available depending on your size and needs
**Servers:** staff included
**Bar facilities:** host or no-host bars with a minimum setup fee; bartender included; cocktail service provided at no charge
**Linens and napkins:** linen tablecloths and napkins; color coordination available
**China and glassware:** beautiful, traditional china and glassware provided
**Cleanup:** provided by Rheinlander
**Decorations:** pre-approved by the banquet staff; tape only; early access for decorating. Ask about our additional decorating services!
**Parking:** free parking; private banquet entrance
**ADA:** Rheinlander is entirely handicap accessible

### Special Services
We specialize in corporate functions. We want your event to be perfect and exactly how you imagined it to be. Our experienced banquet staff will work with you on every detail. Please call for an appointment to view rooms, look at samples or even taste the food!

### BEAUTIFUL BANQUET ROOMS ENHANCED BY DELIGHTFUL ENTERTAINMENT!
The Rheinlander is proudly celebrating over 40 years in Portland. We offer authentic German cuisine and fresh continental specialties including poultry, beef, seafood and pork. Strolling accordionists and singers complement your evening with their beautiful music.

# RiverPlace Hotel

1510 SW Harbor Way • Portland, OR 97201-5105 • 503.228.3233 hotel
503.295.6167 sales & catering • sales@riverplacehotel.com
www.riverplacehotel.com

---

**Capacity:** 10 to 200 guests
**Price Range:** customized menus at varying prices
**Catering:** provided by the hotel exclusively
**Types of Events:** corporate meetings, wedding ceremonies and receptions, dinners, holiday parties, reunions, birthday celebrations, and rehearsal dinners

## Availability and Terms

RiverPlace Hotel's three meeting rooms as well as our waterfront restaurant, Three Degrees, the grand suite, private dining room and courtyard offer a unique variation of meeting space for any event. The flexible space RiverPlace Hotel has to offer may be used for a professional board meeting, corporate function or an exquisite reception; the possibilities are endless. Allow us to help you define your ideas and coordinate your needs.

## Description of Facility and Services

**Seating:** tables and chairs provided
**Servers:** professional servers and bartenders provided
**Bar facilities:** full beverage service available
**Dance floor:** complimentary dance floor
**Linens and napkins**: white and ivory linens and napkins; inquire about color selection
**China and glassware:** china and glassware provided
**Decorations:** please inquire with catering manager
**Cleanup:** included at no extra charge
**Audiovisual:** services and equipment available
**Parking:** valet
**ADA:** fully accessible

## Special Services

Specialized menus can be created by our Executive Chef. Inquire about corporate and group room rates.

## A Waterfront Location in Downtown Portland

RiverPlace Hotel, newly renovated in Spring 2004, showcases the essence of the Pacific Northwest. With river views and craftsman style detailing, we offer a relaxing alternative and a perfect setting for your event.

## RIVERS AT AVALON HOTEL & SPA

*0470 S.W. Hamilton Court • Portland, Oregon 97239*
*Contact: Catering*
*(503) 802-5814; Fax (503) 802-5830*
*www.avalonhotelandspa.com*
*Business Hours: 7am–11pm*

---

**Capacity:** 2,285 square feet
**Catering:** in-house, full-service
**Price Range:** call for pricing—we customize our menus
**Types of Events:** business meetings, wedding receptions, rehearsal dinners, corporate retreats, birthday parties

### Availability and Terms
A 50% deposit is required.

### Description of Facility and Services
**Seating:** up to 150 for standing reception or 100 for sit down
**Servers:** available
**Bar facilities:** full-service bar and bartender
**Dance floor:** available for rent
**Linens:** included
**China and glassware:** provided
**Audiovisual:** available to rent
**Equipment:** available to rent
**Cleanup:** provided
**Parking:** complimentary valet parking
**ADA:** accessible

### Special Services
Located adjacent to the Avalon Hotel & Spa offering 99 guestrooms, full-service spa, salon and fitness club in John's Landing on the Willamette River. Event room blocks and group spa appointments are available.

### LOCATED ON THE SHORES OF THE WILLAMETTE RIVER
Our banquet space is located on the second floor of Rivers Restaurant. Our 2,285 square foot ballroom offers floor to ceiling windows with an outdoor patio, providing spectacular views of the Willamette River and its surroundings. The Avalon Hotel & Spa offers meeting space for up to 14 persons in our suites and up to 25 persons for small receptions. Contact our catering department to reserve your next event.

# ROCK BOTTOM RESTAURANT & BREWERY

*206 S.W. Morrison*
*Portland, Oregon 97204*
*Contact: (503) 796-2739 or (503) 796-0723; Fax (503) 796-1051*
*Business Hours: Mon–Thur 11am–1am; Fri–Sat 11am–2am; Sun 11am–11pm*

---

**Capacity:** Mill Room–up to 30, window area–up to 65, Pool Room–up to 100
**Price Range:** Pool Room Rental–prices and minimum purchase vary; please call for details. Buffets are a per person basis with appetizers, lunch and dinner packages to choose from. We can customize any menu. Kegs available for off-premise events.
**Catering:** eclectic comfort food; in-house catering only
**Types of Events:** meetings, holidays, reunions, rehearsal dinners, events

## Availability and Terms

We welcome all types of events. Parties of 20 or more should make reservations at least one week in advance. A $100 deposit is required at time of booking the party; deposit will be applied toward food and beverage bill. A gratuity of 18% is applied to parties of eight or more.

## Description of Facility and Services

**Seating:** tables and chairs provided for up to 485
**Servers:** full service provided
**Bar facilities:** full bar in separate area
**Dance floor:** available for special functions
**Linens:** white available at no charge
**China and glassware:** included in the cost of food and beverage
**Decorations:** okay to decorate appropriately
**Audiovisual:** available upon request
**Cleanup:** provided by Rock Bottom Brewery

## Special Services

Rock Bottom is conveniently located in the heart of downtown Portland. Our site offers three different venues to choose from when planning your event. Room rental fees, minimum food and beverages may apply. You can even reserve the entire restaurant for your group exclusively, although some guidelines apply.

### "LIFE'S BETTER AT THE BOTTOM"

At Rock Bottom we feature an innovative menu filled with contemporary brewpub favorites complemented by fresh, hand-crafted beers brewed on premise. Our menu options can cater to any taste bud. From wedding rehearsal dinners in the 'Mill Room', to a billiard party in the 'Mezzanine', we're sure to tempt every palate. Let our professional staff arrange your special event, whether it's dinner for two or two hundred, we'll handle every detail. Don't hesitate to call us at (503) 796-2739 or (503) 796-0723 for more information. We look forward to working with you and remember, *"Life's better at the Bottom."*

**ON THE COLUMBIA**

*3839 N.E. Marine Drive*
*Portland, Oregon 97211*
*Contact: Matthew Carter*
*(503) 288-4444; Fax (503) 284-7397*
*Web site: www.saltys.com*

*Restaurant Hours:*
*Lunch Mon–Sat 11:15am–3pm; Dinner Mon–Thur 5–10pm, Fri–Sat 5–10:30pm;*
*Sunday Brunch 9:30am–2pm; Sunday Dinner 4:30–9:30pm; winter hours vary*

---

**Capacity:** Private **Wine Room**: 10-30 seated and 35 reception-style; **North Shore View Room**: 10-150 seated and 200 reception-style
**Price Range:** available online at saltys.com
**Catering:** full-service catering; in-house or off-premise
**Types of Events:** all-day meetings, board meetings, seminars, employee recognition events, retirement and holiday parties, rehearsal dinners, wedding receptions and other special events, business breakfasts, sit-down dinners and luncheons, seafood and brunch buffets, cocktails and hors d'oeuvres

## Availability and Terms

We recommend reserving your space three to six months in advance. But if you need assistance with last minute planning—we can help! A deposit is required to reserve your date. Room fees are waived with a minimum purchase of food and beverage.

## Description of Facility and Services

**Seating:** a variety of table sizes and seating options
**Servers:** after a specified minimum gratuity or 20%, servers provided at no additional charge
**Bar facilities:** full-service bar provided courtesy of Salty's; host/no-host; liquor, beer and wine
**Linens:** house colors available at no extra cost
**China and glassware:** restaurant silver, china and glassware available at no charge
**Audiovisual:** overhead and slide projector with screen; TV, VCR, flip charts available for rent
**Cleanup:** handled by Salty's staff
**Parking:** plenty of free parking; complimentary valet service available Mon–Sat nights
**ADA:** first floor accessible for handicapped; Wine Room and North Shore View Room are on second floor

## Special Services

Our catering director works closely with you to ensure your event's success. We print a personalized menu for you and your guests. We are happy to refer you to florists, DJs and musicians. At Salty's, we pride ourselves on catering to your every whim.

## GIVE YOUR NEXT EVENT A BETTER POINT OF VIEW

Located on the riverfront only 15 minutes from downtown Portland, Salty's provides the perfect recipe for successful business meetings and social events for up to 200 guests. Salty's exceptional Northwest cuisine, warm hospitality, and spectacular views of the mighty Columbia River and majestic Mount Hood will make *your* event a special occasion! We're easy to get to, and ready to serve you the very best seafood, steaks, Sunday Brunch, and riverfront view in Portland.

# SEVEN FEATHERS HOTEL & CASINO RESORT

*146 Chief Miwaleta Lane • Canyonville, Oregon 97417*
*Contact: Sales (800) 548-8461; Fax (541) 839-4222*
*E-mail: sales@sevenfeathers.com; Web site: www.sevenfeathers.com*

**Capacity: Umpqua Grand Ballroom:** 21,340 square feet (1,500 person capacity); eight conference rooms ranging from 450 to 3,350 square feet
**Price Range:** contact sales and convention services staff for pricing information
**Catering:** full-service in-house for meetings, conventions and receptions
**Types of Events:** buffet or sit-down banquets, live entertainment, conferences, conventions, trade shows, weddings and holiday parties

## Availability and Terms

Contact the Sales and Convention Services at (800) 548-8461 ext.1161 for more information.

## Description of Facility and Services

**Seating:** tables and chairs for up to 1,500
**Servers:** full staff available
**Bar facilities:** full-service bar available
**Dance floor:** in-house 30' x 30' dance floor available
**Linens and napkins:** provided; variety of colors may be special ordered
**China and glassware:** provided
**Cleanup:** provided
**Decorations:** allowed with prior approval
**Audiovisual:** LCD projector, overhead, screens, TV, VCR, variety of microphones available
**Equipment:** mobile barbeque, podiums, risers and staging
**Parking:** valet and self-parking available at no charge
**ADA:** meets ADA requirements

## Special Services

Seven Feathers offers a variety of gaming entertainment including 1,000 slots, non-smoking casino area, live Keno, high stakes Bingo, Roulette, Craps, Let It Ride Bonus, Poker, Blackjack, Pai Gow Poker, Three Card Poker and monthly promotions. For an elegant experience in fine dining, The Camas Room features Northwest and Mediterranean cuisine and spectacular Sunday Brunch. The Cow Creek Restaurant is open 24 hours and offers an extensive menu and dinner buffet. Scoops Ice Cream Parlor specializes in a variety of desserts, espresso, deli sandwiches and personal pizzas. Stix Sports Bar has 11 TVs and a full-service menu. Seven Feathers also features live cabaret entertainment.

## FULL SERVICE HOTEL

Seven Feathers Hotel and Casino Resort boasts a full service, 146 room hotel with complimentary 24-hour valet parking, shuttle and concierge service. Extended amenities include a full-service RV park, indoor pool, fitness center, sauna, spas and a video arcade.

# Sheraton Portland Airport HOTEL

*8235 N.E. Airport Way*
*Portland, Oregon 97220-1398*
*Contact: Diane Weber*
*(503) 335-2863*
*E-mail: dweber@sheratonpdx.com*
*Web site: www.sheratonpdx.com*

**Capacity:** 15,175 total square feet accommodating 10 to 500 seated, 750 reception
**Price Range:** $10 to $30 per person for meals; $150 to $2,400 rental
**Catering:** full-service in-house and off-premise available
**Types of Events:** corporate meetings, conventions, symposiums, trade shows, banquets, receptions, graduation night parties

## Availability and Terms

Schedule early to ensure availability. Rental is based on a sliding scale dependent on food and beverage and/or guestrooms required. The cancellation policy varies according to type of event; an advance deposit may be required.

## Description of Facility and Services

**Seating:** tables and chairs provided
**Servers:** included as hotel service
**Bar facilities:** full-service with bartenders; hotel must provide all beverages
**Dance floor:** complimentary
**Linens and napkins:** large selection available at no charge
**China and glassware:** white china; all types of glassware
**Decorations:** many available at no charge
**Cleanup:** included in price
**Audiovisual:** meeting rooms are high-speed internet ready; large selection of rental equipment available in-house
**Equipment:** podiums, risers, easels and dance floor provided at no charge; wireless high-speed internet access in all meeting rooms
**Parking:** complimentary
**ADA:** fully complied

## Special Services

Sheraton Portland Airport Hotel offers 213 superior guestrooms including nine suites with honor bar, internet access and voice mail, Club Level and Smart rooms include continental breakfast and evening reception, complete business center, concierge service, restaurant and lounges, 24-hour room service, fitness center with therapy pool, and 24-hour complimentary airport shuttle service. Convenient airport light rail access to downtown. Points available for Starwood Preffered Planner.

***Restaurant and Convention Center—***
***Portland Airport/I-205***
*11707 N.E. Airport Way*
*Portland, Oregon 97220-1075*
*Contact: Sales/Catering Office*
*(503) 252-7500, ext 270*
*E-mail: portland205@shiloinns.com*
*Business Hours:*
*Mon–Fri 8am–5:30pm;*
*Sat by appointment*

---

**Capacity:** 10,402 square feet of flexible meeting and banquet space
**Price Range:** packages to fit most budgets
**Catering:** full-service at our deluxe hotel
**Types of Events**: business meetings to formal affairs

## Availability and Terms

You are invited to visit our facility to discuss your needs.

## Description of Facility and Services

**Seating:** banquets of up to 400 guests
**Servers:** professional, full-service staff for all events
**Bar facilities:** hosted or no-host bars and table service
**Entertainment:** musician and DJ referrals available
**Dance floor:** wood floor available for a minimal setup fee
**Linens:** available to complement your colors
**China and glassware:** included; styled to complement formal and informal themes
**Cleanup:** setup and cleanup by our staff
**Decorations:** chandeliers, mirrored walls, table and buffet decorations included
**Guestroom accommodations:** 200 Suites; special wedding packages and group rates available
**Parking:** free parking available on site
**ADA:** fully accessible

## CONVENIENT LOCATION AND PROFESSIONAL STAFF

Located conveniently to I-205, Portland Airport, Vancouver and Downtown Portland, this beautiful property offers spacious accommodations and wonderful family dining. An indoor heated pool, a spa, steam room and fitness center are open 24 hours a day to delight any guest. Free 24 hour Portland Airport shuttle.

Our professional catering coordinators will assist you in planning your event. We offer the convenience of a full-service banquet facility, restaurant and deluxe hotel on one property.

Children under 12 stay free at Shilo Inns with an adult. Enjoy a complimentary Barista breakfast. All rooms come with a microwave, refrigerator, hair dryer and first run movies and entertainment. Call toll free 1-800-222-2244 or visit our Web site for online pictures, information and reservations at www.shiloinns.com.

# SPIRIT MOUNTAIN CASINO

*P.O. Box 39 • Grand Ronde, Oregon 97347*
*Contact: Stephanie Miller, Sales and Marketing Coordinator*
*(800) 760-7977 ext.3034*
*Business Hours: Mon–Fri 9am–5pm, Casino Hours: 24 hours*
*Web site: www.spiritmountain.com*

**Capacity:** The Legends' banquet facility is available for private functions 6am to Midnight daily. **Rogue River Room:** 2,500 square feet of space divides into two equal rooms, comfortably seating up to 180 people in its entirety; **Kalapuya Room:** 2,300 sq.ft. also divides into two sections, seating up to 150. 25 person minimum required.

**Price Range:** The full room rental fee is $350, or $175 per half room, per day. This fee is reduced to a set-up fee of $50 with a minimum of a $450 food service order. Menu prices include gratuity.

**Catering:** full service, in house

**Types of Events:** meetings, seminars, conventions, luncheons, dinners, receptions, parties, weddings, and corporate functions.

## Availability and Terms

Contact Banquet Sales at (800) 760-7977 ext. 3034, Online RFT available at spiritmountain.com

## Description of Services and Facility

**Servers:** provided

**Seating:** A variety of setup choices are available in each of the function rooms including rounds, hollow square, u-shape, conference, classroom and theater seating.

**Stage/dance floor:** complimentary with advance notice

**Linens, napkins, china and glassware:** provided

**Decorations:** allowed with prior approval

**Audiovisual:** podium, microphone, TV/VCR, overhead projector, slide projector, LCD projector, screen, flip chart, white board, dance floor and stage

**Cleanup:** provided

**Parking:** ample free parking, including complimentary valet service; **ADA:** fully complies

## SPIRIT MOUNTAIN LODGE

Spirit Mountain Lodge features Northwest décor and furnishings with original Native American art. The renowned wineries of Polk and Yamhill Counties, and the beautiful Oregon Coast are just a short drive away. Bell service, valet parking, in-room coffee, in-room safes, handicapped accessible rooms and hearing impaired kits are provided at no charge.

Beginning in Spring 2005, we will have 254 rooms available as well as a free continental breakfast for all lodge guests, and a business center with high-speed Internet connections, faxing and copying capabilities.

The Summit View Lounge offers live entertainment every weekend. Headline entertainment is showcased throughout the year in our spacious 1,600-seat concert hall. Playworld, a supervised childrens' entertainment area, is available, as well as an exciting video arcade.

*2945 N.W. Jetty • Lincoln City, Oregon 97367*
*Contact: Group Sales (541) 994-2191 or 800 452-2159; Fax (541) 994-2727*
*Web site: www.surftidesinn.com; E-mail: surftides@charter.net*
*Business/Office Hours: Mon–Fri 8am–5pm, or call for appointment*

---

**Capacity:** meeting and banquet facilities up to 140 reception; 120 seated
**Price Range:** meeting room prices vary by season and days of week.
**Catering:** full-service in house catering
**Types of Events:** all occasions — meetings, seminars, receptions, sit-down, buffets or any custom event

## Availability and Terms

We suggest that you book as far in advance as possible to ensure availability. Direct billing available upon approval. Deposit and 30 days cancellation notice required.

## Description of Facility and Services

**Seating:** tables and chairs for up to 120; reception style for up to 140; 2,170 sq. ft.
**Servers:** set-up, full service, tear down
**Bar facilities:** full service, host/no host; inn provides liquor and bartender
**Dance floor:** 15 x 9 ft., electrical hook-ups available
**Linens:** cloth linens and napkins available
**China:** china and glassware are provided
**Audiovisual:** TV/VCR, screen, overhead
**Equipment:** podium, whiteboard, easel available
**Cleanup:** included in catering costs
**Parking:** ample free parking
**ADA:** fully accessible
**Special Services:** Surftides Inn has 153 smoke-free guest rooms, most of which are oceanfront (bedroom units, studios and suites) indoor pool, spa, sauna and steam room, fitness center, lighted surf, balconies, fireplaces/in-room Jacuzzis available and handicapped beach access. Oceanview Ki West Restaurant and Lounge and banquet facilities are fully accessible to all for all occasions.

### *CLOSE TO EVERYTHING,*
### *YET NOTHING COMES CLOSE TO US!*

This lovely inn features everything you need to make your conference, meeting or special occasion perfect. In addition to the Ki West Banquet and Conference Room, the Cascade Head Room and Terrace Room can each accommodate smaller meetings of up to 35 people. Overlooking the sparkling indoor pool, the state-of-the-art fitness room features a Trimline elliptical, treadmill, multi-station gym and complete set of weights to get your day off to a good start. The comfortable guest rooms, night lighted surf and oceanfront balconies provide a peaceful and relaxing culmination to your days events.

*7125 S.W. Nyberg Road (Exit 289 off I-5)*
*Tualatin, Oregon 97062*
*Contact: Sales & Catering Office*
*(503) 692-5800, (800) 551-9167; Fax (503) 404-1950*
*Web site: www.Sweetbrier.com*
*Office Hours: Mon–Fri 7:30am–5:30pm; Sat 9am–1pm*

---

**Capacity:** from 5 to 400 guests; 4,000 square feet of meeting space
**Price Range:** please call for current prices; individual and custom menus available
**Catering:** full-service in-house catering
**Types of Events:** meetings, breakfast, lunch and dinner receptions, sit-down or buffet

## Availability and Terms

Four separate rooms are available; we can seat 250 for dinner or 400 for a reception. Please contact the sales and catering office to discuss space availability.

## Description of Facility and Services

**Seating:** tables and chairs provided
**Servers:** included in price
**Bar facilities:** full-service bar available; $25 service fee
**Dance floor:** 225-square-foot dance floor; PA systems and risers available for a fee
**Linens:** white linen tablecloths and colored napkins; white skirting
**China and glassware:** white china; variety of glassware
**Decorations:** creative catering staff to assist you
**Cleanup:** provided by hotel
**Audiovisual:** available upon request
**Equipment:** all meeting equipment available upon request
**Parking:** ample free parking
**ADA:** fully accessible

## Hotel Features

The Sweetbrier Inn & Suites is a two-story "country inn" located only 10 minutes south of downtown Portland. Offering 131 tastefully decorated guest rooms including 32 executive suites that provide a high level of warmth and comfort. Our beautifully landscaped grounds create a true picture of Oregon's beauty. Some of our standard amenities include free local phone calls, complimentary continental breakfast, touch-tone phones with data port capabilities, and in-room coffeemakers. Our executive suites have two televisions, oversized workstations, two-line phones, microwaves, refrigerators, and private patios. Our hotel features a newly renovated full-service bistro and live jazz bar with some of Portland's finest jazz artists playing four nights a week, a 24-hour fitness center, heated outdoor swimming pool, room service, ample free parking, dry cleaning service, and complimentary laundry facilities. Special group rates available. AAA rated–Three Diamond.

© Holland Studios

# TIFFANY CENTER

*1410 S.W. Morrison • Portland, Oregon 97205*
*(503) 222-0703 or (503) 248-9305*
*Office Hours: Monday–Friday 9am-5pm.*
*Appointments recommended; after hours and Saturday appointments available*

---

**Capacity:** from 10 to 1,200 people; seven rooms and two elegant grand ballrooms ranging from 200 to 6,918 square feet

**Price Range:** call for price schedule

**Catering:** exclusively by Rafati's Elegance in Catering, prepared on-site in their commercially licensed kitchen. Rafati's full-service catering can assist you with your selection of the perfect menu for your corporate event. From continental breakfasts to casual or formal reception services, all events are customized to reflect the needs of your organization. Rafati's offers personalized menu planning in all price ranges.

**Types of Events:** corporate meetings, seminars, conferences, receptions, dinners, private parties, holiday parties, dances, concerts, theater productions, exhibits and fund-raising events

## Availability and Terms

The Tiffany Center has three ballrooms with dance floors and stages as well as several smaller meeting and conference rooms. Early reservations are suggested, but short notice reservations will be accommodated with space availability. A refundable deposit is required at the time of booking. Client must provide liability insurance.

## Description of Facility and Services

**Seating:** table and chair setup included in room rental
**Servers:** provided by Rafati's Elegance in Catering
**Bar facilities:** provided by Rafati's Elegance in Catering; fully licensed
**Dance floor:** accommodates up to 700 people
**Parking:** convenient street and commercial lot parking; located on MAX line
**ADA:** all event rooms are fully ADA accessible

- Central air conditioning in second floor Ballroom; spot cooling available in fourth floor Ballroom

## Special Services

The Tiffany Center's expert staff can provide you with complete meeting and event planning services. From audiovisual needs, theme decor and decorated ice carvings to candle and floral centerpieces, balloons and musicians and much more.

## PORTLAND'S PREMIER EVENT FACILITY

The Tiffany Center features traditional charm and elegance in a centrally located historic downtown building. The Tiffany Center offers your organization a variety of meeting spaces that will fulfill all your corporate requirements. From large ballrooms to breakout rooms, the Tiffany Center is the perfect facility for your corporate functions.

**See page 217 under Catering Services.**

## TIMBERLINE LODGE

*Timberline, Oregon 97028*
*Sales Office: (503) 219-3192; Fax 295-1855*
*Business Hours:*
*Mon–Fri 8am-5pm or by appointment*
www.timberlinelodge.com
*E-mail: sales@timberlinelodge.com*

**Capacity:** up to 250 banquet, 400 reception or theater-style; 4 meeting/banquet rooms, outdoor patio and day lodge facilities plus Silcox Hut accommodates 42
**Price Range:** price is determined by the event and specific menu selection
**Catering:** in-house only
**Types of Events:** meetings, conferences, seminars, retreats, social gatherings, buffet, sit-down, cocktails, overnight lodging, ski events—you name it!

### Availability and Terms

All meeting rooms have been recently refurbished to coincide with guest room upgrades! The Raven's Nest (1,400 square feet), complete with soaring ceilings and large picture windows with views of Mount Hood and Jefferson, is perfect for social functions as well as informal meetings. Ideal for meetings or meals, Ullman Hall (2,300 square feet), is divisible into two sections and features windows with spectacular views, a dance floor and recessed screen. An adjacent patio allows for winter ski-in meetings and summer outdoor festivities. The historic Barlow Room (1,600 square feet), with its unique, original decor, offers state-of-the-art projection capabilities and is versatile for all uses. The Day Lodge is also available seasonally for trade shows and as additional breakout space. For a truly uncommon experience, Silcox Hut is available for overnight lodging, meetings and group retreats. This exclusive retreat, located 1,000 feet above the Lodge, offers bunkroom accommodations, hearty mountain-style meals and a Great Room with a massive stone fireplace perfect for any gathering. Please contact the Portland Sales Office for a complete Conference Packet or visit our Web site at www.timberlinelodge.com/Groups/groups.asp

### Description of Facility and Services

**Seating:** rooms can be arranged in any style to meet your event requirements
**Servers:** friendly service staff included
**Bar facilities:** full-service bars available
**Audiovisual:** full selection of audiovisual services available; please inquire for pricing
**Parking:** ample parking available; Sno-Park permit required during the winter months
**ADA:** yes, within the limitations of a historical building

### Special Services

Timberline, a National Historical Landmark, has 70 guest rooms that accommodate up to 150 guests. Amenities include a sauna, hydro-spa, and year-round outdoor swimming pool. Timberline is also home to a full-service ski area with the longest ski season in North America. Nearby activities include championship golf, hiking, horseback riding, windsurfing and mountain biking. Our microbrewery, the Mt. Hood Brewing Company, offers tours, tastings and pub-style fare.

### TIMBERLINE—HALFWAY UP THE HILL TOWARD HEAVEN

This spectacular alpine resort, nestled midway to the summit of Mount Hood, is a favorite destination for skiers and non-skiers alike from around the world. Unique lodging, gourmet dining, excellent skiing and panoramic views of the Cascade Mountain Range welcome guests year-round. Located 65 miles east of Portland, Oregon.

# the Treasury

*326 S.W. Broadway Street, Portland, Oregon*
*(503) 226-1240 • www.treasuryballroom.com*
*Mailing Address:*
*P.O. Box 5982, Portland, Oregon 97228*

---

**Capacity:** Ballroom: up to 300; Board Room: up to 50
**Price Range:** package availability is based on a per person price
**Catering:** in-house caterer
**Type of Events:** including but not limited to corporate functions, private parties, fundraisers, meetings, conferences, weddings, and receptions

## Availability and Terms

Early reservations are recommended; however, we will make every effort to accommodate short-notice reservations. Deposits are required.

## Description of Facility and Services

**Seating:** tables and designer chairs provided
**Dance floor:** marble floor; stage setup available
**China, Linens, Glassware and Bar Service:** provided by caterer
**Parking:** on-site parking garage or in several nearby lots
**ADA:** accessible

## Special Services

Offering full event planning services and entertainment packages, including casino parties, murder mysteries, game shows, comedy hypnosis, music and more. A/V equipment also available.

Discover The Treasury Ballroom and Board Room, located in the historic U.S. National Bank Building. This elegant terra cotta building features giant columns, lions' heads, winged figures, urns, and a rooftop terrace.

A grand staircase descends into the Ballroom, which features neo-classical architecture, arches, and floors and columns of Italian marble. A steel vault door to the safe deposit area, turn-of-the-century bar, restoration light fixtures, stained glass and rich velvet curtains complete the extraordinary and unique atmosphere. There is a luxurious lounge and a catering kitchen.

The magnificent Board Room, designed by Pietro Belluschi, features elegant woodwork and backlit stained glass windows. Gold cherubs on the chandelier fly above the large hardwood table and accent the grand marble fireplace. Enhancing the Board Room is a high-end sound system, video conferencing, and high-speed Internet access. Behind the Board Room is a prep/warming kitchen.

# *Tuality Health Education Center*

*Facilities for your special events.*

*A member of the Tuality Healthcare family.*

*334 S.E. Eighth Avenue*
*Hillsboro, Oregon 97123*
*(503) 681-1700*
*Business Hours: Mon–Fri 9am–5pm*

**Capacity:** rooms range in size from 270–3,100 square feet and can accommodate up to 400 people, or 250 in banquet/seating format
**Price Range:** price varies according to event
**Catering:** choose from one of our preferred caterers
**Types of Events:** meetings, seminars, banquets, parties, receptions

## Availability and Terms

A 50% rental deposit and signed license agreement reserves your space up to one year in advance. Day, evening and weekend space is available. Minimal kitchen fee per person.

## Description of Facility and Services

**Seating:** tables and chairs provided and set up to your specification
**Servers:** provided by caterer
**Bar facilities:** provided by caterer
**Dance floor:** dance floor available up to 18' x 18'
**Linens:** provided by caterer
**China and glassware:** white Wedgwood china, variety of glassware available
**Decorations:** no rice, birdseed or confetti; enclosed dripless candles only
**Audiovisual:** video/data projector, 35mm slide dissolvers, wireless microphones, sound system, satellite receivers, assisted listening/interpreting system
**Equipment:** podium, 10' x 30' stage
**Cleanup:** handled by caterer
**Parking:** ample free parking
**ADA:** building fully accessible

## PERFECT FOR SMALL OR LARGE EVENTS

The Tuality Health Education Center features a beautiful sunlit foyer area that is perfect for cake and buffet service tables. The combination of skylights and foliage in our lobby is a perfect setting for your guests to mingle. A selection of different sizes of classrooms and conference rooms with moveable walls allow for creating a space that is just the right size for your event. Our variety of microphones and the large screen audiovisual projection system assures that all of your guests will see and hear whatever is presented.

# ULTRAZONE

## Portland's Best Laser Tag

*16074 S.E. McLoughlin Boulevard*
*Milwaukie, Oregon 97267*
*Contact: Eric Lelack or Lee Sturman*
*(503) 652-1122; Fax (503) 652-5204*
*E-mail: lasertag@ultrazoneportland.com • Web site: www.ultrazoneportland.com*

**Capacity:** up to 150
**Price Range:** a variety of complete packages are available; please call for current prices
**Catering:** full-service catering available
**Types of Events:** business meetings, office parties, team-building events, birthday parties, morale boosting, sales meetings, performance reward

### Availability and Terms

Please make your reservations as early as possible. Visa and MasterCard accepted.

### Description of Facility and Services

**Seating:** tables and chairs provided for up to 60
**Servers:** provided by Ultrazone
**Dance floor:** LaserTag arena can be used a 5,000-square-foot, two-level dance floor
**Audiovisual:** provided on request
**Cleanup:** provided by Ultrazone
**Parking:** ample free parking
**ADA:** fully accessible

### ULTRAZONE—THE FUN BUSINESS MEETING

Break the routine and inject a dose of fun and excitement into your business meeting. **Ultrazone** is combination of tag and hide& seek with a high-tech twist. Everyone wears a special vest outfitted with flashing lights and sensors. Using a real laser, players score points by "tagging" opponents and "capturing" opposing teams' bases. Special computers track events and tally points. Action takes place in **Portland's largest and only multi-level arena**. Experience fog-filled mazes and electronic wizardry. Ultrazone is heart-racing, adrenaline-pumping non-stop action.

**Join the growing list of companies that have taken the Ultrazone challenge.**

- Hewlett Packard
- Horizon Airlines
- Tektronix
- American Honda
- Burger King
- Commercial Credit
- AT&T Cellular
- Civil Air Patrol
- Boyd Coffee
- Safeco Insurance
- Will Vinton Studios
- In Focus
- Starbucks
- Thomason Auto Group
- Nautilus Group
- Intel
- Red Lion Hotels
- Shari's Restaurants
- Home Depot
- Sprint
- Adventist Medical
- Ikon
- The Good Guys
- Voicestream Wireless
- Zellerbach
- Nortel
- ADP
- Quaker Oats
- Wells Fargo Bank
- Pacificorp
- U.S. Bank
- Western Wireless
- Mentor Graphics
- Standard Insurance
- Phoenix Inn
- Burgerville
- Prestige Care
- Electric Lightwave
- Louisiana Pacific
- Kaiser Permanente
- LSI Logic
- Safeway
- RR Donnelley
- The Christie School
- Regal Cinemas

*120 N.W. 23rd Avenue • Portland, Oregon 97210*
*Contact: Stephanie Brindley (503) 226-8980; The Uptown Billiards Club (503) 226-6909*
*Web site: www.uptownbilliards.com*

---

**Capacity:** 10 to 200 for parties
**Catering:** In-house chef; updated menu available on the Internet
**Types of Events:** Specializing in office parties, client entertaining, holiday events, wedding receptions, teambuilding and sales-team functions; we have billiards, casino and ping-pong equipment for parties up to 200 people on-premise

## Availability and Terms

The Club's unique attraction is its 10 mahogany pool tables. Two of these tables are located in our semi-private Parlor Room, which also accommodates games of darts and ping-pong. A half wall and heavy velvet drapes separate the Parlor Room from the casual, comfortable seating arrangements in our Library area. The curtain can remain open to accommodate larger groups or be drawn to provide a quiet, intimate setting for smaller groups.

## Description of Facility and Services

**Seating:** 10 to 200 for parties
**"No Nickel-and-Diming" policy:** Our straightforward room rates include all incidentals such as linens, cleanup, china, glassware, etc.
**Service:** Above and beyond is the policy; the finest in Portland is the result. There is an 18% service charge on food and beverage.
**Bar facilities:** Full-service by cocktail staff or from our turn-of-the-century bar
**Dance floor:** 70-person capacity, expandable
**Decorations:** Uptown Billiards is decorated in the style of the "Old English Gentlemen's Club"; holiday decorations are up on Dec. 1; you are welcome to decorate for your party
**Meeting and audiovisual services:** 6'x 8' screen with projector and cordless microphone
**Additional services:** Wine tastings hosted by local experts, tournaments orchestrated for no charge, theme and upscale menus tailored to fit your needs and more!
**Parking:** Three Pay & Park lots are available within a two block radius

## HAVE SOME FUN THIS YEAR…IN STYLE!

Crafted in the tradition of the classic late 19th century billiards hall, the ambiance and character of the Uptown Billiards Club will elevate your event above the realm of boring, run-of-the-mill banquets. With a Library filled with overstuffed chairs and couches and gleaming mahogany pool tables lit by antique and brass chandeliers, we have created an unparalleled atmosphere in which to host the most memorable social and corporate affairs. From incredible food tailored to fit your group, to atmosphere and service, let us surpass your expectations.

# Washington County FAIR COMPLEX

*873 N.E. 34th Street • Hillsboro, Oregon 97124*
*Contact: Lisa DuPré (503) 648-1416; Fax (503) 648-7208*
*Business Hours: Mon–Fri 8am–5pm*
*Web site: www.faircomplex.com*

---

**Capacity:** 40 to 1,500
**Price Range:** varies depending on event; please call
**Catering:** no in-house catering; can assist with selection of caterer, if requested
**Types of Events:** indoor and outdoor facilities for weddings and receptions, trade shows, seminars, business events, concerts, corporate picnics, livestock events, AND MUCH MORE!

## Availability and Terms

All bookings are encouraged as early as possible. A deposit is required. The Fair Complex features a room small enough for a quiet gathering of up to 40, a Main Exhibit Hall that hosts trade shows comfortably or a banquet of 1,500 (catering kitchen), many covered outdoor facilities (one with stage), and room in the amphitheater for 4,000. Public address systems available in two halls.

## Description of Facility and Services

**Seating:** tables and seating provided for most facilities
**Servers:** caterer to provide
**Bar facilities:** you provide bartender and liquor liability; OLCC permit required for any sale of alcohol
**Dance floors:** polished concrete for 100 to 500 depending on the facility
**Linens, china and glassware:** available from caterer or you provide
**Decorations:** please inquire about restrictions
**Cleanup:** you provide or Fair Complex provides for a charge
**Equipment:** podium, easel, and risers available
**Parking:** free parking for up to 10,000
**ADA:** fully complied

## Special Services

We provide event staff on site to make sure everything is taken care of. Staging, extra tables and chairs, and setup and take down can be provided.

## A FACILITY FOR ALL NEEDS

The Washington County Fair Complex has a facility, or that special open space, to accommodate any type of event one can imagine. Glass shows, car shows, trade shows and concerts all happen at the Fair Complex! Every Fair Complex employee is dedicated to making your event a success!

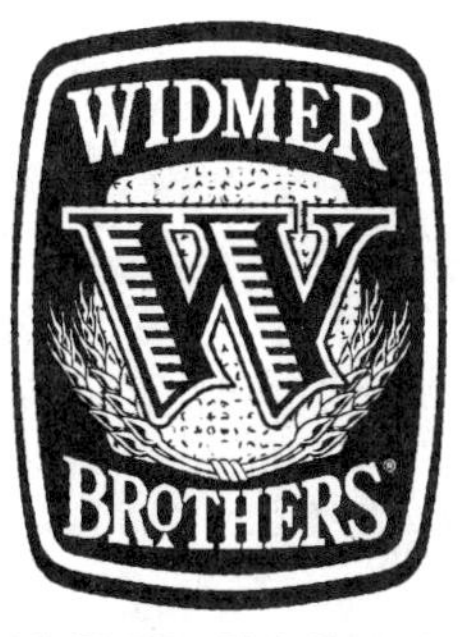


## WIDMER GASTHAUS

*955 N. Russell • Portland, Oregon 97227*
*Contact: Gasthaus Managers (503) 281-3333; Fax (503) 331-7242*
*Business Hours: Mon–Thurs 11am–11pm, Fri–Sat 11am–1am, Sun noon–9pm*

---

**Capacity:** private room, 45 guests; parties greater than 45 require special arrangements
**Price Range:** $15–$25 per person
**Catering:** in-house only
**Types of Events:** rehearsal dinners, birthdays, retirements, holiday parties, business dinners, or any other event where great beer and delicious food will make your party complete

### Availability and Terms

All parties require a nonrefundable $200 deposit to secure a date and will be considered tentative until receipt of deposit. A food and beverage minimum of $500 is required Sunday through Thursday; $750 minimum on Friday and Saturday. Monday evening and daytime minimums vary. Please call for details. A 17% gratuity is applied to all food and beverage including no host bar.

### Description of Facility and Services

**Seating:** tables and chairs for up to 45; up to 75 requires special arrangements.
**Servers:** provided.
**Bar facilities:** hand-crafted beers brewed on location as well as a variety of wines and soft drinks available.
**Dance floor:** not available.
**Linens:** white linen is provided on food and beverage tables during banquets with an array of colors available for formal dinners at a nominal fee.
**Decorations:** no nails, tacks or confetti please.
**Audiovisual:** large screen TV, VCR, DVD, and DMX sound system.
**Equipment:** overhead and slide projectors and other equipment available at a minimal charge.
**Cleanup:** included.
**Parking:** plenty of on-street parking as well as two parking lots.
**ADA:** yes.

### FRIENDLY SETTING COUPLED WITH FINE BEER AND WINE

Widmer Gasthaus is a friendly place to enjoy fine food and our excellent handcrafted beers. The Gasthaus is housed in a turn-of-the-century brick building, adjacent to the famous Widmer Brewery. Our chef and staff are experienced in all types of events, from formal dining to Super Bowl parties, so let us make your next celebration one to remember! All information regarding the Gasthaus and its menus can be found on our web site at www.widmer.com. Our managers will be happy to answer any questions you may have regarding availability or menu planning. Until then, PROST!

**Capacity:** private rooms accommodate up to 35 guests for seated dining or up to 50 for cocktail/reception-style; main dining room accommodates up to 130 guests seated or you can book the entire restaurant for up to 180 guests; the train station lobby can accommodate up to 800 guests and the "rose" garden 300 reception style

**Price Range:** menus available in varying price ranges to meet your expectations; room charges may apply

**Catering:** full-service catering; home, office or event site

**Types of Events:** corporate board meetings, from breakfast to dinner; receptions, rehearsal dinners, box lunches, open house, theme or corporate promotional events, family celebrations and monthly association meetings for lunch or dinner

## Availability and Terms

Wilfs offers a variety of rooms of varying sizes to accommodate your event, from an intimate sit-down lunch or dinner, to a large corporate gala. Our Beefeater Room is ideal for up to 20 guests. The Wine Vault is best for groups up to 35, with our main Dining Room accommodating up to 130, the historic station lobby 800 guests or the "rose" garden 300. All rooms are decorated in a rich, lush, comfortable décor to complement the Historic Union Station. Deposits required, cancellation terms vary.

## Description of Facility and Services

**Seating:** tables and chairs for up to 180 on-site; off-premise, rentals available
**Servers:** wait-staff provided; off-premise at additional charge
**Bar facilities:** full-service bar on-site with liquor, wine, beer, nonalcoholic, bartender, and liquor liability; off-site Wilfs or host can provide liquor, liability to be discussed
**Dance floor:** 30- to 100-person capacity dance floor available at additional charge
**Linens:** cloth napkins and tablecloths in a variety of colors
**China and glassware:** ivory china; appropriate glassware
**Cleanup:** included in rental charge
**Parking:** free "reserved" parking for Wilf's or valet ordered for a fee; **ADA:** accessible

## THE GEM OF THE CITY...WILFS RESTAURANT AT UNION STATION

Union Station and its famous clock tower, is home to Wilfs Restaurant and Bar, a minute from the Pearl District and Downtown. Wilfs, a sustainable company, offers only the freshest, organic Northwest ingredients to create a menu reflective of American/Continental cuisine, with a flare that makes it unique to our region. The brick interior of Wilfs creates a warm, inviting feeling while Portland's best jazz artists perform; you linger and enjoy the artwork from the Pearl District galleries. Or imagine the Union Station Rose Garden, with lush flowers as your backdrop, dinner being served under the treetops, while music fills the air. Wilfs has also partnered with the Lawrence Gallery in the Pearl District, to offer a unique event site. The Lawrence Gallery features the finest artists world wide, and an exquisite outdoor water garden, all creating the perfect setting for 20-400 guests. Visit **wilfs.citysearch.com** for photos.

*10323 Schuler Road • Aurora, Oregon 97002*
*Contact: Laurel and Scott Cookman*
*(503) 678-2195*
*E-mail: w.gables@juno.com*
*Web site: www.willamettegables.com*

## Special events in an intimate country setting on the banks of the Willamette River

Willamette Gables is a five-acre country estate on the banks of the Willamette River, 30 minutes south of Portland and 30 minutes north of Salem. This beautiful southern plantation-style home provides the perfect backdrop for your special event or meeting.

The adjacent gardens and grounds overlook the meandering Willamette River, offering gorgeous views and solitude. Willamette Gables specializes in quality customer service and attention to detail.

**Capacity:** 200 outdoors; 10 to 50 seated indoors; 100 reception-style indoors
**Price Range:** please inquire; half-day and full day rates available
**Catering:** choose your own caterer (we reserve the right to approve your selection) or choose from our list
**Types of Events:** meetings, seminars, retreats, private parties, picnics, garden parties, teas, weddings, receptions, anniversaries

## Availability and Terms

Indoor facility is available year round; outdoor setting is available June through September. All reservations must be accompanied by a 50% deposit; the balance is due 30 days prior to your scheduled event. Five bed & breakfast rooms are available for lodging.

## Description of Facility and Services

**Seating: indoor:** tables and chairs provided for up to 50; **outdoor:** provided up to 200
**Servers:** provided by caterer
**Bar facilities:** caterer or renter provides licensed bartender and liability insurance; beer , wine and champagne only
**Dance floor:** inquire about availability
**Linens and napkins:** provided by caterer
**China and glassware:** provided for up to 50 at no charge
**Setup and tear down:** provided; caterers are expected to provide their own cleanup and trash removal
**Decorations:** many items are provided; little decoration needed; no rice, birdseed or confetti
**Sound system:** responsibility of client
**Event coordination services:** available for an additional fee
**Covered Area:** 40′ x 40′ canopy (upon request) available for an additional fee
**Parking:** ample parking; parking attendants included in the fee

## Special Services

- **Five Bed and Breakfast rooms available, all with private baths**

*4033 S.W. Canyon Road*
*Portland, Oregon 97221*
*Contact: Facilities Coordinator*
*503-488-2101; Fax 503-228-4608*
*Office Hours: Mon–Fri 8:30am–4:30pm*
*www.worldforestry.org*

**Capacity:** banquet, 40-250; classroom, 35-175; conference, 50-300; stand-up reception, inside—200–400, outside plaza—1,000
**Price Range:** price varies by type of facility and time; please call for specific pricing.
**Catering:** preferred caterers, full kitchens available; caterer referral list on request
**Types of Events:** seminars, conferences, banquets, trade shows, board meetings, formal dinners and buffets, breakfast and luncheon meetings, workshops, receptions

## Availability and Terms

Located in Portland's Washington Park, our three meeting halls and 10,000-sq-.ft. outdoor plaza are available year-round, seven days a week for day and evening events. Our 30,000 sq.-ft . museum is open after-hours for stand-up receptions. A deposit is required for booking.

## Description of Facility and Services

**Seating:** Miller Hall: 300 chairs, 25 eight-foot tables, 30 five-foot round tables; Cheatham Hall: 200 chairs, 25 eight-foot tables; David Douglas Room: 50 chairs
**Servers:** provided by caterer
**Bar facilities:** liquor allowed, OLCC regulations apply
**Dance floor:** Cheatham Hall, 18′ x 18′ dance floor available
**Stage:** Miller Hall, 12 sections, 3′ x 4′ portable stage, two sets of steps
**Linens and napkins:** provided by client or caterer
**China and glassware:** provided by client or caterer
**Decorations:** check with Facilities Coordinator
**Audiovisual:** PA system, microphone, screen
**Cleanup:** client or caterer to remove everything brought into facility
**Parking:** ample parking, shared lot with Oregon Zoo; on MAX line (easy access from hotels)
**ADA:** meets most ADA requirements

## A BEAUTIFUL SERENE SETTING

Escape to Portland's beautiful Washington Park where the World Forestry Center offers a quiet, sylvan setting for your social or business event. Enjoy the natural warmth of wood tones in Miller and Cheatham Halls which are inviting spaces with large, open ceilings. Select from our extensive preferred caterer list to use our full kitchen facilities. When the season permits, gaze into a star-studded evening from our outdoor plaza.

## World Trade Conference Center

*25 S.W. Salmon Street*
*Portland, Oregon 97204*
*Reservations: (503) 464-8688*
*Office Hours: Mon–Fri 8am–5pm*

The World Trade Conference Center offers 13 conference rooms with varying sizes, and two fabulous covered indoor/outdoor areas that are unique to Portland, making our venue an excellent choice for any event.

**Capacity:** Indoor space can accommodate up to 400 reception, 300 seated; Outdoor Covered Plaza; 800 reception, 500 seated; Outdoor Skybridge Terrace overlooking waterfront; 500 reception 300 seated; Theater 220 seated.
**Price Range:** Pricing varies based on specific event requests - please call to inquire
**Catering:** The World Trade Center is a full service facility with an Executive Chef on staff.
**Types of Events:** Corporate conferences, seminars, meetings, luncheons plated and buffet, formal dinners and buffets, holiday parties, breakfasts and brunches wedding receptions and other social events.

### Availability and Terms

Please inquire for a current copy of our menus and terms of service.

### Description of Facility and Services

**Seating:** Seating capacity based on room(s) selected and chair arrangement.
**Bar facilities:** Full beverage service provided.
**Decorations:** Creative themed events welcomed. The World Trade Center offers a standard elegant holiday décor.
**Audio Visual:** Full service professional audio visual services available.
**Parking:** Underground daytime and evening parking available in building.
**ADA:** Entire building is ADA accessible.

### Special Services

The World Trade Center prides itself on excellent service, culinary expertise and the uniqueness of our space. We offer a variety of menus as well as the opportunity to work with our Executive Chef and create themed parties and events. Our experienced sales staff takes a heartfelt interest in each event and customizes to the client's desires.

### Where the World Meets

The World Trade Center offers distinctive urban elegance through our unique space, attentive service and culinary excellence. Located in downtown Portland, with easy access from I-84 and I-5, the World Trade Center is an ideal location for all types of events. The spectacular views of the Willamette River, Mt. Hood and Portland's landmark bridges create an atmosphere that is unmatched in the area.

### To Find Us

We want to help you plan your next event. Call to talk with any of our experienced sales managers for a tour or more information. You can also see us online at www.WTCPD.com or stop by — we are located between Front and First Avenue and Salmon and Taylor Streets across from Tom McCall Waterfront Park.

# Notes

# Notes

# Notes

Banquet, Meeting & Event Sites – Smaller Venues

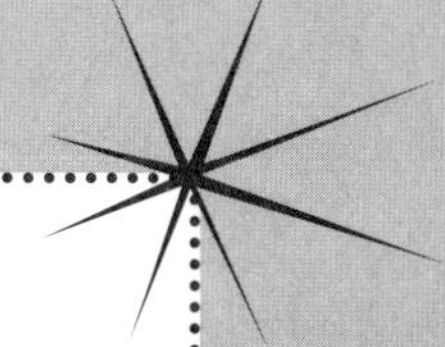

# Banquet, Meeting & Event Sites – Smaller Venues

BravoPortland.com

*Contact: Carolyn Campbell*
*5509 N.E. 30th*
*Portland, Oregon 97211*
*503-493-9497*

*www.thecoresource.com*
*carolyn@thecoresource.com*

**Capacity:** Groups ranging from 8-80 depending on event.
**Price Range:** Varies depending on space and services used.
**Catering:** We work with some of the best caterers in the city, and welcome the caterer of your choice upon approval.
**Types of Events:** Seminars, retreats, celebrations, board meetings, fundraisers, professional meetings, weddings.

## Availability and Terms

Call for availability. All events require a nonrefundable deposit to secure the date. Amount varies depending on rooms used. Client provides liability insurance.

## Description of Facilities and Services:

**Seating:** flexible space and room design
**Servers:** provided through caterer
**Bar facilities:** provided through caterer
**Dance floor:** dance floor available
**China and glassware:** provided through caterer
**Audio/visual:** additional equipment included; video projector available for a nominal fee
**Parking:** ample street parking and lot available

## Spacious, Comfortable, Innovative

Designed in a contemporary, timeless motif, The Core Source provides a relaxing, inspiring space for individuals, groups and organizations to create and celebrate. Minutes away from downtown, yet tucked away from the hustle-bustle, our artful setting is perfect for meetings, seminars, celebrations, retreats and fundraisers. Combining recycled materials with fine art, we've created a uniquely flexible setting. You can choose individual rooms or reserve the entire space to suit your specific needs. Visit the web site for pictures and details.

## Custom Services

We also provide customized programs and services to bring your ideas from concept to completion with clarity and impact. Please visit our site to find out more about these services.

- coaching & workshop facilitation specializing in visioning, speaking, presenting, selling
- editing, web design & speech writing
- event design & recognition celebrations

**Where art, business & community meet**

*3520 S.E.Powell Blvd.*
*Portland, Oregon 97202*
*Contact: Donata 503-239-5220*
*Fax 503-239-7978*

---

**Capacity:** Up to 40 in private dining room. Restaurant seats up to 110 and is available during the day from 11:30am–2:30pm.

**Price Range:** Per person pricing with flexibility needed to fit any budget. Pricing varies with menu selection. Please call for a banquet menu. **ROOM CHARGE IS COMPLIMENTARY WITH FOOD/DRINK ORDER MINIMUM.**

**Catering:** Full service catering on our premises, special menu for off site catering. **SPECIALIZING IN PIZZA, PASTA, LASAGNA, ANTIPASTO, AND SALADS.**

**Types of Events: WE DO IT ALL!** Holiday Parties, Business Dinners, Retirement Galas, Birthday Parties, Family Reunions, or any other type of gathering requiring great food, great service, and a vast selection of entrees.

## Availability and Terms

All reservations require a $100 non-refundable deposit. We recommend that you reserve your party at least two months in advance, however we can always assist you with last minute accommodations. An 18% gratuity is applied to all events.

## Description of Facilities and Services

DeNicola's is a family owned restaurant that has been part of the Portland dining scene for the last 26 years. The family friendly atmosphere, attention to detail and consistency in quality and service keep our customers coming back year after year. Dress is casual, however, we can spiff up very easily.

**Seating:** Arrangements are flexible, depending upon your needs.

**Service:** Our staff provides experienced and professional servers. Off-site we prefer to serve buffet style. We will provide set-up.

**Bar facilities:** Beer and wine available.

**Linens:** Cloth linens per DeNicola's atmosphere.

**China and glassware:** Provided.

**Decorations:** Clients may decorate prior to their event. No confetti, nails, or tacks please.

**Audiovisual:** Some available – please ask for information.

**Parking:** Full parking lot behind restaurant.

**ADA:** Accessible.

## "THE ITALIAN FLAVOR YOU REMEMBER"

We offer simple Italian fare with great flavor that has been heralded by many long time customers. Time and time again we are compared to the home-style Italian neighborhood restaurants on the east coast. *"The food is simply the best."*

## AOL City Guide customers voted DeNicola's as:

"The Best Italian Restaurant 2004." • "The Best Pizza 2004."
"The Best Family Friendly Restaurant 2004."

# MALLORY HOTEL

*729 S.W. 15th Avenue • Portland, Oregon 97205*
*503-223-6311, 800-228-8657*
*Fax 503-827-0453*
*info@malloryhotel.com*
*www.malloryhotel.com*

---

*Classic...Charming...Elegant...Affordable*

Built in 1912, the **Mallory** is Portland's premier uptown Hotel. This classic and architecturally significant boutique hotel offers traditional decor and ambiance. Located on the corner of S.W. 15th and Yamhill, adjacent to the MAX light rail, the Mallory is ideally situated within walking distance of downtown and the trendy Northwest and Pearl districts.

**Capacity:** 1,782 square feet of meeting and banquet space. **The Crystal Room** accommodates up to 85 for plated meal service or 100 for receptions and meetings. **The Garden Room** accommodates up to 26 for plated meal service or 35 for receptions. **The Executive Room** accommodates up to 16 for plated meal service or 24 for receptions.

**Price Range:** Room fees may apply depending upon food and beverage purchase.

**Catering:** $9.95 to $35.95 per person plus 17% gratuity.

**Types of Events:** weddings, receptions, rehearsal dinners, anniversary parties, reunions, fundraisers, corporate events, holiday parties, theme parties and awards banquets

## Availability and Terms

Call for availability information. Signed contract and 25% deposit are required to secure a reservation.

## Description of Facility and Services

**Included:** licensed servers and bartenders; set up/clean up, tables, chairs, linens, cloth napkins, skirting, glassware, silverware, dinnerware, chafing dishes, mirror and votive center pieces

**Liquor:** provided in-house; served by in-house licensed bartenders; corkage available with fee.

**Dance floor:** available for an additional fee; please inquire for availability and fees.

**Decorations:** clients may decorate prior to their event if availability allows. Our staff may secure other arrangements such as risers, staging, etc., through outside vendors.

**Audiovisual**: equipment and services available; fees vary, please inquire.

**Internet:** complimentary high-speed wireless Internet access available.

**ADA:** compliant

## Guest Rooms and Suites

130 deluxe guest rooms, including 13 suites. Overnight guests enjoy complimentary continental breakfast, free parking, fitness center, daily newspaper, HBO, pay-per-view movies and free local calls. Check-out is always at 1 pm. Other amenities include in-room refrigerators, safes, iron and ironing board. Group and corporate rates are available. High-speed wireless Internet access.

**Parking and Ground Transportation:** Mallory Park Garage is across the street and is complimentary for overnight guests and guests attending functions at the hotel. MAX light rail is adjacent to the hotel on Yamhill Street.

HISTORICAL SOCIETY & MUSEUM

17677 NW Springville Road • Portland, OR 97229

Contact: Mark Granlund, 503-645-5353 • 503-516-0449 cell • 503-645-5650 fax
Web: www.washingtoncountymuseum.org; E-mail: markgranlund@juno.com

---

**Capacity:** Perfect for small receptions and events of 50-100 people.
**Price Range:** Varies according to rental space and size of group; please call for specific information.
**Location:** Located on the beautiful Portland Community College Rock Creek Campus in rural Washington County.
**Catering:** Preferred caterers' list provided on request.
**Types of Events:** Social or business meetings, receptions, reunions, parties.

### Availability and Terms:

Reserve as early as possible. We can sometimes host events on short-term notice. A 25% deposit is required to reserve the date and space.

### Description of Facility and Services:

**Seating:** Tables and chairs available from caterer.
**Servers:** Appropriate service staff provided with catering service.
**Bar Facilities:** Alcoholic beverages allowed.
**Parking:** Plenty of available parking in PCC lot
**ADA:** Fully accessible.

## MAKE YOUR NEXT EVENT AN HISTORICAL OCCASION IN OUR BEAUTIFUL REMODELED VENUE

The recently remodeled Washington County Museum, located on Portland Community College's Rock Creek Campus, is ready for you and your guests to enjoy.

We're perfect for small receptions and events, featuring special group guided tours, outstanding professionally designed exhibits, and a beautiful gallery with flexible space to accommodate your event's needs.

**Make your next event an historical one!**
**Call Mark Granlund at (503) 645-5353 to reserve today.**

# Notes

# Bartending & Wine Service

BravoPortland.com

# BARTENDING & WINE SERVICE

**Liquor laws and liability:** With today's strict liquor laws, it's always smart to check into who assumes the liability for any alcoholic beverage service. Although the event facility and/or the caterer may carry liability insurance, the host or coordinator of the function may still be considered liable. Make sure all parties involved with the event are properly insured and consult with an insurance agent to make sure you have appropriate coverage for yourself.

**Oregon and Washington Liquor Control Commission Laws: In Oregon** private hosted bars featuring hard alcohol, beer, and wine do not require any special licensing. Private no-host bars may only feature beer and wine and do require a special day license. OLCC does not allow private no-host service of hard alcohol. Only OLCC licensed food and beverage establishments and caterers may sell hard alcohol. **In Washington** private hosted bars featuring hard alcohol, beer, and wine do require a WLCC Banquet Permit. The permit must be obtained one week in advance at any Washington state liquor store. Only WLCC licensed food and beverage establishments may provide no-host bars. For more information regarding these issues, contact: Oregon Liquor Control Commission at (503) 872-5070 or Washington Liquor Control Commission at (360) 260-6115.

**Private hosted bars:** If you are serving hard liquor (alcohol other than beer or wine) at a hosted bar, you should consider having a state-licensed bartender. Licensed servers have a permit from the State's Liquor Control Board.

If you have a no-host bar where money changes hands, it is the law that you must have a server who has a permit from the State's Liquor Control Board showing that the bartender has completed alcohol-server education.

**Advantages of hiring professional beverage servers:** Beverage and catering service companies provide professionally trained staff who can handle complete bar services at your event. They take care of the purchasing, bar setup and cleanup, serving, and liability. It costs a little more but may be worth it to ensure the bar will be handled in a professional and legal manner. These people are trained to detect if someone should not be served more, or if someone is underage. This service also allows you to enjoy the event without worrying about your guests.

**Oregon Alcohol Service Laws:** Any contracted bartender for pay is required to have the OLCC permit to serve alcohol. Volunteer servers do not need a service permit. **Washington Alcohol Service Laws:** Bartenders are not required to have a permit to serve alcohol for a private function.

**Beverages in bulk or case discounts:** How do you get a good selection of beverages on a budget? Distributors, wine shops, and some stores offer variety and savings when purchasing in bulk. In some instances, unused beverages may be returned for a refund. However, keep in mind that some sites will charge a corkage fee to bring in your own alcohol and others don't allow outside beverages at all.

**Control liquor and keep consumption costs down:** Have a no-host bar. Shorten the cocktail reception by 15 minutes. Serve beer, wine, water and soft drinks only; eliminate hard liquor from hosted receptions. Avoid serving salty foods during hosted bars (pretzels, peanuts, etc.). Instruct caterers or waiters to uncork wine bottles only as needed. As a healthy alternative, offer a juice bar or an espresso bar.

# HELVETIA VINEYARDS

Helvetia Vineyards and Winery
23269 N.W. Yungen Road
Hillsboro, Oregon 97124
503-647-5169
e-mail: info@helvetiawinery.com
Web site: www.helvetiawinery.com

*100 year-old Jakob Yungen Farmhouse on the grounds of Helvetia Winery and Vineyards.*

---

## FINE WILLAMETTE VALLEY WINES

**WINE TOURS AND EVENTS:** Your country farm and winery experience just 25 minutes from downtown Portland and 10 minutes from high-tech Hillsboro. The grounds surrounding our historical farmhouse are available for wine tasting events and picnics with a minimum wine purchase. Take a break from the business at hand and tour the Christmas tree farm, vineyards and winery. A perfect setting to learn about wine and winemaking in a relaxed country atmosphere.

**WINE CATERING:** Helvetia Winery offers a variety of fine vintage wines from our own and neighboring vineyards for wine tasting at your event in your location. Order wines at special case prices and we will assist you and your guests in appreciating the finer points of Oregon wines such as the importance of vintage, winemaking styles and aging.

**CUSTOMIZED LABELS:** A memento for a special event. Business meetings and conventions, presentations, retirement dinners and special thank you's are enhanced by a bottle of fine wine with your message on your own label. Because of federal regulations, please allow six weeks for delivery.

*"The north wind howls here every time it frosts.*
*However, the grapes often ripen full and wonderful."*

– Jakob Yungen writing to his
Swiss relatives in 1917

**www.helvetiawinery.com**

# Personal Bartenders

*A touch of class to any event*

**(503) 637-3379**

---

## High Quality Service

- Professional, friendly and knowledgeable bartenders
- Flexible and willing to help with planning, set up, serve, breakdown and coordinating your event
- Able to bartend from very special to very casual events
- Willing to cater to your special needs
- Referrals from satisfied customers available upon request

## Experience

- All bartenders are registered and have server permits with OLCC (Oregon) and WLC (Washington)
- Presents and displays drinks menus
- Offers pick up of beverages and supplies for your event
- Member of ACEP (Association of Catering and Event Professionals)

## Style to Any Event

- Company Parties/New Company Ownership
- Banquets/Award Dinners
- Weddings/Anniversary Celebrations
- Holiday Destivals
- Birthday Parties (Surprise someone!!!)
- Barbeques/Picnics
- Family Reunions
- Hawaiian Luaus
- Casino Parties

***For superior service that allows you to have a wonderful experience at your own event***

*(503) 236-6439 • www.bestinbrew.com*

---

Add pizzazz to your next event with gourmet espresso!

**Appassionato** – Perfect for small groups and areas with limited space. This service provides regular and decaf espresso, whole and skim milk, half & half, bittersweet chocolate, and four flavors of syrups. Iced drinks not available with this service. $230 for the first 2 hours. $75 for each additional hour. 40 cups per hour.

**Supremo** – Our most popular service. This service provides regular and decaf espresso, whole, skim and soy milk, half & half, nine flavors of syrups, bittersweet & white chocolate, and chai. Iced drinks are available upon request at no additional cost. $260 for the first 2 hours. $100 for each additional hour. 50 cups per hour. Please call for a quote for larger parties.

**Magnifico** – Like bringing the café to your event. This service offers regular and decaf espresso, whole, skim and soy milk, half & half, 12 flavored syrups, bittersweet & white chocolate, Italian sodas, iced & chai tea, lemonade, blended coffee drinks, and two flavors of fruit smoothies. Something for everyone! $100 set-up fee. $2.50 per drink. $250 minimum for the first 2 hours. $100 minimum for each additional hour.

**Caffeterra** – Delicious Torrefazione Italia drip coffee and Barnes & Watson teas. $15 per 2-liter of coffee. $10 per 2-liter of hot water and eight assorted tea bags. $15 per gallon of iced tea. Minimum 2-2 liter purchase.

We pride ourselves on serving high quality, Torrefazione Italia espresso drinks served by a professional barista. All services come with paper cups, stirrers, napkins, sugar, Sweet 'N Low®, Equal®, and nutmeg, cinnamon and cocoa shakers.

We can accommodate intimate parties to groups of over 1,000. Our licensed mobile espresso trailer is perfect for high volume, outdoor events.

For more information please call us at (503) 236-6439 or visit www.bestinbrew.com. Prices may change without notice.

**Bridgetown Coffee Company**
**Catering Division**
*3460 N.W. Industrial • Portland, Oregon 97210*
*(503) 224-3330; Fax (503) 224-9529; cell (971) 219-6984*
*E-mail: catering@bridgetowncoffee.com*
*Web site: www.bridgetowncoffee.com*

---

## LET US WIRE UP THE COMPANY BRASS & SPICE UP YOUR EVENT

### Enhance any Occasion

Bridgetown Coffee Company's hand-sculpted mobile brass and copper espresso machine and our *two new* brushed silver and black dome espresso machines will add an elegant flourish to any occasion! It has been the centerpiece at galas, weddings, business openings, office and staff appreciation events or just about any high profile occasion. It's a unique and universal way to please everyone!

### Service

Our formally dressed, skilled barista will arrive promptly at the venue of your choice to prepare specialty espresso drinks, hot and cold. A standard 110-volt electrical outlet is all you need and we bring the rest! It's your very own coffee kiosk.

### Cost

Packages are customized to fit your needs.

### Corporate Gifts

Bridgetown redefines the spirit of corporate gift giving. We can create a gift package today for your most discriminating client. Come to our warehouse and pick out what you want and we will put it together in a basket or box ~ your choice! (Large quantity and delivery/shipping available.)

### Coffee & Hot Beverage Catering

Bridgetown's high quality coffee, roasted fresh daily, brewed just for you, with all the condiments and cups included. We bring it in five-gallon black and gold cambros that serve up to 85 cups. Besides gourmet coffee, regular and decaffeinated, we offer orange juice, tea, cider, hot chocolate, mulling spice, or hot water for individual teas and chai packets. Give us a call for pricing and a proposal!

**FOR INFORMATION AND RESERVATIONS, CALL (503) 224-3330 TODAY!**

**Get on our calendar before the HOLIDAYS!**

# ESPRESSO VOLARE!
## ESPRESSO CATERING

*Contact: Myra Furnish Lee*
*(503) 246-3398; Fax (503)245-0373*
*E-mail: EspressoVolare@comcast.net*

---

### Description of Service

Personal and professional espresso catering service for groups of all sizes and events of all types, from morning meetings to evening occasions. You provide the electrical service, we do the rest. Serving Cappuccinos, Lattes, Mochas; we bring 12 flavors plus four sugar free; decaf and regular; hot or iced; assorted teas and chai lattes; hot chocolate and steamers; nonfat, 1%, 2%, whole and soy milk. Also available: individual juices, pastries, bagels, fruit salad or platters, Italian soda bar, box lunches and elegant desserts.

### Types of Events

Including but not limited to:

- Business Seminars
- Employee Appreciation
- Wedding Receptions
- Trade Shows
- Auctions
- Open Houses
- Grad Night Parties
- Holiday Parties
- Anniversaries

### References

A sampling of some of our clients:

- Portland Teachers Credit Union
- Verizon Wireless
- Fishel's Furniture
- Standard Insurance
- Portland Marriott
- Louis Dreyfus Property Group
- Portland Hilton
- Boeing
- Legacy Hospitals
- The Benson Hotel
- Walsh Construction Co.
- Saks Fifth Avenue

### Popular Locations we have Served

- Oregon Coast
- Portland Art Museum
- Jenkins Estate
- Portland Performing Arts Center
- Oregon Zoo
- The Pittock Mansion
- Leach Botanical Garden
- Tiffany Center
- Oregon History Center
- OMSI

### Our Experience Counts

We are a full-time professional business serving all of Oregon and Southwest Washington. Having been involved in the catering and service industry since 1985, we have chosen to specialize exclusively in espresso catering since 1992. We will gladly work with your selected caterer or location. Please call us for more details **(503) 246-3398**.

A special *thank you* to our wonderful and loyal customers for their 12 years of support. We look forward to a continued relationship. ***Great coffee and great service are our business.***

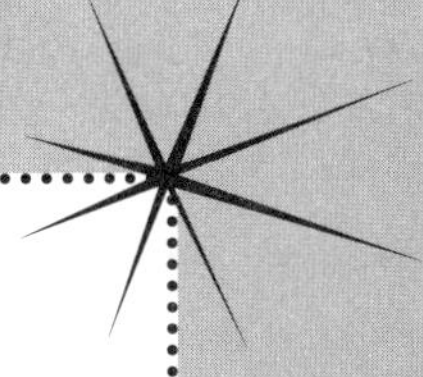

# Boats & Trains

Portland Spirit

Willamette Star

Crystal Dolphin

110 SE Caruthers Portland, OR 97214
503-226-2517 • 800-224-3901
E-mail: sales@portlandspirit.com • www.portlandspirit.com

The fleet of the Portland Spirit will provide a unique, memorable experience for your next event. Portland Spirit cruises are ideal for entertaining guests for corporate events, reunions, conventions, weddings and more. Cruise with us for a breakfast or luncheon meeting, anniversary party, or gala holiday event. Our knowledgeable sales staff and professional event planners will handle all the details, making your planning process easy and stress-free!
**Price Range:** prices vary – please inquire
**Catering:** in-house, food minimums apply

## Portland Spirit

Our flagship yacht combines a classic nautical experience with a fine-dining atmosphere. One-deck rentals, private charters of the entire vessel and public group reservations are available. Two levels are fully enclosed and climate controlled, each with a grand piano. The Columbia Deck has a built-in marble dance floor and open air viewing deck.
**Capacity:** up to 540 guests
**Seating:** tables and chairs for 340 plus outside seating

## Willamette Star

Elegance and style has been custom built into the Willamette Star, from its solid cherry wood interior to brass accents and plush carpeting. The Willamette Star has two enclosed, temperature-controlled levels, two outdoor viewing decks, piano and a sound system.
**Capacity:** up to 144 guests
**Seating:** tables and chairs for 100 plus outside and bar seating

## Crystal Dolphin

This sleek and luxurious vessel provides a bright, contemporary setting for any event. The Crystal Dolphin features three fully enclosed and climate controlled levels, a grand piano, outdoor viewing decks and sound system
**Capacity:** up to 120 guests
**Seating:** tables and chairs for 50 plus outside and lounge seating

## Description of Vessel Services and Facilities

**Linens:** linen tablecloths and napkins provided
**China:** house china and glassware provided
**Servers:** included with food and bar service
**Bar facilities:** full service bar, liquor, bartenders and liability insurance
**Cleanup:** provided; **Parking:** commercial and street parking available
**ADA:** limited with assistance; please call for more information

# PORTLAND STREETCAR AND VINTAGE TROLLEY

*Contact: Sarah Fuller, Director of Fun 503.323.7363; directoroffun@hotmail.com*

## ALL ABOARD!

For a unique gathering, consider hosting a function on board Vintage Trolley or Portland Streetcar. There are many creative ways these cars can be used with large or small groups. Party ideas are limited only by your imagination. We will be happy to work with you to customize your special event. When scheduling, please allow at least 14 days advance notice. Charters are subject to approval by rail operations. The charter price varies based on client specifications.

Catering and entertainment are not included in the charter cost. You may use the caterer of your choice or provide your own refreshments. Arrangements for catering, entertainment or complete event planning are available for an additional fee.

## Vintage Trolley

The fine craftsmanship and elegant styles of the classic trolley cars provide a charming glimpse of Portland's past. Four hand-crafted streetcars, replicas of the Council Crest trolleys from the turn of the century serve as both transportation and an attraction in Portland.

Two specially designed serving tables are available for use in the trolley, however use of these will affect available seating. The trolleys can accommodate up to 70 people, depending on usage. On board is a PA system for your taped music, or to provide an efficient system for your announcements. A conductor rides along and is available to provide a historic perspective on the trolley and sites along the route. Vintage Trolley merchandise may be purchased to use as favors for your guests.

Vintage Trolley charters operate along the MAX route from downtown Portland to Gresham, however we do not operate west of the tunnel. Charters on this route are available on weekdays from 9:30am to midnight (excluding rush hours from 3pm to 6:30pm) and from 6:30am to midnight on weekends. Vintage Trolley charters are also available along the new Portland Streetcar route (see route description below) and are available from 6:30am to midnight on both weekdays and weekends on this route.

## Portland Streetcar

Charters are available on board the modern Czech Republic streetcars along the Portland Streetcar route. This route is a loop from Northwest Portland through the Pearl District to Portland State University. These cars are larger and can accommodate approximately 125 people. Serving tables are available for your use.

Portland Streetcar charters are available weekdays after 6:30pm and from 6:30am to midnight on weekends (excluding Saturday from 3pm to 6pm.)

**To charter either Vintage Trolley or Portland Streetcar, contact**
**Sarah Fuller, Director of Fun**
**503.323.7363 or directoroffun@hotmail.com**

# STERNWHEELER "COLUMBIA GORGE" & MARINE PARK

*Sales Office: P.O. Box 307*
*Cascade Locks, Oregon 97014*
*(541) 374-8427; (800) 643-1354*
*Web site: www.sternwheeler.com; E-mail: sales@sternwheeler.com*

Owned & operated by the Port of Cascade Locks

**Capacity:** 350 passengers
**Price Range:** varies depending on event and length of cruise; two hour minimum; please call
**Catering:** full range of catering services provided including menu selections for champagne brunch, luncheon, dinner, hors d'oeuvres and theme parties
**Types of Events:** private charter meal and excursion cruises, company picnics (park only), holiday parties, casino cruises, weddings, fund raisers, meetings, conventions

## Availability and Terms

The Sternwheeler "Columbia Gorge" offers two fully enclosed heated decks, providing a comfortable setting for any time of year. Marine Park offers accommodations for groups of 50 to 1,000, as well as a three-acre private island. A 25% nonrefundable deposit is required upon booking; final payment is due 14–30 days prior to scheduled event, depending on season.

## Description of Facility and Services

**Seating:** tables, chairs, and standard linens provided
**Servers:** provided
**Bar facilities:** two to three full-service bars with bartenders available
**Dance floor:** dance area available; full electrical hookup
**Linens and napkins:** vinyl linens and cloth napkins; color coordination available–please inquire
**China and glassware:** house china available with our catering service
**Decorations:** elegant turn-of-the-century motif requires little decoration
**Audiovisual:** available; please call a sales representative
**Cleanup:** provided courtesy of the Sternwheeler crew
**Parking:** *Cascade Locks Marine Park:* free parking
**ADA:** disabled accessible

## Special Services

With the beauty of the gorge and an abundance of breathtaking views to choose from, the Sternwheeler "Columbia Gorge" and Marine Park continue to provide a unique venue for meetings, banquets, or any event. We can coordinate your event from start to finish, including transportation, catering and entertainment. Please call our sales office for more details.

# THE STERNWHEELER ROSE

*6211 N. Ensign*
*Portland, Oregon 97217*
*(503) 286-ROSE (7673)*
*Business Hours: Mon–Fri 9am–5pm*

## The Sternwheeler Rose

Cruising aboard *The Sternwheeler Rose* is a unique way to make your event special. It's also a festive place to host business meetings, customer appreciations, company picnics, receptions, anniversaries and birthday celebrations. Or, treat your group to a cruise with the Christmas ships for your Christmas party.

Our professional caterer will provide you with breakfast, lunch, dinner or hors d'oeuvre menu suggestions. Of course, you are also welcome to create your own menu. You're limited only by your imagination and budget! Additionally, our staff, crew and captains are available to help you plan every step and execute every detail to make your cruise a wonderful and memorable event.

**Capacity:** up to 130 people; you may reserve the entire boat for your private cruise
**Price Range:** prices vary—please inquire
**Catering:** licensed, in-house catering available; flexible menus
**Types of Events:** breakfast, lunch, dinner or cocktail cruises, business meetings, corporate parties, receptions, weddings, anniversaries, birthday parties.

### Availability and Terms

*The Sternwheeler Rose* is Portland's finest year-round charter boat. It cruises on the Willamette river. A deposit of 50% is required. Terms are available.

### Description of Facility and Services

**Boarding location:** OMSI; other boarding sites can be scheduled
**Seating:** tables and chairs provided
**Servers:** provided
**Bar facilities:** full-service bar available
**Dance floor:** floor for up to 80 people; electrical hookups available
**Linens and napkins:** all colors of linen tablecloths and cloth napkins available at additional cost; white linens at no charge
**China and glassware:** glass plates, glasses and barware available
**Decorations:** No candles, confetti or propane allowed
**Equipment:** podium, easel, risers available upon request
**Cleanup:** complete cleanup courtesy of The Sternwheeler Rose with catering
**Parking:** free at OMSI

### Special Services

Be sure to ask about decorations both for ideas and logistics

**Please call if you would like more information or a tour.**
**(503) 286-7673**

**Visit us at www.sternwheelerrose.com**

# Notes

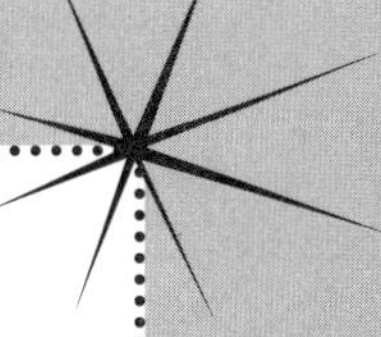

# Business Publications & Media

- *Radio Station Listings*
- *Television Station Listings*
- *Newspaper & Magazine Listings*

# WRITING A PRESS RELEASE

Press Releases are one of your more effective mediums of advertising. Press stories are usually presented in the paper, television, radio or trade publications because of a special interest to the audience. There are a variety of reasons to send out a press release: Grand opening, new office site, an event, new product, exciting news, etc.

Public relations can be like Russian roulette, sometimes you get the coverage and other times you don't. When you do get the story, it can be worth ten times more than advertising. Always send a press release,whether you think there is a story there or not. If the newspaper or television station needs a last-minute story they may publish your release verbatim, or call you to do a story the day of the event.

## Timing

- You may want to plan your event when nothing else of significance is happening. Larger, more public events and happenings will always take priority over a smaller event.
- You cannot predict disaster or national news stories, but these can happen and can bump even a story that had been planned and written already.
- In some cases when you send your press release determines if you will receive exposure before or after the event. You may just send info about the event, or invite the press to a press party, or invite the press to cover the actual event.
- Press Releases should be sent out two weeks prior to the event. Call to confirm the release was received and then follow-up with enthusiasm about the event, to see if you can answer any questions or provide any additional information.

## Planning

- The more information you collect; facts, figures, interesting points, etc. the better job you can do writing a press release.
- Creative writing is a must.
- Media list: There are hundreds of newspapers, radio stations, television and trade publications. You can choose to send press information to all or just send to a selected list. Then keep this list for future use. Refer to the list of all local media in this chapter. (Note: always update and call-down media list prior to using- updates are recommended every six months)
- During the prior call-down, confirm who the appropriate department and person or editor to send information to. You can develop an ongoing relationship with these persons for future events and happenings.
- When the Press arrives at an event–a fact sheet is helpful for them to take back to their office; fact sheets include details surrounding the event, information about the organization and goals for the event.

## Writing and Developing

- Creative angle to press release: Inserting a sample of product, photo. Press releases can be fun in a creative format-using special paper, ink, mounting on foam core, etc. (there are creative firms in this Guide listed under "Signage, Design & Printing" that can help with the entire public relations campaign).
- Try to write the press release in a journalistic manner (no first person). If written well, sometimes the press release will be published word-for-word.
- Keep it brief and to the facts; make sure facts are accurate and specific
- Format for the press release is listed in the front of this Guide "Planning a Meeting or Event, Promotions and Publicity."

# The Business Journal

*851 S.W. Sixth Avenue, Suite 500*
*Portland, Oregon 97204*
*Contact: Craig Wessel, Publisher*
*Rob Smith, Editor for press releases*
*Doug Horton, Marketing Manager for subscriptions*
*George Vaughan, Director of Sales for advertising*
*Phone (503) 274-8733; Fax (503) 227-2650*

---

Established in 1984, *The Business Journal* is a weekly newspaper that covers local business news. It is written for business executives and publishes stories about specific industries, trends and people. It is considered a "must read" by professionals, and its award-winning editorial makes *The Business Journal* the best news source for local business in Greater Portland.

## Editorial

The Business Journal has dedicated coverage of the hospitality industry. Editorial sections specifically relating to events and meetings include:

- Meetings, a focus section
- Travel, a focus section
- Hospitality, a focus section
- Top 25 Hotels and Motels list
- Top 25 Meeting Facilities list
- Top 25 Meeting Facilities-out of area list
- Top 25 Restaurants list
- Top 25 Resorts list
- Top 25 conventions list

## Circulation

- 13,000 total circulation
- 58,000 readers

## Readership

- 77% read four out of four issues
- 64% consider *The Business Journal* their primary source of local business news

## Subscriber Information

*The Business Journal* subscribers are key decision-makers for their companies.

- 57% in top management
- 70% work in small companies
- Facilities used for off-site meetings: hotels—56%, restaurants—52%, meeting facilities—41%, resorts—25%
- Use of local hotels for: meeting rooms—49%, banquet facilities—38%,
- Median age: 50 years
- 81% college graduates
- Average household income: $204,000
- 73% drink Oregon wine
- 54% drink Oregon microbrews

**www.portland.bizjournals.com**

# Meetings | west

*550 Montgomery Street, Suite 750*
*San Francisco, California 94111*
*Phone 800.358.0388, Fax 415.788.1358*

***For Advertising Information:***
*Shawne Hightower, Regional Sales Manager*
*Lynne Richardson, Associate Publisher*

***For Editorial:***
*Tyler Davidson, Editorial Director*

***For Subscriptions:***
*Heidi Miller, Circulation Supervisor 319.364.6167*

*Web site: www.meetingsfocus.com*

---

*Meetings West* delivers news, features and the most thorough destination information on the western United States, western Canada and Mexico meetings markets to a national audience of planning professionals who book meetings in these regions. Key editorial topics include: hotel and conference facilities; interesting event venues; renovation updates; industry trends; and topical articles of general interest.

- 26,000 qualified subscribers; BPA audited
- Annual planning directory, *Meetings West Guide*
- Three to four in-depth destination features each month

## Hot Topics for 2005

| | |
|---|---|
| **January** | Events Datebook, Meetings Market Report, Planners' Best Bets, Pacific Northwest |
| **February** | Conference Centers, Dude Ranches, Incentives |
| **March** | Summer Mountain Resorts, University Venues |
| **April** | Convention Centers, Historic Places, Luxury Hotels, **Oregon** |
| **May** | Small Meetings, Special Venues, Government Meetings |
| **June** | Affordable Meetings/Value Destinations, Hip Hotels, Spas |
| **July** | All Inclusives, Team Building, Sports Meetings |
| **August** | Coastal Meetings, Assoc. Meetings, Best of the West Awards |
| **September** | Washington, Winter Mountain Resorts, Incentives, Shipboard Meetings |
| **October** | Attractions/Theme Parks, Gaming, CVB Update, High-Tech Meetings, **Portland — Bonus Distribution at Bravo!** |
| **November** | Airline Update, Airport Properties, Desert Meetings |
| **December** | Golf & Tennis Resorts, New & Renovated Properties |

**Visit our award-winning web site, MeetingsFocus.com.**

***Call for advertising rates.***

## RADIO STATIONS

**KBMS Radio - 1480 am**
P.O. Box 251
Vancouver, WA 98666
(360) 699-1881

**KBNP Radio - 1410 am/**www.kbnp.com
278 SW Arthur Rd.
Portland, OR 97201
(503) 223-6769

**KGON Radio - 92.5 fm/**www.kgon.com
**KFXX Radio - 910am**
**KNRK Radio - 94.7 fm/**www.knrk.com
**KISN Radio - 97.1 fm/**www.kisnfm.com
**KRSK Radio - 101.9 fm**
0700 S.W. Bancroft St.
Portland, OR 97239
(503) 223-1441

**KBOO Radio - 90.7 fm/**www.kboo.org
20 S.E. Eighth Ave.
Portland, OR 97214
(503) 231-8032

**KFIS - 104.1 fm/**www.104thefish.com
5110 S.E. Stark
Portland, OR 97215
(503) 231-7800

**KKCW Radio - 103 fm/**www.k103.com
**KKRZ Radio - 100.3 fm/**www.z100portland.com
**KEX Radio - 1190 am/**www.1190kex.com
4949 S.W. Macadam Ave.
Portland, OR 97201
(503) 225-1190

**KINK Radio - 102 fm/**www.kinkfm102.com
1501 S.W. Jefferson
Portland, OR 97201
(503) 517-6000

**K-LOVE Christian Music Radio -**
**1040 am, 88.7 fm & 96.3 fm/**www.k-love.com
1425 N. Market Blvd.
Sacramento, CA 95834
(800) 525-5683

**KMDH Radio**
Mt. Hood Community College
26000 S.E. Stark St.
Gresham, OR 97030
(503) 491-7271

**KMUZ Radio**
24 S. "A" St. Ste.C
Washougal, WA 98671
(503) 227-2156

**KOPB Radio - 91.5 fm**
7140 S.W. Macadam Ave.
Portland, OR 97219
(503) 244-9900

**KWJJ Radio - 99.5 fm/**www.kwjj.com
**KOTK Radio -1080 am**
2000 S.W. First Ave., Ste. 300
Portland, OR 97201
(503) 228-4393

**KPDQ Radio - 93.7 fm/**www.kpdq.com
5110 S.E. Stark
Portland, OR 97215
(503) 231-7800

**KUFO Radio - 101.1 fm/**www.kufo.com
**KVMX Radio - 107.5 fm**
2040 S.W. First Ave.
Portland, OR 97201
(503) 222-1011

**KUIK Radio - 1360 am/**www.kuik.com
P.O. Box 566
Hillsboro, OR 97123
(503) 640-1360

**KUPL Radio - 98.7 fm/**www.kupl.com
**KLTH Radio - 106.7 fm/**www.literock1067.com
222 S.W. Columbia, Ste. 350
Portland, OR 97201
(503) 223-0300

**KWBY Radio - 940 am/**
**KCKX Radio - 1460 am**
P.O. Box 158
Woodburn, OR 97071
(503) 981-9400

**KXL Radio - 750 am/**www.kxl.com
**KXJM Radio - 95.5 fm/**www.jamminfm.com
0234 S.W. Bancroft St.
Portland, OR 97239
(503) 243-7595; Fax (503) 417-7660

## TELEVISION STATIONS

**KATU-TV (ABC)**
P.O. Box 2
Portland, OR 97207
2153 N.E. Sandy Blvd.
Portland, OR 97232
(503) 231-4222; Fax (503) 231-4626
www.katu.com

**KGW-TV (NBC)**
1501 S.W. Jefferson
Portland, OR 97201
(503) 226-5111; Fax (503) 226-5059
www.kgw.com

**KNMT-TV**
432 N.E. 74th Ave.
Portland, OR 97213
(503) 252-0792; Fax (503) 256-4205

**KOIN-TV (CBS)**
222 S.W. Columbia St.
Portland, OR 97201
(503) 464-0600; Fax (503) 464-0806
www.koin.com

**KOPB-TV**
7140 S.W. Macadam Ave.
Portland, OR 97219
(503) 244-9900; Fax (503) 293-1919
www.opb.org

**KPTV-TV Fox 12**
211 S.E. Caruthers
Portland, OR 97214
(503) 230-1200; Fax (503) 230-1065
www.kptv.com

**KWBP-TV**
10255 S.W. Arctic Drive
Beaverton, OR 97005
(503) 644-3232; Fax (503) 626-3576
www.wb32tv.com

**Portland Cable Access**
2766 N.E. MLK Jr. Blvd.
Portland, OR 97212
(503) 288-1515; Fax (503) 288-8173
www.pcatv.org

## NEWSPAPERS

**The Battleground Reflector**
P.O. Box 2020
Battleground, WA 98604
(360) 687-5151; Fax (360) 687-5162
Contact: Marvin Case
www.thereflector.com

**Bee – Sellwood**
1837 S.E. Harold Rd.
Portland, OR 97202-4932
(503) 232-2326; Fax (503) 692-5653
Contact: Eric Norberg
www.readthebee.com

**The Business Journal**
851 S.W. 6th Ave., Suite 500
Portland, OR 97204
(503) 274-8733; Fax (503) 227-2650
Contact: Dan Cook
www.bizjournals.com
*See page 189*

**The Clackamas County Review**
16207 S.E. McLoughlin Blvd.
Milwaukie, OR 97267
(503) 786-1996; Fax (503) 786-6977
Contact: Michael Russell
www.clackamasreview.com

**The Columbian**
P.O. Box 180
Vancouver, WA 98666
(503) 224-0654; Fax (503) 699-6033
Contact: Scott Campbell
www.columbian.com

**Community Newspapers**
P.O. Box 370
Beaverton, OR 97075
(503) 684-0360; Fax (503) 620-3433
Contact: Steve Clark

**Corvallis Gazette-Times**
P.O. Box 368
Corvallis, OR 97339
(541) 753-2641; Fax (541) 758-9505
Contact: Rob Priewe
www.gtconnect.com

**Gresham Outlook**
1190 N.E. Division St.
P.O. Box 747
Gresham, OR 97030
(503) 665-2181; Fax (503) 665-2187
Contact: Dean Rhodes
www.theoutlookonline.com

**Hillsboro Argus**
P.O. Box 588
Hillsboro, OR 97123
(503) 648-1131; Fax (503) 648-9191
Contact: Gary Stutzman

**Hollywood Star**
2000 N.E. 42nd Ave.
Portland, OR 97213
(503) 282-9392
Contact: Nancy Woods

**Hospitality News**
P.O. Box 21027
Salem, OR 97307
(503) 390-8343; Fax (503) 390-8344
Contact: Brenda Carlos

**Just Out**
P.O. Box 14400
Portland, OR 97293
(503) 236-1252; Fax (503) 236-1257
Contact: Marty Davis
www.justout.com

**Lake Oswego Review**
P.O. Box 548
Lake Oswego, OR 97034
(503) 635-8811; Fax (503) 635-8817
Contact: Martin Forbes
www.lakeoswegoreview.com

**Oregon City News**
16207 S.E. McLoughlin Blvd.
Milwaukie, OR 97267
(503) 786-1996; Fax (503) 786-6977
Contact: Michael Russell

**The Oregonian**
1320 S.W. Broadway
Portland, OR 97201
(503) 221-8100; Fax (503) 227-5306
Contact: Fred Stickel
www.theoregonian.com

**Portland Observer**
P.O. Box 3137
Portland, OR 97208
(503) 288-0033; Fax (503) 288-0015
Contact: Charles Washington
www.portlandobserver.com

**The Skanner**
P.O. Box 5455
Portland, OR 97228
(503) 285-5555; Fax (503) 285-2900
Contact: Bobbie Foster
www.theskanner.com

**Statesman Journal**
P.O. Box 13009
Salem, OR 97309
(800) 452-2511; Fax (503) 399-6706
Contact: Dick Hughs
www.statsmanjournal.com

**West Linn Tidings**
P.O. Box 548
Lake Oswego, OR 97034
(503) 635-8811; Fax (503) 635-8817
Contact: Ray Pitz
www.westlinntidings.com

**Willamette Week**
822 S.W. 10th Ave.
Portland, OR 97205
(503) 243-2122; Fax (503) 243-1115
Contact: John Schrag
www.wweek.com

## MAGAZINES

**Meetings West**
550 Montgomery St., Ste. 750
San Francisco, CA 94111
(800) 358-0388; Fax (415) 788-1905
www.meetingsmedia.com
*See page 190*

**Oregon Business Magazine**
610 S.W. Broadway, Ste. 200
Portland, OR 97205
(503) 223-0304; Fax (503) 221-6544

**Portland Magazine**
P.O. Box 1685
Clackamas, OR 97015
(503) 558-8289
www.portlandmagazine.com

**Portland Monthly**
600 NW 14th Avenue, Suite 100
Portland, Oregon 97209
503-222-5144
www.portland-monthly.com

# Notes

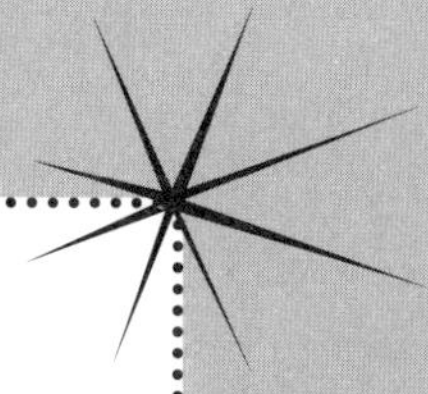

# Casinos & On-Site Casino Parties

BravoPortland.com

RESORT

*1777 N.W. 44th Street*
*Lincoln City, Oregon 97367*
*Contact: Steve Chrisman*
*(541) 996-5925, (888) CHINOOK ext. 5925*
*stevec@chinookwindsgaming.com • www.chinookwindscasino.com*
*Business Hours: 8am–6pm; messages taken 24 hours*

**Capacity:** groups from 20 to 2,000; over 44,000 square feet total; main room, 20,000 square feet accommodating 1,610 theater-style and 1,120 sit-down; eight rooms with 3,000+ square feet; five rooms, 550+ square feet; additional showroom space available: 15,000 square feet, theatre seating for 1,400 or 60 trade show booths (depending on setup)
**Price Range:** prices vary depending on menu selection and size of event
**Catering:** Full-service, in-house catering
**Types of Events:** any type of function: 20 to 2,000 people; dinners, receptions, trade shows, conventions, meetings, fundraisers, seminars, conferences, weddings, reunions; breakout rooms available

## Availability and Terms

We encourage you to book early to ensure availability.

## Description of Facility and Services

**Seating:** various styles for up to 1200
**Servers:** provided by Chinook Winds
**Bar facilities:** full-service bar and bartender
**Dance floor:** in-house floor can be rented
**Linens:** provided; variety of colors to choose from at a minimal charge
**China:** provided; variety to choose from
**Decorations:** various themes to choose from
**Audio/Visual:** complete equipment available upon request
**Parking:** abundant free parking and valet service, free hotel shuttles
**ADA:** meets all ADA requirements

## Special Services

Our 4-star chef and professional staff work to produce a magnificent event that your company will be proud of. Other amenities include full-service Business Center, childcare, arcade, ocean view, buffet, deli, private gaming tournaments, golf and wedding packages, fine dining.

## FLEXIBLE MEETING SPACES

The newest resort on the Oregon coast, Chinook Winds Casino and Convention Center overlooks the picturesque Pacific Ocean and offers over 44,000 square feet of meeting space. The recent acquisition of the adjacent 247 room oceanfront hotel (formerly Shilo) makes us an even more spectacular location. Our host of services provide for a wide range of needs and afford the meeting planner creativity and flexibility with their event. The main conference area opens to 20,000 sq. ft. of carpeted meeting space. The ample room can be divided into as many as six rooms of over 3,000 sq. ft. each. Also available are three meeting/breakout rooms and a full-service Business Center. An additional 15,000 sq. ft. is available in the showroom to accommodate trade shows or theatre style seating for up to 1,400. All these options add up to 44,000 sq. ft.! Just minutes from great golf, outlet shopping and nature's impressive splendors, let us make your next event fresh and exciting while you watch your attendance rise. We don't just say *It's Better At The Beach,* we prove it.

*12888 188th Avenue, S.W.*
*Rochester, Washington 98579*
*(800) 720-1788*
*E-mail: banquets@luckyeagle.com*
*Web site: www.luckyeagle.com*
*Directions: Just 30 minutes south of Olympia.*
*I-5 exit 88/88-B, west on Hwy 12 to*
*Anderson Road, Rochester*

---

**Capacity:** Groups from 6-700; Over 12,056 square feet total; Event Center - 6,750 sq ft accommodating 1,200 theater style, seats 650; (2) rooms with over 1,300 sq ft; (3) rooms with over 500 sq ft, seats 40-50; (2) smaller rooms for intimate gatherings of 16-32.
**Price Range:** menus for every budget, please contact event coordinator
**Catering:** full service, in-house and off-site to the location of your choice
**Types of Events:** corporate meetings, banquets, luncheons, holiday parties, wedding receptions, award ceremonies, trade shows, fundraisers, conferences

## Availability and Terms

The Lucky Eagle Casino has everything you need for the perfect group gathering. Free bus shuttle service is available in certain areas. Please contact for more information.

## Description of Facility and Services

**Seating:** eight different banquet rooms with seating for 6-700 guests
**Servers:** provided
**Dance Floor:** available at an additional charge
**Linens/China:** provided
**Decorations:** allowed with prior approval
**Parking:** plenty of free parking
**Cleanup:** provided
**Audio Visual Equipment:** available at an additional charge

## THE EXCITING EVENT SPECIALISTS!

Wedding receptions. Award ceremonies. Company banquets. Holiday parties. The Lucky Eagle Casino is the ideal venue for your next function. Our spacious banquet rooms have a total capacity of 700 guests, allowing us to meet the needs of groups both large and small. What's more, the Lucky Eagle has four different restaurants on site, and our talented chefs offer a wider range of menu choices than any other banquet facility in the area. And entertainment? Your guests can play to their heart's content at our fabulous casino, or dance the night away in our special event center. We can help you plan your event at our facility, or provide complete catering services at the location of your choice. Simply put, the Lucky Eagle Casino Banquet & Catering staff just gives you more!

## Luxury Hotel Coming in 2005.

**Visit our website in the days ahead for updates on our hotel construction. Then plan to play and stay at Lucky Eagle Casino.**

An enterprise of the Confederated Tribes of Grand Ronde

# SPIRIT MOUNTAIN CASINO

*P.O. Box 39 • Grand Ronde, Oregon 97347*
*Contact: Stephanie Miller, Sales and Marketing Coordinator*
*(800) 760-7977 ext.3034*
*Business Hours: Mon–Fri 9am–5pm, Casino Hours: 24 hours*
*Web site: www.spiritmountain.com*

---

**Capacity:** The Legends' banquet facility is available for private functions 6am to Midnight daily. **Rogue River Room:** 2,500 square feet of space divides into two equal rooms, comfortably seating up to 180 people in its entirety; **Kalapuya Room:** 2,300 sq.ft. also divides into two sections, seating up to 150. 25 person minimum required.

**Price Range:** The full room rental fee is $350, or $175 per half room, per day. This fee is reduced to a set-up fee of $50 with a minimum of a $450 food service order. Menu prices include gratuity.

**Catering:** full service, in house

**Types of Events:** meetings, seminars, conventions, luncheons, dinners, receptions, parties, weddings, and corporate functions.

## Availability and Terms

Contact Banquet Sales at (800) 760-7977 ext. 3034, Online RFT available at spiritmountain.com

## Description of Services and Facility

**Servers:** provided

**Seating:** A variety of setup choices are available in each of the function rooms including rounds, hollow square, u-shape, conference, classroom and theater seating.

**Stage/dance floor:** complimentary with advance notice

**Linens, napkins, china and glassware:** provided

**Decorations:** allowed with prior approval

**Audiovisual:** podium, microphone, TV/VCR, overhead projector, slide projector, LCD projector, screen, flip chart, white board, dance floor and stage

**Cleanup:** provided

**Parking:** ample free parking, including complimentary valet service; **ADA:** fully complies

## SPIRIT MOUNTAIN LODGE

Spirit Mountain Lodge features Northwest décor and furnishings with original Native American art. The renowned wineries of Polk and Yamhill Counties, and the beautiful Oregon Coast are just a short drive away. Bell service, valet parking, in-room coffee, in-room safes, handicapped accessible rooms and hearing impaired kits are provided at no charge.

Beginning in Spring 2005, we will have 254 rooms available as well as a free continental breakfast for all lodge guests, and a business center with high-speed Internet connections, faxing and copying capabilities.

The Summit View Lounge offers live entertainment every weekend. Headline entertainment is showcased throughout the year in our spacious 1,600-seat concert hall. Playworld, a supervised childrens' entertainment area, is available, as well as an exciting video arcade.

# UPTOWN CASINO EVENTS

120 NW 23rd
PORTLAND, OR 97210
CONTACT: Drew Podolak
503-819-9708
FAX: 503-282-8008
www.uptowncasino.com

---

***Don't gamble...***

*on your company party, reunion, reception graduation night or private affair...*

***Play it safe with***
**Uptown Casino Events!**

## Experience

Our staff is well versed in all elements of event production and will ensure that the casino portion of your evening is tailored to fit your group's specific needs — flowing seamlessly into the big picture of your group's event.

## Better Gaming Equipment

Uptown Casino Events has the finest, most elegant gaming equipment in the Portland area. Hand crafted tables, casino quality chips, and the best accessories for a true casino gaming experience!

## Lower Prices

With our exceptional equipment, friendly staff, and prices that can't be beat…what more could you ask for? Per table pricing for poker, blackjack, craps and roulette to accommodate all event sizes.

## Better Service

Although games and activities go a long way in providing atmosphere, only personalities can be "The Life of Your Party." We hire and train a very personable crew.

## One Phone Call

Is all it takes to plan your entire event. Let our sister company, The Uptown Billiards Club, take care of your off-site catering and/or entertainment needs and receive onsite gaming prices. Hold your event at the Billiards Club's unique facility and receive a 15% discount on the gaming portion of the evening.

**Call Uptown Casino Events**
**for an evening you will never forget!**

**(503) 819-9708**

*2318 N.W. Vaughn Street • Portland, Oregon 97210*
*(503) 224-0134; Fax (503) 224-0278 or Toll-free (800) 346-7280*
***www.wildbills.com***

Voted the most popular form of entertainment by event planners nationwide, casino parties are perfect for:

Fund Raisers • Company Parties • Reunions • Conventions • Grad Nights
Client Appreciation Parties • Holiday Parties • Picnics • Private Parties

Wild Bill's is the leader in the Northwest for providing exciting casino action for all types of events. From the first meeting to the conclusion of the event, Wild Bill's Casino is there to make sure your first "Casino Night" is a big success!

Your guests wager with Wild Bill's Bucks at games like blackjack, craps and roulette, all run by our friendly, professional dealers. It's all in fun, with no real gambling.

## Wild Bill's Casino Provides:

Over 22 years of casino party experience in the Northwest
Professional quality gaming tables such as Blackjack, Craps, Roulette, Texas Hold'em, Caribbean Stud Poker, Let it Ride, Money Wheel, 3-Card Poker and Slots
Extensively trained dealers, including Casino Supervisors and Relief Dealers
All the supplies you need to run the event such as cards, chips, dice, scrip, drawing tickets or vouchers, as well as delivery, setup and pickup
Outstanding customer service

## Here's What Our Clients Have To Say

*"The staff at Wild Bill's was phenomenal! Not only did you live up to your reputation, you have exceeded it."*

~ Reynolds Education Foundation

*"...a tremendous service and a terrific party. Everyone had a good time."*

~ Texpo

*"Fantastic organization – professional, fun and organized!"*

~ Gentle Dental

## Additional Entertainment Options

- Comedy Hypnosis
- Game Shows
- Inflatable Games
- Murder Mysteries
- Video Horse Racing
- Mini Auto Racing
- $10,000 Putting Challenge
- DJ / Karaoke

Member: Assoc. of Catering and Event Professionals, National Assoc. of Casino & Theme Party Operators, Meeting Professionals International, International Special Events Society, and the Portland Oregon Visitor's Association

**See page 310 under Interactive Entertainment.**

BravoPortland.com

# EVENT CATERING

**Food and beverages can make a major contribution to the success of an event.** In addition to breakfast (full or continental), lunch or dinner, food and beverage functions can include theme events, receptions, cocktail parties, and refreshment breaks. Most often at any event or meeting, the food has a lasting impression on your attendees. Whether it was too cold, not enough, or absolutely great, you will hear about it. Include regional or local specialties as often as possible for a memorable touch. Be health conscious and try to offer a variety of foods that are nutritionally balanced and colorful. Remember to include vegetarian option. Avoid heavy sauces and keep lunch light to keep attendees alert! On hot days, provide a lot of water, juices and fresh fruit.

**You are not limited to printed menu options.** Either give the food and beverage providers a budget to come up with options or give them an idea of what you want and ask them to determine the cost.

**It is important not to run out of food.** Some attendees will have one plate at a buffet, and others will go back for thirds. Customize your menu and quantities based on the types of attendees. Ask your caterer's opinion as to whether served portions or banquet style is the best for your event.

**Meal guarantees:** Facilities usually require a "guarantee" for the number of guests that will need to be served at each meal function. The guarantee is usually required at least 48 hours in advance of the event. After the guarantee has been given, the facility will allow you to increase the numbers but not decrease.

**Catering guidelines:** Ask the caterers what their guidelines are and how they figure them. How do they take care of extra people? Get several estimates if you are using an outside caterer–the price, portions, and what is or isn't included may vary for the same menu. Make sure the prices quoted will be valid the day of your event or have them commit to a percentage cap that can't be increased. For example, the price of beef may rise, but the caterer would guarantee quoted beef prices within 10%.

**What a caterer supplies:** Caterers can generally supply serviceware, flatware, dishes, cups, and table linens. They also normally provide servers, bartenders, and clean-up crew. Be sure to check what items and services are included.

**Delivery of food:** If the caterer delivers the food, make sure it is transported in warmers and coolers to ensure that it stays at the appropriate temperature.

**Saving dollars:** Order bottled beverages served by consumption and at the end of the event count the empty bottles to make certain you are charged the correct amount. Avoid labor intensive foods. Replace a full breakfast with a continental breakfast; it won't be as heavy and people can snack throughout the meeting.

**Beverage conversion:** One gallon coffee = (20) 8 oz. cups. One bottle of wine= (5) 6 oz. glasses. One full-size beer keg = 15 gallons, or (200) 10 oz. or (160) 12 oz. glasses.

**IMPORTANT NOTE:** Do not leave food out for long periods of time unless hot food is in chafing dishes and cold food is on ice.

# AN ELEGANT AFFAIR

*P.O. Box 80013 • Portland, Oregon 97280*
*Contact: Melody*
*(503) 245-2802; Fax (503) 246-4309*
*E-mail: melody@anelegantaffaircatering.com*

---

***You are cordially invited to experience An Elegant Affair…Your Next Event!***

## Types of Menus and Specialties

Catering is our only business. An Elegant Affair catering will carefully plan, prepare, and present a tantalizing bill of fare created specifically to fit your budget and needs. Whether it's a business meeting brunch, open house luncheon, holiday hors d'oeuvres cocktail party, or formal board meeting dinner, we are committed to making your affair an elegant one!

## Services and Cost

- **Menu planning:** Our seasoned staff can prepare any type of cuisine in our fully licensed catering kitchen, and we are happy to design a menu that will suit your special occasion.
- **Estimating number of guests:** We can help you determine how many guests to expect to ensure accurate food quantities are ordered.
- **Cost:** Our prices are determined on a per-person basis and vary upon menu selection. A 35% deposit is required to reserve your date. The balance is due before the event.
- **Beverage service:** Alcoholic and nonalcoholic beverages are available.
- **Linens and napkins:** Buffet table linen and skirting no charge; paper products no charge; white and colored linen tablecloths and napkins available.
- **Serviceware:** Silver serving trays available no charge; china, glassware, paper, and plastic available.
- **Servers:** We supply experienced, professional servers and bartenders in formal black and white attire. Setup, serving, and complete cleanup of all food and beverages are always provided.

**For your entertaining ease, let AN ELEGANT AFFAIR handle your next catered event.**

(You'll find hosting a special occasion will never be easier or more enjoyable.)

**Call today for a complimentary consultation!**
**(503) 245-2802**

*fresh creative organic*

*503-233-8539*
*www.artemisfoods.com*

---

*Exceptional cuisine with local, seasonal and organic ingredients.*
*Outstanding Service*

## Full Service and Drop off Catering for any event, large or small.

The same thoughtful consideration and preparation goes into our drop off catering as in our full service catering. Below is a sampling of the types of catering we offer:

- Coffee Service and Breakfasts
- Business Lunches and Boxed Lunches
- Holiday Parties
- Dinner Parties
- Gallery Openings and Open Houses
- Retirement Parties
- Cooking Classes in a "Dinner Party Style" for Business Entertainment
- Cocktail Receptions
- Weddings

## Menus:

We offer seasonal menus for breakfast, snacks, desserts, boxed lunches, full lunch and dinner, from casual to spectacular. Our award winning chef/owner, Grace Pae is accomplished at creating fabulous food that is elegant yet simple, celebrating the bounty of the Northwest and borrowing from many different World cuisines. Artemis Foods focuses on using organic and local ingredients, meats, wines, coffee, juices, etc. as much as possible. We offer reusable plates and cutlery and recycled paper products.

***For any day and everyday, let us always eat good food!***

## Service:

Ask for Greta Collias Molitor, our office manger, or Grace to help you with all the details. We pay attention to our clients needs and budget. We will make your event perfect. From coordinating linens and china to setting up stages, podiums, staging and tenting. We have the resources to provide any event with the best and most complete set up. Check out some of the outstanding venues at which Artemis Foods may cater your event:
**Ecotrust Conference Center, World Forestry Center, Portland Japanese Garden, PICA, Jenkins Estate, Wilsonville Training Center, Contemporary Gallery of Arts, Leach Botanical Gardens, Earth Advantage National Center.**

***On the City of Portland's List of Sustainable Caterers***

BAJA BestMex GRILL™

www.baja-grill.com

VISIT OUR WEBSITE for all of our MENUS

827 SW Second Avenue ~ Portland, Oregon 97204

(503) 224-0370 Fax (503) 224-3919

| RESTAURANT | CATERING |
| --- | --- |
| Mon–Fri Lunch | 24/7 (with advance notice) |

## BAJA CASUAL TO MODERN SOUTHWESTERN CUISINE

**~ Company Picnics ~ Cinco de Mayo ~ Holiday Parties ~**
**~ Office Meetings ~ Box Lunches ~ Grand Openings ~ Weddings ~**

## ¡ GUARANTEED TO KNOCK YOUR SOMBRERO OFF!

**Baja Grill** redefines "Mexican Food." We put the **"Love"** back into it with our new approach to traditional Mexican Food. We start with only the **freshest ingredients,** prepared in a **wholesome** and **flavorful** way. **Extra touches** going above and beyond carries through with our team's **awesome attitude, personal attention** and **flexibility.** In the rare case that we don't meet or exceed your expectations, just let us know and we'll make it right for you!

## ¡ BAJA BEACH PARTY!

| | | | |
| --- | --- | --- | --- |
| Citrus Grilled Chicken | Grilled Ahi Tuna | Grilled Veggies | Grilled Carne Asada |
| Casita Style Potato Salad | Southwest Slaw | Baja Shrimp Cocktail | BBQ Black Beans |
| Cilantro Lime Pesto Rice | Kids Quesadillas | Nachos para Ninos | Fire Roasted Salsa |

## Location

~ The all new Downtown **Baja Terrace**… Casual and elegant fiestas up to 225
~ Your place… "The Sky's the limit!"

## RENT OUR MARGARITA MACHINE ¡HAVE CANTINA WILL TRAVEL!

~ We have ALL the Best Mexican Beers and Keg packages.
~ Servers- From setup, to serving, to clean up.
~ Rental coordination at no additional charge: Tents, tables, chairs, china, linens and much more.

## Cost

We provide you with quality and value… Doing as much or even as little as you require. Drop off catering, full service or come down and pick it up. Basic Catering Menu charges are based on per person and per item selection, plus 18% service charge for basic catering.

## Our Mission

We strive to be the best **CATERER** and **FIESTA MAKER** possible. No matter what! Be it a party of five or 5,000. We treat our clients and their guests like old friends. Serving the best quality of food and outstanding beverages. Our staff shows the utmost attention to detail in making ALL of our fiestas a success. We make ordering for corporate and private catering accurate, simple and user friendly! We'll bring you the finest and freshest ingredients crafted with striking presentation, served with precision and care. We love what we do… We think you will too!

**BEST OF CITYSEARCH 2004**
**VOTED BEST MEXICAN FOOD IN PORTLAND**

2118 NW Glisan Street
Portland, OR 97210
Call Carla at 503-750-5467
www.bezinfulcatering.com

---

Be Zinful Catering delivers a menu rich in flavor, design and creativity, spiked with a healthy dose of local ingredients. Our catering staff is trained to serve events of all sizes — from small to large, from casual to sophisticated, we can make any event successful. Whether hosting a buffet breakfast, planning an afternoon reception or serving a sit-down dinner, Be Zinful will creatively present your food, deliver and set-up in a timely manner and graciously assist you with any special requests.

**Menu:** Our catering staff is flexible with menu development and will work within your budget. Executive Chef, Kevin Kennedy is skilled at developing a menu to fit your needs, whether it is themed, traditional, or contemporary selections. We also have several menus to help in making your selection and you can find these by visiting our website at bezinfulcatering.com, visiting our deli on NW 21st & Glisan or calling us.

**Event Types:** Corporate parties, workshops, seminars, lectures, board meetings, fundraisers, and receptions, executive box lunches, cocktail parties, in-house dinner parties, holiday parties, wine dinners, themed events and more.

**Cost:** Menu is priced on per-guest count and can vary depending on menu selection, but the price per guest includes **the following amenities free of charge:**
- China
- Flatware
- Linen

**Additional Services:** We offer full liquor, beer, wine and champagne selections as well as non-alcoholic beverages. We are fully licensed by OLCC and carry liability insurance.

Our catering staff is skilled in developing a memorable event and can assist with any and all steps involved in planning your event. Some of our additional services include:
- Designing, printing and mailing invitations
- Party favors
- Theme development

**Event Facilities:** Be Zinful is happy to cater at the location of your choice. We also have exclusive catering availability at Montgomery Park in northwest Portland, and The Museum of the Oregon Territory in Oregon City.

**Executive Chef:** The menu is the creation of northwest acclaimed Chef, Kevin Kennedy. Chef Kennedy possesses over 20 years of culinary experience. He boasts a resume that includes an Executive Chef title at Salishan Lodge, The Pavilion Grill, Captain Whidbey Inn, Sun Mountain Lodge and La Casa Del Zoro. He is heavily involved in the Portland community and has organized such local charitable events as the 2002 Iron Chef Competition, the Oregon Pinot Noir Camp and the annual International Pinot Noir Celebration.

# Café Allegro

## Allegro Catering

*12386 S.W. Main Street*
*Tigard, Oregon 97223*
*503.684.0130 • www.allegro.net*

---

**Capacity:** Off-premise: unlimited; Back Room 55; Back Room W/Patio 75; Whole Restaurant 120

**Pricing:** Per person pricing within your budget; Room charge is in most cases free with food/drink order minimum

**Catering:**
- Extensive Italian menu: meats, pasta, salads, etc.
- Extensive fresh menus—made custom to your needs and budget
- Family style, full service and buffet

**Events:** Rehearsal dinners, receptions, company parties, team and group events

**Terms:** Flexible with short notice, deposit before event; cash, check, credit cards

**Services:** Full service, bar service, paper or china, glass stemware, party planning, etc.

**Sample Menu Ideas:**
- Jumbo Prawns wrapped with pepper bacon
- Mini Calzone: "Finger Food Style" Italian, chicken, shrimp or veggie
- Smoked Salmon stuffed Mushrooms
- Antipasto: Italian style meats, cheeses, olives
- Salads: Caesar, pasta, fruit, Greek, etc.
- Ginger-spiced porkloin skewers
- Hot pasta dishes (ask for details)
- Chicken Roll-up ala-gorgonzola proscuito
- Grilled, fillet, salmon, prawns, scallops, etc.
- Many, many other items made to order

Cafe Allegro is housed in a turn-of-the-century 1900 building in historic Old Town Tigard. The atmosphere is quaint and cozy with lots of personality!

*Allegro Catering:* great food, great service, easy to work with.
Please call the Chef or Doug at **503.684.0130**
**allegro.net**

*12003 N.E. Ainsworth Circle, Suite A*
*Portland, Oregon 97220*
*Contact: Christian or Annette Joly*
*(503) 252-1718; Fax (503) 252-0178*
*Business Hours: Mon–Fri 7am–7pm*
***Web site: www.caperscafe.com***

## If You're Entertaining Very Important People… We Deliver

When you want to electrify a crowd, nothing causes quite the stir like food prepared by Capers Cafe and Catering Company. Bold, imaginative food… presented with both precision and panache. You've probably got some great ideas. So do we. And together we will plan an event that's destined to be remembered and implemented precisely as planned. All foods are prepared from fresh Northwest products with emphasis on taste and appearance.

## Banquet and Reception Site

Capers is able to accommodate private rehearsal dinners and receptions.

## Cost

Cost is based on the food selection and type of event. All costs are itemized and on a per person basis. A 50% deposit is required upon confirmation of event. Cancellations may be made 10 days prior to the event.

## Experience

With 25 years experience in the industry, Christian Joly has prepared international events for 2,000, as well as intimate dinners for two.

## Services

Capers Cafe and Catering Company is a fully licensed and insured caterer, capable of providing any style of food and beverage that a customer may require. Seven days a week.

## Food Preparation and Equipment

Capers Cafe and Catering Company prepares all foods with flair, putting heavy emphasis on taste and visual appearance.

## Serving Attendants

To ensure a successful event, we provide all the necessary professionals to prepare, serve, and clean up. Gratuities are optional.

## OUR FOODS AND SERVICES ARE 100% GUARANTEED

Capers Cafe and Catering Company is an extremely successful business because of its employees. Our staff believes in satisfying all the needs of our customers. We never take shortcuts and guarantee our foods and services 100%, or we return your money. ***We are at your service.***

*"We have an ongoing commitment to provide our clients with unsurpassed food quality, service & presentation"*
*– Sandy Robinson, Owner*

**SPECIAL EVENT & FULL SERVICE CATERING COMPANY**

503 238-8889 • Fax 503 238-8893
Kitchen Address: 611 SE Grant Street, Portland, Oregon 97214
Mailing Address: P O Box 42264, Portland, Oregon 97242
Web site: www.caibpdx.com • E-mail: dorothy@caibpdx.com

---

## *What We Do…*

Elaborate & Unique Special Events, Corporate Meetings & Conferences, In-Home Parties, Gourmet Box Lunches, Christmas & Holiday Parties, Weddings & BBQs from 10 to 2,000 guests! Our team of Event Planners, Chefs, Professional Service Staff & Bartenders will create a memorable event your guests will be sure to enjoy!

## *Menus We Design & Foods We Serve…*

Catering At Its Best is proud to offer a wide range of traditional, ethnic and unique themed menus. From Grand Buffets, Sit Down Galas & Tray Passed Hors D'Oeuvres parties. Our chefs use only the freshest and highest quality ingredients, offering delicious and artistic culinary creations! Vegetarian and special dietary menus are available upon request. Choose from one of our enticing menus or let us design a custom menu to compliment your special event! Our specialties include Applewood Smoked Salmon, Pan Asian, Mediterranean & American ("comfort food") cuisine, as well as an in-house pastry department.

## *Services We Provide…*

Catering At Its Best can provide you with all of the necessary "extras" that will make your next event a memorable affair. Our Catering Consultants will work with you every step of the way to ensure that your event is a complete success. Our basic services include delivery, set up, service and clean up of your event.

*Other services (additional fees may apply) include:*

- Customized Event Planning, Site Selection & On Site Event Manager
- Complete Event Coordination: Theme Design Services, Rentals, Props, Floral, Valet Parking & Entertainment
- Experienced, Professional Servers and OLCC Licensed Bartenders

## *Venues…*

Whether it's your office, home, park or ballroom, we are adaptable to any location. We are an approved or exclusive caterer at these locations in and around the Portland area:
The Portland Center For The Performing Arts, Montgomery Park, Pittock Mansion, Oregon Sports Hall of Fame, Portland Classical Chinese Garden, Urban Wineworks, Historic Portland City Hall, Forestry Discovery Center, Elk Cove Vineyards, Norse Hall, The Sternwheeler Rose, Paradigm Conference Center, The Jenkins Estate, Kingstad Center for Meetings & Events, Oregon Historical Society and more!

***Voted BEST FOOD @ 2004 BRAVO! TRADE SHOW!***

*736 S.E. Powell • Portland, Oregon 97202*
*(503) 222-4553; (503) 493-1960 Fax*
*E-mail: CDJCatering@aol.com*

---

## NO THEME TOO EXOTIC; NO CUISINE TOO ESOTERIC

Chef du Jour has been a full-service caterer for Portland-Metro and surrounding areas for the past 13 years. Each event we do can be tailored to our clients' whims.

We utilize the freshest product of the season—including growing our own herbs and edible flowers and specialty vegetables for selected use. Wild game, seasonal mushrooms, nuts and fruits are standard ingredients. In recent events, we have provided pheasant and salmon, exotic fish including whole Mahi Mahi flown in from Hawaii, kosher meats, spit roasted pig, rotisserie lamb, sushi and (fire code permitting) flaming desserts.

We have produced wedding receptions in wineries, on yachts, in outdoor venues, under tents, in conservatories and in warehouses. We have provided plated and buffet dinners for large and small groups alike, both corporate and social.

Many unique client challenges have been solved by our skill, knowledge and creativity. For every event we plan a multitude of details for the client including:

- Full Beverage Service
- Rental equipment
- Serviceware
- Floral
- Food design
- Mobile cooking equipment
- Tenting
- Floor plans
- Lighting
- Special theme props
- Music
- Mobile refrigeration
- Backdrops

Chef du Jour is a fully licensed, full-service caterer. We can provide alcohol, linens, glassware, centerpieces or anything else you need for your event. We have a professionally trained staff, attractive and healthy food and innovative food styling. We also offer decorating and florist services, pickup and delivery.

## CATERING WITH A DIFFERENCE!

# Classic Fare Catering
## With you in mind!

Contact us @ 503-375-7026; fax 503-315-2948
Bethany @ bigelow-bethany@aramark.com
Crystal @ hoover-crystal@aramark.com

---

We specialize in quality and service. Let us delight you with our professionalism, our focus on food safety and our endless creativity! Email or call for a catering brochure, look over our menu…if you need something and don't see it here, just ask. Custom orders are no problem.

### Featuring
Now available to you for any of your events or parties is our Chocolate Fountain! Enjoy a variety of tasty treats dipped by you into the flowing fountain of chocolate.

### Events
Weddings, receptions, holiday parties, themed events, meetings, box lunches and all other parties and events even last minute ones!

### Specialties
We invite you to be our guest as we indulge your taste buds with a scrumptious breakfast, bountiful luncheon or splendid dinner party! From dropping off coffee and muffins to providing tuxedoed wait staff, hand-passed hors d' oeuvres to hundreds of enchanted guests, we have solutions for your catering needs. It is our goal to customize our products and services to match your individual requirements and provide you and your guests with a truly memorable experience!

### Catering Services
Catering services may include but is not limited to: china, silverware, stemware, linens, staffing, setup, cleanup, paper products, balloons, décor…

### Cost and Terms
Cost is based on menu selection along with the number of guests attending your event. A 50% deposit is due with your signed Order Confirmation Form. We request a final count no less than three business days prior to your event. The balance is due upon receipt of invoice.

**Proud Members of the Oregon Food Alliance**

*9037 S.W. Burnham Street • Tigard, Oregon 97223*
*Contact: Steve DeAngelo (503) 620-9020*
*Available for catering seven days a week*
*Visit our Web site: www.cateringbydeangelos.com*
*Fax (503) 620-3964*

## Types of Menus and Specialty

DeAngelo's offers all types of menus from self-serve buffets to full-service formal sit-down affairs. We are well-known for our Gourmet Pizza Feeds, Pasta Bars and Western Barbecues. All foods are scratch prepared. Low-fat and vegetarian menus are happily accommodated. A wide range of ethnic menus are available, such as Asian, Italian, Mexican, African, and Caribbean. Give DeAngelo's Catering a call when planning your next fund raiser, social or corporate event, or if you're in need of concession services, product sampling or beverage management.

## Cost and Experience

Price is based on a per-person basis for full-service events; however, many other options are available. DeAngelo's Catering prides itself on quality food at an affordable price. Delivery service available. Food tasting and references provided upon request.

## Services

DeAngelo's is licensed and insured to serve alcoholic beverages. Complete event coordination and site-analysis service available. To complete your event theme, props are available for rent, with all full-service buffets are decorated at no charge. Entertainment packages and interactive games can be arranged.

## Presentation and Service Staff

All foods are exquisitely presented using copper chafing dishes along with granite and marble tiles and slabs. Service staff is available for all types of events from formal sit-down dinners to concessions. Attire is always appropriate.

## FLEXIBILITY TO MEET YOUR NEEDS

DeAngelo's is always willing to work with clients to find a menu that fits within their budget and menu guidelines. We offer flexibility to adapt to special needs and requests. With our wide range of menus and services, we can accommodate your requests.

**Decorations provided FREE**
**with all full-service buffets!**

**Voted Best Caterer at the 1999 Bravo! Meeting & Event Planners' Trade Show!**

***A founding member of the Association of Catering & Event Professionals.***

---

Let's admit it – most caterers make great food. That is why we do it! What makes DIVINE CATERING different is a professional, personable staff and attention to detail that will ensure that your breakfast meeting, training lunch, open house or holiday party is not only a success, but sets the standard!

We enjoy working with our clients time after time! We consider it our top priority to exceed your expectations with our flawless execution, excellent service and food that will leave your staff and clients talking about it even after they go home. DIVINE CATERING has delighted clients at events ranging from softball games to multi-course plated dinners and everything in between, with our distinctive Northwest cuisine.

## Count On Us:

- To share our experience in event planning
- To design unique menus to fit your taste and budget
- To supply linens and accessories or coordinate rentals based on your ideas & needs
- To recommend wines, hors d' oeuvres, entrees and delectable desserts (just to name a few)
- To worry for you (who wants to worry about details during an event – that's our job!)

We don't like surprises, unless it's a party, and you probably don't either, so you can expect us to be up front about our pricing and capabilities. We arrive early and stay until the last crumb is cleaned up! Our clients rely on us to deliver a complete catering experience. They enjoy working with us and appreciate our great lines of communication. We look forward to you feeling the same.

***Our job is to make you look good.***
***(Delicious food is just a fringe benefit.)***

**DIVINE CATERING**
**503-280-1191**

We enjoy sharing our customer's feedback, so please ask us for references.

# EAT YOUR HEART OUT CATERING

*Monica Grinnell, Proprietor since 1975*
*1230 S.E. Seventh*
*Portland, Oregon 97214*
*Kitchen/Voice Mail: (503) 232-4408*
*Fax (503) 232-0778*
*E-mail: party@eatyourheartout.biz*
*www.eatyourheartout.biz*

---

Eat Your Heart Out Catering, established in 1975, has had the pleasure to be hired by some of the finest corporations and private clients in the Northwest. Our experience includes almost 30 years of planning catering events; running the former Eat Your Heart Out Restaurant; designing and packaging a line of herbed vinegars; cooking with such noted chefs as Julia Child, Marcella Hazan, Craig Claiborne, Annie Somerville, and Pierre Franey; teaching cooking classes; and appearing on local television and at local events demonstrating and teaching cooking techniques. We would be glad to furnish a client list or letters of recommendation, and we are happy to show you our beautiful portfolio.

## Types of Menus and Specialties

Maybe you want to be involved in the menu, or just sit back and be dazzled by choices ranging from Tuscan Tenderloin of Beef with Oregon Pinot Noir Sauce and Grilled New Zealand Baby Lamb Chops, to Caviar Éclairs with Lemon Crème Fraiche and Gougere Dungeness Crab Puffs with dried Bing Cherries. At the heart of it, Monica Grinnell, the owner, was trained as an interior designer, so food design and presentation are as important as the delicious flavors we create. Most recently, Chloe Crinnell has joined her mother in running the kitchen after gaining culinary experience at Portland area restaurants, San Francisco's famous Greene Restaurant, and the Bay Area's premiere catering company, Paula Le Duc. Most importantly, we specialize in you because we know that you want to remember your event as a wonderful and impressive experience.

## Food Presentation, Equipment and Staff

Eat Your Heart Out Catering is a full service and licensed caterer, both for food and alcohol service. We provide dishes, linens, disposable products if you need them, all serving pieces both traditional and unusual, flowers, ice sculptures, and even props for special themes. Our staff includes trained chefs, charming bartenders, and efficient servers. We hope you will show off your good taste with our good taste!

**www.eatyourheartout.biz**

# JAKE'S CATERING
AT THE
# GOVERNOR
HOTEL

*611 S.W. 10th Avenue*
*Portland, Oregon 97205*
*(503) 241-2125; Fax (503) 220-1849*
*Web site: www.JakesCatering.com*

## Type of Menus and Specialty

Jake's Catering at The Governor Hotel is part of the McCormick & Schmick Restaurant Group and "Jake's Famous Crawfish." Jake's is one of the most respected dining institutions in the Portland area, and Jake's Catering at The Governor Hotel upholds this prestigious reputation.

Known for offering extensive Pacific Northwest menu selections, including fresh seafood, pasta, poultry and prime cut steaks, Jake's Catering at The Governor Hotel has the flexibility and talent to cater to your needs.

From stand-up cocktail/appetizer receptions to fabulous buffet presentations, to complete sit-down dinners for groups and gatherings of all sizes, Jake's Catering at The Governor Hotel is always poised and ready to serve.

Enjoy delicious hors d'oeuvres and entrees, delectable desserts and specialty theme menus (upon request), all prepared by our talented chefs and served by our friendly and professional staff.

Customers are encouraged to review our catering menus and to tour the elegant banquet facilities at The Governor Hotel to fully appreciate the total scope of menu options, facilities, and full-service capabilities.

## Cost

We base our cost on a per-person count and the type of menu developed. We require a 50% deposit to confirm your event and payment in full 72 hours prior to event for estimated charges. We ask for a guaranteed number of guests three business days prior to the event.

## Services

Jake's Catering at The Governor Hotel is the exclusive caterer at The Governor Hotel, which features twelve exquisite banquet rooms with an Italian Renaissance decor and the capability to host groups from as small as 10 people up to 450 (seated) and 600 (stand-up reception).

Jake's Catering at The Governor Hotel also provides off-premise catering services.

### A REPUTATION FOR QUALITY AND A RESPECT FOR TRADITION

You are guaranteed the finest quality of food and presentation, a friendly and professional staff, and a personalized customer service. Trust your important event to one of Portland's long-time favorites to ensure a truly memorable and successful experience.

**See page 112 under Banquet, Meeting & Event Sites.**

## Types of Menus and Specialty

Premieré Catering offers fine dining in any location, customized to fit your style of entertaining, culinary tastes, and budget. We offer location catering at its finest…on a mountain top, at the beach, or in the boardroom…the possibilities are endless. Let Premieré Catering make your next event a true culinary success. We specialize in on-site cooking (ask for details). Nothing compares to freshly prepared foods at your event. Your guests will notice the fresh flavors and quality of your menu.

## Services

Premieré Catering is a full-service caterer, providing everything needed for a successful event.

- Event planning and site selection
- Licensed to serve alcoholic beverages
- Rental coordination (china, glassware, silverware, tables, chairs, tents)
- Props and decorations
- Entertainment (bands, disc jockeys, musicians)

## Cost and Experience

Price is based on the type of services required and menu selection. Please call for price quotations for next event. Regardless of the type of event or service required, you can count on the reputation Premieré Catering has earned, with over 20 years experience in the event business.

Premieré Catering has been awarded some of Portland's largest and most important corporate events. From Intel's 25th anniversary party with over 10,000 guests, to private corporate chalets and Indy Kart Races for the Rose Festival; from Tektronix's 50th anniversary party, to the Hillsboro Air Show. With this experience, we are able to accommodate both large and small events. We will show you how well experience pays off.

## Serving Attendants

Premieré Catering provides all the service staff required to make your event successful. From setup to cleanup, you will find our staff efficient, friendly, and professional. Attendants are dressed in traditional black-and-white attire unless otherwise specified.

**CALL TODAY FOR MORE INFORMATION**
**(503) 235-0274**

*Elegance in Catering*

*TIFFANY CENTER*
*1410 S.W. Morrison, Suite 600 • Portland, Oregon 97205-1930*
*(503) 248-9305; Fax (503) 243-7147*
*E-mail: rafatis@coho.net • Web site: rafatis.citysearch.com*

## Types of Menus and Specialty

Rafati's full-service catering staff can assist you with the selection of the perfect menu for your function. From corporate picnics in the park, formal dinner service, the needs of the corporate board, that special holiday celebration or new product introduction to the most unique or casual of corporate meetings and/or receptions, box and buffet luncheons—we've done it all. Our portfolios are filled with pictures of our work—Northwest and other American Regional cuisines to Continental and Ethnic, mirror displays, theme buffet presentations, formal dinner services and elegant hors d'oeuvres passed on silver trays.

## Cost

The cost is determined by the menu selection, level of desired service and number of guests.

## Experience

Operating under the Rafati's name since 1983, our actual catering and food service experience spans more than 25 years. Experience has made flexibility our hallmark.

## Food Preparation and Equipment

Rafati's specializes in delicious, freshly prepared foods set in an elegant, lavish and stylish display. From silver, copper, crystal and mirrors to baskets, china, fresh flowers and theme props—we provide all service equipment needs.

## Special Services

**Service attendants:** trained, professionally uniformed service staff to set up, serve and clean up; OLCC licensed, professionally uniformed and equipped bartenders

**Beverages:** we offer full liquor, extensive wine and champagne selections, bottled and keg beer (domestic, micro and imported) and a full selection of chilled nonalcoholic beverages; OLCC licensed with liquor liability insurance

**Dishes and glassware:** china, glassware standard, disposables on request

**Napkins and linens:** linen cloths, napkins and table skirting in range of colors; paper products in selection of colors

**Other:** fresh flowers; table, hall and theme decorations; ice carvings—full event services.

## WHEN GOOD TASTE AND EXPERIENCE COUNT ...COUNT ON RAFATI'S

Rafati's is the exclusive caterer for the Tiffany Center—a centrally located, historic building featuring event floors and conference space of traditional charm and elegance with gilded mirrors, polished woods and emerald accents. From our fully licensed commercial kitchen we also provide elegant catering services to many other facilities, corporate sites and other venues in the Portland Metro area. Our attention to detail, safe food-handling practices, award-winning chefs, trained professional servers, bartenders and experienced event planners are all dedicated to ensuring your complete satisfaction—guaranteed.

## ROSE QUARTER CATERING

**503-797-9947**
**rosequartercatering@rosequarter.com**

---

## Let Us Cater Your Event!

As the exclusive caterer to the Rose Garden and the Memorial Coliseum, Rose Quarter Catering is committed to providing you with the highest quality food and a professional staff for your dining experience. Whether the size of your group is 10 people or 10,000, we have the experience and the facilities to meet all your catering and party needs.

- Free Room Rent*
- Free Parking in Rose Quarter Garages*
- Easy access to Tri-Met system
- Inclusive Pricing
- No additional linen charges
- No additional taxes
- No added labor or service charges
- The Rose Room is our premier dining room with seating for 325.

The Rose Room, which overlooks the Rose Quarter Commons and the Memorial Coliseum, is the ideal setting for breakfast meetings, lunch meetings, anniversary parties and wedding receptions.

For smaller groups we have several rooms in both the Rose Garden and the Memorial Coliseum. In the Rose Garden, the Private Dining Room and the Suite Conference Room can accommodate your small group of 36 or fewer people. Meeting Rooms in the Memorial Coliseum can accommodate 10 – 10,000 people.

The Exhibit Hall can accommodate very large groups in any number of configurations. Hold your Winter Carnival or Summer Picnic in the Exhibit Hall and you can put the entire event in a single room.

***Contact Rose Quarter Catering Representatives for specific information**
**503-797-9947**
**email rosequartercatering@rosequarter.com**

**The Taste:** Discover a world of difference with Salvador Molly's! Whether it's a corporate meeting, wedding, company picnic or private party, our innovative chefs explore cuisines from around the world for new ideas and tastes and combine these with the finest and freshest Northwest ingredients.

**The Look:** Décor, flowers, site selection, entertainment and all of the many details combine to create a look for your event that is uniquely yours. Our experienced, creative event staff will help every step of the way.

**The Feel:** Great food, stunning décor, the perfect location and exciting entertainment create a magical event that your guests will remember forever. Let us help create that for you.

## Pacific Northwest Buffet

- Horseradish Asiago Encrusted Salmon with hazelnut mustard sauce ( add $2 per person)
- Pan Seared Pork Loin with peppered pear relish
  *or*
- Apple Wood Smoked Chicken Breast with amber hops, rhubarb and dried cherry chutney
- Honeyed Vegetable Wild and White Rice
- Artichoke, Mushroom and Baby Lima Saute
- Grilled Romaine Salad with Oregonzola blue cheese, hazelnuts and prosciutto maple vinaigrette
- Rustic Baked Breads with sweet cream butter
- Hood River Oatmeal Apple Crisp

*$17.50 per person*

## Gala Events Plated Menu

- Poached Pears, Maytag Blue Cheese, Filberts and Currants tossed with Field Greens and a light sherry vinaigrette
- Swordfish en Papillotte with Sambuca Butter
- Roasted Fennel and Asparagus
- Wasabi Mashed Potatoes
- Grilled Triple Ginger Pound Cake with Minted Ginger Mango

*Market price*

**Corporate Clients** include: Mentor Graphics, AT&T Wireless, Nike, Gartner, Tazo, Adidas, Davis Wright Tremaine, DeLoitte and Touche, Intel and many others.

**Locations:** We are on the exclusive caterers list at Portland Art Museum, Oregon Historical Society, Montgomery Park, Rex Hill Vineyard, Museum of the Oregon Territories, the Treasury, Lake House at Blue Lake park, Pittock Mansion, Molly's Loft on Belmont, Jenkins Estate, Bridgeport Brewpub and other fine facilities.

**Cost:** We will work within any budget parameters. Price based on a per person or per piece count, food selection, and service requirements.

120 NW 23rd Avenue
Portland OR 97210
503-226-8980
info@uptowncatering.com
*www.uptowncatering.com*

---

Uptown has been exceeding the expectations of Portland's most discriminating clientele for almost a decade. Our knack for making the party a pleasure for you, the host, as well as your guests is what makes us special. Food is the easy part: throw a couple of great chefs into a kitchen, add a dab of creativity, a little genius and let them practice 365 days a year…they'll turn out great food.

## Our Promise

We aspire to throw the best tasting, most fun, well-serviced parties in town. Rest assured that Uptown Catering will use the same care and attention we afforded The White House, The Governor, both Senators and every Fortune 500 company in Oregon. Our promise to you…

- Attentive, experienced event professionals to assist you with ALL of your event needs
- A custom designed menu and event based upon your individual party needs
- Affordability- Because we own our own equipment, we are more effective and can afford to charge significantly less than most caterers
- Unparalleled quality of food, service and staff (oh, and we like to have fun too)

Because we are better, because we are cheaper and because we've spent nearly a decade "walking in your shoes," let Uptown Catering's chefs dazzle your guests with great food while the rest of our team goes to work taking the pressures off of you. After all, it's your party!

*5222 NE Sacramento • Portland, Oregon 97213*
*503-437-1786*
*www.wildplumcatering.com*

---

The professional, experienced staff of Wild Plum Catering loves food and thoroughly enjoys creating spectacular menus and events.

## Count on Wild Plum Catering to:

- provide detailed attention to every aspect of your event—planning to clean up
- personally plan a menu that suits your exact tastes and budget
- prepare your meal as tastefully and beautifully as if it were to be served at our own table
- follow the highest professional standards—from safety and sanitation, to recycling and using sustainable materials

## When only the best of the Northwest will do

Our menus are designed with creativity and appreciation for the finest ingredients we can find and feature the very best of the Northwest's variety from the sea, farms and vineyards.

## Experience, service and attention to detail

From corporate breakfasts to black-tie receptions, Wild Plum Catering puts more than thirty years of experience in catering and restaurants toward every detail of your event. We have the pleasure of working with some of Portland's finest coordinators, venues and organizations and we are fully licensed and insured.

**Large or small, formal or casual, for the chairman of the board or friends at home, Wild Plum Catering delights in exceeding your expectations of food, service, quality and price.**

**Wild Plum Catering 503-437-1786**

# *Yours Truly* CATERERS

*1628 S.W. Jefferson*
*Portland, Oregon 97201*
*Contact: Barbara La Valla*
*503-226-6266, Fax 503-226-7616*
*www.yourstrulycaterers.com*

---

## A PORTLAND TRADITION WITH A STANDARD OF EXCELLENCE

As Portland's oldest catering company, Yours Truly Caterers provide you with everything you need for Breakfast Meetings to Corporate Parties. From simple meals to elegant banquets, you can rely on us to give you the best in food and service. We will work with you to design a menu and service plan that suits your needs and budget. We pride ourselves on our commitment to our clients. From first contact to the day after your party, we pledge to make your event special.

Yours Truly is a family owned and operated business. Barbara La Valla (former hostess on Channel 6's KOIN Kitchen) and son, Scott La Valla (graduate of Portland's own Western Culinary Institute) utilize their outstanding culinary and catering skills to help prospective clients plan the "perfect" event.

Yours Truly prides itself on providing the most fully trained, efficient, and professional staff who handle everything from setting up your event to service and clean up. We are licensed and insured to serve wine, beer as well a full bar.

We use our own china, silverware and dishes, which are included free with our service. With the purchase of Dale's Catering, Yours Truly now offers a wider selection of choices for all of your catering needs.

Our onsite café, Sal's Bistro & Espresso, specializes in sandwiches, homemade soups and quiche.

Sal's is open Monday through Friday from 7am–4pm. Sal's is also proud to offer truffles from Theobroma.

**Call Yours Truly Caterers today!**
When your special event arrives you'll be able to relax and…
Feel like a guest at your own party!

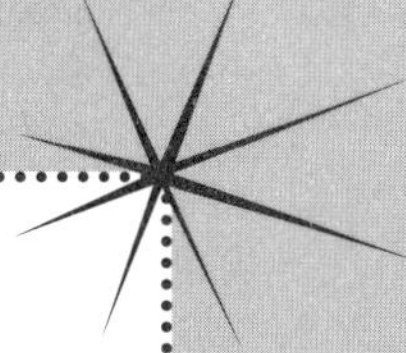

# Child Care

BravoPortland.com

**Professional childcare provided for your event**
**Wedding ceremonies, Corporate events, Conferences, Meetings, Seminars, Holiday parties, Concerts, and Individual hotel guests**
*Contact: Michelle Davenport*
*Office: 503.518.CCSI (2274);*
*Fax: 503.518.0880*
*E-mail: michelle@munchkincare.com*
*Web site: www.munchkincare.com*

---

**You've reserved the hall, the speakers, and the band...**
**Now, what are you going to do with the children?**

At **Creative Childcare Solutions**, we believe children should be allowed to be children—not act like "little adults." That's why we offer on-site childcare for your special event or your out-of-town hotel guests. We go wherever you are.

We would love to assume that all children will behave appropriately when need be, but we know that is not always realistic. Parents enjoying themselves at a special occasion can get distracted from watching their children and problems can arise. That's where we come in! We provide care for individual families or a group of children so everyone can enjoy themselves. You provide the space and we will do the rest.

**Prior to your event**, we can provide online preregistration or an inquiry form to see what specific childcare needs your company will have. Preregistration allows our company to communicate directly with your clients to answer their questions, reserve a space for their child, accept payments, and put the parents' minds at ease.

**During the event**, we will keep the children entertained with arts & crafts, toys, games, and music. We can decorate the room in our theme or we can implement your theme into our activities or just provide crafts and entertainment under a big tent while parents visit.

**Creative Childcare Solutions** will customize each special event to meet your unique needs. We provide safe, fun care for children of all ages and group sizes: from one child in a hotel room to several hundred children at a corporate picnic. We send you only qualified caregivers who bring with them many years of childcare expertise, CPR and First Aid Certification, and an element of fun and professionalism. No teenage sitters!

For your next event, let the kids be kids and let the adults relax in the knowledge that their children are nearby in a safe, exciting, loving environment with **Creative Childcare Solutions, Inc**. We carry **commercial liability insurance** for your peace of mind.

COST—Custom designed to meet your specific needs. Call today to receive a more specific quote based on your unique needs. Visa, MasterCard, AmExpress accepted.

TERMS—One contact person required for planning. Retainer required for bookings.

# Convention & Exhibition Facilities

BravoPortland.com

Convention & Exhibition Facilities

# QUESTIONS TO ASK YOUR FACILITY

Coordinating a trade show is a large task. Your facility coordinator will be your partner for several months. Make sure that you have good communication with your facility and coordinator. It is important for you to find out in the beginning whether the facility can meet your needs. Here is a list of the information that you should get from the facility in advance of booking your trade show:

- Complete floor plan (entrances, loading dock, improvements, etc.)
- Exhibition floor space (total square footage)
- Heights of ceilings (lighting)
- Does the facility meet ADA (Americans with Disabilities Act) requirements?
- Are meeting and banquet rooms available? How far from exhibit space?
- Are there accessible loading and unloading areas?
- Limitations that exhibitors need to be aware of (weight, loading area dimensions, etc.)
- Are there freight elevators and ramps (how many floors to exhibit space, size of elevator, weight limitations)?
- Are there elevators, stairs, and escalators (location, and how many)?
- Are there storage facilities available (if so, cost)?
- What are the insurance requirements?
- Cost of facility (deposit, and terms of payment)
- What services are available? Who is recommended? What are union requirements? (labor rates of electricians, carpenters, decorators, security etc.)
- Additional expenses (telephones, parking, fax machine, press room, utilities, computers, typewriters, show management, desk/office, storage, etc.)
- What are regulations concerning: licenses, liability, fire, building codes, alcohol, cleanup, etc.
- Exhibitors information: shipping address, check-in and checkout procedures, earliest setup time, latest takedown time, inspection dates and times, etc.)
- Types of admission: open/free of charge, badge, charge, etc.
- Key contact for security, theft reporting, off-hour contact

**Exhibit Professionals:** This is a fast growing industry. There are many professional companies that can help you accomplish your tasks. Exposition service contractors can provide all the services listed here, or you can develop your own team of experts. Exhibit services include: Furniture, floor coverings, accessories, pipe and drape, utilities, floor plans, signage, audio visual equipment, staffing, flower/ plant rentals, cleaning service, security services, exhibit design and construction, lighting, sound, communications, photographic services, business service centers, postal packing services and consulting (you will find most of these services in this guide).

# DESCHUTES COUNTY FAIR & EXPO CENTER

*3800 S.W. Airport Way • Redmond, Oregon 97756*
*Contact: Roxia Thornton Todoroff, Director of Sales (866) 800-EXPO, (541) 548-2711*
*Fax (541)923-1652; Office hours: Mon–Fri 8am-5pm*
*E-mail: roxiat@deschutes.org; Web site: www.expo.deschutes.org*

---

**Capacity:** Northwest Premiere Convention & Exhibition Facility: Event Center, 40,000 sq. ft. arena floor, 28,250 sq. ft. concourse, concert seating up to 7,500, arena seating up to 4,000, 274 trade show booth space. Three Sister Conference Center & High Desert Activity Center: meeting rooms total 46,420 sq. ft. divisible into fourteen individual rooms, ceiling height is 14'. Three main halls can accommodate 1,200 – 1,600 theatre style.
**Price range:** Please call for current rates.
**Catering:** Exclusive on-site catering is provided by C&D Event Management, ensuring exceptional quality and a dedication to excellence.
**Types of Events:** conventions, trade shows, meetings, banquets, weddings, receptions, performances, concerts and sporting events

## Availability and Terms

Please call for available dates. A 20% deposit is required to contract space with full prepayment 60 days prior to event date. Guarantees seven days prior to event with final guarantee 72 hours in advance.

## Description of Facility and Services

**Seating:** tables and chairs available
**Servers:** provided by C&D Event Management
**Bar facilities:** provided by C & D Event Management
**Linens and napkins:** provided by C&D Event Management
**China and glassware:** provided by C&D Event Management
**Cleanup:** provided by staff
**Trade Show Services:** A perimeter road gives easy access to the back of each building with 14' roll-up doors for easy load-in/load out. All buildings are climate controlled with built-in sound systems; conference center features power, telephone and data port connections in floor on 20 ft. squares.
**Banquet & Conference Services:** equipment, classroom, banquet tables and chairs, staging, podium, house sound and microphones available
**Lodging:** assistance with lodging through CVB and Visitor's Association
**Parking:** parking for over 4,000 with direct access to Conference & Event Center; additional 100 acres of parking for Expo Center
**ADA:** fully accessible; meets all ADA requirements

We really can do it all and are eager to share what we know will exceed your expectations.

# expo

PORTLAND METROPOLITAN EXPOSITION CENTER

*2060 N. Marine Drive*
*Portland, OR 97217*
*(503) 736-5200*
*Fax (503) 736-5201*
*Web site: www.expocenter.org*
*E-mail: info@expocenter.org*

**Capacity:** Exhibit halls ranging in size from 4,400 sq. ft. to 108,000 sq. ft. of flat-floor and column-free consumer trade show space. Meeting rooms accommodating from 10 up to 300 people in varied and comfortable settings. Please see charts and facility diagram.

**Price Range:** Contact us at 503.736.5200 or via www.expocenter.org for a direct price quote.

**Catering:** Full-service catering and concessions services provided exclusively by ARAMARK / Giacometti Partners Ltd. Select from a vast array of available menu choices or create your own menu along with our Executive Chef. Contact Ed Strong, Aramark General Manager at 503.736.5230.

**Types of Events:** Consumer trade shows, catered local meetings and meals, festivals, concerts and conferences. Large or small, the Expo Center can make your event experience easy.

## Availability and Terms

Call 503.736.5200 or via www.expocenter.org for date and space availability. A Nonrefundable deposit is required with executed license agreement. Balance due 30 days prior to event.

## Description of Facility and Services

**Seating:** Various tables and chairs are available. For details, contact your Event Manager.

**Facility equipment:** Flip charts, easels, bulletin boards – see www.expocenter.org for details.

**Audio-visual equipment**: House paging and a small AV inventory are available for meeting rooms.

**Parking:** 2,200 parking spaces or 825,000 sq. ft. of space. Discount exhibitor rates offered.

| Exhibit Hall Space | Dimensions | Sq. Ft. | Ceiling Height | 10' x 10' Exhibits | Max Seating Capacities | | |
|---|---|---|---|---|---|---|---|
| | | | | | Theatre | Classroom | Banquet |
| Hall A | 400'x120' | 48,000 | 15' | 246 | 2726 | 1680 | 1860 |
| Hall B | 300'x120' | 36,000 | 15' | 226 | 2700 | 1656 | 1440 |
| Hall C | 300'x200' | 60,000 | 25' | 333 | 4736 | 3000 | 2880 |
| Hall D | 300'x240' | 72,000 | 30' | 386 | 7000 | 3208 | 4620 |
| Hall D1 | 300'x120' | 36,000 | 30' | 193 | 3500 | 1640 | 2100 |
| Hall D2 | 300'x120' | 36,000 | 30' | 193 | 3500 | 1640 | 2100 |
| Hall E | 360'x300' | 108,000 | 30' | 640 | 9000 | 5280 | 6240 |
| Hall E1 | 360'x150' | 54,000 | 30' | 319 | 4500 | 2680 | 2880 |
| Hall E2 | 360'x150' | 54,400 | 30' | 321 | 4500 | 2680 | 2880 |
| East Hall (Hall A) | 40'x110' | 4,400 | 18' | 22 | 336 | 260 | 240 |
| Connector (Halls D & E) | 30'x150' | 4,500 | 30' | 16 | 350 | 204 | 220 |

# Portland Metropolitan Expo Center – The Versatility of Space

With the newly completed Hall D, the Portland Expo Center has grown to become Oregon's largest consumer trade show facility with over 330,000 sq. ft. of multi-use exhibition space and 6,900 sq. ft. of meeting rooms. In addition to Hall D's eight new meeting rooms, spacious foyer, and the 72,000 sq. ft. of column free space, clients can revel in our new full-service kitchen while choosing from a delectable array of wonderful offerings from ARAMARK's Executive Chef, Joshua Sperl. The flexibility of our many exhibit halls provide you with limitless possibilities. Whether you're producing a large consumer trade show for thousands or a small luncheon meeting for fifty, the Expo Center can handle it – with service and style. Please call us at (503) 736-5200 or visit www.expocenter.org for more detailed information.

***Light Rail is Here!****— Ride the Interstate Max Light Rail directly to the Expo Center. Visit trimet.org for schedules and times.*

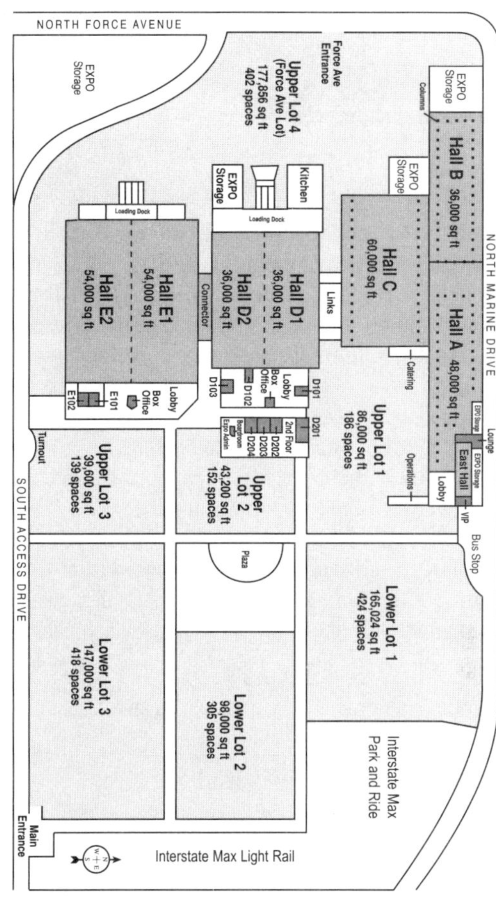


| Meeting Room Space | Dimensions | Sq. Ft. | Ceiling Height | Max Seating Capacities | | | |
|---|---|---|---|---|---|---|---|
| | | | | Theatre | Classroom | Banquet | Conference |
| Lounge (Hall A) | | 1,500 | 9' | N/A | N/A | 62 | N/A |
| Boardroom (Hall D) | 12'x17' | 204 | 9' | 25 | 12 | 12 | 12 |
| Rm D101 | 26'x19' | 494 | 14' | 60 | 24 | 20 | 28 |
| Rm D102 | 15'x22' | 330 | 14' | 33 | 21 | 20 | 21 |
| Rm D103 | 29'x29' | 841 | 14' | 98 | 48 | 50 | 40 |
| Rm D201 | 26'x50' | 1300 | 14' | 162 | 72 | 80 | 58 |
| Rm D202 | 28'x28' | 784 | 14' | 88 | 48 | 40 | 40 |
| Rm D203 | 28'x29' | 812 | 14' | 94 | 48 | 50 | 40 |
| Rm D204 | 28'x28' | 784 | 14' | 88 | 48 | 40 | 40 |
| Rms. D202-4 | 28' x 85' | 2,380 | 14' | 300 | 156 | 160 | 88 |
| Rm E101 | 21'x25' | 525 | 14' | 60 | 24 | 30 | 28 |
| Rm E102 | 24'x25' | 600 | 14' | 68 | 36 | 40 | 34 |
| Rms. E101-2 | 45' x 25' | 1,125 | 14' | 138 | 63 | 80 | 46 |

# OREGON CONVENTION CENTER & ARAMARK – GIACOMETTI PARTNERS, LTD.

*777 N.E. Martin Luther King Jr. Blvd.*
*Portland, OR 97232*
*Contact: OCC Sales 503/235-7575*
*Web site: www.oregoncc.org*

---

**Capacity:** **Individual Meeting Rooms:** Located directly across from the exhibit areas, 50 combinable meeting rooms totaling 54,000 square feet accommodate from 10 to 700 people. **Portland Ballroom:** Totaling 34,300 square feet divisible into eight separate rooms to accommodate from 250 to 3,500 people; **Oregon Ballroom:** Totaling 25,200 square feet divisible into four separate rooms to accommodate from 250 to 2,500 people. **Exhibit Halls:** Five combinable halls, 30,000 square feet to 255,000 square feet; **Skyview Terrace:** Located at the base of the towers, the Skyview Terrace can accommodate from 50 to 200 people for reception-style events.

**Types of Events:** We can accommodate a wide variety of events—from an intimate VIP meeting for 12 to a trade show for 60,000.

**Price Range:** Price is determined by event size and specific menu.

**Catering:** Full-service catering provided exclusively by ARAMARK/ Giacometti Partners Limited. In addition to the wide variety of menu suggestions, the ARAMARK catering department together with our executive chef can create a special menu to suit your needs.

## Availability and Terms

Terms and conditions vary with each event. Local events can be guaranteed for dates as far as 18 months prior to the event.

## Description of Facility and Services

**Seating:** Tables, chairs and head tables provided complimentary.

**Facility equipment:** Registration tables, coat racks, water stations, lecterns, podiums, staging and other essentials are available. Call for pricing and inventory.

**Audio Visual:** Our in-house Audio/Visual team can provide the necessary equipment and technical assistance for any type of event, offering you the utmost in convenience and service at a competitive price.

**Parking:** 800 spaces available in the underground parking garage, 225 exhibitor spaces in the adjacent parking lots.

**Linens and napkins:** Wide variety of colors; various types.

**China and glassware:** White china; stemmed glassware provided complimentary.

**Decorations:** Contract decorators available for exhibitors, booths, etc; ARAMARK/GPL can provide water fountains, multi-tiered buffet tables, mirrored bases, floral displays, "theme" breaks and food displays; ice sculptures, floral arrangements, silver service, and votive candles available.

**Getting Around:** Portland's MAX light-rail system makes getting around easy. It can pick you up or drop you off right at our front door—and it's free within most of the downtown area! Arriving from out of town? OCC is just eight short miles from the airport, and MAX can even bring you to us or take you home.

**Sustainability:** The center was acknowledged for its forward thinking expansion design and was selected for the BEST Award (Business for an Environmentally Sustainable Tomorrow) by the City of Portland's Office of Sustainable Development for water conservation and its innovative rain garden. The facility's many sustainable design features and the staff's commitment to continuous improvement of its practices have created a very "green" venue.

**Network and Internet Access:** OCC provides state of the art local area networking as well as high-speed wired and wireless (Wi-Fi) Internet access throughout the entire facility. We also have the flexibility to add additional lines to accommodate specialized requirements.

**In-House Services Provide Additional Convenience and Savings:** Full Service Catering/Concessions with on-site Executive Chef, Professional Audio/Visual Services Team, FedEx Kinko's, Starbucks and a variety of retail shops!

| Facility Specs |
|---|
| 255,000 sq. ft. of exhibit space |
| 60,000 sq. ft. of ballroom space - "Portland" and "Oregon" Ballrooms |
| 54,000 sq. ft. of meeting space - 50 meeting rooms |
| 19 loading docks |
| 800 total parking spaces in the underground garage |
| 225 exhibitor parking spaces available on-site |

The Oregon Convention Center features a one million square foot campus with 255,000 gross square feet of contiguous exhibit space, making it the largest such facility in the Pacific Northwest. Two beautiful grand ballrooms of 25,200 GSF and 34,300 GSF and 50 premier meeting rooms compliment the exhibit space. Add in high speed wired and wireless (Wi-Fi) Internet connections throughout, on-site parking on two levels in our underground garage, extraordinary meals served up by ARAMARK/Giacometti Partners Ltd. and award-winning customer service, we are confident we can become your preferred meeting destination.

The OCC is located within Portland's city center, right around the corner from famous restaurants, popular cultural attractions and wide-ranging entertainment. The surrounding area's scenery, some of the most spectacular on the planet, is artfully complimented by the décor and atmosphere of the center's spacious interiors. From the start, you will realize that the OCC isn't only a great place to be, but a place where great things can happen.

**The Oregon Convention Center: At The Center of Success.**
**Call us soon at (503) 235-7575 or visit our website www.oregoncc.org**

***Experience** the Difference of an Oregon State University Event!*

OSU
Oregon State
UNIVERSITY

**OSU Conferences and Events**
**100 LaSells Stewart Center, Corvallis, OR 97331**
**1-800-678-6311, 541-737-9300, Fax 541-737-9315**
Email: conferences@oregonstate.edu
Website: http://oregonstate.edu/conferences

---

Nestled in the heart of Oregon's Willamette Valley, Oregon State University is uniquely situated between large cities, mountains, and the Pacific Ocean. While our meeting space will impress you, it is our commitment to service that will make your Oregon State University experience unlike any other. Groups of 12 to 1,200 can be accommodated with ease in a variety of meeting spaces.

- ***World-Class Facilities:*** Over 80,000 square feet of flexible meeting space, plus state-of-the-art technology at your disposal.
- ***Exciting Activities:*** Award-winning wineries; golf at OSU's Trysting Tree Golf Club; experiential education and teambuilding at the OSU Challenge Course; and newly remodeled recreational facilities with an indoor climbing center!
- ***Unparalleled Service:*** Our conference planners will ensure that every detail of your event is handled with care.
- ***Exceptional Catering and Dining:*** Customer-choice catering in the conference facilities, plus economical on-campus dining options.
- ***Luxurious Accommodations:*** Space for 3,000 residence hall guests during the summer months, plus limited year-round housing. 128-room Hilton Garden Inn located next to the conference facilities, plus 900 additional hotel rooms nearby.

## OSU Conferences and Events

1,200-seat and 200-seat auditoriums
500-seat ballroom
14,000 sq. ft. of exhibit space
15 breakout rooms for groups of 12 to 1,200
Summer and year-round residence hall accommodations

**Let us tailor a bid to suit your needs! 1-800-678-6311**

*Please also see Corvallis Tourism under Event Professional Organizations on page 318.*

# ROSE QUARTER

Rose Garden • Memorial Coliseum • Rose Quarter Commons

*Contact: Cathy Walsh*
*E-mail: facilitysales@rosequarter.com*
*Business Hours: Mon–Fri 8:30am–5:30pm*
*Rose Quarter Event Hotline (503) 321-3211*

*One Center Court, Suite 150*

*Portland, Oregon 97227*
*503.235.8771; Fax 503.736.5120*
*www.rosequarter.com/facility*

---

**ROSE QUARTER CAMPUS**

The Rose Quarter Campus consists of three facilities: the Rose Garden, Memorial Coliseum and the Rose Quarter Commons. The Rose Quarter has exceptional meeting and conference facilities, making it the perfect location for client entertaining, a corporate meeting or employee appreciation event. The Memorial Coliseum and the Rose Garden together include 13 exceptional meeting rooms which are ideal for dinners, receptions, lectures and meetings.

**ROSE GARDEN**

The Rose Garden, a 20,000-plus seat arena, offers a brilliant array of world-class entertainment features. The "Theater of the Clouds" set, with its spectacular theater curtains, allows you a more intimate setting for small groups and can accommodate up to 6,500.

**MEMORIAL COLISEUM**

The Memorial Coliseum has exceptional meeting and conference capabilities complete with its own exhibit space.

| | |
|---|---|
| Entire Arena Bowl | 12,000 Capacity |
| Arena Half House Configuration | 1,000–6,000 Capacity |
| Half Court Basketball Configuration | 500 Capacity |
| Entire Memorial Coliseum | Arena Bowl, 40,000 sq ft<br>Exhibit Hall and 7 Meeting Rooms |

**ROSE QUARTER COMMONS:**

The Rose Quarter Commons is an outdoor, paved plaza and can accommodate everything from open-air concerts with seating for 3,000 to outdoor festival and fairs for up to 5,000 people.

**ROSE GARDEN BANQUET ROOMS:**

- Rose Room – 270 banquet
- Legends Restaurant – 200 banquet
- Widmer Room – 50 banquet
- Players Sports Bar – 225 banquet
- Garden Club – 128 banquet
- Preferred Dining Room – 36 banquet

**MEMORIAL COLISEUM MEETING ROOMS:**

- Georgia Pacific —350 banquet
- US Plywood — 120 banquet
- Weyerhaeuser — 120 banquet
- Fountain — 80 banquet
- Simpson — 80 banquet
- International Paper — 80 banquet
- Pope & Talbot — 64 banquet

# SEASIDE CIVIC AND CONVENTION CENTER

*415 First Avenue • Seaside, Oregon 97138*
*(503) 738-8585 or (800) 394-3303; Fax (503) 738-0198*
*Office Hours: Mon–Fri 8am–5pm*
*E-mail: sales@seasideconvention.com Web site: www.seasideconvention.com*

## THE PERFECT MEETING PLACE

Seaside has it all! Superb meeting and convention facilities, great food, wonderful accommodations and spectacular coastal scenery. The Convention Center is located within walking distance to downtown and a marvelous variety of over 1,400 guest rooms. These include top-notch suites with spectacular oceanviews and cozy bed and breakfast inns complete with fireplaces and sundecks. Recreation and relaxation opportunities abound, as will your delegates enthusiasm for Seaside.

**Capacity:** from 25 to 1,950 people
**Catering:** 25 years experience from our in-house caterer "Oregon Fine Foods;" full service bar available. No service and gratuity charge
**Types of Events:** conventions, trade shows, meetings, receptions, banquets

## Description of Facility and Services

A professional staff with cumulative experience totaling more than 50 years in convention and meeting planning. Personal attention is our profession. The Convention Center is a nonsmoking facility. For availability and terms, please contact our Director of Sales.
**Audiovisual equipment:** a full range of audio visual equipment, sound and lighting, "wi-fi;" most AV equipment free of charge
**Parking:** ample free parking available
**ADA:** compliant

Seaside Civic and Convention Center—overlooking the scenic Necanicum River and Quatat Marine Park, and just three blocks from the beach and Promenade—affords more than 22, 000 total square feet of very flexible meeting space.

| LOCATION | Square feet | Approx. Dimens. | Ceiling Height | Theater | Classroom | Reception | Banquet | Exhibits |
|---|---|---|---|---|---|---|---|---|
| Main and Exhibit Hall | 15,180 | | | 1,300 | 600 | 1,950 | 1,300 | 100 |
| Main Hall | 10,500 | 105'x100' | 20' | 900 | 480 | 900 | 800 | 72 |
| Exhibit Hall | 4,680 | 65'x72' | 12' | 400 | 240 | 500 | 336 | 28 |
| Riverview | 1,944 | 72'x27' | 10' | 120 | 80 | 100 | 120 | |
| A/B/C (each) | 648 | 24'x27' | 10' | 40 | 24 | 35 | 30 | |
| Seaside | 1,944 | 72'x27' | 10' | 120 | 80 | 100 | 100 | |
| A/B/C (each) | 648 | 24'x27' | 10' | 40 | 24 | 35 | 30 | |
| Seahorse | 1,540 | 22'x70' | 8' | 80 | 48 | 100 | 80 | |
| A/B/C/D (each) | 385 | 22'x17' | 8' | 20 | 16 | 25 | 20 | |
| Haystack | 850 | 17'x50' | 8' | 45 | 36 | 60 | 60 | |
| A/B/C (each) | 283 | 17'x17' | 8' | 15 | 12 | 20 | 20 | |
| Seamist | 540 | 20'x48' | 8' | 50 | 32 | 55 | 40 | 5 |

# SEASIDE CIVIC & CONVENTION CENTER



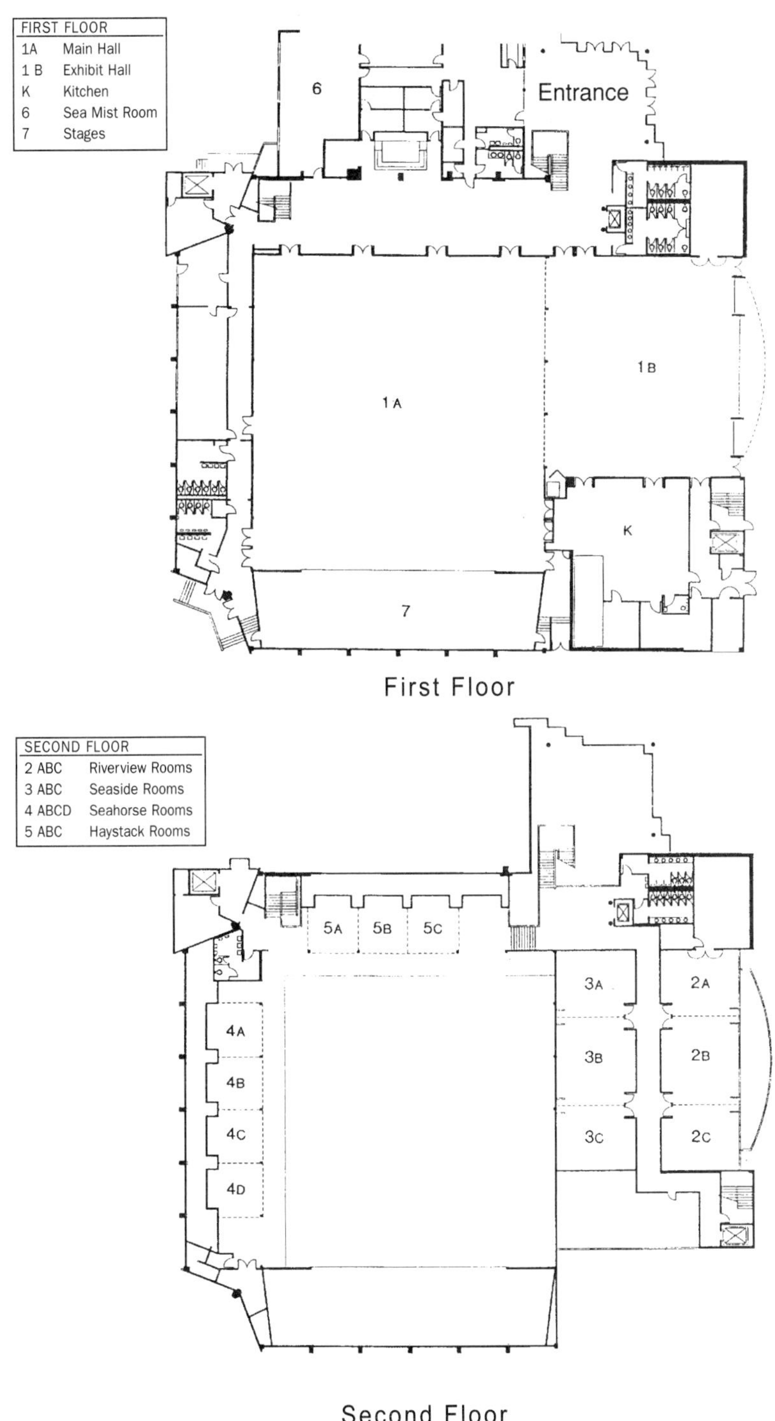


First Floor

Second Floor

200 Commercial Street SE
Salem, Oregon 97301
1-877-589-1700
www.salemconferencecenter.org

The Salem, Oregon Conference Center is like no other meeting facility in the Willamette Valley region. It is the result of a strong commitment to create a center of extraordinary quality from the flowing integration of the conference center and hotel, to the combination of classic appointments and forward-looking technology.

## The Gem

In all, 14 different rooms totaling 29,400 square feet can be configured for any combination of theatre, banquet space, trade show space, or classroom activity.

The second floor 11,400 square-foot Ballroom can accommodate up to 1,600 guests, and the first floor 8,750 square-foot Great Hall accommodates up to 1,200 guests.

## The Hotel

At the end of the day, visitors will enjoy refined hospitality at the adjoining 193-suite business-class hotel. Each luxurious guestroom and suite offers separate living, sleeping and executive work areas. To unwind, visitors can choose fine dining, the executive lounge, the indoor pool and spa, or the fitness center without leaving the facility.

## Brilliant Technology

Architectural accents of glass, steel and brushed aluminum will hint at the deep technology embedded in every corner of the conference facility. The most demanding exhibitors will find gigabit fiber, 10/100 Ethernet and Wi-Fi wireless available on both levels. 10/100 nodes can be configured for voice or data as required. The high-speed Wi-Fi hot spot network covers the entire interior of the conference center, so Wi-Fi enabled PDAs and laptops, and the visitors that use them, can connect. Underneath it all, a robust multi-mode fiber network ensures high-load reliability and performance decades into the future.

## The Setting

A stroll begins in the heart of Salem's historic downtown, bordered to the east by the state Capitol Plaza, and to the west by the Willamette River. An eclectic mix of shops, bakeries, art galleries, antique and fashion stores, craft and music stores and casual eateries are within blocks of the center.

Blocks away, Riverfront Park is home to the Willamette Queen sternwheeler like those that helped build Old Salem in the 1800s. There's a carousel with hand carved horses, a natural amphitheater, and miles of trails and paths along the Willamette River. Further afield, 25 wineries dot the surrounding hills, a mere 30 minutes downtown Salem.

For more information, please contact Donna Meyers, Director of Sales at 1-877-589-1700, or donna@salemconferencecenter.org.

You can download a free meeting planner kit, or fill out an online meeting RFP request by visiting www.salemconferencecenter.org. We look forward to working with you to create an event that will be, by any measure, flawless.

# WILLAMETTE EVENTS CENTER AT THE LINN COUNTY FAIR AND EXPO

## *"A PLACE TO PRESENT YOUR BEST..."*

*I-5 and Knox Butte Road • Albany, Oregon 97322*
*Contact: Jill Ingalls*
*(541) 926-4314, (800) 858-2005; Fax (541) 926-8630*
*E-mail: fairexpo@co.linn.or.us; Web site: www.co.linn.or.us/fairexpo*
*Office Hours: 8:30am–5pm; facility staffed 24 hours*

---

**Capacity:** Willamette Events Center can accommodate up to 6,000 guests; conferences from 10 to 400 in 48,600 sq. ft.; three additional buildings totalling five acres under cover
**Price Range:** $140–$2,200
**Catering:** select from eight providers, contracted and flexible
**Types of Events:** conventions, conferences, workshops, training seminars, parties, board meetings, expositions, livestock show/sales, horse shows, and more

### Availability and Terms
Currently booking into 2006. Please call for availability.

### Description of Facility and Services
**Seating:** provided according to event
**Servers:** provided; contracted
**Bar facilities:** contracted through caterer
**Dance floor:** available at market rate
**Linens:** available in a variety of colors
**China and glassware:** contracted
**Decorations:** some limitations apply
**Audiovisual:** slide projector, overhead, TV/VCR
**Equipment:** A/V carts, cords, podiums, sound; anything can be arranged
**Parking:** approximately 2,000 public parking spaces available; additional vendor/exhibitor parking; loading dock
**ADA:** compliant
- New lodging adjacent to facility

### Special Services
"...our best is present in this place." Service is extreme here! On-site assistance with local contacts and arrangements. The Linn County Fair and Expo Center is a full-service conference center, exhibit hall, and fairgrounds facility with a professional "can do" staff.

Located adjacent to lodging, near restaurants, shopping and recreational opportunities. Next to 10,000 seat amphitheater and wooded park with a lake.

# DEVELOPING A TRADE SHOW

**Market Analysis:** Bringing together the right buyers and sellers. Your success with exhibits will be based on both the interest your attendees have in the exhibitors' products and services, and future sales. If you have had a show before, it is best to survey the attendees to analyze the type of attendee you are attracting. Sample questions include: How did you hear about the show? What is your age? Will you use the products or services presented at the show? What did you like or dislike about the show?

**Site Selection:** How much exhibit space is available?; How many exhibits will fit?; How accessible is the space for load-in and load-out?; Are professional decorators available? Needed?

Exhibits are becoming more and more an integral part of meetings and conventions. This is often due to the revenue they bring to a meeting from exhibitors' fees. The exhibit program is a complement to the convention and as much time should be spent planning the exhibit portion as the other vital parts of a meeting.

**Exhibitor Promotion:** Be sure the exhibitors have as much information as they need about your attendees, as well as what needs the exhibitors can expect from the attendees. Also, be sure the exhibitors have all of the detailed information: the size of the booth, the layout of the booths, the exhibit hours, the color of pipe and drape, the booth inclusions, available utilities, and advertising that is available and/or provided.

**Communicate often:** Exhibitors need to be kept up to date with highlights of the program, list of exhibitors, numbers of attendees. They will also need an exhibitor packet that will give them details on all the official contractors they may order through. For example, forms to order flowers, tables, crate storage, shipping, electricity, etc.

**Attendance Promotions:** You are obligated to deliver visitors to the exhibitors. You may use direct mail, advertising in newspapers, television, newsletters, and magazines. Be sure to include the name of the event, date, time, location, description of products displayed, fees (if any), and any special attractions.

**On-Site:** Prepare an operations manual. This will be the exact details of how you want to run the exhibit portion, including the times, dates, location, and who is responsible for what.

**Evaluations and Follow-up:** A simple questionnaire to gather timely information from your exhibitors will be worth a lot as a planning tool. Find out how the exhibitors did and how you can improve the experience.

*3720 N.W. Yeon Avenue*
*Portland, Oregon 97210*
*(503) 228-6800; Fax (503) 228-6808*
*Contact: Marc Beyer • E-mail: mbeyer@dwatradeshow.com*
*Web site: www.dwatradeshow.com*

---

**DWA Trade Show & Exposition Services is a Full Service Trade Show, Convention and Special Event Contractor.**

DWA has been in business since 1977. We are a locally owned and operated company with a very knowledgeable staff that has years of experience in the trade show industry. We have a large inventory of equipment warehoused in our 65,000 square foot facility in Northwest Portland. We are conveniently located just 10 minutes from the Oregon Convention Center, Portland Exposition Center, the Rose Quarter, and many other event facilities, giving us the ability to respond immediately to any emergency that may arise.

## DWA Services

- Floor Plans and CAD Design
- Special Events
- Exhibit Installation and Dismantling
- Freight Handling and Storage
- Graphics/Banners
- Rental Exhibits
- Booth Equipment
- Booth Furnishings
- Aisle and Booth Carpet
- Entrance Units
- Registration Furnishings
- Aisle Signs

**DWA Trade Show and Exposition Services—**
***Quality at an affordable price and***
***where the customer is our number one priority!***

# EMERALD STAFFING

## www.emeraldstaffing.com

Kruse Woods II
5335 Southwest Meadows Road
Suite 210
Lake Oswego, Oregon 97035

Contact: John Burton, Jr., CPC Tel. 503.941.4788 Fax. 503.941.4799

johnjr@emeraldstaffing.com

---

### Emerald Staffing Offers Professional Staffing To Meet All Your Needs…

We specialize in taking the worry out of project management. We have been staffing for temporary, temp to hire and direct placement since 1978. We match your requirements with our employee's abilities. On each new assignment, our friendly staff will call to verify the arrival and progress of our employee assigned to you. In addition to event management, registration and tradeshow services, we also specialize in the following areas:

- Administration
- Clerical/Reception
- Customer Service
- Accounting
- Data Entry
- Insurance
- Mortgage Industry
- Sales
  - Technology Sector
  - Industrial Market
- Medical
  - Front/Back Office
  - Paraprofessional

### Our Commitment:

Our entire staff is committed to total client satisfaction. We listen, we respond, and stand behind you! We value your business and know you will be pleased with our performance. Call today and see for yourself why Top Local and National Companies call Emerald first!

**Staffing Since 1978**

*Portable & Modular Displays & Graphics*
*Portland - Seattle*

*503.624.2905, 866.624.2905*
*Fax 503.624.2904*
*www.exhibitsnw.com*

---

## Hardware Solutions

- New & Used Exhibit Sales
- Elaborate Custom Modular Exhibits
- Banner Stands
- Fabric Structures
- Portable Chairs/Tables
- Table Coverings
- Transport Cases
- Projector Screens
- Portable Table Top & Full-Height Exhibits
- Truss
- Point of Purchase Displays
- Flooring Solutions
- Literature Racks
- Lighting Options
- Monitor Stands

## Graphic Services

- Large Format Murals
- Dye Sublimation on Fabric
- Dimensional Graphics
- Rigid & Flexible Applications
- Photo, Inkjet & Lambda
- In-System & Detachable Graphics
- Vinyl Application
- Translucent (backlit) & Opaque
- Banners
- Continuous Tone Output

## Rental Services

- Custom Rental Design
- Pop-up & Panel Backwall Systems
- Counters, Towers & Lighting
- Truss Systems

## Exhibit Management Services

- Show Service Order Coordination
- Storage
- Shipping Management
- Nationwide Exhibit Installation & Dismantle

***Visit our new web site***

**www.exhibitsnw.com**

TouchPoll Orlando, Inc.
*A Nationwide Survey Company*
TEL: 407-897-5259
www.touchpollorlando.com
info@touchpollorlando.com

---

The TouchPoll Survey System provides an affordable opportunity to collect meaningful feedback from the people who are important to your business or organization. People touch their answers right onto the touch screen – quickly and easily, without all the traditional hassle. We help a wide variety of businesses:

- Conventions
- Trade Shows
- Banks
- Restaurants
- Sports Events
- Museums
- Libraries
- Transportation
- Theme Parks
- Media
- Shopping Malls
- Retailers
- Government Agencies
- Municipalities
- Real Estate
- Human Resources
- Meetings
- and more

It's fun for the respondent, and it also reduces interviewer bias and data entry errors associated with paper surveys. The TouchPoll System collects, tabulates and reports information faster, more accurately and with better results than traditional survey methods. Results are always available right at your fingertips.

We are a nationwide, exclusive provider of survey and research services utilizing this advanced touch screen data collection system. Let us help you get the valuable feedback you need, so you can make informed business decisions.

TouchPoll is fast and it's fun! By using a custom TouchPoll survey, you can get the feedback that really counts.

## A few survey features and benefits:

- Questions are 100% customizable
- Respondents can choose answers or type 'free-form' comments
- Feedback is current—not from a 'faded memory'
- Touchscreen provides higher response rates
- Results can be tabulated immediately—great for wrap-up meetings

Why not take advantage of an easy and affordable way to collect the feedback that really counts? Call us today to learn more.

TouchPoll Orlando, Inc.
*A Nationwide Survey Company*
TEL: 407-897-5259
www.touchpollorlando.com
info@touchpollorlando.com

*1400 N.W. 15th Avenue*
*Portland, Oregon 97209*
*(503) 294-0412; Fax (503) 294-0616*
*Business Hours: Mon–Sat 8:30am–6pm*
*Appointments Available Any Hour*
*www.wcep.com*

## Services

West Coast Event Productions is the Northwest's premier idea center for all events and special occasions. We specialize in the custom planning and design of convention and exhibition installation. We also offer design and rental services and custom fabrication of staging, lighting, sound, special effects, audio visual presentations, signage, and theme production. We tailor events and trade shows to mirror your corporate identity or direction.

## Convention and Exposition Services

**Pipe and drape/skirting/carpeting:** Our drape and matching table skirting covers a spectrum of vivid colors creating the ideal backdrop or setting for a booth, room divider, stage backdrop, or imaginative decorating. Skirting comes in a variety of different styles such as box pleats or straight wraps. Our selection of carpeting covers drab floors in a variety of colors and styles.

## Fabrication Inventory

At West Coast Event Productions we pride ourselves in designing award-winning exhibit booths that identify an individual company's uniqueness among the competition. We create and produce designs that compel people to take notice of you. West Coast Event Productions has the resources to not only create a winning trade show display, we can provide you with banners, interiors and exterior signage, props, and speciality tabletop decor.

**Sound systems, lighting and audio visual:** West Coast Event Productions has a complete inventory of sound equipment from amplifiers, microphone and mixing consoles to CD players, Karaoke machines and high end data projectors. We offer a variety of unique lighting fixtures and special effects including Lycian spotlights, fog machines, image projectors and much more. Our audio visual division offers large screen projection televisions, podiums, and 35mm and overhead projectors with screens for all meeting room events.

**Staging and dance floors:** You'll find an assortment of floors including elegant oak parquet, black and white checks, and floors with custom designed images at West Coast. Elevated foundations include meeting room risers, three-tier big band staging, and custom installations with attractive carpeting and color-coordinated skirting.

## Props

West Coast offers a surprisingly large selection of props and accessories to supplement your tradeshow and convention needs. Select from existing inventory or work with our in-house designers and production staff to build something custom, you'll find what you need at West Coast Event Productions.

## West Coast Event Productions

Celebrating our 20 year anniversary, West Coast is dedicated to providing you with a service that is unmatched anywhere. Our commitment, attention to detail and experience in the event production field has propelled West Coast Event Productions into one of the most celebrated event companies in the Northwest.

**See page 430 under Rental Services.**
**See page 471 under Themes & Props.**

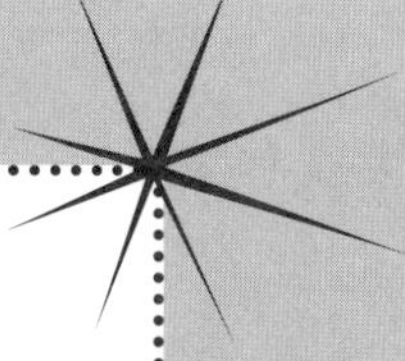

# Decorations & Party Supplies

- *Balloon Decor*
- *Disposable Cameras*

# DECORATIONS & PARTY SUPPLIES

**Kinds of party supplies:** Be sure to stop by a party supply store for many great ideas. You will discover fun ways to decorate–from crepe paper to balloons in every color imaginable. A party supply store can help you with special themes and ideas for decorating tables, walls, ceilings and floors!

**Case or bulk discounts:** Be sure to inquire about discounts when buying large quantities of items. You may want to consider renting a tank of helium so you can coordinate your own balloon decorations and save money.

**Special-occasion decorations:** Party shops carry a large selection of party decorations and accessories for theme events, birthdays, anniversaries, etc. Theme-coordinated decorations are very popular–matching plates, napkins, cups, invitations, plus many other accessories. Gift supplies include coordinated wrapping paper, ribbon, gift bags, tissue, cards and more.

**Balloon ideas:** Balloons are an inexpensive means of decorating and provide a dramatic visual effect. Balloons often are used to enhance a room and can also be used to hide flaws in walls or ceilings. Balloons can be sculpted in any shape you desire. Arches made with helium balloons enhance entrances, dance floors, and buffet tables. A fun idea is to have a balloon release with special notes inside the balloons. These are certified balloon specialists to help you decide how to decorate with balloons. **NOTE: Some facilities do not allow balloons. Check to be sure they are allowed before you place your balloon order.**

**Colors of balloons:** Balloons come in a wide variety of colors, sizes, and styles. A special theme color can be created by placing a balloon of one color inside another of a different color.

**Imprinted balloons:** Balloons can be imprinted with your business logo or event name and date.

**Rental decorations:** Rental decorations come in a variety of choices–ficus trees with twinkle lights, waterfalls, and fountains. You can create any visual effect you want with the right decorations. An underwater theme is fun with live fish in bowls on the tables as centerpieces. Netting and garland for seaweed hanging from the ceiling creates the illusion of being underwater. Refer to rental companies in this Guide in the "Event Rentals" section or party supply stores.

*6650 N.W. Kaiser Rd • Portland, Oregon 97229*
*Contact: Cheryl Skoric, CBA*
*503.629.5827; Fax 503.645.9404*
***Oregon's First Certified Balloon Artist***
*Business Hours: to suit your schedule,*
*day or evening by appointment*
*www.bouquetsandballoons.com*

---

## More than your ordinary florist
## Flowers ❀ Balloons ❀ Theme Creation

*We offer beautiful floral arrangements, but we are experts in creating balloon themes.*

Corporate Events • Conventions • Trade Shows • Banquets • Theme Parties • Special Events • Company Picnics • Grand Openings • Carnivals & Fairs • Shopping Mall Promotions •

### As Corporate Specialists

Bouquets & Balloons offers services designed to simplify your job while providing you with imaginative ideas and unsurpassed service.

• Free consultation at the event site, your location, or ours

### Theme Parties

Balloons are the perfect decorating alternative for any occasion or event. Arches, columns, swags, balloon drops and sculptures can highlight the focal points of your event and give the room an air of festivity and elegance. Try Futuristic, Tropical, Fantasy, Carnival, Mardi Gras, Wine Fest, '50s, Under the Sea and Western, just to name a few.

### Special Effects

Do you want to create Excitement? Exploding Balloons filled with confetti, balloons, movie tickets or anything else you desire, exploded over the crowd will inspire them. Do you have something that you would like to hide until a specific time? Try the Exploding Wall. Sure to be a crowd pleaser.

### Balloon Ideas

Logos • Chinese Lanterns • Cactus • Tumbleweeds • Wagons • Santa Claus • Snowmen
Tin Soldiers • Sea Horses • Octopus • Fish • Waves • Bubbles • Dance Canopies

### Floral Ideas

Stage Decor • Buffet Flowers • Centerpieces • Podium Arrangements
Head Table Arrangements • Presentation Bouquets • Corsages • Boutonnieres
• Sign-in Table Arrangement

**Note:** Some facilities do not allow helium-filled balloons. But if you like the looks of balloons, check with us, we specialize in air-filled balloon decorations.

**WWW.CNGDISPOSABLECAMERA.COM**

*408 S.W. Augustus Drive, Dallas, Oregon 97338*
*(888) 431-3463; Fax (775) 459-3750*
*E-mail: disposablecamera@prodigy.net*

---

## Disposable Cameras for All Occasions

**(Now Available – Reusable 35mm Cameras at Disposable Camera prices)**

Have you ever been at a special event and wish you had a camera? Well now you can! At CnG Disposable Cameras we have a wonderful collection of uniquely designed, new, totally reusable cameras for your special occasion. The new reusable cameras are available at the same pricing as disposable cameras. They are more durable and can be used over and over again. Our cameras come already loaded with film and are ready to use. We offer the LARGEST SELECTION of specially designed cameras.

Each camera is affordable and always ready for action. All cameras come with the highest quality film, ensuring your pictures will come out every time.

We can provide both custom designed cameras and personalized cameras to meet your specific needs.

## Special Designed Cameras Include:

Accident, Baby, Bar Mitzvah, Bat Mitzvah, Birthday, Christmas, Custom corporate Designs, Document, Everyday, Graduation, Golf, Halloween, Holiday, Kids, Long Range, Memories, New Year's, Party, Prom, Reunion, Special Day, Tropical, Underwater, Valentines, USA and Wedding.

**See our LARGE SELECTION of pre-designed cameras on our web site, or call us to have a camera designed for your event.**

**www.cngdisposablecamera.com**

50 SE Yamhill (at Water Avenue) • Portland, Oregon 97214

**503.239.7007** • 800•321•6047 • 503.239.0956 fax • www.lippmancompany.com

*Discover our central east side location – just six blocks north of OMSI at the base of the Morrison Bridge.*

*Open Monday - Friday 9:00 - 6:00 & Saturday 9:00 - 5:00*

---

**Family owned and operated since 1948**

## Party Supplies:

- Our friendly and creative staff is here to assist you with your party planning needs. From decorations to party favors, paper products, balloons and rentals, you're sure to find everything you need to create a party for all to remember.

## Balloons:

- 1000 square foot balloon room features the largest selection of foil and latex balloons and balloon supplies in the State. The Lippman Company offers an extensive inventory of balloon designs, colors, and sizes. Our distribution department offers a full color catalog, with seasonal supplements – join our mailing list!
- Our expert staff can custom design balloon sculptures, and décor to make any occasion unique. Call ahead for a balloon bouquet to go!

## Helium Tank Rental:

- We carry a wide selection of helium tank sizes for rent and sale. Pick up a tank for your party, or set up a Lippman Company account with regular delivery for your corporate needs.

## Small Toys:

- Come play with our toys! We stock over 300 small toys and trinkets in bulk quantities with volume pricing by the dozen and gross. Our selection includes seasonal and themed toys ideal for your school carnival, corporate event, or party favor.

## Theme Parties and Rentals:

- From Celebrity Stand-Ups to Tiki Gods and Mod Furnishings, The Lippman Company's huge selection of rental items will exceed your expectations! Themes include: Western, Casino, Tropical, 1950s, 60s and 70s, Halloween, Hollywood, Mardi Gras, Fiesta, and more!

## Event Space Rental:

- Newly finished 3,000 square foot event space features bamboo floors, flexible lighting and sound system, two ADA restrooms and large staging kitchen.

# Notes

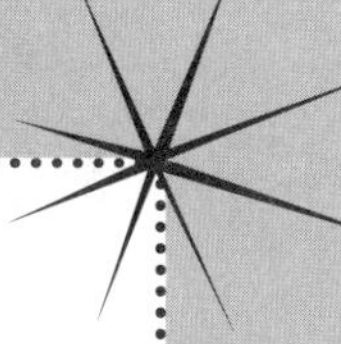

# Desserts & Logo Chocolates

- *Chocolate Fountains*

*4733 S.E. Hawthorne*
*Portland, Oregon 97215*
*www.jacivas.com*
*(503) 234-8115; Fax (503) 234-6076*
*Business Hours: Mon–Sat 7:30am–6pm*

---

***United States Pastry Alliance gold medal winner***
***Winner of the Austin Family Business Award***
***Featured on national Food Network's "Food Finds"***
***Recipient of Master Chocolatier Award***

## Chocolate Logos…A Tasteful Business Approach

JaCiva's can take your company logo and turn it into a chocolate gift to be used as client gifts for holiday or promotional items at trade shows. Wrappers for chocolate bars can also be printed with the company name and any message. Everyone loves getting chocolate and will remember your name with logo chocolates.

## Cakes and Pastries Available

If you're looking for a beautiful cake for your corporate or social event, that is exquisite looking as well as luscious inside…then JaCiva's is your answer. We are always happy to personalize your cakes and cookies with company logo or inscriptions.

You can also select from our scrumptious selection of pastries. We offer muffins and danish for your breakfast and brunch meetings. Victorian cookies for that afternoon tea, and European pastries for evening events.

## Molded Chocolate Items

For special events or holidays JaCiva's offers special chocolate items such as chess sets, tools, golf and tennis items, edible chocolate boxes filled with truffles and chocolate life-sized turkeys filled with holiday chocolates and candies. Place your orders early.

## Ordering

Early ordering is suggested, especially for large orders.

**CALL FOR A CONSULTATION WITH JACIVA'S**

# Northwest Chocolate Fountains

503.617.6923
www.nwchocolatefountains.com
E-mail: info@nwchocolatefountains.com

## What to Expect

A chocolate fountain can ensure that any occasion is made more elegant, delightful, and memorable. It is an unforgettable conversation piece that will enhance any event from weddings, showers, birthdays, anniversaries and holiday parties, to corporate events and fund-raisers. The possibilities are limited only by your imagination.

As the aroma of chocolate fills the air, your guests will smile in anticipation of dipping a delicious selection of fruits, pastries, marshmallows, or pretzels into the warm cascading chocolate. The possibilities are endless, however, the results are always the same . . . delightful, decadent and entertaining!

## The Fountains

A fountain service includes your choice of premium dark, milk or white chocolate, 2.5 hours of service, delivery, set up, break down and cleaning of the fountain, decorative table accents and skewers. To assure the success of your chocolate fountain experience an attendant will assist your guests during your event.

**Small Fountain:** Serving up to 100 guests, this is a wonderful size for smaller receptions, home parties or work place celebrations. This fountain includes 10 pounds of premium chocolate and 300 skewers for dipping items.

**Medium Fountain:** Serving up to 200 guests, the medium fountain is the preferred size for wedding receptions or corporate events. This fountain includes 20 pounds of premium chocolate and 500 skewers for dipping items.

Additional chocolate and time can be purchased for your special event.

## Experience

Catherine Camp is the owner and operator of Northwest Chocolate Fountains. To each event she brings over 20 years of experience in Hotel and Corporate Management. Ensuring your special occasion goes as you have envisioned, one of her core priorities is to establish a clear line of communication with you and your caterer to fulfill your expectations. Catherine takes great pride in creating a presentation that brings both you and your guests sweet indulgence and delight.

# Promotional Treats

*P.O. Box 19691*
*Portland, Oregon 97280*
*(503) 246-4743*
*Fax (503) 246-4754*
*E-mail: protreats@aol.com; www.promotionaltreats.com*

## Have Something to Say?

Say it with chocolate. Deliver your message in a way they'll remember. Put your name, message, or logo straight into the chocolate. We work with you to create just the right product to promote the theme of your event—because your event is special. At Promotional Treats, you'll find that our candy looks as good as it tastes.

## Product Offering

- Centerpieces
- Chocolate dishes filled with chocolate delights
- Chocolate floral bouquets
- Chocolate promotional items
- Corporate gifts
- Custom molded chocolate
- Custom boxed candy
- Corporate logos
- Table favors
- Truffles

## Event Suggestions

- Corporate events
- Employee incentives
- Grand openings
- Holidays
- Office parties
- Sales promotions
- Thank you gifts
- Weddings/Anniversaries

Our chocolate gift items serve as a gift, a decoration and a dessert.

**So Remember—**
**A Touch of Chocolate for Every Event**

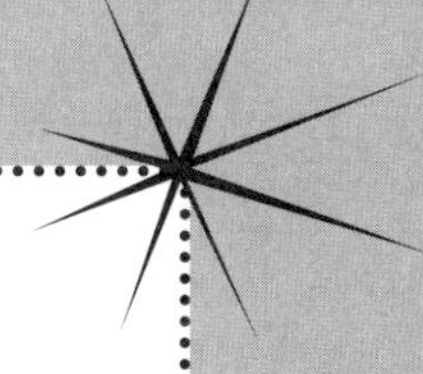

# Entertainers & Performers

- *Caricature Artist*
- *Improvisational Comedy*
- *Comedians*
- *Country Dance Instruction*
- *Entertainment Planning Service*
- *Santa for Hire*
- *Magicians*
- *Yo-Yo Artist*

503-238-4301 www.barbarapikuscaricatures.com

## Celebrate with Style

From a black tie event to a child's birthday party, capture the moment with Oregon's favorite caricature artist, Barbara Pikus. Since 1994 Barbara has created magical caricatures for guests attending:

| **Corporate Events:** | **Private Events:** |
|---|---|
| **Parties, Picnics** | **Parties, Picnics** |
| **Tradeshows** | **Wedding Receptions** |
| **Conventions** | **Reunions** |
| **Grand Openings** | **Bar/Bat Mitzvahs** |
| **Cruises** | **Graduation Parties** |

Ten drawings per hour…Drawings are black and white, front or three-quarter view, face and shoulders.

## Custom Cards

Barbara Pikus designs cards for all occasions. Please see examples on web site.

## Clients:

Nike, Intel, Yoshida Group, Wells Fargo, AAA, Merant, Market Transport, Portland Spirit, Columbia River Yacht Club, University Club, Riverplace Athletic Club, Spirit Mountain Casino, Providence Portland Medical Center, Sheraton Airport Hotel, Hayden's Lakefront Grill, Miller Nash and Preston Gates & Ellis LLP

## Praise for Barbara Pikus

"Barbara is consistently a fun, crowd pleaser who captures the moment with her drawings. She's a pleasure to work with and a true professional."

**Bob Baskette, Event Planner**
**Portland Spirit**

"Professional and uplifting attitude. Her talent is very much in demand."

**Spirit Mountain Casino**

"Barbara was a joy to work with. She really did a lot to bring out the best in people even when they were shy about sitting in her chair."

**Key Technology**

## Awards

National Caricaturists Convention, Las Vegas , Winner of "Best Likeness" Award.

# brainwaves

IMPROVISATIONAL COMEDY

*3721 SE 13th Ave., #7*
*Portland, Oregon 97202*
*(503) 796-9550*
*Web site: www.brainwavesimprov.com*

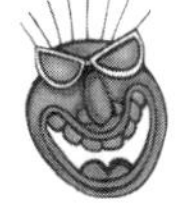

## What is Brainwaves?

Brainwaves Improvisational Comedy is a unique form of entertainment that can make your next event a hilarious success. Made up entirely of professional comic actors, Brainwaves plays corporate functions, colleges, theaters and special events all over the country. Brainwaves first formed in 1986, so the cast has years of experience adapting their performance to fit the needs of you and your audience. This familiarity gives the B'wavers what the *Oregonian* calls, *"An almost psychic connection in their comedy."* Since it is improvisational, the cast can incorporate anything about your company or event theme into the show. Brainwavers can also perform for any size group in nearly any venue, including conference rooms, banquet halls, auditoriums, cruise ships, and even outdoor picnics.

## What Happens in a Show?

A Brainwaves show consists of scenes based on suggestions from your audience. These may include a live-action soap opera based on the life of a favorite employee, the wit and wisdom of a two headed psychic, who can answer any question about the future of your company or a plethora of other improvised scenes that are geared to make you laugh. The show can be any length from 15 to 90 minutes and beyond.

## Who Has Already Booked a Brainwaves Show?

Corporations and colleges that have enjoyed our professional, inoffensive, and consistently funny brand of humor include: Nike, Columbia Sportswear, Starbucks Coffee Co., Leo Burnett, Indiana State University, Hewlett Packard, First Interstate Bank, Oregon Medical Association, PGE, Old Spaghetti Factory, Univ. of Nebraska, Minnesota State Fair, Port of Seattle, Toro, Creighton University, St. Mary's Academy, METRO, Wells Fargo, M-Financial, Deloitte & Touche and many more. Brainwaves has showcased at the Chicago Improv Festival and even performed with the Oregon Symphony to help answer the question, "Can Classical Music Be Funny?"

## Like to Check Out a Live Show?

Brainwaves performs regularly at the Electric Company Theater, 2512 SE Gladstone.
Call (503) 796-9550 for dates and passes.

**WE'LL MAKE YOU LAUGH!**

# CJ'S COUNTRY DANCE INSTRUCTION

**Want to Liven Up Your Event ?**
**Make Your Gathering a Memorable One**

**Energetic Country Western Dance Instruction**
**to get your party up and Boot Scootin'**

Web site: www.cjscountrydance.com
Contact: Connie Jo Collins (360) 892-1406 or E-mail: conniejo@cjscountrydance.com

---

If you're looking for entertainment and the opportunity for socializing during your event, Country Dance Lessons are just the ticket.

Country Western Dance is fun and easy to learn. Choose Partner or Line Dances.

No group is too large or too small. Experience teaching groups of 400+ at one time.

## EXPERIENCE:

Connie Jo specializes in instruction for the beginning level student. She has been teaching Country Dance since 1985 at weekly lessons, conventions, corporate and community events, graduation parties, wedding receptions, private family parties and more.

**WEBSITE:** www.cjscountrydance.com

**FOR RATES:** Contact Connie Jo Collins (360) 892-1406 or
E-Mail: conniejo@cjscountrydance.com

## LOOKING FOR COUNTRY MUSIC FOR YOUR EVENT?

Live Country Bands: The Buckles, Cross Country, Last Rodeo Band & more contact ConnieJo
D.J.: Rich's Porta-Party – Specializing in Country and Vintage Rock & Roll (503) 621-3074

*Office:*
*3308 East Burnside Street*
*Portland, Oregon 97214*
*Contact: Patrick Short*
*503.236.8888*
*Fax 503.235.6291*

***Regular performances:***
*Fridays and Saturdays at The ComedySportz Arena*
*1963 N.W. Kearney Street • Portland*
*Web site: www.portlandcomedy.com*

---

## Over 10 Years and 2000 Shows in Portland — But *What* is ComedySportz?

ComedySportz is competitive improvisational comedy — a battle of wits between two teams of professional "actletes" playing a variety of fast-paced scenes and games based on suggestions from your audience. It's funny, topical (your folks make all of the suggestions) and CLEAN! Seeing a ComedySportz match is like seeing a sporting event—energy, excitement, fan involvement — with the additional payoff of laughter. A referee is on-hand to explain games, get suggestions from the fans, time the action, and keep things clean. After the National Anthem, the coin is tossed and the action begins. You might see your boss portrayed as a Shakespearean hero, and an office problem solved as part of a Grand Opera, or a sales goal laid out as a Broadway musical. It could happen!

## What are Suitable ComedySportz Events?

Corporate or office parties, picnics, sales promotions, customer conferences, trade shows, project wind-ups — because we are so portable and flexible, we can play in almost any event or space you dream up. ComedySportz is suitable for all audiences — we're sensitive to your needs and we understand that laughter doesn't have to come at the expense of members of your audience. Because ComedySportz is funny without making fun of who people are, we are the only comedy entertainment truly appropriate for professional settings. Planners from such companies as Tektronix, Pacificorp, Coca-Cola, Good Samaritan Ministries, Mentor Graphics, Intel, Hewlett-Packard, Legacy, Verizon Wireless, Providence, Standard Insurance, Boyd's Coffee and the Oregon Food Bank have looked like geniuses by choosing ComedySportz.

## This Sounds Interesting and Fun—But How Can I Be Sure?

See a regular ComedySportz show! We perform each Friday and Saturday at The Comedy Sportz Arena in Northwest Portland. Make a reservation by calling 503.236.8888 and bringing this Bravo! Resource Guide along. Not only will one of our "actletes" gladly autograph it, but you'll get two free tickets to check us out and have a blast! See for yourself!

## Group Unity Training Seminars (G.U.T.S.)

Group Unity Training Seminars are powerful tools for the competitive business landscape. It's one thing to want a strong team that can take advantage of opportunity — it takes G.U.T.S. to make it happen! We've built powerful teams with our clients and customers in hundreds of situations over the past 20 years. The process is fun and the results are real. We tailor half-day, full day and series to meet your objectives, to help you become a focused, improvising organization. Check our website and call us to find out how — 503.236.8888.

speaker

# *GAIL HAND*

*The Power of Laughter*

**humorist**

*3439 N.E. Sandy Blvd. #104 • Portland, Oregon 97232*
*503-284-2342*
*E-mail:gail@gailhand.com*
*www.gailhand.com • www.thepoweroflaughter.com*

---

**Wouldn't it be great if your program was full of useful content AND was really funny?**

Visit Gail's Interactive Website: **www.thepoweroflaughter.com**

Gail is the author of *The Power of Laughter, Seven Secrets to Living and Laughing in a Stressful World.*

Gail utilizes her years of comedy experience in her program. Audiences rave about her interactive, upbeat style of humor.

## The Power of Laughter Topics

- *Seven Secrets to Living and Laughing Every Day*
- *21 Secrets Guaranteed to Make you Irresistible to Your Prospects*
- *How to Laugh Your Way to More Productivity and Profit*
- *Creative Ways to Honor and Celebrate Differences*
- *How to Put Laughter to Work in the Workplace*
- *Seven Secrets to Living and Laughing in Health Care*

*"Our emergency department loved her interactive program!"*
*— Meeting Planner, OHSU*

**Certified Laughter Leader with the World Laughter Tour**
**Add a Laughter Yoga Program to your next event!!**

**Toll free (888) 664-4904**

**Email: greg@gregbennick.com**

**Website: www.gregbennick.com**

---

## Juggler — Unicyclist — Comedian — Emcee

Greg Bennick is the most versatile entertainer in the Pacific Northwest. Able to perform stage shows, strolling, or appear as a Master of Ceremonies, Greg is an interactive comedian who blends an incredible variety of skills with a thorough knowledge of the corporate marketplace. Read on to discover more about the Pacific Northwest's best "corporate comedic strategist."

### Client specific...

Whether riding a six foot unicycle or juggling seven balls, Greg makes sure that his comedy and overall delivery are interwoven with the initiatives and messages that the client wants conveyed. Greg meets with all clients in advance of the event, preferably onsite, in order to understand completely what the purchaser has in mind.

### Corporate "safe"...

Always tasteful, Greg's humor is crafted with corporate audiences in mind. His dynamic stage presence and amazing skills have been a hit with Microsoft, Boeing, Timex, Sheraton Hotels, State Farm Insurance, Planet Hollywood, Remington, Nike, AT&T, Pfizer, FAO Schwartz, Nintendo, and hundreds of others since 1983.

### Always professional...

Greg Bennick is committed to providing quality entertainment. His shows are backed by a $2,000,000 insurance policy. Meeting planners will find working with Greg to be a breeze. His show is entirely self contained and includes a full sound system. He is always willing to go the extra distance to ensure a successful event.

### Proven success!

*"Our 300 attendees were thoroughly entertained by your performance, as evidenced by the STANDING OVATION at the conclusion of your show!"*

—Steven L. Sanderson, United Way of America

**Call for a full promotional packet, references, or to reserve dates.**

**PO Box 86474**
**503-788-3826**
**Portland, OR 97286**
**www.pdxentertainment.com**

---

***PDX Entertainment*** PDX Entertainment is constantly working to be the best entertainment planning service in the Northwest! Our experience makes PDX Entertainment the favorite of Oregon and Washington's premier companies and events. We offer valuable planning assistance including:

- **Entertainment Contracting**
- **Scheduling**
- **Theme Development**
- **Custom Mascots & Costumes**
- **Stage Management**
- **Technical Assistance**

***PDX Entertainment*** is the **"Perfect Pick for Professional Performances"**

- CLOWNS
- JUGGLERS
- STILT WALKERS
- BALLOON ARTISTS
- FACE PAINTERS
- MAGICIANS
- UNICYCLISTS
- HYPNOTISTS
- BELLY DANCERS
- FIRE EATERS
- COSTUMED CHARACTERS
- CELEBRITY IMPERSONATORS
- GAME SHOWS
- MUSIC AND MORE!

We specialize in finding the perfect performers for any event. Our pledge is to find your event the highest quality entertainment at the most economical price. We work hard so you don't have to! We ask the right questions to ensure a hassle free event. At ***PDX Entertainment*** your satisfaction is our goal!

**Pick the perfect performer online!**
**www.PDXEntertainment.com**
**Call us to get the party started!**
**503-788-3826**

# SANTA FOR HIRE

*(360) 693-8562*
*Web site: www.redraccoon1.com*
*E-mail: mail@redraccoon1.com*

Bring smiles to the faces of young and old as you let Santa into your heart and event this year!

Rob Figley doesn't just look like Santa, to thousands of children and adults in the Pacific Northwest, he IS Santa!!!

From his home in Vancouver, Santa Rob entertains businesses and families alike. Whether it is a corporate event, an office party, a neighborhood gathering or a family's home, nothing beats a visit from Santa! He is the merriest elf in town. Candy canes for all and a sit on Santa's lap will soften up even Scrooge!

Santa Rob is a non-denominational Christian minister who is ordained in the states of Oregon and Washington.

**Specializing in Company Christmas Parties,
Neighborhood Events and Home Visits!!!**

***It is NOT too early to call NOW
and get the date you want for your visit!!!***

*(206) 232-9129 www.steffansoule.com*
***magic@steffansoule.com***

---

**Fast-Paced Magic** guaranteed to succeed with the modern corporate audience!

**Steffan Soule's Magic** is recognized by a Kennedy Center Award. He has performed on National Television, and his work for corporate events is outstanding.

**Online Videos** at www.steffansoule.com provide quick access to numerous ways to include magic at special events.

**Online Price List** gives you all the details and simplifies your planning and producing process.

**Incredible Magic Shows** for all ages, close-up and on stage.

**Now serving Portland!** Offices in Seattle & Vancouver.

***When*** *Microsoft introduced Windows... when Lattice created an event for their upper management... when the Benson Hotel wanted to impress their corporate clients... when Nike needed interactive entertainment with no language barrier for their foreign customers, employees and press... when Paul Allen wanted to enliven a party, and when Bill Gates wanted a private show for Steve Balmer,* ***Steffan Soule's Magic was there.***

**(206) 232-9129**
**www.steffansoule.com * magic@steffansoule.com**

***Create an atmosphere of astonishment and wonder...***
Bring the **award-winning MAGIC** of **Tim Alexander** to your event!

Your audience will laugh with amazement as I perform **classics of magic** and **original tricks** manipulating balls, bills, coins, cards, rope, rings, and every day objects close-up or on stage. **Things will appear, multiply, transform, and vanish at my fingertips, *and in your guests' hands!***

**Strolling:** Close-up or table-to-table Magic is perfect for:
**• Receptions • Cocktails • Fairs • Buffets**

**Parlor Show:** Stand-up Magic is the ideal entertainment for:
**• Meetings • Banquets • Parties • Holiday Gatherings**

**Stage Show:** Marvelous for family audiences:
**• Sleight-of-Hand • Live Bunny! • Levitation • Music**

Your guests will be delighted by my visual artistry, tasteful music and 19th century styling. Mystery, humor and sleight-of-hand combine to create a uniquely entertaining and **unforgettable magical experience!**

**"Your tricks were original and unique...Truly top notch!"**
*–Kenny Ruffo, CoMotion Venture Capital*

**"Judging from the looks of awe and puzzlement, and the gasps of surprise, everyone who crossed paths with you enjoyed your amazing art."**
*–Nancy Buley, J. Frank Schmidt & Son Co.*

**"Thank you very much for providing such great entertainment...a pleasant delightful evening...As the organizer of the party, it was great to hear so many positive comments!"**
*–Kazuko Arai Mahoney, James Gray Co.*

**"...top local entertainer..."**
*–Portland Family Magazine*

# WORLD CHAMPION YO-YO ARTIST TOMMY MOORE

*800.368.1726 • 503.675.9300*

**www.yotom.com**

WaLk tHe DOG

**Over 1,000 professional performances since 1995**
**23 states from Oregon to the NY harbor**
**Entertainer • Humorist • Life of the Party**

- Spectacular yo-yo demonstration includes galaxy of world's best tricks
- Hands-on instruction — learn great yo-yo tricks
- Yo-yos have your logo, name and message imprinted on side — your choice of colors

## Call Tommy Moore for:

• After dinner entertainment • picnic • trade show • party • convention • cocktail hour • sporting event • award travel • sales meeting • cruise • festival • open house • tour • school

*"...trade show superstar!"*

– Mark Brandyberry, National Restaurant Association
Trade Show Chicago

*"The amazing Tommy Moore wowed onlookers with a combination of classic yo-yo tricks and cheerful patter."*

– David Shayt, Smithsonian Museum of American History
Washington D.C.

*"You were a smash! Thanks for making our science of toys a success."*

– Tracy Flynn, Oregon Museum of Science & Industry
Portland

*"It put a feather in my cap for hiring you."*

– Lindsay Martinez, Produce Marketing Association Trade Show
Atlanta

*"Best after dinner entertainer we've ever had!"*

– Vicki Long, COMSYS Inc.
Beaverton

**Call now...schedule fills fast**

# Notes

# Notes

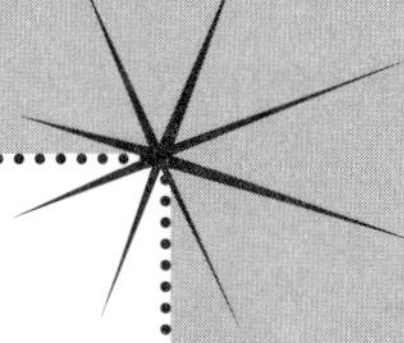

# Entertainment – Bands

# HIRING A BAND

**Deciding on a band:** Every band should have a music list available for you to review. This will be helpful in deciding on a band. You may want to ask if the band is currently playing somewhere, and then you can listen to their music live and observe their stage presence before you make a final decision.

**Reserving a band:** Reserve a band or orchestra for your event immediately, especially if the date of your affair falls during peak party seasons like Christmas or New Year's. Popular bands and orchestras are often reserved up to a year in advance.

**Written contract:** It is advisable to get a written contract stating exactly what you have agreed upon: date, number of hours, the total cost, and so on.

**Setup requirements:** The formality, facility, and size of your event will determine the type of music that is appropriate. Inquire about whether the site can accommodate dancing and has the area necessary for the musicians to set up and perform. Be very specific about getting the space and electrical requirements from the band so that you can accurately relay the information to your contact person at the facility.

**Cutoff hours:** When you make all the final arrangements with your facility, be sure to ask if they have any specified time limitations for music. Some facilities require that music be stopped as early as 10pm for the comfort of neighboring homes, businesses, or other guests.

**Background music and dancing music:** Remember when reserving your music that the first hour of your event is a time for introductions and mingling with guests. If your band begins playing immediately, you'll want to make sure that the music is background-type music that doesn't overwhelm and interfere with conversations. The band can be instructed or signaled to pick up the pace of the music for dancing at a certain time.

**NOTE:** Make sure your contract is sound, and that your event won't be bumped for a larger engagement. A deposit is usually required.

# A DANCING PENGUIN BAND

*(503) 282-3421 • www.AdancingPenguin.com*

---

## Sinatra & Swing, Rock, Motown & Disco!

Band leader, Kim Ralphs, has assembled an exciting group of professional musicians that play a wide variety of popular styles. Usually, they begin with tasty jazz instrumentals, and the romantic melodies of Gershwin, Cole Porter, and Duke Ellington.

For dancing, you'll enjoy Big-Band Swing, and sassy Latin versions of Glenn Miller and Harry Connick Jr. The band also offers Rat-Pack style vocal tributes to Dean Martin, Frank Sinatra and Tony Bennett.

For more excitement and variety, the band adds vocalist LaRhonda Steele. Her musical roots are in Gospel, and plainly evident in her dynamic and heartfelt renditions of Rock, R&B, Blues and Disco hits.

LaRhonda has sung with many of the finest bands in the area including the Swingline Cubs and the No Delay Band. She has appeared with "Boogie Cat" Norman Sylvester at the Mt. Hood Festival of Jazz, and Portland's Waterfront Blues Festival. LaRhonda regularly performs at the Candlelight Bar with the band, Ocean 503.

And if you're after a bigger sound, the band can add a three piece horn section (sax, trumpet, trombone). A lot of music in a medium sized group!

A Dancing Penguin Band has played all the finest hotels and country clubs in the area, and are often recommended by event planners and talent agents. With a thoroughly professional attitude, they will offer their experience to help make your event a success. They will gladly make announcements for you, and help coordinate your party. Standard attire is a Penguin suit (black tuxedos).

**LISTEN TO WHAT THE PROFESSIONALS SAY:**

*"The Penguins are fun...I always enjoy seeing them here."*
Dennis Yamnitsky, F&B Manager, **Oswego Lake Country Club**

*"They play here often, and always do a great job...highly recommended."*
Susan O'Neill, **Waverley Country Club**

*"All the music that I have listened to, over the years and all the conventions that I have gone to, I can truly say that this band was the best!"*
Colleen Greenen, Convention Sales Manager, **Portland Oregon Visitors Association**

*"Impeccably professional and experienced...a pleasure to work with."*
Nancy Tice, **Northwest Artist Management**

***Call for a free consultation and demo CD***
***Visa & Mastercard accepted***

**P.S. . . . We can add a DJ for even more variety! See page 291 under DJs.**

# Another Night with Johnny MARTIN

*www.johnnymartin.com*
*503.228.3620*

---

Whether coordinating a dance party or romantic dinner, this is the entertainer for your event!

***"Having been to many events, I can say it is unusual to see a dance floor packed all evening long. You make that happen. Your music is so danceable and you are so entertaining. You bring an energy, style and repertoire that really pulls a diverse guest list like ours together on the dance floor. Our guests in their 20's and those in their 70's had a wonderful time. Johnny, thank you so much. Working with you has been smooth as can be – a real pleasure. We have really appreciated your professionalism and good humor."***
— Meriss Sumrall CEO / The Library Foundation '04

***"Wonderfully Sinatra with just enough Johnny to keep you begging for more."***
— Lee Cline/Entertainment Director/Spirit Mtn.Casino 2003

***"Johnny Martin is a consummate entertainer, who brings life to the stage in a groovy style that combines the casual cool of a lounge act with the fun of big band showmanship."***
—Eric Cila/VISCOUNT BALLROOM '00

***"Just Fabulous!"***
—David Kahn/GM Indiana Pacers '99

A distinctive voice and playful stage presence put this slender vocalist at the top of agent's submission list. Imagine Frank Sinatra and Louis Prima rolled into one. Make your reservations early and let your clients know you care enough to book the best.

The fun begins with **Johnny Martin!**
**call Pacific Talent Agency 503.228.3620**

## Satisfied Client List:

**INTEL**
**SEVEN FEATHERS CASINO**
**MUSEUM AFTER HOURS**
**EUGENE CELEBRATION**
**SPIRIT MOUNTAIN CASINO**
**HEATHMAN HOTEL**
**ZOO LA-LA**
**VISCOUNT BALLROOM**
**MULTNOMAH ATHLETIC CLUB**
**CHINOOK WINDS CASINO**

## Partial Song List:

**LUCK BE A LADY**
**DAY IN, DAY OUT**
**JUST A GIGOLO**
**LET'S FALL IN LOVE**
**THE SUMMER WIND**
**JUMP, JIVE AN' WAIL**
**OLD DEVIL MOON**
**MACK THE KNIFE**
**L.O.V.E.**
**BEYOND THE SEA & MORE...**

# BYLL DAVIS & FRIENDS

(503) 644-3493

## Type of Music

Byll Davis & Friends offers complete flexibility in all styles and eras of music, including ethnic, Big Band, good time rock 'n' roll and Top 40.

## Instrumentation

Byll Davis can accommodate your needs with one to eight musicians. Dress is usually formal, but we'll dress to suit the occasion. Call for more details.

## Experience

Byll Davis has a master's degree in music, has participated in several successful road tours and has led and performed in bands that specialize in Big Band, rock 'n' roll, Top 40 and variety and society musical styles. The Byll Davis & Friends ensemble has performed in literally thousands of engagements locally for a wide variety of events and audiences.

## Musical Style and Audience Rapport

The following comments represent the kind of feedback Byll Davis & Friends receives:

*"Byll, you were fabulous as always and a delight to work with."*

*"It was the perfect band for the evening…many, many compliments from our guests."*

*"Your selections for our event were based on your ability to adjust and come through with what people like."*

*"Your music was so good it made it difficult to keep the outsiders from crashing in."*

## Free Consultation

If hiring a band is new to you, or if you want to find out more about Byll Davis & Friends, make an appointment to meet with Byll. The service is free, the information invaluable.

## Cost and Terms

Prices, space and electrical requirements will vary depending on the size of the band and location of engagement. Please call for additional information.

**RELIABLE**
**APPROPRIATE**
**PRICED RIGHT**
**FUN ! ! ! !**

**(503) 644-3493**

# Dance Machine™

**Lasting • Memorable • Events**

ph. 503.827.7370
fx. 503.590.6983
info@dancemachinetheband.com
www.dancemachinetheband.com

---

**Your entertainment will greatly impact your event**
**Let us engage your guests**

Adding live entertainment to your event may be the most important choice you make. Studies show guests stay longer if they enjoy the entertainment. Our music and interaction invites your guests to join the celebration.

## Music Variety

Dance Machine is a six-piece variety band that performs hit music spanning over six decades. Our music includes jazz standards, rhythm and blues, Motown, disco, rock and roll, top 40 and current chart hits. Our energy and enthusiasm is contagious and guests can't help but join us on the dance floor.

We play music for everyone and we craft our performance to fit the mood of your engagement. We can provide live easy listening music for things such as dinner or a cocktail hour – and when it is time to get your guests moving we are ready to provide the spark.

## Instrumentation

Our interactive and fun band features exceptional male & female lead vocals, rich vocal harmonies, tenor/soprano saxophone, keyboard/synthesizer, bass and guitar, drums and accent percussion. We bring all the elements to your event including sound and lighting equipment.

## Our Specialty

We have experience entertaining for events of all types and sizes including: private parties, fundraisers, corporate events, holiday parties, theme parties, wedding receptions and festivals. We can comfortably handle any indoor or outdoor venue. We understand the demands of a well-planned event. We will provide you a professional, tasteful, and polished performance.

## Services and Terms

We welcome you to use our PA for toasts, activities or announcements. We also provide Master of Ceremony services if you wish. Our pricing is extremely competitive and is determined by month, day, time, location and duration. Please call or email us to discuss Dance Machine's availability for your event.

*Visit Dance Machine on the Web*
*www.DanceMachineTheBand.com*
*listen to Mp3s, bios, testimonials, song list*

**Too cool for words. Simply, this is class entertainment.** David Cooley's onstage charm and blazing talent make his group one of the Northwest's most **diverse, fun** and **engaging** bands for receptions, dinner dances and major event entertainment. Together with an impressive repertoire of **swing** music, **R & B** vocals, **pop** standards and **rock & roll** classics, this charismatic performer constitutes the **perfect professional package**. Cooley knows his business, and whether providing subtle background music, festive reception entertainment, or a wide variety of dance music, he's got the right stuff. **Special requests are always welcome**.

## Experience

Hired entertainment can make or break an event. David Cooley has been responsible for successful events and receptions for 15 years. Cooley is a **champion-grade singer** and band leader with a canny sense of style and pace. His performance credits include venues in **Europe, Asia, Canada,** and throughout the **United States**.

## Instruments

From a **quartet, five, six, seven, or eight-piece group**, the David Cooley Band comes as you like it. These variations allow great flexibility in choosing the appropriate sound and style to compliment your event. **(Solo piano, duo & trio units also available.)**

## Special Services

David Cooley is an **accomplished Emcee**. On hand to make announcements, David is available to coordinate greetings and speeches by individuals from your group. We are happy to honor and humor any VIPs with special song requests.

## Cost and Terms

Pricing is flexible, according to the size of the band, venue and location. **Please contact our office for an estimate: (503) 227.1866 or (360) 693.1707**

## Credits

MassMutual • Oregon Symphony • Nat. Auto Dealers Assn. • Portland Street of Dreams
Microsoft • Seattle Street of Dreams • Nat. Public Power Assn. • OR State Fair • Clark Co. Fair
Nike • Multnomah Club • Pioneer Courthouse Square • Davis Wright Tremaine • ARCO Co.
Washington Athletic Club • Toyota Corp. • Boullion Aviation • Honeywell International
NW Natural • Oswego Lake Country Club • Columbia Tower Club • University Club
WSU Foundation • University of Portland • Crystal Ballroom • Lane Powell Spears Lubersky

***Planning an extraordinary event?***
***Call now: 503.227.1866 or 360.693.1707***
***The David Cooley Band has the magic to make it happen.***

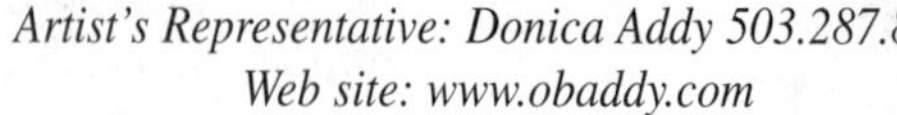


*Artist's Representative: Donica Addy 503.287.8729*
*Web site: www.obaddy.com*

**Share OB's Story:** Addy is a self taught percussionist from Ghana, West Africa. OB's (pronounced "O""B") first love of music is reggae and when he blends his traditional rhythms with the music he loves out comes a unique sound that is all his own. His artistry on the authentic drums of Africa has gained him a formidable reputation among musicians and audiences alike. In 1994, he formed I & I, Reggae inna Afrikan Stylee Band. Along with accomplished musicians, the six member band loves to entertain and delight audiences with their music. I & I means "us", you and me, giving equal respect to all. This is happy music with heartbeat drum and bass rhythms, and sweet soul lyrics and melodies. Instrumentation consists of Congas, percussion, saxophone, rhythm & bass guitars, drums, keyboards and vocals. People tell us all the time that they did not know they even liked reggae music until they heard us. So break out of your comfort zone and let the collective excitement of these musicians simply compel your audience to dance, sing or howl with delight.

**Type of Service:** We have thrilled audiences at ~ Corporate Events~ Private Parties~ Weddings~ Receptions ~Concerts~ Fundraisers~ Wineries~ Colleges~ Conventions~ Corporate Parties ~ Clubs~ Libraries~ So you can see, if you need music...no matter the type of event, OB has a way of designing the performance to fit perfectly for your needs. Making every performance unforgettable for your audience.

**Who Books Us:** I & I has opened or appeared with such reggae icons as Burning Spear, The Wailers, Lucky Dube, Jimmy Cliff, Culture, Toots & the Maytals, Desmond Dekker, Steel Pulse, Sister Carol, Meditations...and so many more, many having us back time and time again.

**Headlined or Performed:** Portland Trailblazers, Rose Quarter, ESPN, Oregon Convention Center, Bumbershoot, Bite of Portland (six years), World Nike Games, Street of Dreams, Oregon Country Fair, World Folklife Festival, NXNW tour, Pioneer Courthouse Square, Community Events, Salem Art Fair, Artquake, Crystal Ballroom, Roseland Theatre...I & I has performed thousands of shows to the accolades of thrilled audiences throughout the Pacific Northwest.

***"It is rare that we have a group which initiates such a GREAT response as we received to your performance. It was a fun evening for all."*** ~ Reed College Fine Arts Board

***"What the audience likes, he does more."*** ~ Positively Entertainment

***"What great, professional, sincere people that you are. The band was wonderful and Donica you're the best. The Power Is in the Drums."*** ~ Calvin Walker, Musician, Producer

**Worth Every Penny:** Prices are competitive yet flexible dependent on size of band, location, sound requirements and length of performance. Please contact us for an estimate.

**Other Notes of Interest:** OB also teaches and conducts drumming workshops. Performs with his Traditional African Drum and Dance Troupe, Wala, and he also DJs for events wanting reggae and world/ethnic music. OB's self titled CD is available and he is currently working on his next recording. Please call if you would be interested in any of these services.

# METRO

*Contact: Becky Stroebel*
*503-590-5840*
*www.sterlingtalent.com*

---

Experience the energy and excitement of METRO, Portland's new highly acclaimed all-star band, featuring music for all ages from easy listening jazz to dance tunes of the 90's.

**Style:** Metro's musical style is self-described as "Urban, R&B, Funk, Soul, Groove Music," but no matter how you define their musical format, people agree that Metro sets itself apart from other bands with their enthusiasm to carefully tailor each performance to the needs and preferences of their audiences.

**Flexibility:** Metro can expand from a five-piece group to a dazzling eight-piece show band at your request to fit varied budgets and room sizes.

**Experience:** Just a few of Metro's happy clients include Sunriver Resort, Kaiser Permanente, The 2004 Tigard Festival of Balloons, 2004 Newberg Old Fashioned Festival, 2004 Tualatin Crawfish Festival, 2004 Ft. Vancouver 4th of July Celebration, Nike Summerfest, Bacchus Restaurant, Inn At The Quay and many corporate, convention, wedding and private party clients.

*"We are a group that likes to dance and Metro had people on the dance floor from the very first song, straight through to the very last song."*

—Vickie Bowden, Healthcare Financial Management Association

*"The music really set the stage for a festive and fun atmosphere"*

—Jackie Personett, CCFA NW Chapter

*"Metro was a huge hit with our festival audience! They offered the perfect blend of high energy cover tunes and smooth jazz originals"*

—R. Johnson, Tigard Festival of Balloons

To hear a demo of this versatile band, please go to **WWW.STERLINGTALENT.COM**. Call Becky Stroebel today for a free promotional package and pricing information.

# NOAH PETERSON

*Contact: Peterson Entertainment*
*P.O. BOX 86066*
*Portland, Oregon 97286*
*503-703-9516*
*www.noahpeterson.com*

---

Noah Peterson plays jazz, the excitement he creates when playing is tangible; it passes through the audience; completing the circuit. The electric moment; where fact, fiction and fantasy fall away and the truth is revealed and reveled in, a celebration of the now; Jazz, real Jazz, good Jazz.

Saxophonist and band leader, Noah Peterson is a seasoned veteran of blues, rock, pop and military bands who offers a clear, true voice and a new vision. A true professional in every sense, his groups reflect his vision at the center of their improvisations. Turning pop tunes into jazz classics; polishing jazz standards into bright new gems. At home in any size venue from clubs to stadium concert stages, Noah's music will bring the best out of your event audience. Utilizing the best of the Northwest talent pool, Noah often features up and coming talents as well as regional stars. He is creative and flexible in assembling the right ensemble for your event. A few of the available combos are duo, trio, quartets and larger. His talented musicians offer the perfect balance to Peterson's fine horn playing; they are light to Noah's shadow, as they groove to the mystic depths of his untamed saxophone. Like the best high wire act these gentlemen perform without a net.

The repertoire embraces the best in jazz and popular music. Songs that touch and delight their audience come dancing from the horn of Noah Peterson. Romantic indigo moods to funky festivals of sound; the man makes every performance come alive with an inner fire his audiences never forget.

If you need a fun, professional act to enliven your upcoming event or celebration contact Noah Peterson today. Please remember that dates are confirmed with a first called, first served policy, so to make sure your dates are booked – don't delay.

**www.noahpeterson.com**

# PATRICK LAMB PRODUCTIONS

*Contact: Samantha Howie*
*(503) 335-0790; Fax (503) 892-0790*
*E-mail: samantha@patricklamb.com*
*www.patricklamb.com*

## Types of Music and Demo

Imagine the sound of sweet saxophone permeating the atmosphere of your event. Patrick is versatile and plays music appropriate for the occasion including jazz, blues, motown, 70s retro, disco and original music of his own. His invitation to play at the White House and appearances at major festivals around the U.S. have given his career momentum. His new release, *Sunshine Alley*, is commercially available. Patrick has a funky, versatile group which can tune itself for the needs of almost *any occasion*. From traditional, relaxed background jazz, needed for a dinner party, to '70s party down retro, funk, R&B and motown, Patrick's band is a consistent crowd-pleaser. Please call for a promotional package, demo tape and/or more information.

## Instrumentation and Personnel

High quality professional musicians including saxophone, male/female vocals, bass, drums, guitar, percussion, piano/organ as appropriate for the size and intimacy of the occasion.

## Experience

You might be familiar with Patrick's music from his many appearances which include: The Mount Hood Festival of Jazz, The Bite,Intel, IBM, Keiser Permanente, Sony Duplication, Lake Oswego Concert Series, Nordstrom, or the private parties he has played including one for FOX49. Or you might have heard his new "Top 10 in the Northwest" release on KINK. Patrick has also toured and recorded with recording artists Tom Grant and Grammy recipient Diane Schuur, opening at festivals for people like George Benson, Wynton Marseilles, Branford Marseilles, B.B. King, and many others. Patrick has experience in all aspects of the music business form touring, recording, and playing for all kinds of different occasions.

## Cost and Terms

Prices are competitive and computed on an individual basis depending on month, day, time, and length of engagement. Our PA and lighting systems are always available for your use. Call for quotations.

## Testimonials

*"Patrick Lamb's music adds so much to any event or to any venue. He is someone you want to follow and listen to wherever he plays. Any event or venue would greatly benefit from his appearance because of his reputation, his crowd appeal, and the draw that he brings in. Patrick Lamb is simply the greatest!"* —Teri Joly, Concentrex, Portland, OR

*"I want to thank you for your beautiful holiday performance at the White House. Your appearance helped to make our 1996 Christmas holiday program truly memorable."*
—Ann Stock, social secretary, White House, Washington, D.C.

## SWINGLINE CUBS

*1414 N.E. 115th Ave. • Vancouver, Washington 98684*
*Contact: Joe Millward (360) 254-3187 • Fax (360) 604-8392*
*E-mail: joe@swinglinecubs.com*
*Web site: swinglinecubs.com*

### Showmanship

The Swingline Cubs shows are designed to get the audience involved with the entertainers and work well for possible "theme" parties. Each show runs about an hour and fifteen minutes, and we can follow up the shows with a set or two of variety music for dancing. We use our own PA and lights as well as a follow spot for the shows. Here is a short description of our shows:

### Las Vegas Swing Show

Our Swing show, which is a Las Vegas style show featuring Michkael and Tarshene performing jazz standards mixed with newer pop tunes. We prefer to do this show in a "supper club" type atmosphere, utilizing a spotlight. Michkael and Tarshene leave the stage and walk amongst the audience, talking to them, getting them involved with the show. We dress in tuxedos with Michkael and Ruppert changing formal outfits during the show.

### 70's & 80's Show

This show really shows off Michkael's choreography skills. Covering tunes from the Disco 70's (KC and the Sunshine Band, Donna Summer, Barry White, Cool and the Gang...) to groups from the 80's (Journey, The Cars, Michael Jackson, Baby Face, Prince, etc...). Tarshene and Michkael's dance routines will have your audience screaming for more. Relive those 80's dance steps with us.

### Swingline Cubs Present "That Great Motown Sound"

Our third show is a Motown-R&B show featuring Michkael and Tarshene perfoming tunes from the 60's to 80's from The Temptations, Stevie Wonder, The Supremes and Smokey Robinson just to name a few. They get together and sing some great duets from Tammie Terrel and Marvin Gaye...We invite people to dance as it is impossible to sit still to this great dance music!

### Experience

In the last 15 years, we have played for well over 1,000 events of all kinds. Our client list includes: Portland Trail Blazers, Peter Jacobsen Productions, Oregon Symphony, Hewlett Packard, NIKE, Intel, Jantzen, Boys and Girls Aid Society, American Cancer Society, Doernbecher Children's Hospital, Komen Foundation, University of Oregon, Oregon Health Sciences University, University of Portland, Mayor Vera Katz, Portland Oregon Visitors Association, Reed College, The Bite, Rose Festival, Fort Vancouver Fourth of July, FEI Corporation, Merrill-Lynch… and hundreds more.

### Personnel and Instrumentation

The "Cubs" are a continuously rehearsed, eight-piece, same-member band. Exceptional vocalist, Tarshene Daugherty, is featured with Michkael Bateman. Instrumentation includes piano/organ/snythesizer, trumpet/flugelhorn, sax/flute, guitar, bass and drums.

### Cost and Terms

Prices are always competitive. Please call for a quotation.

# Notes

# Notes

# Entertainment – Consultants

BravoPortland.com

"The Best Party Bands!"

Casino Parties

Viva Mexico Mariachi

# CELEBRATION MUSIC & EVENTS

*6916 S.E. 17th Avenue*
*Portland, Oregon 97202*
*Contact: Peggy or Michael Winkle*
*(503) 234-2492; Fax (503) 233-0835*

***E-mail:***
*info@cmevents.com*
***Web site:** www.cmevents.com*

---

Celebration Music & Events has been providing quality entertainment to the Northwest since 1980. We represent nearly 600 local and regional acts ranging from Acrobats to Zydeco bands and have had the pleasure of working with many fine corporations.

Since 1980 we have had the pleasure of working with many fine corporations, clubs and organizations such as these: Nike, Hilton Hotels, Marriott Hotels, United Grocers, Oswego Lake Country Club, OHSU, Muscular Dystrophy Assn., Hewlett Packard, Waverley Country Club, Doernbecher Children's Hospital, Portland Junior League, Assistance League of Portland, Adidas Corporation, The University Club, Mentor Graphics and many more.

## Partial Artist Roster (A complete listing @ www.cmevents.com)

**Variety Bands:** Pressure Point, Swingline Cubs, Power of Ten, Design, Patrick Lamb Band, 24-7, Caramel Chocolates, Nuance, SLAM, Two Much and more.

**Big Band/Swing:** Lily Wilde, Art Abrams, Woody Hite, HB Radke & The Jet City Swingers, Johnny Martin and more.

**Blues:** Lloyd Jones, Paul Delay, Linda Hornbuckle, Curtis Salgado, Norman Sylvester and more.

**Country:** The Derailers, The Countrypolitans, Shorty & The Mustangs, Sam Hill and more.

**Jazz:** Dan Balmer, Tom Grant, Tall Jazz, Rebecca Kilgore, Marilyn Keller, Patrick Lamb, The Cool Set, Michael Allen Harrison, The Woolies and more.

**Show Bands:** Hit Explosion, Body & Soul, Johnny Limbo & The Lugnuts, The Retros, Pepe' & The Bottle Blondes, The Beatniks, M-PACT and more.

**Original & Specialty Musical Acts:** Pink Martini, Higher Ground, Curare, The Instigators, 3 Leg Torso, The Clumsy Lovers, Billy's Brass Band, The Trail Band, The Dickens Carolers and more.

**Ethnic Musical Acts:** Reggae, Greek, Calypso, African Drum, Steel Drum, Mariachi, Klezmer, Salsa, Polka, Polynesian, Cajun/Zydeco, Native American and more.

**Solo Musicians & Classical:** Piano, Organ, Violin, Harp, Accordion, String Quartets and more.

**Miscellaneous Entertainment Options:** Comedians, DJ Service, Karaoke, Casinos, Game Show To Go, Interactive Games, Portable Golf, Magicians, Clowns, Celebrity Impersonators, Digital Photography, Fortune Tellers, Numerologists, Fire Breathers, Santa Claus, Mother Goose, Balloon Artists, Face Painters, Caricaturists and more.

Let the dedicated professionals at Celebration Music & Events help you with all of your entertainment needs. Let's work together and make your event the best that it can be! For more information, call us at **(503) 234-2492** or visit our web site @ **www.cmevents.com.**

# Northwest Artist Management

## Musicians, Concerts & Fine Events

*Contact: Nancy Anne Tice (503) 774-2511; Fax (503) 774-2511*
*E-mail: nwartmgt@bigplanet.com; Web site: www.nwam.com*

---

Since 1989 Northwest Artist Management has been proud to offer the finest in Classical, Jazz and International music for Concerts, Corporate Entertaining and Fine Occasions of all kinds. From Arias to Zydeco, soloists to elegant dance bands and hot jazz ensembles, we can accommodate just about any entertainment need or musical preference, including assistance with technical details.

**EXCLUSIVELY REPRESENTING RUPPERT BLAIZE**

### THEME PARTIES ARE OUR SPECIALTY

We are knowledgeable about all music, from the **Grand Baroque** period to the hottest **Top 40**. We coordinate the musical entertainment, food and decorations to create exciting and memorable events and sizzling nights on the dance floor.

All of the artists on our roster are gifted, polished professionals with many years of experience helping our clients "custom-design" every detail of their musical needs. We are available to consult with you personally to help select the perfect ensemble and repertoire that will create and enhance the mood and ambiance of your event and accommodate the needs of your guests. Call for free promotional literature, demo CDs.

### DANCE BANDS

**You name it, we've got it:** from Swing to Vintage Rock-n-roll, Motown, Funk, R&B, Latin, Blues, Country, Caribbean, Folk, Top 40 and Variety. **Featuring Ruppert Blaize.**

### INTERNATIONAL ROSTER

**Go ahead, use your imagination!** African and Cuban Rhythms, Caribbean, Reggae and Steel Pan bands, Brazilian, Latin, Salsa, Irish, Italian, Mexican, Klezmer and Israeli, Cajun/Zydeco, Bagpipes, Flamenco, Medieval and Renaissance, Blues, Bluegrass, Hawaiian, German Oompah, Dixieland, and Barbershop Quartets. **Featuring THE BRIDIES, the fiery dueling fiddles from Michael Flatley's *Lord of the Dance* and *Riverdance shows.***

### WESTERN ENTERTAINMENT

**Put the Yahoo into your next Western Night Party!** Old Time Fiddlers, Honky-Tonk Piano, Singing Cowboys, Bluegrass and Jug Bands, Folk Ensembles with Folk/Square Dance Callers, Country/Rock Bands with Line Dance Instructors and Lewis & Clark Speakers, and musical programs with **The Trail Band.**

### JAZZ and CABARET THEATER

Elegant, sparkling after-dinner entertainment highlighting the magical memories of Broadway, Hollywood, the Symphony Pops, and the Big Band Era of the 30s, 40s and 50s. Soloists to 18-piece Big Bands. Vocalists, Latin, Mainstream Standards, and the finest in contemporary Jazz for listening and dancing. **FEATURING JOHN ENGLISH, *"THE VOICE,"* who sings a TRIBUTE TO FRANK SINATRA.**

### ALSO

Many Classical favorites such as String Quartets, Harps, Small Chamber Ensembles, Strolling Musicians, DJs, Caricature Artists, Clowns, Magicians, Comedians, and much, much **MORE**...

**MEMBER OF:**

POVA, Jazz Society of Oregon, North Clackamas Chamber of Commerce, Convention and Visitors Bureau of Washington County.

# PACIFIC TALENT INC.

*5410 SW Macadam Avenue, Suite 280 • Portland, Oregon 97239 USA*
*(503) 228-3620; Fax (503) 228-0480*
*E-mail: inbox@pacifictalent.com • Web site: www.pacifictalent.com*

***Total Entertainment and Event Production Services since 1975***

## ARTIST ROSTER (Partial List)

**Northwest Recording Artists:** Pink Martini • Curtis Salgado • Linda Hornbuckle • Stephanie Schneiderman • Craig Carothers • Paul deLay • Lloyd Jones • Aaron Meyer • Duffy Bishop • Terry Robb • Rubberneck • Quarterflash • Sequel • Colorfield

**Jazz &World Music:** Tom Grant • Michael Allen Harrison • Boka Marimba • Mary Kadderly • Obo Addy • Bobby Torres Ensemble • Mariachi Viva Mexico • Ron Steen • Mel Brown • Tall Jazz • Dan Balmer • Balafon • Darrell Grant • Sam Bamboo • Sandin Wilson

**Country:** Misty River • McKenzie River • Tim Schneider • Up Country • The Last Rodeo Band • Melody Guy

**Variety:** Nuance • Swingline Cubs • Night Flight • Design • The Antics • Opus 5 • PDX • Wiseguys • Two Much • Metro • Off The Record

**Big Band Swing:** Woody Hite Big Band • The Broadway 9 • Art Abrams Swing Machine

**Special Attractions:** Johnny Martin • The Trail Band • Super Diamond • Pepe & The Bottle Blondes • Hit Explosion • The Beatniks • Johnny Limbo & The Lugnuts • Riverboat Jazz Band • The Dickens Carolers • Soul Vaccination • Joe Stoddard • 5 Guys Named Moe • The Alderwood Strings • Billy's Brass Band • Lions Of Batucada • m-pact • The Retros • The Suffering Gaels • The Coats • 3 Leg Torso • Patrick Lamb Band • Cool Ade • Sneakin Out • Tim Ellis and Jim Walker • Billy Scene & The Kooltones

**Miscellaneous:** Comedians • DJ and Karaoke • Family Entertainment • Magicians and Illusionists • Keynote Speakers and Seminars • Murder Mysteries

## NATIONAL ARTISTS *for Conventions and Corporate Events* (Partial List)

B.B. King • George Benson • Chicago • Natalie Cole • Harry Connick Jr.• Sheryl Crow • Chris Isaak • Lyle Lovett • Kenny Loggins • Dixie Chicks • Manhattan Transfer • Donna Summer • Peter Paul & Mary • Bonnie Raitt • The Pointer Sisters • Earth, Wind & Fire • Rita Rudner • James Taylor • The Temptations • Shania Twain • Smokey Robinson • Jerry Seinfield • Bruce Horsby • Willie Nelson • Huey Lewis • The Smothers Brothers

## SPECIAL EVENTS

We work with only the most talented and world-class performers to provide you with the experience of a lifetime. Phenomenal headliners, exciting dance bands, fantastic comedians, charming interactive characters and fully staged and choreographed musical and theatrical stage shows are all sure to captivate your audience. We pride ourselves on providing a diverse set of ideas for our clients. For corporate events, conventions, fundraisers, receptions or private parties, we are the experts in making your event a very special and memorable occasion.

## BIO — ANDY GILBERT

Andy Gilbert established Pacific Talent Inc. in 1975. Since then, he has guided the company to become the largest talent-booking agency in Oregon. Andy has produced numerous corporate events, conventions, and festivals throughout the Northwest for 500 to 250,000 persons in attendance. Andy is experienced and knowledgeable with regard to available talent and industry acquisition procedures, all associated talent production requirements, full event production budgeting and accounting, and media relations.

High Street

Bob Miller's Almost All-Star Band

Michael John

*P.O. Box 231059*
*Tigard, Oregon 97281*
*Becky Stroebel, President*
*Phone: 503-590-5840*
*www.sterlingtalent.com*
*email:sterlingtalent@aol.com*

## 6 excellent reasons why should you call Sterling Talent to help you with your next event :

1. **We do not believe Customer Service is a thing of the past.** Your business is important to us, and top quality entertainment options combined with detailed customer service is the reason you should choose Sterling Talent over our competitors.
2. **Creative and refreshing new ideas are our specialty.** We want to get to know you and help you discover innovative new entertainment ideas that can make your event unique and memorable.
3. **Picky, picky, picky**...yes, the rumor is true. We are one of the most discriminating agencies in the business. If we recommend a band or artist for your event, you can bank on the fact that they are top flight professionals with a desire to make your event a success in every way.
4. **Whatever your budget, we have entertainment options your company will rave about!**
5. **One stop shopping...**in today's hectic world, we can simplify yours! We are happy to help you handle everything from entertainment ideas to catering, event planning, flowers, sound and light production, staging and decorations.
6. **We are the exclusive agency representing 3 of the West Coast's top acts...**
   Portland's favorite Radio star, **Bob Miller and His Almost All-Star Band** – this high energy 8 piece show band, complete with a 4 piece horn section, 2 lead singers, and Bob himself offers a long list of funk driven dance hits from the 60's and 70's.

   **High Street Band** – If you haven't seen this spectacular 10 piece, in your face, Jazz, Swing, R&B and variety show extravaganza...what are you waiting for? Check out their video on our web site.

   **Michael John** – Refreshingly hilarious and musically gifted, this popular entertainer artfully blends his gift of music with his ability to manipulate your guests into becoming part of the show. Be prepared to laugh, sing and look like a hero for booking such a spectacular and memorable entertainer for your event.

Finally...**don't take our word for it! See for yourself** why Sterling Talent, Inc. should be your first choice in entertainment ideas. Go to **WWW.STERLINGTALENT.COM**, click on any of the artist's pictures, and get ready to listen to page after page of reasons why Sterling Talent has more satisfied clients than any entertainment agency in the Pacific NW.

Call for your free consultation today!

Bands • Musicians • Comedy • National Acts • Speakers
Novelty Acts • Theme Parties • Wedding Music

# Notes

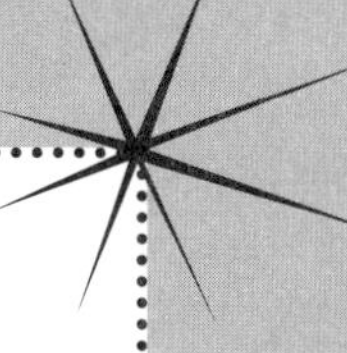

# Entertainment – Disc Jockeys

# HIRING A DISC JOCKEY

**Deciding on a disc jockey:** Be sure to meet with disc jockeys in person. Make sure the person you meet is the one you are hiring for your event. Ask to see the equipment and portfolios or presentations of their shows so you know what to expect. If they do more than one show per day, check to make sure they have the appropriate equipment setups for two or more shows. The disc jockey should be able to provide you with a list of music available so that you can pre-select favorites you want played. Be sure there is a good mix of music so that people of all ages can enjoy and participate.

**Written contract:** It is advisable to get a written contract stating exactly what you have agreed upon: date, number of hours, types of equipment, who will be doing the show, the total cost, what is included, and so on.

**Emcee:** Be sure to ask whether your disc jockey can act as the emcee at your event. This will help the event flow smoothly.

**Volume of music:** With your disc jockey, discuss the selection of music you would like, as well as the volume at which it should be played. Keep the volume of music low for the first hour of your event, allowing guests to mingle and ensuring that the sound level is comfortable for older guests. Then when the dancing begins, the volume can be increased.

**Setup requirements:** Inquire about whether the site can accommodate dancing. Find out whether your disc jockey needs early access to the room and what the space and electrical requirements are. Make sure your facility contact knows about these needs and that they can be met.

**Cutoff hours:** When you make all the final arrangements with your facility, be sure to ask if they have any specified time limitations for music. Some facilities require that music be stopped as early as 10pm for the comfort of neighboring homes, businesses, or other guests.

**Special effects and requests:** Most disc jockeys are glad to play special songs if they are requested. Also inquire about any special effects they can supply, such as lighting, strobes, mirror balls, and fog.

# A DANCING PENGUIN MUSIC

## LIVE MUSIC & DJ

*(503) 282-3421 • www.ADancingPenguin.com*

**LIVE PIANO WITH A DJ WILL MAKE YOUR EVENT SPECIAL!**

---

Since 1989, we have built a great reputation with superb customer service and attention to detail. Over half of our clients come to us from referals. We listen to you!

Playing the right song at the right time keeps the dance floor full and your guests happy. Swing, country, rock, disco, 80's, current hits or oldies, it's up to you!

You'll have total control of music styles and volume.

We can e-mail you a songlist, and let you pick every tune. Or you can tell us your favorite recording artists, and we'll do the rest.

Master of ceremonies and help coordinating your event are included.

Black tuxedo is standard attire (Penguin suit).

Ceremony music a specialty. Free demo CD, or check our website.

Also available: electric piano, sax, flute, cello, drums, and vocalists.

## LISTEN TO WHAT THE PROFESSIONALS SAY:

*"The Penguins are fun DJs. I always enjoy seeing them here."*
Dennis Yamnitsky, F&B Manager, **Oswego Lake Country Club**

*"They play here often, and always do a great job...highly recommended."*
Susan O'Neil, **Waverley Country Club**

*"Whenever I need a DJ, A Dancing Penguin Music is the first company I call."*
Nancy Tice, **Northwest Artist Management**

*"The piano and DJ combination really adds a touch of class to your event."*
Charlotte Seybold, event planner, **Special Occasion Consulting**

***Call for a free consultation and demo CD!***
***Visa and Mastercard welcome***

**See page 271 for details on "A Dancing Penguin Band".**

503.295.2212

WWW.DEEJAYENTERTAINMENT.COM

SPECIALIZING IN WEDDINGS

---

## Type of Music

DeeJay Entertainment can play a wide variety of music at your special event, including Top 40, Country, 70s/80s Retro, Classic Rock, and Oldies. Every crowd is different and every event is unique. DeeJay Entertainment reacts with the appropriate selections every time.

## Experience

DeeJay Entertainment is fortunate to represent some of the most experienced and professional disc jockeys available in the Portland Metro area. Our dedicated and professional entertainers take pride in the success of each and every event. DeeJay Entertainment is owned and operated by radio stations: Z100, K103, 105.9 The River, 1190 KEX, and AM620 KPOJ.
Our relationship with these stations brings a higher level of credibility and professionalism to our performances. You can feel confident when you choose us to play at your event.

## Demo

The most complete information is available on our web site, **www.deejayentertainment.com**. In addition to packages and rates, you will also find a sample song list and comments from customers who have used our service.

## Cost and Terms

Each package is designed to give you exactly what you are looking for from your DJ. DeeJay Entertainment wedding packages include the DJ, a state-of-the-art sound system, and a cordless microphone. Rates start as low as $295. We can also provide music at your wedding ceremony.

**PROFESSIONAL...**
**EXPERIENCED...**
**RECOMMENDED...**

Most of the events scheduled with DeeJay Entertainment are referrals, so we encourage you to check on availability as soon as you have set a date. We invite you to call with questions or schedule an appointment with one of our representatives.

*Experience you can trust*

***503.331.9195***
*Toll-Free 866.530.1110*
*www.prodjsoregon.com*

---

- When calling PRO DJs Oregon, you will talk personally to owner Chris Taylor, who has over **25 years experience** in the entertainment industry. Chris will answer all your questions, putting you at ease and providing you with tools to create your best possible event.
- Upon selecting PRO DJs Oregon you will have phone and email **access to your DJ** in preparation for your event. Our DJ's are experienced, attentive, professional, and personable...some with international DJ experience.
- Consider PRO DJs Oregon for all your DJ services: Weddings, corporate functions, commitment ceremonies, community and church events, school events, private parties, and emcee.
- Our **interactive web site** allows you to plan your event with our user-friendly **event planner**.
- Also see our web site for rates, music list, references, and our **Satisfaction Guarantee**.

**PRO DJs Oregon.**

**Consistent, Reliable, Experience You Can Trust.**

Visa and MasterCard welcome.

Call us or visit our web site at prodjsoregon.com

Professional Shows for All Occasion

Extensive Musical Selections

# SAILING ON PRODUCTIONS

*8207 N.E. 95th Street • Vancouver, Washington 98662*
*Tel/Fax 360-892-9701 /Cell 360-608-0677*
*E-mail: rocky@rockyrhodes.com; Web site: www.sailingonproductions.com*

---

## Type of Music

With over 2,000 CDs and 25,000-plus karaoke songs, (over 11,000 in English and 14,000 in other languages), Rocky & Associates can provide music from all eras as well as ethnic music (i.e. Hispanic, Japanese, Hawaiian, Italian, Jewish, Greek, many other Asian languages, German, Irish, etc.). Theme shows are Rocky's specialty.

## Equipment

With a state-of-the-art system, which includes special effects, sound and lighting, Rocky can cater your look and sound to be intimate or Vegas-style. Designed to fit in all settings with a look of class, professionalism is the word.

## Experience

A Pacific Northwest tradition since 1983 and having performed nationally since the 1960s, Rocky brings years of experience to every event. Rocky has a resume and portfolio to prove why he can be versatile enough for birthdays, anniversaries, weddings, divorce parties (yes! I have played them), bar mitzvahs, bat mitzvahs, family gatherings, quinceaneras and corporate events.

## Cost and Terms

A basic charge of $500 will give you up to five hours of entertainment with no extra charge for setup or travel, unless the event is outside the Portland/ Vancouver area. The distance will determine the travel fee. Any show for less than three hours can be negotiated. Overtime is $50 an hour. A 50% nonrefundable deposit is required in advance to hold the date and the cost includes all sound, lighting and karaoke.

## Settings and Requirements

There is no setting too demanding for this show. The only needs are one electrical outlet (two would be beneficial), and a space of at least 8x10 ft.

## Versatility

The uniqueness to Rocky's show is his versatility and one-on-one service to each client. No two shows are exactly alike, and the ability to adapt to each client's need has made him marketable worldwide. No request is too difficult, and if we don't have it, you can bring it to be played. Only the client's satisfaction is the main concern of Sailing On Productions.

For further details and/or booking arrangements, please contact
ROCKY RHODES at the above listed address and/or telephone numbers.
Online information also available.

**ULTIMATE ENTERTAINMENT**
**Portland's Premier**
**Full Service DJ Company**
*916 S.E. 29th*
*Portland, Oregon 97214*
*(503) 234-3055, (888) 332-6246*
*E-mail: Claraswe@Sprynet.com*
*Web site: www.ultimatedjs.com*

**Find Us On The Web: ultimatedjs.com**

## Type of Music

We feel strongly about giving you the right music. Songs that are proven to get your guests up and dancing. That's why we provide you with a catalog of the biggest party songs of all time. Choose from any era…Big Band, Country, '50s & '60s, '70s & '80s, R&B, Top 40, Classic Rock and more! All music is on compact disc to provide clear digital sound. Special requests are always welcome.

## Equipment

What's great music without great sound? At Ultimate Entertainment, we use sound systems that contain the finest audio components available. Sound checks are made before guests arrive to ensure excellent sound at every location, both indoors and out. We have a wireless microphone at every event for your convenience. For nighttime functions, a dazzling array of lighting is an option you may choose to enhance your celebration. From the smallest backyard to the largest banquet hall, Ultimate Entertainment has the equipment to handle any situation effectively and efficiently.

## Experience

Ultimately, it's our people that make the difference. When you choose Ultimate Entertainment, you get more than a DJ, you get our 15 years of experience, quality, and professionalism. We entertain and energize your guests. We play your style of music, handle your activities, and make all of your announcements.

## Cost and Terms

Our price is based on a four hour event. This includes cocktail/dinner music and dance music. Dance floor lighting is available for an additional charge. Only a $100 nonrefundable deposit holds your date. Please call us to learn more about availability and price information.

## Special Services

Our disc jockeys are trained event coordinators and will handle your special activities during your event. Whether you are looking for an "interactive host" or a "low key DJ," our DJs can help you with your function. Ultimate Entertainment also has: mobile game shows, karaoke, special effect lighting, fog machines, snow machines, and party kits (novelty items… leis, sunglasses, inflatable guitars, saxophones, and beach balls).

**THE ULTIMATE ENTERTAINMENT FOR YOUR…**

Holiday Party
Awards Banquet
Retirement Party
Grand Opening
Company Picnic
Convention
Theme Party
Trade Show

# Notes

# Entertainment – Musicians

# *Harpist Ellen Lindquist*

*(503) 626-4277*
*E-mail: harpmuse@aol.com*
*Web site: www.bravoevent.com/or/ellenlindquist*

© Adams & Faith Photography

## DISCOVER THE AMBIANCE AND ELEGANCE OF HARP MUSIC AT YOUR NEXT SPECIAL EVENT

### Types of Music

Harp music adds elegance and magic to any event. Ellen's repertoire spans many decades to include Classical, Love Songs, Movie Themes, Show Tunes, Oldies and New Age. Her repertoire ensures each celebration is personal, unique and will create the desired ambiance for any occasion.

### Harp Music is Perfect for

- Awards/Recognition Ceremonies
- Board Functions
- Sales Milestones
- Receptions
- Holiday Parties
- Banquets
- Retirement Parties
- Fundraising

### Experience

With over 20 years of professional experience, Ellen knows what her clients want and expect. She has played at hundreds of functions in the Portland/Vancouver area and will work with you to blend the music with the type of event. She has played with the Columbia Symphony, Portland Chamber Orchestra, Eugene Symphony, Oregon Festival of American Music, Ernest Bloch Music Fest and Peter Britt. Her experience includes working on cruise ships, hotels in Japan and she has played with celebrities from Kenny Rogers to the Moody Blues. She was trained at the Julliard School of Music in New York and California State University Northridge.

## LET HARP MUSIC CREATE THAT EVERLASTING MEMORY

Call for a free brochure, references and prices.

# GEORGE MITCHELL

Piano ❖ Keyboards
503-239-5223
503-230-0129 Fax
*www.georgemitchellmusic.com*

## Types of Music

**George Mitchell** delivers some of the best jazz piano throughout the region's most popular venues. He is a superb pianist, whose musical knowledge and style spans jazz, pop, classics and standards.

Mitchell is the keyboardist of choice for virtually every Northwest band leader, and for guest artists performing with the Portland Symphony or acts booked at local jazz venues and festivals. In 2004, Mitchell was invited to perform at the prestigious **10 Grands Concert**, and is featured on the lively compilation CD of top pianists from around the USA. In 2003, Mitchell released his long-awaited second CD ***Play Zone*** – a collection of refreshing, original compositions and jazz standards. It showcases Mitchell's unique styling, and features some of Portland's best jazz artists.

Mitchell is available for solo performances, and will provide duo, trio or quartet combinations upon request. Please visit **www.georgemitchellmusic.com** to hear a sampling of his music and performance style.

## Experience

**George Mitchell** has been pop superstar Diana Ross' first-call pianist for more than 20 years. He continues to tour with her musical ensemble which performs at hundreds of concerts worldwide, as well as extensive touring throughout the United States.

Mitchell's keyboard talents were featured in command performances for the Queen of England, and at Super Concerts in T'ai-Pei and Japan, with Ms. Ross and renowned opera singers Jose Carreras and Placido Domingo. He has made numerous appearances as an ensemble player on top-rated television and radio shows including: *The Tonight Show, Late Night with David Letterman, NBC's Today Show* and *Oprah.*

Recently, he played with Diana Ross at the 2002 command concert for Prince Charles in Hyde Park, London; a 2001 private benefit and farewell salute to Bill Clinton in Los Angeles; a 2001 private performance in Los Angeles honoring Motown founder Berry Gordy; and the 2000 VH1 Divas Live from Madison Square Garden, New York, NY.

## Costs and Terms

Performance rates will vary depending on venue, length of engagement, sound requirements and size of group requested. Please call for a quotation.

## Available Recordings

| | | |
|---|---|---|
| 2004 | *10 Grands Concert* | MAH Records |
| 2003 | *Play Zone* | Origin Arts, OA2 Records |
| 1997 | *Perspectives* | PHD, Libran Music BMI |

# MUSIC FOR OCCASIONS

Weddings • Receptions • Events
Bach to Beatles
*Carol M. Hawes* ***(503) 254-3740***

**Piano, Organ, Portable Keyboard** ***and the...***

---

## Types of Music

The sweet harmonies of **Satin Strings** will greet your guests and create an elegant ambiance for your important event. **This versatile group offers everything you need** from traditional string quartet and trio, with flute, or added trumpet fanfare, to having a small orchestra, including piano or organ. **We help you choose** the right soloist or combination of musicians and the right music **for almost any event**. We specialize in light classical background music but in keeping with our motto **"Bach to Beatles,"** we play music fom the timeless strains of Pachelbel's "Canon in D" to serious string quartet music, current ballads and pops, Broadway tunes, waltzes and tangos, ragtime, soft jazz, hymns and holiday songs. We love to play for you and will make every effort to find your requests.

**The Satin Strings pianist / organist** performs the same styles of music including contemporary Christian praise songs and Jewish songs. She is an accomplished church musician having played for thousands of religious services, weddings and funerals. She frequently performs background music at corporate events or private parties, receptions and dinners. She is experienced at playing sing-a-long parties in various settings and retirement communities.

## Experience

The **Satin Strings Quartet** was formed in 1984 by four professional musicians who were performing as individuals in various orchestras and chamber groups throughout the Northwest. **We were the featured quartet at the Greater Portland Bridal Faire in 1984** and several successive years. We have since been performing continuously in the greater Portland/Vancouver area. Please call if you have questions.

## Cost

Call or E-mail **satinstr@quik.com** for a demo CD, price and music list. Contract always provided. **Visit www.satinstringsmusic.com**

**Member American Guild of Organists and American Federation of Musicians**

## ANDREW (ANDY) GUZIE,
## solo guitar

*(503) 771-2621 • E-mail: aguzie@quik.com*
*www.portland.quik.com/aguzie*

### Types of Music

Intricate finger-style arrangements of jazz standards, pop and easy listening favorites inspired by great guitarists such as Charlie Byrd, Antonio Carlos Jobim and Joe Pass. Andy also plays selections from the classical and Spanish guitar repertoire and sets an ideal mood for conversation and dining.

### Experience and Cost

Andy earned a masters degree in music from the University of Oregon. He has played professionally for over 25 years, most recently in the Portland area for receptions, dinner parties and weddings at many popular venues. More information and demo clips, visit his web site. Fees start at $175.

**www.portland.quik.com/aguzie**
**Or type Andy Guzie into any search engine.**

---

## Aurora Strings

*Quartets, Trios, Duos and Soloists*
*Contact: Kjersten Oquist (503) 491-1802*
*E-mail: kjerstenoquist@aol.com*

Portland's premier string ensemble, Aurora Strings (formerly the Mezzanotte Strings) specializes in major event and wedding performance, and combines musical excellence, a wealth of experience, and personalized attention to create an elegant ambiance for your celebration. Whether you are planning a gala, fundraiser, or a more relaxed gathering, Aurora Strings will add polish and style to your festivities.

### Type of Music

While the group specializes in classical and baroque music, our extensive repertoire also includes jazz standards, pop tunes, Broadway hits, and holiday music. From Bach to the Beatles, we continuously update our repertoire to bring you the finest music. If we don't already have your favorite piece, we can arrange it for you.

### Experience

The members of The Aurora Strings are career professionals who perform with Portland's numerous orchestras and ensembles, and have played countless engagements together in the area's most prestigious locales.

Quotes given include musicians in formal attire, length of engagement, travel allowance if applicable, and all consultations. We will be pleased to provide you with a complimentary demo cd, repertoire list, and further information.

## VIOLIN & CELLO DUO/STRING TRIO & QUARTET

# Duo con Brio

*Corey Averill (503) 526-3908; Cell Phone (503) 887-4448*
*Web site: www.duoconbrio.com; E-mail: singandbow@comcast.net*

### Types of Music

Duo con Brio is a professional ensemble founded by cellist Corey Averill. The duo may be augmented to a string trio or quartet; flute, harp and trumpet are also available. We have a large repertoire, from Baroque to Contemporary, and we pride ourselves on fulfilling most special song requests at no additional fee.

### Experience and Cost

Formed in 1989, the Duo has performed more than 1,000 weddings and other special occasions. Over the years we have performed both locally and abroad in Europe and Asia. Duo con Brio has played a number of memorable events, including performances on Tri-Met's MAX, the opening for NW Portland's Fred Meyer, a Nike International Croquet Tournament, the University of Phoenix graduation ceremonies, OHSU conventions, marriage proposals at Blue Lake Park, and weddings in Oxbow Park (with a deer wandering through the service). We offer a wide range of services, including free consultations and a demo CD. We look forward to assisting you with your special event. We accept Visa and Mastercard.

$150 – Solo Cello/1st hour ($75 each add. hr)
$275 – Duo/1st hour ($135 each add. hr.)
$375 – Trio/1st hour ($170 each add. hr)
$475 – Quartet/1st hour ($195 each add. hr.)

---

## PIANO • KEYBOARDS • VOCALS

## SUSY WOLFSON

*(503) 662-5420 • Web site: www.havemusicwilltravel.net*

### Solo Background

Susy Wolfson is a musician of uncommon versatility. She is equally comfortable as a solo pianist or accompanying her own vocals, moving smoothly from contemporary styles, jazz standards, rock 'n' roll or rhythm & blues to classical music. Her background includes a magna cum laude performance degree from the prestigious Indiana University School of Music and performances at numerous festivals and engagements including the Spoleto Festival in Italy as well as many years as a freelance musician.

### Trio/Quartet/Quintet

Using the classic format of the piano trio plus guitar (with vocals or instrumental only), these musicians are in constant demand for receptions, corporate events, country clubs and winery festivals. From black tie and smooth jazz one night to a kick-off-your shoes rock 'n' roll dance the next, this group will keep 'em dancing! Their song list ranges from Duke Ellington to Sheryl Crow to Stevie Ray Vaughn… and all points in between!

### Performance Combinations

- **Solo Piano or Keyboard**
- **Trio/Quartet/Quintet** (vocals, keyboard, guitar, bass, drums—optional saxophone or flute)
- **Vocals and Piano/Keyboard**
- **Flute and Piano Duo** (vocals optional)
- **Klezmer Band**

*Demos, song lists and references for all musical combinations are available upon request.*

# THE PROP SHOP

*5406 N. Albina Avenue, Portland, Oregon 97217*
*(503) 283-8828; Fax (503) 283-3651*
*www.propshop.com / info@propshop.com*

***Whether it's to surprise, overwhelm, impress or just entertain, surround your guests in beauty and style and you will invoke confidence in your message—confidence in your organization!***

The Prop Shop is a nationally recognized, award-winning creative event design and production company. Our team of expert designers and planners deliver unprecedented results.

We pride ourselves on working closely with our clients guiding them in a direction that will make the most of any budget or venue. The formula is simple—we approach each event as a unique opportunity to showcase your vision using our resources, creativity, team philosophy and most importantly, experience.

## Design

Our signature design services include branding of a corporate image throughout all company functions, from fun-filled employee picnics to synchronized multi-city product launches. The Prop Shop can provide rendering and fabrication of custom props, scenery, staging, backdrops, floral, linens, signage and lighting.

## Décor

Our warehouses hold a plethora of unique sets, backdrops and props, as well as our theatrical designer's workshop and specialty divisions.

## Productions

Our team is equipped with unparalleled national resources and can produce a breadth of events, including corporate meetings, conventions, new product launches, employee appreciations, educational seminars, team building experiences, fundraisers, awards ceremonies, galas, holiday celebrations and picnics.

## Awards

Event Solutions Magazine's Spotlight Award for Designer of the Year 2004
Jack Rosenberg Community Service Award 2003-2004
Bravo! 2002 Best Theme Decor
POVA 2001 Members' Choice Award Most Significant Contribution from a Member

## Memberships

MPI, ISES, POVA, ACEP, CVBWCO & WVDO

# Event Planners

# CALABRIA EVENTS

www.calabriaevents.com
email:calabria.events@gmail.com
(503) 806-2972

Make your event a success! Add Calabria Events to your next occasion and take out the worry and extra work. Our services are available so that you can enjoy your event as much as your guests.

### *Private Dinner Parties and Wine Tastings*

Entertaining at Home? Stuck in the Kitchen?
Calabria Events will coordinate with you and take care of the entire evening (including menu creation, shopping, wine pairing, serving and cleanup) We do the work so you can sit back, relax and enjoy your guests!

### *Wine Tours*

Experience Oregon through our personalized wine tours. A great way to entertain guests and clients, our luxury cars can accommodate large groups or just a couple looking for a romantic getaway. Various packages are available.

### *Corporate Events and Retreats*

Let us design your next corporate event – Golf Tournaments, Auctions, Teambuilding Retreats and Holiday Parties are just a few of the ideas you may consider. Call for a free consultation!

**www.calabriaevents.com**

CLASS ACT

EVENT COORDINATORS, INC.

**CLASS ACT, Event Coordinators**
***Full-Service Event Planners***
***Portland*** *(503) 295-7890*
***Salem*** *(503) 371-8904*
***Corvallis*** *(541) 766-2961*
*Fax (503) 589-9166*
*E-mail: events@classactevents.net*
*Web site: www.classactevents.net*

---

## Planning a Special Event?

Since 1987, Class Act has been designing and coordinating some of the most creative and memorable corporate events in the area.

From budgeting to floor plans to entertainment, event management is a demanding job that calls for impeccable taste, exacting attention to detail and a thorough knowledge of available resources. Class Act eliminates the uncertainty and anxiety related to planning meetings and receptions leaving you free to enjoy the planning process as well as the event.

## Sampling of Events

- Company Picnics
- Business Meetings
- Conferences
- Conventions
- Trade Shows
- Holiday Parties
- Open Houses
- Seminars
- Ground Breakings
- Employee Appreciations
- Grand Openings
- Golf Tournaments
- Retirements
- Luncheons
- Anniversaries
- Weddings
- Fund-raisers
- Class Reunions

## Who Likes Us? (We don't like to brag…but we will)

A few of our clients include:

- West Coast Bank
- The Oregon Garden Foundation
- Aldrich, Kilbride & Tatone
- James W. Fowler Company
- Merant
- Northwest Trailer Parts
- Northwest Aviation Association
- Oregon State Fiscal Association

Call us today for a complimentary initial consultation.

Please be sure to visit us at our new showroom located at 910 Commercial Street SE in Salem to view the latest in corporate and private event trends and distinctive rentals.

*4800 S.W. Macadam Suite 255 • Portland, Oregon 97239*
*503.225.9995 (voice) / 800.524.7084 (toll-free)*
*503.225.1315 (fax)*
*info@columbia-crossroads.com • www.columbia-crossroads.com*

## WE PROVIDE EVERYTHING...

- DMC Services
- Professional On-site Representatives
- Meet and Greet Services
- Luxury Airport Transfers
- Multi-lingual Guides
- Motorcoach Transportation
- Day Tours
- Pre/Post Multi-Day Tours
- Certified Tour Guides
- Hotel Reservations

## CUSTOMIZED! CUSTOMIZED! CUSTOMIZED!

- Experienced – credentialed staff
- Hands on knowledge
- Value with added extras… hospitality you deserve

Our knowledge of practically every corner of the Northwest gives us the background to find unique venues and events that are memorable for your clients. Whether it is a catered dinner at an exclusive winery, hot-air ballooning over breathtaking scenery, or first-class dinner parties, we can do it all. We can handle any size groups from 10 – 11,000 and we have the formula to make events happen successfully — so relax, and put us to work for you!

Columbia Crossroads will remain behind the scenes while ensuring that everything runs according to plan. We will take good care of you!

***Come experience the best with Columbia Crossroads!***

# EventsEtc...

event planning & decorating

P.O. Box 13070
Portland, Oregon 97213
Contact: Debbie Alvarado
(503) 630-3464 • Fax (503) 630-3465
partywithEE@aol.com

## Events Etcetera Specializes In

- Event and Party Planning
- Event Facilitating
- Theme Props
- Table Décor
- Party Decorations
- Entertainment and Live Music
- Menu Planning and Catering
- Marketing and Consulting
- Games and Activities

## Call Us for Your Upcoming Event (Any Size, Anywhere!)

Theme Parties
Holiday Parties
Unique Grad Parties
Weddings
Fundraisers
Formal Galas
Corporate Events
Summer Company Picnics
Festivals
Anniversary Celebrations
Seasonal Office Décor
Casino Parties

## What Our Customers Say…

- Exceeding expectations!
- Beautiful, elegant events!
- Fun and festive parties!
- Beyond your imagination!
- Excellent personal service!

*1108 SE Grand Avenue, Suite 300 • Portland, OR • 97214*
*Tel: 503-232-6666 • Fax: 503-239-8556*

---

**Theme & Design:** Want to fully engage your audience and make sure they remember your event? We can provide concepts, content assistance, unique meeting formats and audience activities to tie it all together.

**Venue Logistics:** Ever wish you had a larger staff? Our seasoned meeting planners can help you with everything from site surveys to travel arrangements and venue negotiations. They are always on hand when you need support.

**Video & PowerPoint:** Need professional speaker support in a hurry? Tap into our state-of-the-art communications department. Our in-house video suite and graphic designers turn out the good stuff, even when time is short.

**Invitations, Registration & Evaluation:** If you build it, will they come? We can help you generate, qualify and register your audience so your event is enjoyed by a roomful of the right people. We can also help you conduct evaluations that offer valuable insight for follow-up efforts.

**Staging & A/V:** Don't you hate it when a microphone cuts out? With NMC, you get the peace of mind of a veteran technical crew that anticipates your event needs. We're always ready with on-site expertise to ensure your event starts smooth and stays that way.

**Speaker Coaching:** Is everything ready but the speaker? With so many people gathered to listen, it is important to be clear and concise. Our coaches use focused rehearsal techniques to help presenters sharpen their skills and effectively connect with the audience.

**Turnkey Solutions:** Looking for something special? Ask about our ideas for generating product demand, aligning your reseller channels and motivating your sales force.

# THE PROP SHOP

*5406 N. Albina Avenue, Portland, Oregon 97217*
*(503) 283-8828; Fax (503) 283-3651*
*www.propshop.com / info@propshop.com*

---

***Whether it's to surprise, inform, overwhelm, impress or just entertain, surround your guests in beauty and style and you will invoke confidence in your message—confidence in your organization!***

The Prop Shop is a nationally recognized, award-winning creative event design and production company. Our team of expert designers and planners deliver unprecedented results.

We pride ourselves on working closely with our clients guiding them in a direction that will make the most of any budget or venue. The formula is simple—we approach each event as a unique opportunity to showcase your vision using our resources, creativity, team philosophy and most importantly, experience.

## Event Planning

Planning an event can be a daunting task for the uninitiated. Even for the veteran planner, fundraising chair, or the savvy sales director, creating a memorable event has its challenges. The Prop Shop can manage every detail of your event, including, concept development, site selection, caterer, permits, rentals, staffing, audio/visual and entertainment.

## Signature Designs

Our expert design services include branding of a corporate image throughout all company functions, from fun-filled employee picnics to synchronized multi-city product launches. The Prop Shop can provide custom props, scenery, staging, backdrops, floral, linens, signage and lighting. We pride ourselves on our excellent customer service, impeccable attention to detail, innovation, resourcefulness and follow-through.

## Productions

Our team is equipped with unparalleled national resources and can produce a breadth of events, including corporate meetings, conventions, new product launches, employee appreciations, educational seminars, team building experiences, fundraisers, awards ceremonies, galas, holiday celebrations and picnics.

## Awards

Event Solutions Magazine's Spotlight Award for Designer of the Year 2004
Jack Rosenberg Community Service Award 2003-2004
Bravo! 2002 Best Theme Decor
POVA 2001 Members' Choice Award Most Significant Contribution from a Member

## Memberships

MPI, ISES, POVA, ACEP, CVBWCO & WVDO

# soirée

special event planning

*By appointment only*
*2236 S.E. Belmont, Portland, Oregon*

*Mailing address*
*P.O. Box 5982, Portland, Oregon 97228*

*503.230.9311*
*503.230.9312 fax*

*www.bonsoiree.com*

---

**Soirée can plan anything you desire to make your idea of the perfect event a reality! With over ten years experience planning events in the Portland area, we have many contacts and resources to draw from to make your event a success.**

**We focus on coordinating events with style and quality. Paying attention to every detail is what enables Soirée to produce superior events. Effectively managing all aspects is essential for making sure your special event is amazing and flawless. Whether you are planning a small intimate gathering or a grand celebration, we give you our full attention so you feel like you are our only client.**

**We offer a complimentary consultation to access the needs of our future clients. We ask precise questions to determine the goals and expectations of the client and their special event. A custom proposal is prepared based on the planning assistance needed.**

- **View our event showcase and read letters from past clients at www.bonsoiree.com**
- **Please give us a call if you have any questions or would like to set up a complimentary consultation.**

# Sonsational Event Experience

*(360) 802-3724*
*Fax: (360) 802-3770*
*E-mail: info@eventexperience.com*
***Website: www.eventexperience.com***

---

**Your Complete Event Planning Resource**

## Enjoy the Party… Let Us Handle the Details

From your first phone call, we work for you by organizing and planning every last detail of your event in a professional, creative, and timely manner!

## We Specialize In…

**Entertainment:** We have relationships with the finest entertainment acts in the Northwest. With creative entertainment suggestions for every type of function, we can ensure your guests will have an unforgettable experience.

**Inflatables:** Choose from one of the largest inflatable inventories in the country. From bouncers and slides to obstacle courses and game shows, we have something for everyone at your event!

**Catering:** Each Northwest season offers unique and festive culinary options. Our catering menus are regularly updated to provide new specials for you to choose from.

**Venue/Site:** The often overlooked process of site selection should not be left to chance. With our experience of hundreds of events, we can make sure the venue provides exactly what your event needs.

## Our Services Include:

- Team building
- Company picnics
- Employee appreciation
- Morale/Incentive events
- Holiday parties
- Grand openings
- DJ services
- Grad parties
- Family reunions

*"I couldn't be happier with the excellent service provided by Sonsational Events. Their attention to detail, on-site support, and product knowledge is extremely appreciated. They truly are the 'party experts.'"* —Holly Longo, The Boeing Company

# Notes

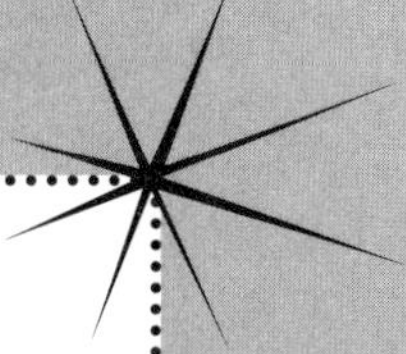

# Event Professional Organizations

ASSOCIATION OF CATERING & EVENT PROFESSIONALS

For those of you working in the catering and special event industry, this is the association for you. And if you're planning an event, we can help with that too!

Please visit our Web site at **www.acep.com.**

## Our Mission Statement

1. To identify and give status to the catering and event planning industry as a whole and to represent its desires and best interests to the community at large.
2. To promote the exchange of common ideas and problems.
3. To develop a cordial relationship among its members.
4. To present to the members programs of educational value relating to the catering, event industries and allied businesses.

## Benefits of Membership

- Networking
- Educational Opportunities
- Online Library
- Complimentary Web Page and Link from our site to yours
- Membership Directory
- Hotline
- Newsletter
- Community Involvement

**For membership information, call *(503) 299-ACEP***
***E-mail: acep@acep.com; Web site: www.acep.com***

**Or call *Olivia Betancourt, 2004 President,* at 503.279.9000**

# COLUMBIA RIVER GORGE VISITORS ASSOCIATION

*2149 W. Cascade*
*P.M.B. #106*
*Hood River, Oregon 97031*
*(800) 98-GORGE*
*E-mail: crgva@gorge.net*
*Web site: www.crgva.org*

---

The Columbia River Gorge National Scenic Area, created in 1986 by an act of Congress, is an area of unique and outstanding beauty. The Gorge has accommodations for every need and activities for every taste. Convention hotel or bed & breakfast, whitewater rafting or historical museum, the Gorge has much to offer.

The Columbia River Gorge Visitors Association, established in 1990, is a unique volunteer organization of visitor industry members working together to market and promote the Gorge. Representing the six counties of Washington and Oregon that are included in the Gorge (Clark, Skamania, Klickitat, Multnomah, Hood River and Wasco), our partnership includes both public and private entities.

## Convention, Event and Tour Planning

- Our membership offers a wide variety of services, from large full-service conference centers accommodating up to 500 attendees to quaint bed and breakfasts for family reunions.
- Attractions can accommodate groups for activities such as vintage dinner train rides, river cruises, whitewater rafting, museum tours, dam and fish hatchery tours and much more.
- Lodging ranges from rustic campsites to luxury hotels. Whatever your needs, we have it in the Columbia River Gorge.

## CRGVA Members Working Together

- Our magazine, *Gorge Guide*, is distributed at many locations and mailed throughout the world. E-mail or call us for a complimentary copy.
- Our web site includes a listing of members, calendar of events and Lewis & Clark information.
- Cooperative advertising for our members in a variety of publications.
- Fulfillment of nearly 22,000 inquiries per year.
- Cooperative participation in Travel and Trade shows.

**We hope to see you soon in the Columbia River Gorge!**

*553 NW Harrison Blvd.*
*Corvallis, Oregon 97330*
*(800) 334-8118 • (541) 757-1544 • (541) 753-2664 fax*
*www.visitcorvallis.com • michelle@visitcorvallis.com*

---

Each year, Corvallis hosts a variety of statewide, regional, national and international conferences, meetings and events. Corvallis Tourism is the catalyst for successful events, partnering with meeting planners to increase attendance while lowering overall costs.

***Call today for your complimentary cost comparison!***

We'll compare details of your past conference with meeting space, food/beverage and lodging options for a future event in Corvallis – with one quick phone call, you're well on your way to a fantastic conference!

Attendees and meeting planners alike appreciate our free customized online hotel registration system – it's convenient, and reduces booking outside the block.

## Why is Corvallis the ideal host city for your next event?

- Corvallis provides 1,000 hotel rooms and more than 90,000 square feet of dedicated meeting space in three conference centers, with banquet accommodation for 500 and theater-style seating for 1,200.
- Oregon State University offers one of the largest public university conference centers in the nation, with 80,000 square feet of meeting space and Hilton Garden Inn headquarter hotel. ***See also the Oregon State University ad on page 232.***
- Salbasgeon Suites and Conference Center provides 4,500 square feet of luxurious meeting space in six rooms, including banquet seating for 120.
- The Ramada Inn and Conference Center's 6,000 square feet of meeting space includes a versatile ballroom accommodating 314 banquet-style.
- Our convenient Willamette Valley location, minutes from I-5, is easily reachable by conference attendees.
- Exciting social activities are available to enhance the overall conference experience, including winery tours, unique downtown shops, championship golf, performing arts, NCAA athletics, and special theme evenings.

***Discover what planners and attendees are raving about!***

Call conference consultant Michelle Boyd today:
**(800) 334-8118**
Submit your RFP online:
**http://www.visitcorvallis.com/meetings/rfp.html**

## CONVENTION & VISITORS ASSOCIATION OF LANE COUNTY OREGON (CVALCO)

*P.O. Box 10286*
*Eugene, Oregon 97440*
*(541) 484-5307, (800) 547-5445*
*Fax (541) 343-6335*
*E-mail: conventionsales@cvalco.org*
*Web site: www.visitlanecounty.org*

---

**CVALCO sales team provides a professional link between the properties, attractions and amenities that will make your meeting or convention a success.**

- **CVALCO** is a full-service convention and visitors bureau
- **CVALCO** will obtain bids from hotel properties and facilities, facilitate tours, and provide a broad cross-section of convention services
- **CVALCO** will match the needs of each meeting with community businesses that can best provide assistance

### Site Profile

Located in the heart of Oregon, Lane County reaches from the snow-covered tops of Willamette National Forest down along the meandering McKenzie and Willamette rivers out to the shoreline of the Pacific Ocean. Matchless beauty, Northwest hospitality, a wealth of recreation and cultural opportunities plus full-service facilities make Lane County a natural meeting destination.

### Accommodations

Lane County has over 4,000 sleeping rooms, with competitive rates, outstanding service standards and hotel meeting rooms ranging in size from 200 to 30,000 square feet. The Lane County Convention Center is over 100,000 square feet and offers complimentary parking.

### Cultural Facilities and Activities

Year-round there is something for everyone in Lane County: white water rafting, opera, ballet, symphony, musical theatre, skiing, dune buggy riding, backpacking, golf, mountain biking and more.

### Transportation

Eugene Airport is just 15 minutes from downtown Eugene/Springfield and offers air service to and from a variety of destinations. Lane County is easily reached by Amtrak and interstate highways as well. Located one hour and 45 minutes from Portland International Airport makes rental car travel an attractive option.

# LINCOLN CITY

VISITOR AND CONVENTION BUREAU

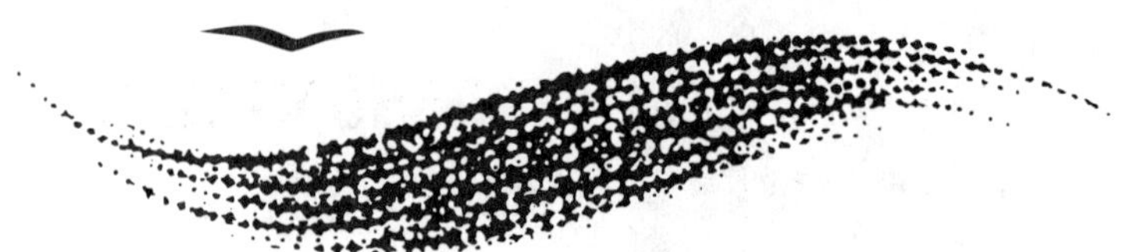

*801 S.W. Hwy 101, Suite #1 • Lincoln City, OR 97367*
*(541) 994-1274/1-800-452-2151; fax (541) 994-2408*
*www.OregonCoast.org*

---

Welcome to Lincoln City, where, ***'The Beach is just the Beginning!'***

Lincoln City is the right site for your meeting, reunion, retreat, wedding, honeymoon, event, party, tour or vacation.

Variety is the option in Lincoln City. We have every lodging choice, from campsite retreats to Four Diamonds, 7.5 miles of public beach, and 690-acre Devils Lake. We have Oregon's finest outlet shopping opportunity, Tanger Outlet Mall, Chinook Winds Casino Resort, art galleries and antiques, fine dining and family entertainment.

Lincoln City has everything you need for business and for pleasure:

**Meetings:** From six to 1600, Lincoln City has a variety of great meeting locations for every sized group. Call for our Meeting Facilities and Services Directory for a list of meeting rooms, their configurations and numbers they can accommodate.

**Retreats:** Vacation Rentals, large or small, make a great place to do business at the beach.

**Reunions:** Bring the whole crew and leave the entertainment up to the Oregon Coast. It's a great place to meet family and friends.

**Weddings and Honeymoons:** Get married on the beach, renew your vows or honeymoon in Oregon's oldest honeymoon spot. Jason Lee brought his bride to Lincoln City in 1837.

**Events, Tours, Parties or Vacation:** Call toll free (800) 452-2151 for our complimentary Visitors Guide to Lincoln City.

***The beach is just the beginning!***

# MEETING PROFESSIONALS INTERNATIONAL

## OREGON CHAPTER

## (503) 768-4299

---

*The purpose of the Meeting Professionals International Oregon Chapter is to provide quality education for its members, to promote professionalism within the meeting industry and to enhance business relationships.*

- Open to all professionals in the meeting industry
- Meetings once each month on Tuesday, September through June
- Annual Regional Conference every March

**For membership information**
**visit our web site mpioc.org or call:**

**Pat Fuller**
**Association Manager**
**(503) 768-4299**
**Email: info@mpioc.org**

*JOIN TODAY AND BECOME PART OF THE ORGANIZATION THAT BENEFITS YOU…*

# Greater Newport Chamber of Commerce

*555 S.W. Coast Highway*
*Newport, Oregon 97365-4934*
*(541) 265-8801, (800) 262-7844*
*Fax (541) 265-5589*
*www.newportchamber.org*

***Newport*** awaits your next business meeting, planning session, convention, retreat, or group tour. In Newport you will find a variety of meeting facilities offering full services—comfortable lodging with terrific views, great restaurants with the freshest seafood you'll ever taste, and miles of wide open beaches.

***Our coastal community*** offers a peaceful, yet exciting setting for any traveler. Not only does Newport offer outstanding meeting facilities, but there are also many activities and attractions that can further enhance your visit to the Central Oregon Coast.

***Our attractions,*** ranging from aquariums to historical museums, complement the natural beauty of the area. Recreational opportunities include crabbing, clamming, fishing, whale watching and marine-based tours just to name a few. Whether you incorporate these activities into your agenda, or offer them during free time, they are bound to make a "splash" with your group.

Group tour guide, slides, color photos, itinerary planning assistance, posters, brochure shells, fam/research tours and maps can all be provided by the Greater Newport Chamber of Commerce. We will help to make your next visit to the beach a huge success!

So, give us a call at (800) 262-7844. We look forward to sharing our special brand of hospitality with you.

## OUR MISSION

The Greater Newport Chamber of Commerce *is organized to unite the efforts of the citizens promoting the civic, commercial, agricultural, tourism, marine and industrial welfare of the City of Newport and its surrounding economic areas.*

## Oregon Festivals & Events Association

*MEMBERSHIP INFO:*
*1-866-451-OFEA (6332)*

*info@oregonfestivals.org*
*www.oregonfestivals.org*

---

The Oregon Festivals & Events Association is the premiere association serving Oregon event professionals across the state.Through the OFEA members enjoy an ever expanding list of valuable benefits and resources that help produce successful events and businesses. Oregon provides a local network of professional peers who understand the value of sharing ideas, answers, creativity, experience and encouragement. Get immediate access to these experts, through membership in Oregon Festivals & Events Association.

### Join the OFEA and receive support services, discounts on advertising, and specialized training for your organization! And so much more!

**Membership in OFEA includes the following great benefits and more:**

- Networking opportunities locally, regionally and nationally
- Highlighted event listings and display advertising discounts in the annual Oregon Event Calendar
- Advanced education, programs and specialized training courses
- Discounts for educational seminars, workshops and courses including the Northwest Festivals & Events Conference held annually in March.
- Links to websites and access to resources gathered collectively

### Who Should Join?

Festival Producers
Non-Profit Event Directors
Parks & Recreation Personnel
City Personnel
Chambers of Commerce
Visitor & Convention Bureaus
Meeting Planners
Industry Suppliers
Entertainers, Agents
Food Service & Concessionaires
Facility Marketers

www.gosgmp.com

---

## Who We Are!

The Society of Government Meeting Professionals (SGMP) is the only nonprofit professional organization involved in both the planning of government meetings and professionals in the hospitality and convention support industry who supply services to government meeting planners.

## Benefits of Membership!

- Encourages and improves communication, understanding, and cooperation between meeting planners and suppliers
- Expands knowledge and abilities of planners and suppliers through formal educational conferences, workshops, and monthly meetings
- Aids planners in locating and evaluating commercial meeting facilities and support services
- Provides up to date statistics regarding per diem rates, regulatory policies, and legislative issues which effect state and federal government meetings
- Check out our web site at www.gosgmp.com

**For membership information contact**
*Gretchen Darnell, Director of Sales*
**Seaside Civic & Convention Center**
*(503) 738-8585*
*sales@seasideconvention.com*

*It's not easy being green.*

# PORTLAND OREGON VISITORS ASSOCIATION

***The convention and visitors bureau of metropolitan Portland***

*1000 S.W. Broadway, Suite 2300*
*Portland, Oregon 97205*
*(503) 275-9750; Fax (503) 275-9774*
*Web site: www.travelportland.com*

---

## POVA AT WORK

*The mission of the Portland Oregon Visitors Association is to strengthen the region's economy by marketing the metropolitan Portland region as a preferred destination for meetings, conventions and leisure travel.*

### 1,000+ Members and Growing

More than 1,000 businesses in the Portland metropolitan area, the state of Oregon and the Pacific Northwest are members of the Portland Oregon Visitors Association (POVA).

### Convention and Tour Business

Members of POVA can market their businesses to the convention/meeting planners and group tour operators visiting Portland and Oregon. The *Portland Oregon Convention & Trade Show Calendar* includes the names, addresses, phone numbers and meeting dates for group meetings in the Portland area.

### Member Networking and Program Events

POVA provides opportunities for members to attend industry meetings and network with more than 100 fellow members. Meetings vary in location, giving members the opportunity to experience venues throughout the Portland metropolitan area.

### Visitor Information Center

Drop by our busy downtown information and services center in Pioneer Courthouse Square and let us help you make decisions about what to see and do in the Portland area. Members' brochures are available for visitors to pick up.

### Three Different Publications

POVA produces Portland's award-winning visitor guide magazine, *Portland Oregon: The Official Visitors Guide*, which is mailed to visitors and convention attendees around the world. In addition, members have the opportunity to advertise in two other POVA publications that are applicable to the pursuit of business for members.

### Professional Sales Staff

A professional staff of convention sales managers, travel industry sales managers, and marketing experts works for members (and for all of us) to bring visitor business to Portland.

**Join the Portland Oregon Visitors Association and put the power of POVA to work for you.**

**For more information, call the POVA Membership Department at (503) 275-9750.**

**SALEM CONVENTION & VISITORS ASSOCIATION**
1313 Mill Street SE
Salem, Oregon 97301
503-581-4325
Fax: 503-581-4540

Toll Free: 800-874-7012
directorofsales@travelsalem.com
www.travelsalem.com

## Inspired Hospitality

Unique venues that meet your exact needs, quality accommodations and professionals who are inspired hosts. These are just a few of the reasons the Salem area should be on your conference "short list." Add to this a location that is both convenient and intensely beautiful, and realize an inspired event of your own.

## Meeting Facilities

With 25 nicely distributed facilities in and around Salem's historic downtown, the city boasts over 450,000 square feet of meeting and exhibit space. With intimate, lovingly restored historic landmarks at one end of the spectrum to ultramodern gems on the other, we enthusiastically host groups from 7 to 7,000.

## Accommodations

The Salem area offers more than 1,700 quality guestrooms ranging from small independent hotels to premier business-class accommodations. Most of our hotel properties have meeting facilities, and many offer "turn-key" service for groups from 10 to 300.

## Transportation

Conveniently located just off I-5 (and half way between the equator and the North Pole), Salem is one of Oregon's most accessible and intimate conference destinations. Portland international Airport is only 50 minutes north of Salem and is serviced by all major airlines. The Salem airport can handle the largest business jets and charter craft up to Boeing 737s size. Amtrak delivers travelers to the center of downtown.

## Intense Beauty and Simple Charm

The Willamette Valley's rich quiltwork of wineries, rivers and historic sites offer discoveries at every turn, and make getting here an experience all its own. Golf opportunities range from breathtaking alpine, to classic parkland layouts along the beautiful Willamette River. For a taste of the old and the new, your group might visit one of the many wineries within Salem, or that grace the surrounding hills. For those who prefer a quiet turn, Salem's historic downtown and offers a charming mix of shops, galleries, restaurants and parks.

## Let Us Help

We'll work as an extension of your team to fashion a meeting that will be truly inspired. The SCVA can help in all aspects of planning including service-related bids, day tours and break-out activities, dining and hotel accommodations, transportation and information packets.

For more information, call Debbie McCune at 800.874.7012 ext. 28 or log onto our meeting professional service center at www.travelsalem.com/balance. Download meeting planner guides, sign up for our electronic newsletter or complete the online RFP for your upcoming event. We look forward to working with you.

## Southern Oregon Visitors Association

*P.O. Box 1645 • Medford, Oregon 97501*
*541-779-4691 • Fax 541-779-4444*
*www.sova.org*

---

The Southern Oregon Visitors Association (SOVA) provides a professional link to the finest meeting and convention facilities throughout Southern Oregon. From the Wild Rivers Coast to the Oregon Outback, we represent more than 200 tourism members in seven Southern Oregon Counties — Jackson, Josephine, Coos, Curry, Douglas, Klamath and Lake.

### TRANSPORTATION

The Southern Oregon area is served by three major highways (Highway 101, Highway 97 and I-5), plus three major airports located in Medford, Klamath and Coos Bay/North Bend.

### FACILITIES AND ATTRACTIONS

Southern Oregon offers numerous unique meeting venues, mountain retreats, ocean get-aways, river and golf resorts, exciting casinos, historical hotels, and downtown business centers all surrounded by an array of attractions… world renowned theatre, numerous championship golf courses, exceptional wineries, jet boating, challenging river rafting, cave exploring, lava beds, fishing, bird watching and whale watching. Combine our outstanding attractions and facilities with our distinct small town charm and friendly and professional service, and you will have your event at a very memorable place.

### SOUTHERN OREGON BUSINESSES

*represented at the Bravo! Trade Show*

***Visitor and Convention Bureaus***
City of Ashland
City of Grants Pass
City of Medford
City of Roseburg

***Meeting Hotels***
Red Lion Inns – Medford
Windmill Inn & Suites of Ashland
Rogue Regency Inn

For a comprehensive look at the top meeting facilities and attractions in Southern Oregon, pick up a copy of SOVA's Meeting and Event Planner. This full color, 24-page planner is your guide to the best meeting facilities in Southern Oregon.

**www.sova.org**

# Convention & Visitors Bureau of Washington County, Oregon

5075 SW Griffith Drive, Suite 120
Beaverton, OR 97005-2921
800-537-3149 Toll Free
503-644-5555 Local
503-644-9784 Fax
www.countrysideofportland.com
sales@countrysideofportland.com

---

## *Washington County, Oregon —"Where Fresh Ideas and Inspiration Grow"*

Over the hills west of downtown Portland the land begins to ripple and roll to the sea. This is the fertile hill country of Washington County, where farms grow fresh produce and businesses grow fresh ideas. In short, it's a natural environment for meetings and events.

***Your convenient and affordable alternative to downtown Portland.***
- Free parking
- Lower room tax
- Convenient, accessible, and affordable light rail transportation just minutes from downtown and within one hour from the airport
- Tax-free shopping

## Meeting and Event Services Offered:
- One phone call to our office provides better pricing options on lodging and meeting space.
- We arrange site tours of hotels, meeting facilities and attractions.
- We assist the client in arranging special group functions.
- We provide complimentary visitor information for your group.
- We can provide an on-site visitor information table at your event registration.
- We offer affordable government lodging and meeting facility rates.

***Washington County, Oregon — "Plant your next event here"***

**800-537-3149** **www.countrysideofportland.com**

# MEETING PLANNING ORGANIZATIONS



MEETING PROFESSIONALS INTERNATIONAL (MPI)

*National phone: (972) 702-3000*

MPI now offers its members their own online service, called MPINet, based on the CompuServe system. MPI's resource center will do research for members and non-members on just about any subject. MPI can also provide destination information through the Worldview program. The local chapter of MPI is a great education and networking group of local meeting planners and suppliers.

***See page 321 in this section about local membership.***

PORTLAND OREGON VISITOR ASSOCIATION (POVA)

*Phone: (503) 275-9750*

As a member of POVA, you can obtain the names of who is in charge of most of the convention and tour groups coming to Portland. POVA also publishes four leading visitor guides to the area and has breakfasts every Thursday featuring informative guest speakers.

***See page 325 in this section about membership.***

AMERICAN HOTEL & LODGING ASSOCIATION (AH&LA)

*Phone: (202) 289-3100*

AMERICAN SOCIETY OF ASSOCIATION EXECUTIVES (ASAE)

*Phone: (202) 626-2723*

AMERICAN SOCIETY OF TRAVEL AGENTS (ASTA)

*Phone: (703) 739-2782*

ASSOCIATION OF CATERING & EVENT PROFESSIONALS (ACEP)

*Phone: (503) 299-2237*

*See page 316*

CONVENTION INDUSTRY COUNCIL (CIC)

*Phone: 1-800-725-8982*

INTERNATIONAL ASSOCIATION OF CONVENTION & VISITOR BUREAUS (IACVB)

*Phone: (202) 296-7888*

INTERNATIONAL ASSOCIATION FOR EXPOSITION MANAGEMENT (IAEM)

*Phone: (972) 458-8002*

OREGON SOCIETY OF ASSOCIATION MANAGEMENT (OSAM)

*Phone: (503) 253-9026*

SOCIETY OF GOVERNMENT MEETING PROFESSIONALS (SGMP)

*E-mail: mmillig@hcs.state.or.us;*

*National phone: (717) 795-7467*

The Oregon chapter of SGMP offers monthly educational meetings and an annual conference with the goal of improving the knowledge, expertise and cost effectiveness for individuals planning and managing government meetings. It is open to planners and suppliers.

*See page 324*

# CONVENTION AND VISITORS INFORMATION BUREAUS

## Oregon and Southwest Washington

**Columbia River Gorge Visitors Association (GVA)**
P.O. Box 106
Hood River, OR 97031
(800) 98-GORGE
*See page 317*

**Convention & Visitors Bureau of Washington County, Oregon**
5075 S.W. Griffith Dr., Ste. 120
Beaverton, OR 97005
(503) 644-5555
www.wcva.org
*See page 328*

**Corvallis Tourism**
553 N.W. Harrison Blvd.
Corvallis, OR 97330
(541) 757-1544
www.visitcorvallis.com
*See page 318*

**Convention & Visitors Association of Lane County Oregon**
P.O. Box 10286
Eugene, OR 97440
(800) 547-5445
www.visitlanecounty.com
*See page 319*

**Lincoln City**
801 S.W. Hwy 101, Ste. 1
Lincoln City, OR 97367
(800) 452-2151
www.oregoncoast.org
*See page 320*

**Medford**
101 E. Eighth St.
Medford, OR 97501
(541) 779-4847

**Oregon's Mt. Hood Territory**
619 Hight St.
Oregon City, OR 97045
(503) 655-8490
www.mthoodterritory.com

**Portland Oregon Visitors Association (POVA)**
1000 S.W. Broadway, Suite 2300
Portland, OR 97205
(503) 275-9750
www.pova.com
*See page 325*

**Roseburg**
P.O. Box 1026
410 S.E. Spruce
Roseburg, OR 97470
(800) 444-9584
www.visitroseburg.com

**Salem**
1313 Mill St., S.E.
Salem, OR 97301
(503) 581-4325
www.travelsalem.com
*See page 326*

**Seaside Visitors Bureau**
7 North Roosevelt
Seaside, OR 97138
(800) 444-6740
www.seasideor.com

**Southern Oregon Visitors Association**
P.O. Box 1645
Medford, Oregon 97501
(541) 779-4691
www.southernoregon.com
*See page 327*

**Southwest Washington Visitors & Convention Bureau**
101 E. Eighth St., Suite 110
Vancouver, WA 98660
www.southwestwashington.com
(877) 600-0800

# CHAMBERS OF COMMERCE

**Albany**
P.O. Box 548
Albany, OR 97321
(541) 926-1517
www.albanychamber.com

**Ashland**
P.O. Box 1360
Ashland, OR 97520
(541) 482-3486
www.ashlandchamber.com

**Beaverton**
4800 S.W. Griffith Dr., Ste. 100
Beaverton, OR 97005
(503) 644-0123
www.beaverton.org

**Canby**
P.O. Box 35
Canby, OR 97013
(503) 266-4600
www.canbyareachamber.com

**Cannon Beach**
P.O. Box 64
Cannon Beach, OR 97110
(503) 436-2623

**Clatskanie**
P.O. Box 635
Clatskanie, OR 97016
(503) 728-2502

**Cornelius**
P.O. Box 681
Cornelius, OR 97113
(503) 359-4037

**Estacada**
475 S.E. Main
Estacada, OR 97023
(503) 630-3483
www.estacadachamber.org

**Forest Grove**
2417 Pacific Ave.
Forest Grove, OR 97116
(503) 357-3006

**Gresham**
701 N.E. Hood Ave.
Gresham, OR 97030
(503) 665-1131
www.greshamchamber.org

**Hillsboro**
334 S.E. Fifth Ave.
Hillsboro, OR 97123
(503) 648-1102
www.hilchamber.org

**Hood River**
405 Portway Ave.
Hood River, OR 97031
(541) 386-2000
www.hoodriver.org
*See page 317*

**Keizer**
980 Chemawa Rd. N.E.
Keizer, OR 97303
(503) 393-9111
www.keizerchamber.com

**Lake Oswego**
P.O. Box 368
Lake Oswego, OR 97034
(503) 636-3634
www.lake-oswego.com

**Lincoln City**
P.O. Box 787
Lincoln City, OR 97367
(541) 994-3070
www.lcchamber.com

**McMinnville**
417 N.W. Adams St.
McMinnville, OR 97128
(503) 472-6196
www.mcminnville.org

**Milwaukie**
7740 S.E. Harmony Rd.
Milwaukie, OR 97222
(503) 654-7777
www.yourchamber.com

**Molalla**
101 N Molalla Avenue
P.O. Box 578
Molalla, OR 97038
(503) 829-6941
www.molallachamber.com

**Mount Angel**
P.O. Box 221
Mount Angel, OR 97362
(503) 845-9440

**Newberg**
415 E. Sheridan
Newberg, OR 97132
(503) 538-2014
www.newberg.org

**Newport**
555 S.W. Coast Hwy.
Newport, OR 97365
(800) 262-7844
www.newportchamber.org
*See page 322*

**Oregon City**
1810 Washington St.
P.O. Box 226
Oregon City, OR 97045
(503) 656-1619
www.oregoncity.org

**Pendleton**
501 S. Main St.
Pendleton, OR 97801
(541) 276-7411
www.visitpendleton.com

**Portland**
520 S.W. Yamhill
Portland, OR 97204
(503) 224-8684
www.portlandalliance.com

**Salem**
1110 Commercial St., N.E.
Salem, OR 97301
(503) 581-1466

**Sherwood**
P.O. Box 805
Sherwood, OR 97140
(503) 625-6751
www.sherwoodchamber.org

**Sunriver**
P.O. Box 3246
Sunriver, OR 97707
(541) 593-8149
www.sunriverchamber.com

**The Dalles**
404 W. Second St.
The Dalles, OR 97058
(800) 255-3385
www.thedalleschamber.com

**Tigard**
12345 S.W. Main St.
Tigard, OR 97223
(503) 639-1656
www.tigardchamber.com

**Troutdale**
P.O. Box 245
330 E. Historic Columbia River Hwy.
Troutdale, OR 97060
(503) 669-7473
www.columbiagorgechamber.com

**Tualatin**
P.O. Box 701
Tualatin, OR 97062
(503) 692-0780
www.tualatinchamber.com

**Vancouver**
1101 Broadway, St. 120
Vancouver, WA 98660
(360) 694-2588
www.vancouverusa.com

**Vernonia**
1001 Bridge
Vernonia, OR 97064
(503) 429-6081
www.vernonia-or.gov

**Welches**
P.O. Box 819
Welches, OR 97067
(503) 622-3017
www.mthood.org

**West Linn**
22500 Salamo Road
West Linn, OR 97068
(503) 657-0331

**Willamina**
105 N.W. Main
Willamina, OR 97396
(503) 876-5777

**Wilsonville**
29600 S.W. Park Pl.
Wilsonville, OR 97070
(503) 682-0411
www.wilsonvillechambers.com

# Notes

# Events & Festivals

# PORTLAND CENTER FOR THE PERFORMING ARTS

*1111 S.W. Broadway • Portland, Oregon 97205*
*Box Office Hours: Mon–Sat 10am–5pm (503) 248-4335; Fax (503) 274-7490*
*E-mail: judy@pcpa.com or andrea@pcpa.com; Web site: www.pcpa.com*

## 2005 PERFORMANCE SCHEDULE

**THE GRADUATE**
January 1-2
Keller Auditorium

**21 DOG YEARS OR DOING TIME @ AMAZON.COM**
January 4-February 4
Winningstad Theatre

**ITZAK PERLMAN RECITAL**
January 5
Arlene Schnitzer Concert Hall

**THE BFG (BIG FRIENDLY GIANT)**
January 9-23
Keller Auditorium

**TERRENCE MCNALLY**
January 19
Arlene Schnitzer Concert Hall

**MADAME BUTTERFLY**
February 5-12
Keller Auditorium

**BRIDGE OF THE GODS**
February 9-27
Winningstad Theatre

**MY FAIR LADY**
February 15-March 12
Newmark Theatre

**BRAHMS SYMPHONY NO. 2**
February 19-21
Arlene Schnitzer Concert Hall

**BEIJING MODERN DANCE**
March 9
Arlene Schnitzer Concert Hall

**STREET SCENE**
March 26-April 2
Keller Auditorium

**SAVION GLOVER**
March 29-30
Arlene Schnitzer Concert Hall

**PATTI LUPONE – "MATTERS OF THE HEART"**
April 5-10
Keller Auditorium

**BEETHOVEN'S EROICA**
April 9-11
Arlene Schnitzer Concert Hall

**RAMONA QUIMBY**
April 17-20
Keller Auditorium

**TASTE OF THE NATION**
April 25
New Theatre Building

**PILOBOLUS DANCE THEATRE**
April 27
Arlene Schnitzer Concert Hall

**TEN GRANDS**
May 6
Arlene Schnitzer Concert Hall

**WINNIE-THE-POOH**
May 6-22
Winningstad Theatre

**PYP'S SPRING CONCERT**
May 7
Arlene Schnitzer Concert Hall

**OBT'S MASTERS AND MODERNS**
May 13-28
Newmark Theatre

**ABDUCTION FROM THE SERAGLIO**
May 14-21
Keller Auditorium

**MAHLER'S SYMPHONY NO. 5**
May 21-23
Arlene Schnitzer Concert Hall

**WONDERFUL TOWN**
May 24-29
Keller Auditorium

**MOVIN' OUT**
June 7-12
Keller Auditorium

**JAZZ BAND CLASSIC**
June 11
Arlene Schnitzer Concert Hall

UNIVERSITY OF OREGON

*Web site: http://center.uoregon.edu/festivalevent*
*E-mail: festivalevent@continue.uoregon.edu*
*(800) 824-2714 or (541) 346-4231; Fax (541) 346-3545*

## PROGRAM OVERVIEW

This program was founded in 1999 to provide professional development opportunities to staff and volunteers working with community festivals, non-profit organizations, recreation sites or businesses that host special events. Over 600 individuals from the northwest region have attended workshops in this program.

Whether you are currently a student or professional, paid or volunteer, there are a variety of options for you to choose from as you pursue your interest in Festival & Event Management:

- Attend occasional workshops for professional development on a specific topic, or to complement a college degree. (Does not require you to pursue the Certificate of Completion.)
- Pursue a "Certificate of Completion in Festival & Event Management" as a professional credential for job advancement. (This requires attending workshops and completing additional work with a festival or event.)
- Meet professional development requirements by receiving Continuing Education Unit (CEU) documentation for your professional membership organization.

## WORKSHOP TOPICS

A variety of topics are covered each year, with selected titles repeating every 18 months. Each September to June cycle includes:

- Foundations of Event Management (a two-day intensive)
- Six one-day sessions from the core topic areas
- A one-day session, on a current topic, with a guest speaker of national reputation
- A behind-the-scenes session, such as the workshop in June 2004 at the Oregon Bach Festival

Workshop titles for 2004-05 include: *Volunteer Management, Marketing* and *Sponsors and Events.*

## WORKSHOP FORMAT

Workshops are generally held on a Friday, approximately once a month, from September to June. Sessions are 8:30am to 4:30pm with refreshments served during the morning and afternoon breaks. Presenters are experienced professionals from around the region, including both urban and rural communities and many types of festivals and events.

## WORKSHOP LOCATIONS

Sessions are regularly offered in Portland and Eugene.

*Mention this listing when registering for a workshop and receive a free UO souvenir when you attend!*

# Notes

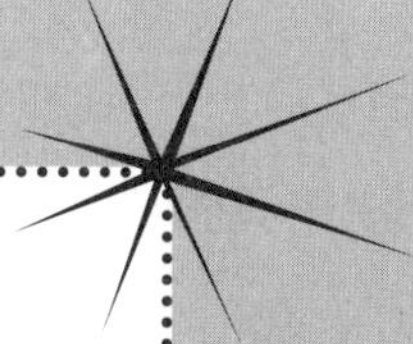

# Executive Gifts & Client/Employee Appreciation

Executive Gifts & Client/Employee Appreciation

BravoPortland.com

# THANK YOU GIFTS & APPRECIATIONS

**Gift and fruit baskets:** The famous welcome basket of fruit has come a long way! Today meeting planners are pressured to provide "VIP" gifts that are creative, easy to travel with, functional, and even recyclable! The fruit basket has evolved into a theme basket for whatever occasion is at hand. Pick the items and the theme, and the basket can be created. Baskets can be personalized, according to hobbies and season, with food additions (coffee, chocolate, etc.). Refer to this section for professionals who custom-design and deliver to your door.

**Thank you gifts**: These are most often given to vendors, speakers and volunteers for doing a good job. After a speaker has presented, many planners send a gift to the speaker's office or hand it to him or her personally. Thanking a vendor or the volunteers who helped create a successful meeting or event is very common. Jewelers and gift stores specialize in gifts like designer pen and pencil sets, crystal or silver pieces, lapel pins, etc.

**Room gifts:** These are usually light snacks, cheese, wine, crackers, and fruit. Logo chocolates are fun to have for a late-night treat. Other items might be momentos of the city, state, or company. Coffee-table books can be easily packed for the return trip home.

**Retirement or acknowledgment gifts:** These gifts or awards are usually very nice and more personal—watches, jewelry, crystal or silver pieces. Many of these gifts have a personal message engraved on them or can be an item that fits the person's style and personality.

**Annual gifts:** The holidays are always busy times for the gift-giving businesses. Thanking clients for their business and thanking vendors for a job well done are reasons to give holiday gifts. Keep in mind these gifts need to be tasteful. A gift given during the year for no particular reason is a nice surprise. Also, a thank-you to a client for a large order or big account is a nice gesture.

**Awards:** Traditional plaques have little purpose aside from placing them on a wall or desk. Today, many awards have a purpose—an engraved clock or a piece of engraved jewelry. It's nice to receive an award you can proudly use and display throughout the year that reminds you of that special acknowledgment you have earned.

**Unique gifts:** There are many unique and specialty gifts that are available including gift certificates for massage therapy, or bringing in a masseuse to your office as a reward for hitting goals. The masseuse can bring the table or massage chair on-site; set up a private office with music and dim lighting and watch your tensions float away. There are also gift certificates to a day spa, with everything from hair care to six-hour spa treatment packages.

## HAIR ARCHITECTS SALON

*8511 S.W. Terwilliger Blvd.*
*Portland, Oregon 97219*
*503-244-4119*
*Tuesday–Friday 9am to 7pm*
*Saturday 9am to 5 pm*

---

## A FULL SERVICE SALON TO MEET ALL CLIENT NEEDS

### Salon Services Available:

**Aesthetician** ~ Facials, Chemical peels, Waxing, Skin Care, Makeup, Eye Treatments and Facial massages for both women and men.

**Nail Services** ~ Spa Manicures & Pedicures, Acrylic Nails, Moisturizing treatments for both the feet and hands, and Nail Care.

**Stylist Services** ~ Deep conditioning treatments, Scalp Massages, Styling, Cuts, Color, Hi-liting, Perming, Relaxing.

### Appreciation packages are available for:

- Weddings/Wedding Party
- Thank Yous
- Promotions /Sales
- New Business / Office Employee Incentives
- Retirement / Secretary's Day
- Happy Birthday / Anniversary
- Seasonal Gifts

Mix and match any salon service to create your own unique way of saying thank you. Some of our best packages are listed below:

- A custom facial and peel, spa manicure and pedicure, and complete hair makeover.
- A custom peel and waxing, moisturizing treatment for feet or hands, deep conditioning treatment for those tired tresses, and style.
- Moisturizing treatment with face, neck, and shoulder massage, spa manicure and pedicure, and choose any hair service.

For a more intimate experience, our packages are available at the office, event location, or home. Special requests, such as food, beverages, and other amenities can be added to any of our packages.

## LET US MAKE YOUR EXPERIENCE WITH US A TRULY MEMORABLE ONE!

# Lucy Palmer Boutique
# &
# Lucy Palmer Specialty Gift Division

***Boutique: 460 Fifth Street***
***Lake Oswego, Oregon 97034***
*Hours: Mon–Sat 10:30am–5pm; Sun Noon–4pm*
*Phone: (503) 534-1435;*
*Web site: www.lucypalmer.com*
*E-mail: lucyp@teleport.com*

***Gift Division/Showroom:***
*5833 Jean Road*
*Lake Oswego, Oregon 97035*
*Hours: Mon–Fri *APPOINTMENT ONLY*
*Phone: (503) 635-6856*
*Fax: (503) 223-2464*

---

Specialty Gift Division—Lucy Palmer Specialty and Corporate Gift Division was created to offer our clients extraordinary gift options. We package fun!

Whether your gift is for personal or business, Lucy Palmer will create a gift that will make a lasting impression.

We offer single item gifts, customized gift packages, auction packages and creative bid packaging, as well as marketing ideas and services.

## Some of our Most Popular Specialty Packages:

- Urban Lounge Party
- Entertaining Package
- Thank God It's Friday!
- Margarita Package
- Instant Birthday Party
- New Home/New Office
- Football Party
- Ultimate Movie Night
- Pizza Night in a Box
- Seasonal Gift Packages
- Queen Spa Package
- Little Miss Fashion
- Hollywood Starlet

Lucy Palmer Boutique— *"The ultimate girl shop."* We offer the very best in accessories for you and your home! One of the Northwest's largest selections of sterling silver jewelry, decorative accessories, lighting, spa and personal care, cards and party, candles and everything you need to entertain in style.

***We look forward to doing business with you soon!***

YOUR GATEWAY TO THE MEDITERRANEAN

©Photo Design

Contact: Leslie Coppock
503-231-8651 or 888-380-8018
E-mail: leslie@olivefarm.com
Website: www.olivefarm.com

Olive Farm Flagship Store
5120 SE Milwaukie Ave
Portland, Oregon 97202

Olive Farm Bellevue Square
274 Bellevue Square
Bellevue, Washington 98004

## ESTATE-BOTTLED OLIVE OIL AND FINE MEDITERRANEAN IMPORTS

Whether you are presenting a Corporate Gift to a key client, sending a special thank you or planning welcome gifts for your next convention, make it a truly exceptional experience by selecting only the best…

**OLIVE FARM** is proud to introduce our unique, comprehensive and cost-effective corporate gift-giving program. We offer the world's best first-cold-pressed estate-bottled Extra Virgin Olive Oils and Mediterranean gourmet foods. Let us custom design the perfect gift to convey your corporate image.

- Choose from a wide selection of estate-bottled olive oils, stuffed olives, spreads, vinegars, dried fruits and nuts, confections, tea, coffee, olive wood pieces, ceramics, spa-line, skin care, accent pieces and much more.
- A beautiful array of pre-made gift baskets and gift collections can be found in our extensive catalog.
- Company logos and promotional items can be incorporated into your baskets or collections, reinforcing marketing efforts and business relationships.
- Personalized cards and messages.
- In-store sampling and tasting at Olive Farm's Flagship Store in Portland and in our newest location at Bellevue Square in the Seattle area.
- Meeting space available in our Portland location for up to 50 people with arrangements for catering, flowers, wine and beverages, and wait staff.
- Monthly cooking classes with top chefs in both our Portland and Bellevue locations. (Gift certificates for our cooking classes make wonderful gifts.)

To arrange an on-site presentation or your own personalized tour and store visit, please contact Leslie Coppock, Corporate Gift Consultant at 503-231-8651 or 888-380-8018.

I look forward to assisting you with all of your gift-giving needs.

The Olive Farm, LLC. 5120 SE Milwaukie Ave. Portland, Oregon 97202

# Promotional Treats

*P.O. Box 19691*
*Portland, Oregon 97280*
*(503) 246-4743*
*Fax (503) 246-4754*
*E-mail: protreats@aol.com; www.promotionaltreats.com*

## Have Something to Say?

Say it with chocolate. Deliver your message in a way they'll remember. Put your name, message, or logo straight into the chocolate. We work with you to create just the right product to promote the theme of your event—because your event is special. At Promotional Treats, you'll find that our candy looks as good as it tastes.

## Product Offering

- Centerpieces
- Chocolate dishes filled with chocolate delights
- Chocolate floral bouquets
- Chocolate promotional items
- Corporate gifts
- Custom molded chocolate
- Custom boxed candy
- Corporate logos
- Table favors
- Truffles

## Event Suggestions

- Corporate events
- Employee incentives
- Grand openings
- Holidays
- Office parties
- Sales promotions
- Thank you gifts
- Weddings/Anniversaries

Our chocolate gift items serve as a gift, a decoration and a dessert.

**So Remember—**
**A Touch of Chocolate for Every Event**

# Ramona's

## BASKETS BEARING GIFTS

*205 Commerce Center*
*11504-K S.E. Mill Plain Boulevard*
*Vancouver, Washington 98684*
*Contact: Ramona Lupo*
*(360) 253-7980, (800) 775-7158;*
*Fax (360) 253-5728*
*E-mail: ramona@ramonasgifts.com*
*Web site: www.ramonasgifts.com*
*Business Hours:*
*Mon–Fri 10am–6pm; Sat 10am–5pm*

## For Over 26 Years...

At Ramona's we take great pleasure in creating baskets bearing gifts of award-winning Northwest wines, microbrews, cheese, sausage, smoked salmon, fresh fruit, pasta, sauces, jams, flowers, plants and the finest chocolate. The offering of gift baskets has a rich heritage in many cultures over thousands of years, and Ramona's continues that tradition. Whether you choose from our Ready To Go, Create Your Own or Custom Design, your gift will be of incomparable quality and style.

## A Sampling

- **Snack Attack:** Perfect for a hotel guest or an office, all Ready To Eat, smoked salmon, cheese, fresh fruit, sausage, crackers, sweets, cookies, soda, wine or beer
- **NW Best:** For the executive or the family, a variety of foods from the bounty of the Pacific Northwest. From sweet to savory, this basket is always popular.
- **Smokey the Fish:** You guessed it, smoked salmon, smoked trout, sturgeon, oysters, salmon jerky, paté, crackers, smoked nuts…add a bottle of wine or brew.
- **Basket in Bloom:** Beautiful live green or flowering plants are surrounded with your choice of gourmet products. Or maybe just a plant in a decorated basket.
- **And more:** Fruit Of The Earth, The Brew Basket, Grape Escape, Coffee Lover's Dream, Primo Pasta
  - Wedding and shower baskets
  - Meeting Snack Paks
  - Table centerpieces and table favors
  - Recognition and guest speakers
  - Trade show display and giveaway baskets
  - Theme Convention Gifts

## Business Gifts

Ramona's offers full-service business gift solutions. We can include your logo on a variety of products for your company gifts, and there are a number of billing options available. Whatever it takes, Ramona's will help enhance your company image. With more than 26 years of "taking care of business" experience, you can trust our expertise in handling business accounts.

Visa, MasterCard, Discover and American Express.
Local delivery and worldwide shipping.

**Visit Ramona's Baskets Bearing Gifts—full service retail store**
**Cascade Park in Vancouver, just off I-205**

***Member of Vancouver and Battleground Chamber of Commerce, S.W. Washington CVB, POVA, Women In Action and HSMAI***

*"The Northwest Products Store"*

**Request a personalized presentation or a quote –** *please contact:*

*Janet Pendergrass & Linda Strand Sisters/Partners*

**Ph: 503-554-9060 or 888-252-0699**

E-mail: jpendergrass@yournw.com (or) lstrand@yournw.com

---

YOUR NORTHWEST . . . *Your Destination for Fine Specialty Foods & Gifts that showcase the Northwest. You will never go hungry for gift ideas again!*

GIFT PACKS, GIFT BASKETS, GIFT BAGS
OREGON MARIONBERRY PRODUCTS
ESTATE GROWN HAZELNUT PRODUCTS
SMOKED WILD SALMON
BERRY PRODUCTS – Fresh From Our Farm
NW FOOD AND WINE
FAMOUS CAKES
BIG SKY CARVERS/BEARFOOTS
NW ARTISTS
NW FAVORITES

PRIVATE LABEL: Add your company logo or message to our fine Berry Preserves and Syrups, Hazelnuts, Confections or Smoked Salmon

**VOLUME DISCOUNTS • GIFT CARDS • RELIABLE DELIVERY**
**INCENTIVE PROGRAMS • ORDERING MADE EASY**

*Visit Our Stores:*
OREGON CONVENTION CENTER 503-233-5665
CLACKAMAS TOWN CENTER 503-653-1717
WOODBURN COMPANY STORES 503-981-5014
DUNDEE, Wine Country 503-554-8101

*Shop Online:* **YOURNW.COM**
Fax: 503-537-9693

*Contact:*
Janet Pendergrass & Linda Strand
*Sisters/Partners*
503-554-9060 or 888-252-0699

E-mail: jpendergrass@yournw.com
lstrand@yournw.com
sales@yournw.com

Mail Us: Your NorthWest
PO Box 1, Dundee, OR 97115

# Florists

# SELECTING A FLORIST

**Selecting a florist:** Most florists have a portfolio of their work. Ask for references and see what customers have to say about them. Choose a florist who will spend time with you. If the florist has not been to the site of the event, you may want to take him or her to view the decor. This ensures that they design arrangements that match the surroundings and can be very helpful when you are discussing your ideas and needs. Your florist can also inform you about what flowers will be in season and styles that will appropriately fit your theme and budget.

**Develop a plan:** Think about your floral design and decorations and write your ideas down. Determine what you will need from the various people involved and have a budget in mind. Ask several florists for formal bids based on your outline, then determine which florist and budget you feel most comfortable with.

**Sample arrangements are a good idea:** It might be a good idea to request a sample arrangement prior to your special event, especially if the order placed is very large and if the idea you are trying out is a new one and photos are not available. This way there will be no surprises the day of the event for florist, decorator and coordinator.

**Meeting with the florist:** You should meet with your florist as soon as possible. A florist can be very helpful in the beginning phases of choosing your theme and can offer decoration ideas that emphasize that theme throughout the event.

**Developing rapport with your florist and decorator:** After several events with the same vendor you can build a great team of idea generators. They begin thinking of ways to add that extra special touch to your events. Your vendors become your extended staff and will do what it takes to accomplish the job, so treat them well and show your appreciation.

**Creative ways of financing flowers and decorations:** For a fund raiser, you can auction the centerpieces right off the tables. At an awards function, the winners can bring home flowers with the award, or you can thank those who helped with the function by giving them the table arrangements. Potted plants also make a long-lasting gift.

**Delivery and setup of flowers:** It is crucial that your flowers be delivered at the right time. They shouldn't arrive earlier than necessary since some facilities are not air conditioned and certain flowers deteriorate rapidly. If your flowers must be in place at a certain time, be sure to tell your florist what time they'll be needed. Always put the location and date on your contract, as well as the desired time of delivery, so there are no questions or last-minute problems. Check to see if the bid includes setup and delivery. If it doesn't, be sure to adjust your budget to include these costs.

# A Floral Affair

Your Event and Wedding Florist

*503.794.9370*
*Web site: www.floralaffair.net*
*E-mail: floralaffair@att.net*

*By Appointment*

***A Floral Affair*** knows when planning and producing important events it is vital that every aspect is carried out professionally and worry free.

***A Floral Affair*** specializes in event floral designs. Whether you are planning a small corporate gathering or a large elaborate affair, you will have confidence in knowing that the floral decorations will be perfect. A complimentary consultation is given in your office or the location of your event. This allows A Floral Affair to gain a full understanding of the important details that will make your event unforgettable. We will work closely with you up until your event, coordinating all the details of the floral décor.

***A Floral Affair's*** clients praise our ability to create unique, high quality displays individually tailored to their specific needs. With 25 years experience in the floral industry, our design styles are truly diverse in contemporary, traditional, European and themed floral designs, incorporating a variety of elements from fresh flowers to novelty items. To achieve a complete look, we can assist you with a variety of rental items to create a one-of-a-kind event. Our competitive pricing allows us to work with any budget to achieve an unforgettable event.

Let ***A Floral Affair*** help you create outstanding events. Call for your complimentary consultation to discuss how we can better serve you and your floral needs.

## PRICING

Prices based on seasonal fresh flowers. Price varies depending on flower choice, quantity of flowers used and size of floral display.

**TABLE CENTERPIECES:**

- Bud Vases $8.50 and up
- Small Centerpiece $12.50 and up
- Medium Centerpiece $25 and up
- Large Centerpiece $45 and up
- Head Table $50 and up

**BUFFET TABLE:** $50 and up

**ENTRANCE DÉCOR:** $75 and up

**PODIUM DECORATIONS:**

- Medium Mixed $75 and up
- Large Mixed $125 and up

**PERSONAL FLOWERS:**

- Corsages $8.50 - $20
- Boutonniere $4.50 - $7.50

**PRESENTATION BOUQUETS:** $20 and up

## ALSO AVAILABLE:

BLOOMING & GREEN PLANTS • BALLOONS • SPRAYS • SILKS • RENTAL EQUIPMENT • STAGE DÉCOR • HOLIDAY DECORATING

***Making your floral decisions a personal and unique experience***

*6650 N.W. Kaiser Rd • Portland, Oregon 97229*
*Contact: Cheryl Skoric, CBA*
*503.629.5827; Fax 503.645.9404*
***Oregon's First Certified Balloon Artist***
*Business Hours: to suit your schedule,*
*day or evening by appointment*
***www.bouquetsandballoons.com***

---

## More than your ordinary florist
## Flowers ❀ Balloons ❀ Theme Creation

*We offer beautiful floral arrangements, but we are experts in creating balloon themes.*

Corporate Events • Conventions • Trade Shows • Banquets • Theme Parties • Special Events • Company Picnics • Grand Openings • Carnivals & Fairs • Shopping Mall Promotions •

### As Corporate Specialists

Bouquets & Balloons offers services designed to simplify your job while providing you with imaginative ideas and unsurpassed service.

• Free consultation at the event site, your location, or ours

### Theme Parties

Balloons are the perfect decorating alternative for any occasion or event. Arches, columns, swags, balloon drops and sculptures can highlight the focal points of your event and give the room an air of festivity and elegance. Try Futuristic, Tropical, Fantasy, Carnival, Mardi Gras, Wine Fest, '50s, Under the Sea and Western, just to name a few.

### Special Effects

Do you want to create Excitement? Exploding Balloons filled with confetti, balloons, movie tickets or anything else you desire, exploded over the crowd will inspire them. Do you have something that you would like to hide until a specific time? Try the Exploding Wall. Sure to be a crowd pleaser.

### Balloon Ideas

Logos • Chinese Lanterns • Cactus • Tumbleweeds • Wagons • Santa Claus • Snowmen • Tin Soldiers • Sea Horses • Octopus • Fish • Waves • Bubbles • Dance Canopies

### Floral Ideas

Stage Decor • Buffet Flowers • Centerpieces • Podium Arrangements •
Head Table Arrangements • Presentation Bouquets • Corsages • Boutonnieres •
Sign-in Table Arrangement

**Note:** Some facilities do not allow helium-filled balloons. But if you like the looks of balloons, check with us, we specialize in air-filled balloon decorations.

Located near the North Park Blocks in the Pearl District, City Flowers has been one of Portland's most beloved flower shops for more than 16 years.

## Want your event to be memorable?

We specialize in big events, and whether you're planning an intimate dinner party or a large-scale business affair, you can trust us to create exciting and original floral designs.

## Friendly, creative designers

Please call or email us for a complimentary consultation. We have a library of albums for you to peruse, and our knowledgeable designers will work with your ideas to flesh out the details of your event. Are you budget-conscious? Let our designers show you creative ways to save money while maintaining the unique "look" of your party. Finally, City Flowers will keep in regular contact with you to answer any questions or make any last-minute changes you may have.

## "Ooos!" and "Ahhs!" guaranteed

"You are miles ahead of the other florists we dealt with in Portland before coming to you. The whole experience was great!" – May 2003

"Everything was right on time and looked great! You were on top of everything and quick to respond. Thank you!" – July 2003

"Wonderful job! I will recommend City Flowers to my family and friends." –November 2003

"We'd recommend City Flowers 10 times over! Thank you for all of your professionalism and vision." – December 2003

## Visit us online!

www.cityflowerspdx.com

# Notes

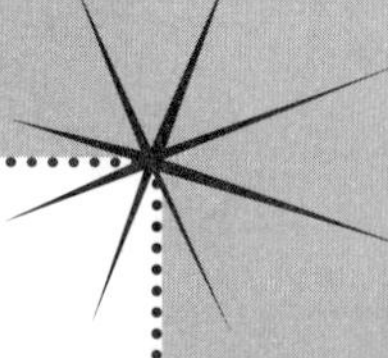

# Golf Courses & Tournaments

- *Public Golf Course Listings*

*24377 N.E. Airport Road*
*Aurora, Oregon 97002*
*503-678-GOLF (4653)*
*www.langdonfarms.com*

Langdon Farms Golf Course is conveniently located 20 minutes south of Portland off I-5. The course is situated on several acres of pristine greens designed from the former farmland of the Langdon Family.

Langdon Farms Golf Club was designed by award winning architects, John Fought and Robert Cupp, and shares course architecture traditions with great courses from around the world. Measuring 6,935 yards from the back tees, but only 5,249 from the forward tees, the course puts a premium on accurate iron shots for low scores, yet remains very playable for the recreational golfer. A commitment to superior playing conditions and excellent drainage make Langdon Farms one of the best places to play every day of the year. Langdon Farms Golf Club has the only all exclusive Nike Golf Shop located in Northwest Oregon.

**www.langdonfarms.com**

---

## Oregon City Golf Club at Lone Oak

*20124 S. Beavercreek Road*
*Oregon City, Oregon 97045*
*Contact: Timber Stevens, Tournament Director (503) 518-2846*
*Business Hours: Mon–Sun 8am–6pm*
*E-mail: timber@ocgolfclub.com*
*wwww.ocgolfclub.com*

Oregon City Golf Club was built in 1922 and is the third oldest public golf course in the state of Oregon still in operation. It was one of the most improved golf courses in the Portland metropolitan area and was recently included in *Golf Digest's* "Places to Play" edition.

The course measures 5,872 yards from the back tees with a rating of 67.9 and a slope of 116. The tree-lined fairways and undulating greens provide a fair test for anyone from the beginning golfer to the top amateurs.

O.C. Golf Club welcomes tournament play. The facilities include a banquet room, patio, gazebo, and courtyard area providing tournaments with a variety of places to gather before or after an event. Other tournament services include cart rental, beverage cart with personalized drink tickets, snack bar area, and more.

Tournaments are already being booked for 2005. Please call (503) 518-2846 as soon as you decide on a date for your event.

# THE RESERVE

VINEYARDS AND GOLF CLUB

*4805 S.W. 229th Avenue • Aloha, Oregon 97007*
*Contact: Ian Sperling, Sales & Marketing Manager*
*(503) 259-2008; Web site: www.reservegolf.com*

## The Reserve – 'Simply the Finest Golf Experience in Portland!'

The Reserve is the premier location for tournaments of all sizes. The conditioning and playability of the courses, as well as the functional nature of the clubhouse, enables group outings with players of mixed abilities to enjoy the day, whether in competition or playing to raise fund for charitable organizations.

### Tournament Pricing Includes

- 18-hole Green Fees, Carts and Range Balls
- Tournament Scoring
- Personalized Cart Signs and Scorecards
- Golf Course Stewards
- Closest to the Pin and Long Drive Competition Signage
- Banquet Facilities
- Beverage Cart
- Tournament Gifts for Each Player

### Additional Services Available

- Tournament Tee Gift Packages
- Golf Clinics, Group Lessons, Swing Solutions Analysis
- Wine Tasting
- Pro Quality Rental Clubs

A tournament may request consecutive tee times for a group of 20 or more players. A deposit is due with the signed contract, and the remaining balance is due 14 days prior to the tournament. Groups may also buy the course for a shotgun start; prices are based on a full field of 144 players. Course prices change throughout the season—please call for further information on tournament pricing and availability.

# Notes

# PUBLIC GOLF COURSES
## Oregon and Southwest Washington

**Broadmoor Golf Course**
3509 N.E. Columbia Blvd.
Portland, OR 97211
(503) 281-1337

**The Cedars Golf Club**
15001 N.E. 181st St.
Brush Prairie, WA 98606
(503) 285-7548 or
(360) 687-4233

**Charbonneau Golf Club**
32000 S.W. Charbonneau Dr.
Wilsonville, OR 97070
(503) 694-1246

**Claremont Golf Course**
15800 N.W. Country Club Dr.
Portland, OR 97229
(503) 690-4589
www.claremontgolf.com

**Colwood National Golf Club**
7313 N.E. Columbia Blvd.
Portland, OR 97218
(503) 254-5515
www.colwoodgolfclub.com

**Creekside Golf Club**
6250 Clubhouse Dr., S.E.
Salem, OR 97306
(503) 363-4653

**Eagle Crest Golf Course**
1522 Cline Falls Rd.
Redmond, OR 97756
(541) 923-2453
www.eagle-crest.com
*See page 440*

**Eastmoreland Golf Course**
2425 S.E. Bybee Blvd.
Portland, OR 97202
(503) 775-2900
www.eastmorelandgrill.com
*See page 91*

**Fairway Village Golf Club**
15509 S.E. Fernwood Dr.
Vancouver, WA 98683
(360) 254-9325

**Forest Hills Golf Course**
36260 S.W. Tongue Ln.
Cornelius, OR 97113
(503) 357-3347

**Glendoveer Golf Club**
14015 N.E. Glisan St.
Portland, OR 97230
(503) 253-7507

**Gresham Golf Course**
2155 N.E. Division St.
Gresham, OR 97030
(503) 665-3352

**Heron Lakes Golf Course (Gray Blue)**
3500 N. Victory Blvd.
Portland, OR 97217
(503) 289-1818
www.heronlakesgolf.com

**Indian Creek Golf Course**
3605 Brookside Dr.
Hood River, OR 97031
(541) 386-7770

**Kah-Nee-Ta Resort Course**
100 Main St./P.O. Box K
Warm Springs, OR 97761
(541) 553-1112
www.kahneeta.com
*See page 445*

**Killarney West Golf Course**
1275 N.W. 334th Ave.
Hillsboro, OR 97124
(503) 648-7634

**King City Golf Course**
15355 S.W. Royalty Pkwy.
Tigard, OR 97224
(503) 639-7986

**Lake Oswego Golf Course**
17525 S.W. Stafford Rd.
Lake Oswego, OR 97034
(503) 636-8228

**Lakeside Golf & Racquet Club**
3245 N.E. 50th Ave.
Lincoln City, OR 97367
(541) 994-8442

**Langdon Farms Golf Club**
24377 N.E. Airport Rd.
Aurora, OR 97002
(503) 678-4653
www.langdonfarms.com
*See page 354*

**Lewis River Golf Course**
3209 Lewis River Rd.
Woodland, WA 98674
(360) 225-8254
www.lewisrivergolf.com
*See page 118*

**Meriwether National Golf Club**
5200 S.W. Rood Bridge Rd.
Hillsboro, OR 97123
(503) 648-4143

**Mint Valley Golf Course**
4002 Pennsylvania St.
Longview, WA 98632
(360) 442-5442

**Mountain View Golf Club**
27195 S.E. Kelso Rd.
Boring, OR 97009
(503) 663-4869

**Oregon City Golf Club**
20124 S. Beavercreek Rd.
Oregon City, OR 97045
(503) 518-2846
*See page 354*

**Orenco Woods Golf Course**
22200 N.W. Birch
Hillsboro, OR 97124
(503) 648-1836

**Persimmon Country Club**
500 S.E. Butler Rd.
Gresham, OR 97080
(503) 661-1800
www.persimmongolf.com

**Pumpkin Ridge Golf Club**
12930 N.W. Old Pumpkin Ridge Rd.
North Plains, OR 97113
(503) 647-9977
www.pumpkinridge.com
*See page 132*

**Quail Run Golf Club**
16725 Northridge Dr.
La Pine, OR 97739
(541) 536-1303

**Red Tail Golf Course**
8200 Scholls Ferry Rd.
Beaverton, OR 97008
(503) 646-5166

**The Reserve Vineyard and Golf Club**
4805 S.W. 229th Ave.
Aloha, OR 97007
(503) 649-2345
*See page 355*

**The Resort at The Mountain**
68010 E. Fairway Ave.
Welches, OR 97067
(800) 669-4653
www.theresort.com
*See page 140*

**Rose City Golf Club**
2200 N.E. 71st Ave.
Portland, OR 97213
(503) 253-4744

**Salishan Lodge & Golf Resort**
7760 N. Hwy. 101
Gleneden Beach, OR 97388
(541) 764-3632
(800) 890-0387
www.salishan.com
*See page 449*

**Skamania Lodge Golf Course**
1131 Skamania Lodge Wy.
Stevenson, WA 98648
(509) 427-2540
skamanialodge.dolce.com
*See page 439*

**Summerfield Golf Course**
10650 S.W. Summerfield Dr.
Tigard, OR 97224
(503) 620-1200

**Three Rivers Golf Course**
2222 S. River Rd.
Kelso, WA 98626
(360) 423-4653

**Top O'Scott Course**
12000 S.E. Stevens Rd.
Portland, OR 97266
(503) 654-5050

**Wildwood Golf Course**
21881 N.W. St. Helens Rd.
Portland, OR 97231
(503) 621-3402

*Please let these golf courses know that you heard about them from the Bravo! Event & Party Resource Guide.*

# Notes

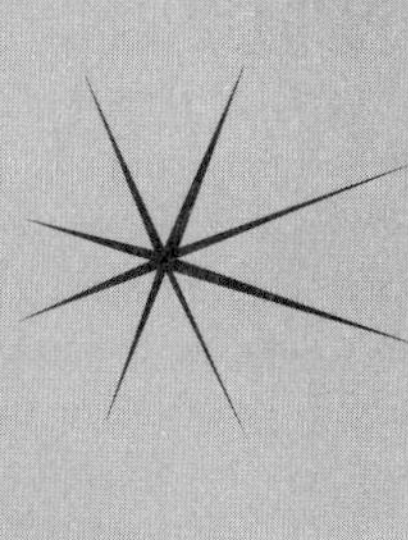

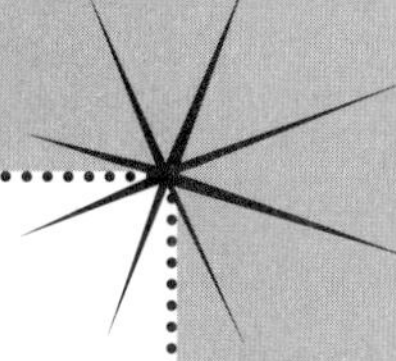

Interactive Entertainment & Team Building

# INTERACTIVE ENTERTAINMENT & TEAM BUILDING

**Why use a theme and audience participative entertainment?** A theme provides interest and coherence for the attendees. Planning is more efficient with a theme, creating an automatically organized process. In addition, the key to successful events is audience participation. The more involved people become in the event they are attending, the more likely they are to enjoy themselves and remember the experience. Attendees may not remember the name of the keynote speaker, but they will remember the "Wacky Olympics" special event!

**When is a theme appropriate?** Anytime you have an event. When done properly, themes can be used to enhance a business meeting, client appreciation, awards event, and even reunions.

**How is a theme chosen?** Define the goals of your event first, what you want to accomplish with the event, who is attending, and what you want them to take away with them. Then, you can decide what theme options may work. Brainstorming with a committee or colleague can be a big help .

**Are theme events expensive?** They don't have to be. It depends on your budget. Some of your theme ideas can be accomplished with a small budget if you and your committee are willing to spend the time. However, a much better use of your time and money may be to use a meeting planner, prop, or entertainment company.

**Decorating tips for theme events:** Consider three to four main areas of the facility for theme props. Main focus areas can include the entryway to the event, stage, guest tables, beverage and food stations, to name a few.

**Interactive and Theme ideas for your next event:**

- Casino Night
- Murder Mystery
- Tropical Island
- Cruise Ship
- African Jungle
- Tropical Rain Forest
- Western/ Wild West
- Medieval Castle
- Hawaiian Luau
- Fabulous 50s
- Great Gatsby Party
- Winter Wonderland
- M•A•S•H
- South of the Border
- Underwater
- Mexican Fiesta
- Mardi Gras
- Circus! Circus!
- International Themes
- Nautical
- The Great Northwest
- Learn to yo-yo

# Airbrush Ink

A Division of Langue Enterprises Inc.

**Temporary Tattoos and Body Art**

503-625-1277

---

**Temporary Tattoos are a great addition to:**

- Corporate Events
- Company Picnics
- Grand Openings
- Birthday Parties

Choose from over 600 unique tattoo designs and nine bright colors appropriate for your specific theme. **Airbrush Ink** can create your company logo for your next corporate event!

***Call us and we'll help make your next event a hit!***
***Fun for all ages!***

**503-625-1277**

Call for a quote!
503.516.3878
www.allaboutfunamerica.com

- -Inflatables
- -Casino Night
- -DJ Services
- -Live Enterainment
- -And much more

---

## THE ONLY CALL YOU NEED TO MAKE FOR ALL YOUR EVENT AND ENTERTAINMENT NEEDS!

Want to create a fun event for your company, staff or customers and don't know where to begin? Call "All About Fun!" We can take care of all your event planning and entertainment needs with our huge selection of entertainment and event planning services.

### INFLATABLE AND INTERACTIVE FUN:

| | | |
|---|---|---|
| GIANT SLIDE | MECHANICAL BULL | OBSTACLE COURSE |
| BAJA RC RACE TRACK | ROCK WALL | VIRTUAL REALITY |
| LAZER TAG | SUMO WRESTLING | BOUNCY BOXING |
| GLADIATOR JOUST | NASCAR RC RACING | BUNGEE RUN |
| BUNGEE TRAMPOLINE | CASH CUBE | DANCE DANCE REVOLUTION |
| KIDS BOUNCES | DUNK TANK | VIDEO GAMES |
| POOL TABLES | FOOSBALL | AIR HOCKEY |
| DOUBLE SHOT | CARNIVAL GAMES | **MUCH MUCH MORE…** |

### CASINO PARTIES:

Everyone loves a chance at "winning big" and "All About Fun" has great casino packages for whatever the occasion:

| | | | |
|---|---|---|---|
| Holiday Parties | Fundraisers | Client Appreciation Parties | Managers Retreats |
| Grad Parties | Private Parties | Birthday Parties | Reunion Events |

Whether you're looking for Black Jack, Poker, Craps or Roulette: we have great equipment and professional dealers with lots of personality to make the event more fun.

### DJ SERVICES:

| | | |
|---|---|---|
| DISK JOCKEY | KARAOKE DJ | KARAOKE DJ/ |
| VIDEO KARAOKE | SOUND EQUIPMENT | GAMESHOW |
| LIGHTING RENTAL | | |

### LIVE ENTERTAINMENT OPTIONS:

| | | |
|---|---|---|
| BANDS AND MUSIC ACTS | CARICATURE ARTISTS | TATTOO ARTIST |
| HYPNOTIST | AIRBRUSH TATTOO | AIRBRUSH T-SHIRTS |
| MAGICIANS | COMEDIANS | JUGGLERS |
| AND MORE…. | | |

**Eddie May Mysteries**
**Hilarious Audience Participation**

# WHODUNITS!

*Great Food!,*
*Side-Splitting Comedy!*
*Mystery! Mayhem! And*

*Served Hot!*

**(503) 524-4366**
*www.eddiemaymysteries.com*
**Have party, will travel!**

---

**DICK TRACEY MEETS SATURDAY NIGHT LIVE!**

Fundraisers! Conventions! Meetings! Cocktail Parties! Birthdays!

**A World Traveled Critically Acclaimed Theater Troupe!**

Masters Of Improvisational Comedy! You'll Die Laughing!

**Play At Our Location Or Yours! We Travel Anywhere!**

Who's Gonna Kick The Bucket? Watch Your Backs!

**Is The Killer Eating At Your Table? Or A Possible Victim?**

Help Detective May Interrogate The Suspects!

**Search The Character's Belongings For Evidence and Clues!**

Solvable Mysteries That Make Sense! Watch– Listen–Examine Solve!

**A Perfect Team Building Opportunity!**

America's Finest Interactive Murder Mystery Parties!

**CAN YOU FIGURE OUT WHODUNIT?**

She was a cold-blooded killer with a pair of icy blues and a heart to match. Now that @#*! cop wants to know why she talked to you all evening. So does your wife.

**"Our faces hurt from laughing so much."**

Pardon me, is that a knife in your back?

**"The president of our association kept asking how we're going to top IT'S A MYSTERY... Well, I honestly don't think we can..."**

As soon as I heard the gun, I knew it meant trouble; but who could have imagined this?

**"...the entire crew were highly professional, courteous, articulate, incredibly funny, and creative beyond belief."**

I'm Detective Richard Sheridan. Don't call me Dick.

**"...remarked that this was the most unforgettable and fun event they have ever attended!"**

Isn't that Mike's favorite golf club next to the body?

**"...the best entertainment we have ever had at a company Christmas party."**

**Toll Free: (866) 621-1500**
**www.itsamystery.com**

# LASERPORT

## ALL NEW LASER TAG ARENA

6540 SW FALLBROOK PLACE • BEAVERTON, OR 97008
OWNERS: JOHN GABEL, BILL BUHLER & PAUL MORRIS
(503) 526-9501; FAX (503) 626-6912
HOURS: MON-THURS NOON-9PM FRIDAY NOON-1AM
SATURDAY 10AM-1AM SUNDAY 11AM-9PM

---

**"DON'T JUST PLAY IT – LIVE IT"**

Our new 18,400 sq.ft. building is uniquely designed to handle corporate functions of all kinds and all sizes. From training seminars to team building, we can accommodate up to 200 people sitting with projection capabilities. With our full service kitchen we can offer a wide range of meal, buffet and/or beverage service options including beer and wine. We have a separate, private room that can easily handle a group of 40 or allow for a breakout; the room is also equipped for PowerPoint presentations. Our all new 5,000 sq. ft. lasertag arena allows for up to 48 players to play comfortably at a time. Great for ice-breaking, get-togethers, after work team activities, or simply a way to reenergize your group after sitting through a particularly long presentation. LASERPORT'S new larger facility offers what no other venue can. Satisfaction Assured – 10 years of Corporate Event Hosting.

**Capacity:** Up to 400

**Price Range:** Corporate packaging of room rental, food, beverages and lasertag are all possible in any combination by contacting our Marketing Department. Posted prices for Lasertag is $7 for the first game and $5 any additional game. We have a weekend special, Friday and Saturday 9pm to midnight, Sunday 6pm to close – three games for $12

**Catering:** Full-service, in-house catering; prices vary with menu selection.

**Types of Events:** Team building and stress reduction make laser tag the perfect corporate outing. Multiple team and customized competitions are possible using our computer-generated game formats, even a "Protect the President" option that adds to the excitement. We can accommodate: training sessions, divisional meetings, sales meetings, management training – almost any corporate group activity can be made memorable by adding the option of lasertag.

### Availability and Terms

We strongly recommend making your reservations as early as possible. Deposit is required upon reservation. We gladly accept all major credit cards.

### Description of Facility and Services:

Two (2) Meeting Rooms, One (1) Full Service Restaurant/Bar. We have a full service restaurant with an extensive menu. Our bar serves beer and wine. Food options include, but not limited to: steak, fresh seafood, pasta, gourmet hamburgers, salads and hand-tossed gourmet pizza.

**Video Games:** We have over 40 of the latest arcade games; quarter operated.

**Server:** We host to the level of the event.

**China and glassware:** Plates, cups, and silverware are provided.

**Decorations:** No limitations.

**Audiovisual:** Provided upon request.

**Parking:** Spacious parking around the whole building; **ADA:** Fully accessible.

## Mad Science of Portland & Vancouver

1015 East Burnside Street
Portland, Oregon 97214
(503) 230-8040; Fax (503) 230-8949
E-mail: info@madscienceportland.com
Web: www.madscienceportland.com

---

### Want to make a LASTING IMPRESSION?

Let Mad Science impress your audience with an unforgettable experience! Our special events entertain families through Spectacular Shows, Fun Stations, and Sensational Workshops.

**Mad Science Special Events...**

- Come to your Event, Holiday Party, Picnic, Show, etc.
- Edu-tain children ages 4-12
- Are suitable for groups of 20-1000+ children
- Range from 45 minutes to a full day in length
- GUARANTEE your satisfaction

**Spectacular Shows:** 30-60 minutes of thrilling, fast-paced, high-energy science presentations that will dazzle the whole family!

- **Fire & Ice** — foggy dry-ice storms... giant balls floating in mid-air... flashy reactions that go POOF!
- **Up, Up & Away**— hot air balloons... fire balls from candles... the Mad Science floating hovercraft...
- **Spin, Pop, Boom!** — water defying gravity...bungee-jumping superheroes... foam bursting into the sky...

**Fun Stations:** Our fascinating science fun stations come equipped with fun and exciting hands-on science activities that are ideal for both indoor and outdoor activities or carnival-type events.

**Sensationally Fun Science Workshops:** Children will learn all about the exciting wonders of science in groups as they rotate from one workshop to another.

*"Mad Science really LIVENS up our holiday parties. The kids keep going back to see what's new to discover! Their staff is very professional and friendly."*

– Claudia Best, Executive Administrator,
Pepsi Bottling Group, Seattle, WA

**Call to find out more and to receive a customized event proposal.**

*Toll-free: 1-888-766-7284*
***Website: www.sonsational.com***

---

## Teambuilding and Morale Events for the 21st Century

***Tired of the ropes course?***
***Or taking the "trust fall" into your co-worker's outstretched arms?***

### Not Your Grandpa's Team Builder…

Our event specialists will work with you to design an event that is centered on your goals. However, unlike those of yesteryear, our teambuilding and morale events will effectively resonate in the modern business environment.

### Go Beyond Traditional Teambuilding…

We provide totally customizable events that will motivate and inspire your people. Activities such as our **GPS Scavenger Hunt**™ and **Madame Tussaud's Murder Mystery**™ build team dynamics in a fun environment. Take it up a notch with our **Team Survivor**™ and **Olympic Gold**™ interactive events. For comprehensive team and leadership development, we offer **Express**™, our tailored corporate program.

*"Your expert staff created the perfect morale event—I couldn't have been happier… I will use Sonsational again and again."* —Jill McKinnis, Product Manager, Microsoft

*"… the perfect program… your creative energy helped make our event a huge success. We shall call you to use your services at another MulvannyG2 Architecture event."*
—Emily Osburn, MulvannyG2 Architecture

*"You and your team do a wonderful job! You are so attuned to the Nike way of doing things and are an extremely valuable vendor partner. I look forward to working with you on many more gigs."* —Jane Mannex, Nike

# UPTOWN CASINO EVENTS

120 NW 23rd
PORTLAND, OR 97210
CONTACT: Drew Podolak
503-819-9708
FAX: 503-282-8008
www.uptowncasino.com

---

***Don't gamble…***

*on your company party, reunion, reception graduation night or private affair…*

***Play it safe with***
**Uptown Casino Events!**

**Experience**
Our staff is well versed in all elements of event production and will ensure that the casino portion of your evening is tailored to fit your group's specific needs — flowing seamlessly into the big picture of your group's event.

**Better Gaming Equipment**
Uptown Casino Events has the finest, most elegant gaming equipment in the Portland area. Hand crafted tables, casino quality chips, and the best accessories for a true casino gaming experience!

**Lower Prices**
With our exceptional equipment, friendly staff, and prices that can't be beat…what more could you ask for? Per table pricing for poker, blackjack, craps and roulette to accommodate all event sizes.

**Better Service**
Although games and activities go a long way in providing atmosphere, only personalities can be "The Life of Your Party." We hire and train a very personable crew.

**One Phone Call**
Is all it takes to plan your entire event. Let our sister company, The Uptown Billiards Club, take care of your off-site catering and/or entertainment needs and receive onsite gaming prices. Hold your event at the Billiards Club's unique facility and receive a 15% discount on the gaming portion of the evening.

**Call Uptown Casino Events**
**for an evening you will never forget!**
**(503) 819-9708**

# ULTRAZONE

**Portland's Best Laser Tag**

*16074 S.E. McLoughlin Boulevard*
*Milwaukie, Oregon 97267*
*Contact: Erick Lelack or Lee Sturman*
*(503) 652-1122; Fax (503) 652-5204*
*E-mail: lasertag@ultrazoneportland.com • Web site: www.ultrazoneportland.com*

## ULTRAZONE—THE FUN BUSINESS MEETING

Break the routine and inject a dose of fun and excitement into your business meeting. **Ultrazone** is combination of tag and hide& seek with a high-tech twist. Everyone wears a special vest outfitted with flashing lights and sensors. Using a real laser, players score points by "tagging" opponents and "capturing" opposing teams' bases. Special computers track events and tally points. Action takes place in **Portland's largest and only multi-level arena**. Experience fog-filled mazes and electronic wizardry. Ultrazone is heart-racing, adrenaline-pumping non-stop action.

## ULTRAZONE—THE ULTIMATE TEAM BUILDING ADVENTURE

- Everyone can play regardless of age or physical strength. No running, climbing or strenuous movements are required.
- Employee relations are improved. Teamwork is promoted by removing boundaries and tensions between employees so they work together to reach a common goal.
- Strategy development skills are sharpened. We demonstrate how teams benefit from working together to develop a strategic plan.
- The dramatic environment leaves a lasting impression on each employee.

## ULTRAZONE—THE BEST LASER TAG IN PORTLAND

Ultrazone is perfect for business meetings, office parties, birthday parties, morale boosting, sales meetings, or as a fun way to just release some steam. Food is available from all-you-can-eat pizza to a formal sit-down dinner. An excellent selection of video games and simulation rides is also available. Reservations are required.

## IS YOUR COMPANY READY TO TAKE THE CHALLENGE?

Join the growing list of companies that have taken the Ultrazone challenge.

- Hewlett Packard
- Horizon Airlines
- Tektronix
- American Honda
- Burger King
- Commercial Credit
- AT&T Cellular
- Civil Air Patrol
- Boyd Coffee
- Safeco Insurance
- Will Vinton Studios
- In Focus
- Starbucks
- Thomason Auto Group
- Nautilus Group
- Intel
- Red Lion Hotels
- Shari's Restaurants
- Home Depot
- Sprint
- Adventist Medical
- Ikon
- The Good Guys
- Voicestream Wireless
- Zellerbach
- Nortel
- ADP
- Quaker Oats
- Wells Fargo Bank
- Pacificorp
- U.S. Bank
- Western Wireless
- Mentor Graphics
- Standard Insurance
- Phoenix Inn
- Burgerville
- Prestige Care
- Electric Lightwave
- Louisiana Pacific
- Kaiser Permanente
- LSI Logic
- Safeway
- RR Donnelley
- The Christie School
- Regal Cinemas

*Since 1982*

*2318 N.W. Vaughn Street • Portland, Oregon 97210*

***(503) 224-0134 or toll-free (800) 346-7280; Fax (503) 224-0278***

***www.wildbills.com***

---

Wild Bill's provides the finest in exciting interactive entertainment for:

Company Parties • Reunions • Conventions • Client Appreciation Parties
Grad Nights • Holiday Parties • Picnics • Private Parties

Everyone has a great time at a Wild Bill's party because we get them involved in the action. You can leave the details to us. Just tell us where and when, and we'll do the rest.

## MURDER MYSTERIES

Cut-throat negotiations. Dirty politics. Killer deadlines. Who would have guessed they would be the highlights of your company party? Whether you have a group of 20 or 200, Wild Bill's can provide a night of unforgettable entertainment. Your guests will get caught up in the twists and turns of the plot as they piece together clues and attempt to solve the crime by interacting with the characters. Let us make a scene at your next party! It'll be a scream.

## GAME SHOWS

Part Hollywood glitter. Part corporate training. And a whole bunch of fun. Our game show production is an evening of high energy, fast paced Hollywood-style entertainment. Your guests are the contestants, competing in our version of your favorite game shows. Questions can come from our extensive trivia library, or we can create a show tailored to your event with questions and answers pertaining to your organization. The possibilities are limitless.

We supply the complete game show set with all the bells, buzzers and whistles, as well as a professional game show emcee, producer, technician, graphics and music.

## Here's What Our Clients Have To Say

*"... outstanding performance... one of the most memorable banquets we have ever had."*

~ Elmers

*"... very professional performance."*

~ Burger King

*"I can't imagine an event that would have been as fun, interactive and appropriate!"*

~ Meeting Professionals International

## Additional Entertainment Options

- Casino Parties
- Video Horse Racing
- DJ / Karaoke
- Comedy Hypnosis
- Inflatable Games
- Team Building Events

Member: Assoc. of Catering and Event Professionals, National Assoc. of Casino & Theme Party Operators, Meeting Professionals International, International Special Events Society, and the Portland Oregon Visitor's Association

**See page 200 under Casinos & On-Site Casino Parties.**

# Notes

# Notes

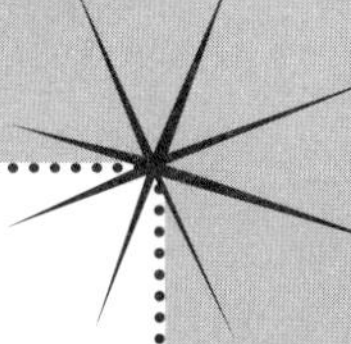

Interactive Games & Inflatables

# Interactive Games & Inflatables

BravoPortland.com

Call for a quote!
503.516.3878
www.allaboutfunamerica.com

-Inflatables
-Casino Night
-DJ Services
-Live Enterainment
-And much more

---

## THE ONLY CALL YOU NEED TO MAKE FOR ALL YOUR EVENT AND ENTERTAINMENT NEEDS!

Want to create a fun event for your company, staff or customers and don't know where to begin? Call "All About Fun!" We can take care of all your event planning and entertainment needs with our huge selection of entertainment and event planning services.

### INFLATABLE AND INTERACTIVE FUN:

| | | |
|---|---|---|
| GIANT SLIDE | MECHANICAL BULL | OBSTACLE COURSE |
| BAJA RC RACE TRACK | ROCK WALL | VIRTUAL REALITY |
| LAZER TAG | SUMO WRESTLING | BOUNCY BOXING |
| GLADIATOR JOUST | NASCAR RC RACING | BUNGEE RUN |
| BUNGEE TRAMPOLINE | CASH CUBE | DANCE DANCE REVOLUTION |
| KIDS BOUNCES | DUNK TANK | VIDEO GAMES |
| POOL TABLES | FOOSBALL | AIR HOCKEY |
| DOUBLE SHOT | CARNIVAL GAMES | **MUCH MUCH MORE...** |

### CASINO PARTIES:

Everyone loves a chance at "winning big" and "All About Fun" has great casino packages for whatever the occasion:

| | | | |
|---|---|---|---|
| Holiday Parties | Fundraisers | Client Appreciation Parties | Managers Retreats |
| Grad Parties | Private Parties | Birthday Parties | Reunion Events |

Whether you're looking for Black Jack, Poker, Craps or Roulette: we have great equipment and professional dealers with lots of personality to make the event more fun.

### DJ SERVICES:

| | | |
|---|---|---|
| DISK JOCKEY | KARAOKE DJ | KARAOKE DJ/ |
| VIDEO KARAOKE | SOUND EQUIPMENT | GAMESHOW |
| LIGHTING RENTAL | | |

### LIVE ENTERTAINMENT OPTIONS:

| | | |
|---|---|---|
| BANDS AND MUSIC ACTS | CARICATURE ARTISTS | TATTOO ARTIST |
| HYPNOTIST | AIRBRUSH TATTOO | AIRBRUSH T-SHIRTS |
| MAGICIANS | COMEDIANS | JUGGLERS |
| AND MORE.... | | |

## "FUN & GAMES" IS OUR BUSINESS!

**When dependability, clean equipment, safety and an energetic staff count… hire the GAMES-TO-GO PROS!**

### ★ Casino Parties-To-Go

Fun for all and all for fun! We bring Las Vegas to your event. We'll provide professional dealers…or you deal.

- ★ Blackjack
- ★ Craps
- ★ Roulette
- ★ Wheel-of-Fortune
- ★ Horse Racing Game
- ★ Giant Slot $ Machine

### ★ MiniGolf-On-Wheels

Luck and skill make this a great activity for all ages. Challenging obstacles. Designed for indoor or outdoor events. We deliver, set up, and provide everything you need.

- ★ 9 or 18-hole miniature golf
- ★ Electronic Golf Challenge

### ★ Games-To-Go-Rentals

New interactive games for all group sizes and age groups. Our energetic staff will keep your event moving and your guests entertained for hours.

- ★ Parachute Adventure, 26′
- ★ Ol' Fashion Picnic Game Package
- ★ Giant Slide
- ★ Soak'um Circus
- ★ Dunk Tank
- ★ Balloon Typhoon
- ★ 40+ Carnival Games
- ★ Carnival Booths
- ★ Kids Tattoo Booth
- ★ Powerpull (Tug O'War)
- ★ Spin Art
- ★ Launcher Wars
- ★ Sea of Balls
- ★ "SeaWeed" 55′ Obstacle Adventure
- ★ "Candy the 55′ Caterpillar"
- ★ Treasure Chest Promotion
- ★ Money Machine
- ★ Electronic Double-Shot Basketball
- ★ Popcorn & Cotton Candy Machines
- ★ Hi-Striker
- ★ 18′ Promotional Balloon
- ★ Super Bouncers

**Games to Go, LLC**
**Recreational Fun To Go!**
***Since 1991***
**(503) 667-7724**
**www.gamestogorentals.com**

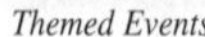

Themed Events

Virtual Reality

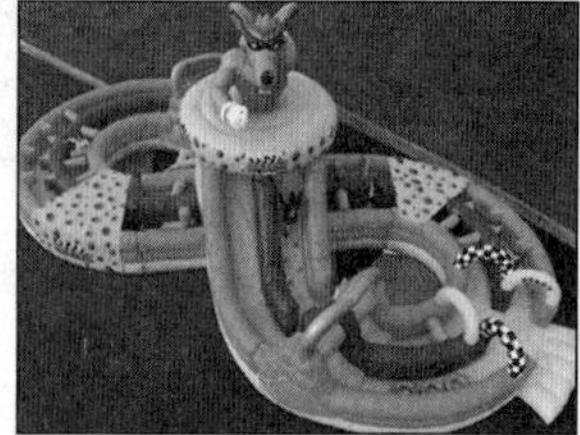

Inflatable Games

# PARTY OUTFITTERS

*Contact: Mark Thibodeau*
***(360) 438-2211***
***(800) 853-5867***
***Web site: www.partyoutfitters.com***

---

**Complete Party and Picnic Packages**
**You relax. We handle the details!**

**Site Selection • Catering • Entertainment • Games • Themes**
**Featuring over 200 games**

## Big Fun for All…

- Bungee Bull Ride
- Virtual Reality Games
- Fire Truck Slide
- Golf Driving Challenge
- Sumo Wrestling
- Climbing Walls
- NASCAN Sprinters
- Speed Pitch
- Batting Cage
- Gladiator Jousting
- Big Time Bouncy Boxing
- Human Gyroscope
- Inflatable Obstacle Course
- Miniature Golf
- Arcade & Video Games
- Rodeo Roper
- Titanic Adventure Challenge
- Mechanical Bull
- Bungee Run
- Tornado Twister Slide
- Laser Tag
- Human Foosball
- 22' and 26' Tall Inflatable Slides
- Survivor Series

## Especially for Kids

- Looney Tunes Bouncer
- Kiddiepillar
- Mickey Bouncer
- Under the Sea
- Moonjumps
- Hoppy Meal Bouncer
- Purple Dragon
- Rocking Pirate Ship
- Choo Choo Express Train
- Space Shuttle Play Space
- Splativity
- Panda Bouncer

## We're the Experts!

Party Outfitters specializes in providing fun, interactive games for special events including: team building, company picnics, trade shows, graduation parties, holiday parties and promotions. When quality, dependability, safety and experience count, hire the pros at Party Outfitters.

## Customer Comments

*"I would like to compliment your staff on doing an excellent job for our Senior All Night party. They arrived early, were very polite and courteous."* —Beverly F., Mossyrock, WA

*"Your staff were prompt and helpful. Their presence was very reassuring that nothing would go wrong…thank you for making it so easy for me to plan an enjoyable day in the sun!"* —Kelly B., Portland, OR

**DELIVERED • INSURED • STAFFED**

**Call for a FREE fun-filled 36-page catalog and RESERVE EARLY:**
**(360) 438-2211, (800) 853-5867**
**Visit our on-line catalog at *www.partyoutfitters.com*.**

## *Portland PartyWorks, Inc.*

*15510 SE Piazza Ave.*
*Clackamas, Oregon 97015*
*503-723-8300; 888-727-8944*
*Email: info@portlandpartyworks.com*
**www.portlandpartyworks.com**

## WE'RE SERIOUS ABOUT FUN!

PartyWorks has one of the largest selections of entertainment on the West Coast. Here's a small sample of what we do!

### Entertainment for All Ages

- Inflatable Games (many)
- Mechanical Bulls
- Giant Slides
- Interactive Games
- Mini NASCAR Racing
- Obstacle Courses
- Bungee Jumpers
- Lazer Tag Productions
- Complete Event Planning
- DJs & Live Music
- Ponies, Petting Zoos
- Game Shows
- Virtual Reality
- Climbing Walls
- Kids Bounces

### Specialty Games:

- Pool Tables
- High Strikers
- Carnival Booths/Games
- Giant Trikes
- Air Hockey Tables
- Golf Games
- Sumo Wrestling
- Water Slides
- Foosball Tables
- Dunk Tanks
- Arcade Games/Pinball
- Photo Props

### Custom Productions & Packages for:

- Company Picnics
- Grad Parties
- Carnivals
- Team Building
- Church Events
- Themed Events
- Broker Discounts
- Harvest Festivals
- Holiday Parties

## Put the Northwest's Most Experienced Entertainment Company to Work for YOU!

PartyWorks has been around longer than any other interactive specialist in the Northwest and has been part of thousands of successful events. We have offices across the country which provide a huge resource for talent and entertainment so no job is too large or too small. From team building and company picnics to festivals and fairs, PartyWorks delivers! When peace of mind matters, choose PartyWorks and enjoy the show!

Top Quality • Clean Equipment • Experienced Staff
Guaranteed Delivery • Local Company

**FULL SERVICE • DELIVERED • STAFFED • INSURED**

*****ASK ABOUT OUR BEST PRICE GUARANTEE*****

Satisfied Customers include Portland TrailBlazers, Fujitsu, Precision Castparts, Hollywood Entertainment, Six Flags Corporation, U of O, Intel, Walt Disney, ESPN, MGM Studios, hundreds of schools & churches and many more!

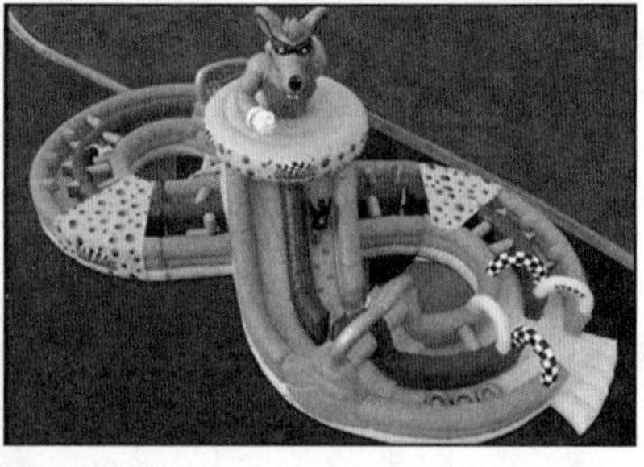

# S&K Inflatable Adventure Rentals

## FUN FOR ALL AGES!

*541-757-1983*

*www.sandk-inflatablerentals.com*

*rick@sandk-inflatablerentals.com*

---

**Created and Inspired by seven-year-old twins Spencer and Koeby, and Their Future**

Slide, jump, race, splash, bounce and squeeze! Welcome to the premier mid-Willamette Valley rental outlet for incredible fun! Kids and adults of all ages will enjoy our exciting inflatables! Owner Rick Bennett is excited to help you with any of your party needs. Please contact Rick at Corvallis Fitness Center (541) 757-1983 for additional information.

## FUN, INTERACTIVE GAMES FOR ANY OCCASION!

- Company Picnics
- Holiday Parties
- Family Reunions
- Church Fundraisers
- Sports Promotions
- Grad/Prom Night
- Festivals/Carnivals
- Trade Shows
- Car Dealerships
- Street Fairs
- Grand Openings
- Day Care Events
- Non-Profit Events
- Team Building
- Themed Events

## COMPETITIVELY PRICED!

**Rental Prices**

***(Includes delivery, set-up, staffing and insurance)***

| | 2 hr | 4 hr | 6 hr |
|---|---|---|---|
| Rat Race | $695 | $895 | $1095 |
| Titanic Slide | $695 | $895 | $1095 |
| Ironman Challenge | $695 | $895 | $1095 |
| Twisted Twister | $695 | $895 | $1095 |
| Rock ’Em - Sock ’Em’ | $295 | $450 | $550 |
| Boxing Ring | $295 | $450 | $550 |
| ‘Lil’ Pumper | $225 | $350 | $475 |
| Entanglement | $225 | $350 | $475 |
| Deluxe Bouncer | $225 | $295 | $495 |
| CrayonLand | $200 | $225 | $325 |
| Backyard Slide (water/ball) | $200 | $225 | $325 |

## SEGWAY RENTALS NOW AVAILABLE!

***Multiple package pricing available. Major credit cards accepted.***

**For a complete list of available inflatables call Rick at 541-757-1983 or check out our web site at www.sandk-inflatablerentals.com**

***SERVING ALL OF OREGON AND SOUTHWEST WASHINGTON***

# Parks & Event Sites

BravoPortland.com

# PLANNING A PICNIC

Planning a company picnic can be easy or difficult depending on several factors: how long you haveto plan, how many you are planning for, the type of activities planned, etc. Here are a few things to remember when you begin planning a company picnic:

- **Remember to book your picnic site early!** Spaces are limited, and some companies book their picnic site up to a year in advance.
- **Confirm dates and times in writing.** Don't assume that since you had your picnic somewhere last year that the space is reserved for you this year. Visit the site and look around to make sure it is presentable and what you need for your event.
- **Develop a committee or committees of volunteers** to help coordinate food and beverages, games and prizes, publicity and sign-ups, entertainment, etc. Get feedback from participants on how the event can be improved from the last year.
- **Be sure your contact at the site has a clear picture of what you want.** Be open to suggestions and solutions from the contact at the site—they have experienced all sizes and types of events at their particular site and can be very helpful with what works and what doesn't.
- **Work with the experienced planners on-site** (if one is not available, then check in the "Meeting and Event Planners" section of this Guide to find one). The only way you'll find the answer to your questions is by asking someone who has been through it before. You may have never coordinated an event like this, so ask questions to figure out the best solutions. There will always be last-minute problems, such as expecting 700 people and having 1,000 show up. Experienced coordinators and planners can handle even the worst problems. DON'T PANIC! When you work with the professionals, they will not disappoint you.
- **Most importantly,** don't make the picnic so complicated that you drain your volunteers of their energy! This is supposed to be a morale-building event, not a burnout.
- **Prizes and promotions:** Don't forget to have a keepsake to take home from the picnic like baseball hats with your company's logo, water bottles, Frisbees, etc. (Refer to "Corporate Gifts & Promotional Items" section of this Guide for more ideas and information).
- **Games and activities:** Sports-related games and activities can add excitement to your event. Employees would especially love the managers in the dunk tank. There are professional companies that can come and set-up games and arrange prizes listed under "Audience Participation" in this Guide.
- **Tents and pavilions:** Picnics are planned for summer fun, but you can never count on the sun to always shine. A tent or pavilion at your site as a back-up to bad weather can ensure a great event come rain or shine.
- **Food for the picnic:** Food choice for a traditional picnic is barbecued hamburgers, ribs, chicken, hot dogs and baked beans and salads. Remember that proper refrigeration can eliminate food spoilage in heat.
- **On-site barbecue trucks:** Special barbecue caterers are using on-site barbecue trucks to store and cook the food right on site. The food is excellent and employees enjoy the event without cooking or helping with cleanup.

# Helvetia Valley Adventures

*Contact: Susan Adkins, with Class Act, Event Coordinators*
*for booking information and a complimentary tour:*
*503.295.7890 • classact@open.org*
*Web site: hvadventures.com*
*Hillsboro, Oregon*

---

**Capacity:** up to 800 people
**Price Range:** please inquire
**Catering:** contact us about our preferred caterer list
**Types of Events:** corporate picnics and events, family reunions and parties, outdoor barbecues, and theme parties

## Availability and Terms

The Farm is a private event site and is available for you on weekends, July through September. Other dates and times are possible by special arrangement.

## Description of Facility and Services

**Seating:** tables and chairs can be rented
**Cleanup:** provided by venue
**Parking:** private parking for up to 800

## PRIVATE PLAYLAND IN THE OREGON COUNTRY

Roloff U-Pick Farms, home of Helvetia Valley Adventures, is a special, private playland, perfect for hosting corporate picnics and events, family reunions, outdoor barbecues and theme parties. Located in the country just outside Hillsboro, there is lots of exciting fun for "kids" of all ages. Events are held for the purpose of promoting Roloff Farms Produce.

**The Adventure Includes:**

-An Old West Town & Underground Secret

-A Medieval Castle

-A Three Story Tree House

-A Pirate Ship docked at the Lagoon

-And so much more!

Come experience Helvetia Valley Adventures for your next special event.

***"If you are looking for a place for family-oriented events, there is nowhere else like it in the country...By far the best outing we have ever had!"***

– Bob Gregg, CEO, Unicru

# Kruger's Farm

*(503) 621-3489*
*17100 NW Sauvie Island Road • Portland, Oregon*
*www.krugersfarm.com, FarmerDon@KrugersFarmMarket.com*

***Located just 20 minutes from downtown Portland on beautiful Sauvie Island.***

**Capacity:** events of all sizes from 10 to 1,000
**Price Range:** $100–$1,500
**Catering:** We have on-site catering available from our grill or you may pick the licensed caterer of your choice to cater an event at the farm.
**Types of Events:** weddings, receptions, BBQs, dinners, corporate events, picnics, parties

## Availability and Terms:

Event spaces at the farm include the gazebo and flower garden lawn, oak tree area and many other open spaces around the property. All of our spaces are outdoors and available from May through the end of October.

## Description of Facility and Services:

**Seating:** provided by caterer
**Servers:** provided by caterer
**Bar facilities:** provided by caterer
**Linens and napkins:** provided by caterer
**Parking:** ample free parking

**About the Farm:** Kruger's Farm is located just 20 minutes from downtown Portland on beautiful Sauvie Island. The farm is a 100-acre working farm with berries and other regional crops. We operate a large farm store that is open from 9am–8pm daily from May through October.

**Charlton House:** The Charlton House is a historic 1903 farm house located on the hill overlooking the farm. The Charlton House lawn is the perfect spot for intimate *al fresco* dinners for as many as 50 people.

**Corn Maze:** Our ten-acre corn maze is available from September 1 through the end of October for private events and rentals. Include a hayride to our pumpkin field, a fresh caramel apple, mini-donuts, hot cider and a visit to our grill and make your event a real celebration of fall.

***Fall Fun – Pumpkins, Corn Maze, Hot Cider & Fresh Caramel Apples***

*21160 N.E. Blue Lake Road • Fairview, Oregon 97024*
*(503) 667-3483 • Email: metroparks@metro.dst.or.us*

---

**Capacity:** Indoors: theatre-style seating for 150, sit-down dinner up to 90; Outdoor Garden: up to 250
**Price Range:** Varies according to time of year and day of week
**Catering:** Executive caterers list or pot luck
**Type of Events:** Including, but not limited to, weddings, receptions, corporate functions, private parties and meetings.

## Availability and Terms

Early reservations are recommended, particularly for summer months. Deposits are required.

## Description of Facility and Services

- Seating: Tables and chairs available
- Servers: Available through caterer
- Linens, china and glassware: available through caterer
- Covered patio
- Picture windows with lake view
- Parking: On-site, private parking
- ADA: Accessible and plenty of handicapped parking

## TAKE TIME OUT TO TAKE CARE OF BUSINESS

Sometimes just getting away from the hustle and bustle of the office can get your employees thinking in new directions. The newly updated Lake House at Blue Lake Park offers a tranquil setting with natural beauty just 10 minutes from Portland International Airport and 20 minutes from downtown Portland.

**WINTER & SUMMER RESORT**

*P.O. Box 280 • Government Camp, Oregon 97028*
*Contact: Karen Norton (503) 222-BOWL (2695) ext. 0*
*Group Sales Office (503) 272-3206 ext. 202; Fax (503) 272-3554*
*Business Hours: Mon–Fri 8am–5pm Web site: www.skibowl.com*

---

**Capacity:** up to 6,000 people (6,000+ with off-mountain shuttle)
**Price Range:** we accommodate a wide variety of budgets
**Catering:** full-service in-house catering or bring your favorite caterer with you
**Types of Events:** company picnics, corporate events, meetings, team building, weddings, private parties and concerts

## Availability and Terms

Reservations are to be made in advance. A deposit of 25% is required upon reservation.

## Description of Facility and Services

**Day lodge:** 2 yurts, 4 day lodges including historic mid-mountain Warming Hut and newly remodeled Multorpor Lodge
**Seating:** tables and chairs provided under six tented picnic areas in addition to the day lodges
**Servers:** professional and friendly staff provided
**Bar facilities:** three full-service host/no-host bars available
**Plates, cups and utensils:** provided with menu at no charge
**Decorations:** theme decorations available for additional charge
**Cleanup:** provided at no additional charge
**Audiovisual and meeting equipment:** available upon request
**Winter activities:** America's Largest Night Ski Area, 65 day runs, 34 night runs, 300 acres of outback gladed terrain, snow tube tow and rentals, adventure park, terrain park, sleigh rides, and sled dog tours. We also specialize in coordinating events, races and obstacle courses.
**Summer activities:** over 20 attractions offering fun for all ages where you're in control: quad sling-shot, 1/2 mile dual alpine slide, two scenic sky chairs servicing nature, interpretive hiking trails, lift-assisted mountain bike park with 40 miles of trails plus rentals and tours, horseback rides, indy karts, disc and miniature golf, space rotation, automated batting cages, zipline, freefall bungee, rapid riser, kiddy jeeps, kiddy canoe ride, indoor super play zone, plus much more.
**Parking:** ample parking available at no charge; free shuttle between east and west locations
**ADA:** complied
**Services:** We can customize any package to meet your needs as well as budget, from no-cost Company Day to closing the facility down exclusively for your company. Our professional and friendly staff knows just what it takes to make your event an unforgettable one. Our event coordinator arranges all the details from transportation to catering, simple decorations to custom themes and provides promotional support for a successful event.

## DISCOVER MT. HOOD SKIBOWL...

Discover Mt. Hood SKIBOWL Summer Action Park. Encompassed in over 1,000 acres and less than an hour drive from Portland, SKIBOWL provides the perfect backdrop for any group setting and features 20 hands-on attractions where you're in control. SKIBOWL offers something for all age groups at affordable prices. Everyone will be able to experience unforgettable fun in the unique alpine environment offered only at Mt. Hood SKIBOWL.

# OAKS PARK HISTORIC DANCE PAVILION

## *at Oaks Park*

*Portland, Oregon 97202*
*Contact:Catering (503) 238-6622*
*Fax (503) 236-9143*
*Web site: www.oakspark.com*
*Business Hours: Mon–Fri 8am–5pm*

---

**Capacity:** dance pavilion with formal seating for 275; festival setup with dancing for 500; outdoor gazebo area for 1,000

**Price Range:** will be determined by event, specific menu choices, and services

**Catering:** our in-house catering menus are individually designed to suit your own taste, personality, and style. Our goal is to give you exactly what you want. If you are using an outside caterer, we will charge you a fee of 20% of their final bill

**Types of Events:** full-line catering, buffet, hors d'oeuvres, and specialty menus

### Availability and Terms

Our indoor facility is available for bookings on any day or evening. Our outdoor gazebo and grounds are extremely popular; please don't hesitate to call and inquire. A deposit of $250 is required on the day of booking.

### Description of Facility and Services

**Seating:** we can formally seat 275 people

**Servers:** we can provide any equipment necessary and the personnel to guarantee your event will run smoothly and at a level of service you expect

**Bar facilities:** Oaks Park Association provides liquor at the liability of the renter; it is Oaks Park's policy to provide a staff bartender

**Dance floor:** 99′x54′ dance floor with a capacity for 400 people

**Linens and napkins:** all colors of linen and cloth napkins and tablecloths available for an additional cost

**Decorations:** we enjoy your personal style—and offer the bonus of fanciful historic carousel horses

**Audiovisual:** available upon request

**Equipment:** podium, easel, and risers available

**Parking:** ample free parking

**ADA:** fully complies

### A PEACEFUL, TRANQUIL SETTING

Join us at our historic riverside park on the Willamette River and let us create a perfect day or evening event for you and your guests. Our facility is ideal for seminars, retreats, corporate dinners, retirement and holiday parties. Children's Christmas parties are a specialty. It is our policy to work with you and offer exemplary step-by-step service all during the event, allowing you to relax and enjoy the party.

**See page 405 under Recreation, Attractions & Sports.**

# STERNWHEELER "COLUMBIA GORGE" & MARINE PARK

*Sales Office: P.O. Box 307*
*Cascade Locks, Oregon 97014*
*(541) 374-8427; (800) 643-1354*
*Web site: www.sternwheeler.com; E-mail: sales@sternwheeler.com*

Owned & operated by the Port of Cascade Locks

**Capacity:** 350 passengers
**Price Range:** varies depending on event and length of cruise; two hour minimum; please call
**Catering:** full range of catering services provided including menu selections for champagne brunch, luncheon, dinner, hors d'oeuvres and theme parties
**Types of Events:** private charter meal and excursion cruises, company picnics (park only), holiday parties, casino cruises, weddings, fund raisers, meetings, conventions

## Availability and Terms

The Sternwheeler "Columbia Gorge" offers two fully enclosed heated decks, providing a comfortable setting for any time of year. Marine Park offers accommodations for groups of 50 to 1,000, as well as a three-acre private island. A 25% nonrefundable deposit is required upon booking; final payment is due 14–30 days prior to scheduled event, depending on season.

## Description of Facility and Services

**Seating:** tables, chairs, and standard linens provided
**Servers:** provided
**Bar facilities:** two to three full-service bars with bartenders available
**Dance floor:** dance area available; full electrical hookup
**Linens and napkins:** vinyl linens and cloth napkins; color coordination available – please inquire
**China and glassware:** house china available with our catering service
**Decorations:** elegant turn-of-the-century motif requires little decoration
**Audiovisual:** available; please call a sales representative
**Cleanup:** provided courtesy of the Sternwheeler crew
**Parking:** *Cascade Locks Marine Park:* free parking
**ADA:** disabled accessible

## Special Services

With the beauty of the gorge and an abundance of breathtaking views to choose from, the Sternwheeler "Columbia Gorge" and Marine Park continue to provide a unique venue for meetings, banquets, or any event. We can coordinate your event from start to finish, including transportation, catering and entertainment. Please call our sales office for more details.

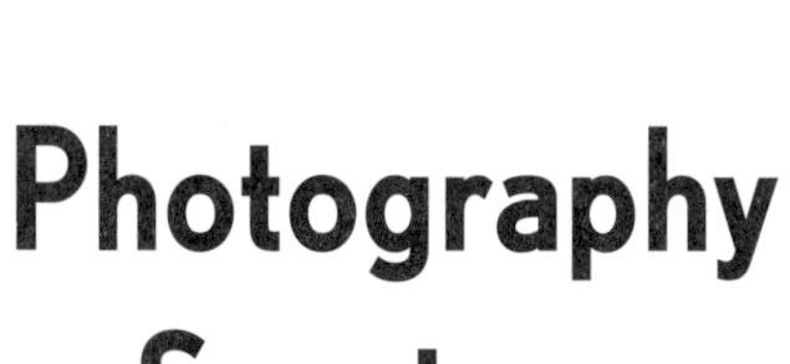


Photography Services

BravoPortland.com

# PHOTOGRAPHY SERVICES

**Why are photographs important?** Photographs capture the results of months of hard work after an event is over. Photographs can thank a sponsor. Photographs of a grand opening or award presentation can be used in press releases after the event. Photographs can be a great keepsake and follow-up thank-you for the supporters who attend the function year after year.

**Selecting a photographer:** Find a photographer whose style you like. Look closely at his or her sample albums and don't be afraid to ask for references. A contract is important to reserve the date and to outline the photography costs. With over 250 photographers currently listed in the phone book, you want to make sure you select the best photographer to meet your specific needs.

**Consulting with your photographer:** When you finally select your photographer, sit down together so you can communicate what you envision your photo session or event photos to look like. Be specific about formal and candid photographs. Be sure you let the photographer know what you are expecting.

**Assigning a photographer's helper:** Save time the day of the event by assigning someone to be the photographer's helper. Submit a list of photographic requests to both the photographer and helper one week before the event so that your helper can guide the photographer to all the right people.

**Why hire a video service?** There are many reasons for hiring a video service. Videotaping an event or meeting is a great way to re-cap the event for people who were not able to attend. The tape can also be used to evaluate the event for ideas for future meetings, or it can be used as a training tool for future employees. Tapes can be given to sponsors or speakers as a thank-you.

**Why hire a professional video service?** The professional has the experience, skills, and technical equipment to produce a high-quality video. Check the types of equipment the video service has: one-camera, two-camera, or three-camera options. Editing and sound options enhance the video and tailor it to the highlights of the event. Take the time to view samples of their work; it will show you the style and quality. Check the background of the company or individual. Have they been professionally trained or self-taught? If it is important to document your event, don't trust an amateur–you have only one shot to get it right.

**Research the different options:** There are one, two, or three camera options. Each will provide a different perspective of the event. With only one camera, you cannot tape more than one thing at a time, and there may be several events happening at once that need attention. In this case, two or more operators may be needed.

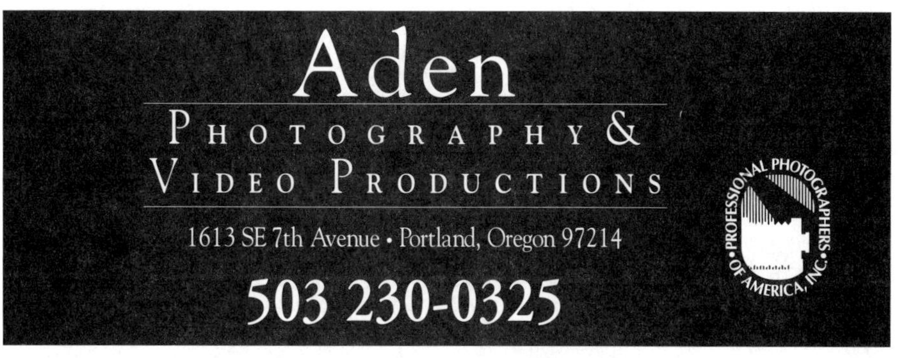


Web Address: **www.adenphoto.com**
E-Mail • **keith@adenphoto.com**

---

## Style

Since 1968, Keith Aden Photography has been serving the greater Portland metro area. Over the years we have built a solid reputation for a professional, assertive, and unobtrusive style that blends perfectly with your event. From international sales meetings to conventions, or political luncheons to company picnics, we can deliver the service that you expect. We are very detail oriented and can tailor our services to fit your budget.

## Services

- Commercial Photography (Digital, 4x5, Medium Format and 35mm)
- Event Photography (Digital or Film)
- Video Production/DVD (Industrial 3 Chip DV or S-VHS Multi-Camera Coverage, Non-Linear or Linear Editing Suites)
- Aerial Photography
- Brochures/Post Cards (Design, Photography and Printing)
- Digital Imaging Services (Professional Digital Cameras)

## SOMEONE WHO CARES

Your choice of a photo or video professional is an important one. It reflects on your reputation as well as your company's reputation. We do not take that lightly! In fact, we put our good reputation on the line every time we take an assignment. And as a former purchasing manager for a national corporation, Keith also understands the needs of business. In short, it is our goal to make everyone look good!

## PROFESSIONAL SERVICE FOR PROFESSIONAL PEOPLE

**1613 S.E. 7th Avenue • Portland, Oregon 97214**
**Studio 503.230.0325 • Fax 503.230.0657 • Toll Free 877.230.0325**

**Member of**

PORTLAND • OREGON VISITORS ASSOCIATION
*the convention and visitors bureau of metropolitan Portland*

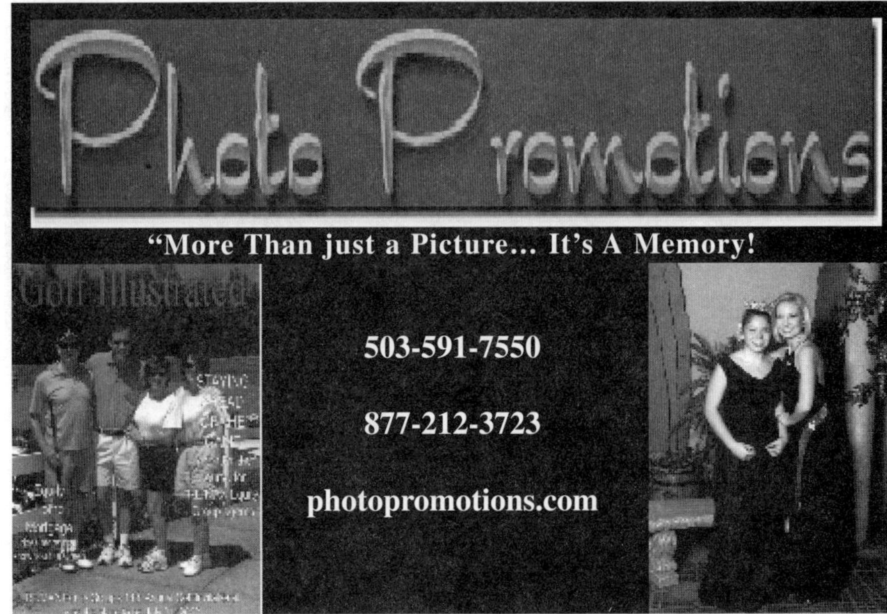


Photo Promotions, the Pacific Northwest's premier event photographer, has been serving customers since 1980.

Our friendly, courteous, professional staff is ready to provide your next event with colorful, high "studio quality" digital photos in a variety of exciting finishing options.

Photo Promotions also has "REAL" Santas, Mrs. Claus and "Custom" Easter Bunnies available to entertain at your next event.

- Take your photos home with you after your event!
- Add a fun border for a custom look (first "customized" border is free)
- Choose from a wide range of print sizes; build your own package
- See your photo before it's processed
- Get extra prints while you wait
- Flat rate charges begin at only $6 per sheet
- No extra charges for group shots
- We accept all major credit cards
- Sepia photos (old fashion), B/W and Green Screen Technology
- Excellent references available

- **Holiday & Theme Parties**
- **Golf Tournaments**
- **Conventions**
- **Dances**
- **Reunions**
- **Trade shows**
- **Bar/Bat Mitzvahs**
- **Fundraisers**
- **Graduations**
- **Auctions**
- **Promotional/Celebrity Events**

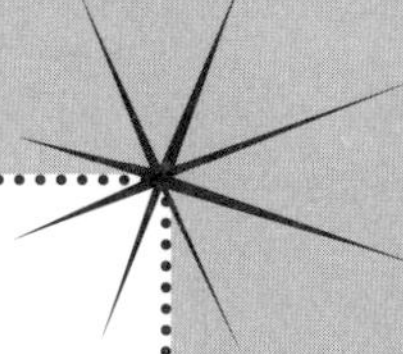

Promotional Items & Screenprinting

Promotional
Items
&
Screenprinting

BravoPortland.com

# PROMOTIONAL ITEMS

**Advertising specialties are the items that make an impression and keep your name in the minds of the attendees long after the event is over**. These gifts, giveaways, awards, or promotional items feature your meeting name, business logo, or your slogan imprinted on them. Traditional types of imprinted giveaways include pens, coffee mugs, hats, t-shirts, etc. The goal today is that these ad specialties be gifts that will have real meaning and function for the people who receive them.

**Get the most from your gift or promotional dollars!** Make sure you investigate all the options and come up with the gift or giveaway that has the most importance and value to your audience. Working with a professional company that offers experience and service is important. The experienced company will have a large enough selection available so you won't have to go all over town looking for the perfect gift.

**When looking for your gift, promotional item, or giveaway, ask yourself the following questions**: How much is the budget? How many pieces will I need? Do I give them to everyone? Do I want a functional or fun item? Is this something I would like to receive? Are the gifts of a quality that reflects your company/meeting standards? What type of imprint is needed on the gifts? What do I want it to say? How much time do I have before I need them?

**There is a fine line between a gimmick and a giveaway**. A gimmick means you have to do something before you receive the "special gift." Everyone is fed up with scams and phony prizes. A gift or promotional item is given without any strings attached.

**Theme and recreational events**. There is an idea for every theme or recreational event: golf balls with the company logo imprinted for a golf tournament, imprinted kerchiefs for a western party, water bottles for a run, travel clocks given to meeting planners reminding them it's time to book a meeting, etc.

**Giveaways in the new millennium can be sophisticated**. Imprinted calculators, watches, duffel bags, golf bags, towels, beach chairs–just about anything is possible. Refer to this section for lots of wonderful ideas.

**Favors:** Meal time is the perfect time to give a souvenir. Something portable like a lapel pin, an imprinted pen, or small box of chocolates or mints. Favors are often a part of the theme of a gala evening. Make it something convenient to carry, not cumbersome.

## Oregon's Premier Provider of Corporate Identity and Printing Solutions

*Offices in Portland, Salem and Eugene*

(503) 620-9898 Fax (503) 670-9292

ideas@eagle411.com www.eagle411.com

---

Since 1971, American Eagle Graphics has taken extraordinary measures as part of our ordinary way of doing business. We've grown by specializing in consultation, marketing, design, sourcing and fulfillment… while delivering unique, creative, on-target results in promotions and print.

An impressive array of products and services are offered to integrate and support your project and brand building needs. We have built a reputation for excellence which has transformed us into a trusted advocate of our clients.

### Promotional Products

Executive Gifts, Corporate Events, Awards, Holiday and/or year end Gifts, Trade Show giveaways, Incentives and Rewards, Recognition, Premiums.

### Apparel

Sport Shirts, Corporate Wear, T-Shirts, Uniforms, Outerwear, Headwear, Golf, Accessories, Licensing, Name Brands, Embroidery and Silk Screening.

### Printed Products

Invitations, Sales Collateral, Signage & Banners, Presentation Folders, Labels, Cards, Documents, Stationery, Envelopes, POP Displays, Brochures and more.

### Services

Concept Development, Direct Importing, Fulfillment, Warehousing, E-stores, E-Commerce, Creative Graphics, Project Management.

Do you have a special or unique project? Let one of our local representatives stop by and consult with you to make sure you get the right item to fulfill the intended purpose… at the right budget.

**A single source** providing multiple solutions.

Women-owned and operated since 1996

*2701 N.W. Vaughn, Suite 102*
*Portland, OR 97210*
*Ph: (503) 525-0253*
*Fax: (503) 525-0279*

Member

---

Picture this...Your own creative support team, dedicated to your purpose, willing to go to whatever lengths needed to get the job done, working round the clock (minus a few hours for beauty sleep...we are women after all!)

Identity Matters is the solution to your promotional challenge – Creative ideas? We have them! Tight turn times? We beat them! Budget constraints? Bring it on!!!

## PRODUCTS & SERVICES TO SET YOU APART:

### PROMOTIONAL MARKETING PRODUCTS

- Mugs, mouse pads, pens, padfolios, office accessories, customized food and candy gifts, golf and sporting accessories and things you've never thought of – always within budget and on-time

### SCREEN PRINTING & EMBROIDERED APPAREL

- Shirts, jackets, hats, fleece, t-shirts, sweatshirts, sportswear and golf towels

### LASER ENGRAVING & ETCHING

- Trophies, recognition plaques, executive gifts, crystal and glass awards

### TRADE SHOW GIVEAWAYS & SUPPLIES

- Bags, lanyards, booth giveaways, and badges

***Too much to do, last minute requests, don't know what to get? Identity Matters can do the work for you:***

- Online research and quote request availability
- Creative consultation and rush order capability
- Electronic order acknowledgements and price quotes
- Credit card acceptance for billing

Our team at Identity Matters is looking forward to making you shine; we provide the finishing touch that will make your event, product and company remembered.

***"It's not who you know, it's who knows you"***

***www.identitymatters.net***

*503-736-0111 • 503-736-0930 fax*
*www.withamanddickey.com • info@withamanddickey.com*

---

**Full Service Printing, High Speed Copying, Graphic Design services,**
**Promotional Products, Direct Mail...**
**All under one roof.**

## Full Service Printing

Take advantage of the wide variety of sheetfed offset presses that Witham & Dickey employs to produce virtually any project you may have. From small runs of business cards up to full color catalogs and manuals, we have the equipment and skilled manpower to get your job printed.

## High Speed Copying

Witham & Dickey has recently upgraded our digital end to offer even more capabilities to our customers. Runs of 10,000 – 50,000 high speed black and white copies are produced in a few hours. Also inquire about the different ways in which our digital color copiers can work for your next short run color project.

## Graphic Design Services

Our art department is well equipped to handle all your design and pre-press needs. With the latest in computer equipment for both Macintosh and Windows based computers as well as Adobe and Quark products, we have the tools to create any design you may have envisioned.

## Promotional Products

Get your name out...your message across...your voice heard with apparel and accessories you can easily embellish. We offer hundreds of shirt, sweater and jacket styles in a myriad of hues, plus brief bags, hats, pens, cups, magnets, lapels and so much more. All prominent places to put your logo or message.

## Direct Mail

Witham & Dickey is one of the largest political printers on the West Coast with experience coordinating mailing services all across the country. You can rely on Witham & Dickey when it comes to your direct mail marketing needs. Call us and see just how easy it is to get your name and products out to your customers.

***"Envision the possibilities"***

A division of Paper Power, Inc.

**www.wowpromo.com**

WOW! Promotions
1421 NW 14th Ave.
Portland, OR 97209

Phone 503-221-9585
Fax 503-221-9702
Toll Free 888-221-4657

***As a full-service promotional products company, WOW! Promotions develops clever event related gifts and give-aways sure to build excitement and recognition.***

---

**Customer Service:** With over 20 years experience in the print and promotional products industry, our customer service representatives are knowledgeable and professional. We pride ourselves on good value, quality products, and on-time deliveries.

**Creative Design Services:** If you want unique, outstanding ideas, our design team is up to the challenge. Good ideas leave lasting impressions. Let us develop a memorable promotion for your next event.

**Products:** With hundreds of thousands of promotional products to choose from, we can cover all your needs, from small trade show hand-outs to corporate apparel, to a multi-product brand awareness blitz. Our product ideas will create interest, leave a lasting impression and build recognition.

**Warehousing/Fulfillment Services:** Our fulfillment department has the ability to do handwork/assembly, warehouse, pick and pack, and manage your inventory. We can package your merchandise and ship directly to your clients or to any remote location.

Fulfillment might include assembling a theme gift of several related items where we label or tag each piece with the theme brand, package for presentation, box for shipping and address from your mailing list.

**Mailing Services:** WOW! Promotions has the ability to take your mail list and fulfill an order straight through to your clients. The package can be sent via US mail or any shipping service including overnight delivery. We have been handling mailings for over 10 years. Make it easy on yourself and let WOW! Promotions develop a clever invitation or impressive announcement and take care of the mailing too!

***We're in the business of making your Promotions say "WOW!"***

# Notes

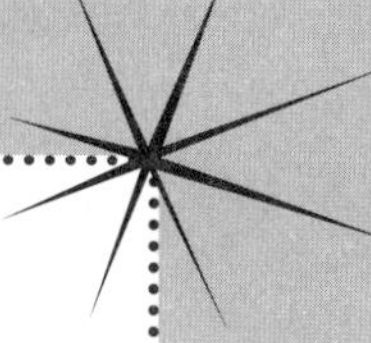



# Recreation, Attractions & Sports

# RECREATION, ATTRACTIONS & SPORTS

**The Pacific Northwest is overflowing with attractions:** From Mt. Hood to the coast, there are endless attractions and activities. The majestic mountains are only an hour-and-a-half away. The miles of beaches are an hour's drive. Award-winning wines at local wineries and brew pubs are cropping up all over the state. The performing arts, museums, scenic and historical sites will keep you busy. Throw in the recreation, sporting events and transportation and there is something for everyone and unique venues for your next event or meeting.

**Tours:** There are many types of sightseeing tours available, these are fun activities to include spouses. Just some of the tours that are available are: tours of local brew pubs and sampling, Wine Country tours- Oregon is rich with some of the finest wines, and the vineyards are absolutely beautiful to tour. There are shopping tours on antique row, and scenic and historical tours of all Oregon's history.

**Destination Management Companies (DMC):** These companies are hired by conventions and out-of-state planners. They specialize in packaging group and VIP events. They can customize local activities to fit the planner's need (you will find these companies in the Event Planner section).

**Local celebrations and sporting events:** Take advantage of local celebrations, sporting events, and theatre schedules to provide "group" activities for free time or for individuals to attend. Sporting activities can be attended as a spectator or local "celebrities" can assist in your programming, offering hands-on windsurfing instruction, rafting trips, or ski excursions for your guests' free time.

**Utilize historical sites and attractions as venues for your special events:** Have a cocktail reception at an aquarium, or a dinner in a museum. Often the exhibits are interesting "decor" at no additional costs. Docents can serve as greeters, and guests can learn something new.

**Audience participation activities:** Recreational activities for company events are becoming more and more popular. The company picnic is becoming more interesting. There are corporate-outing events like ski days, paintball tournaments, laser tag for team-building, and mini "Indy car race tracks." The more interesting an event is, the better the attendance.

## FAMILY FUN CENTER AND BULLWINKLE'S RESTAURANT

*29111 S.W. Town Center Loop, W. • Wilsonville, Oregon 97070*
*(503) 685-5000; Fax (503) 685-9694; Web site: www.fun-center.com*
***Open year-round;** Business Hours: winter: Noon–9pm; summer 10am–10pm*

---

**Capacity:** amusement park, 2,000; **New Meeting Rooms** will be open early 2005 (350 capacity); Bullwinkle's Restaurant dining room 180 people. Private rentals available (recommended 800 people or more).
**Price Range:** $9–$32 per person
**Catering:** in-house
**Types of Events:** corporate meetings, company picnics, seminars, trade shows, wedding receptions, social functions, birthday parties, team parties and more.

### Great Food and Entertainment for All Ages
This amazing 6-acre amusement park is located in the city of Wilsonville (I-5, exit 283). The Family Fun Center and Bullwinkle's Restaurant provide a fun and clean atmosphere, safe attractions, great food and entertainment for all ages.

### Buffet Packages
Bullwinkle's Restaurant provides a variety of buffet options: pizza buffet, an old-fashioned barbecue buffet.

### Indoor Attractions
- **LazerXtreme:** laser tag arena
- **Max Flight Simulator:** this roller coaster simulator will knock your socks off!
- **Kidopolis:** four-level soft play area for children 5 feet and under
- **Frog Hopper:** ride the hopper high into the air, then bounce your way down
- **Arcade:** two-story arcade with more than 100 games
- **Animation Performance:** on stage in Bullwinkle's Family Restaurant

### Outdoor Attractions
- **Miniature Golf:** two 18-hole courses
- **Go Karts:**double seater cars
- **Bumper Boats:** enjoy a wild ride on motorized boats
- **Batting Cages:** eight batting cages ranging from 40 to 70 mph (slow and fast pitch)
- **Sling Shot Bungee** (does not operate when raining)
- **28' Climbing Tower** (does not operate when raining)

### Availability and Terms
First come, first served. Reservations available during all operating hours. After-hour packages also are available. Deposits are required.

### Special Services
Please call the group sales office at (503) 685-5000 ext. 21 to schedule a VIP tour of the park. Ask about our birthday packages, corporate packages and group discount packages. The Family Fun Center is open year-round, rain or shine.

*77 N.E. Holland Street • Portland, Oregon 97211*
*503.283.3380; Fax 503.283.6647*
*E-mail: info@grapeescapetours.com*
*www.GrapeEscapeTours.com*

---

We provide fun, personalized escapes to the Oregon Wine Country for team building events, special group occasions and corporate retreats. Whether you choose an Afternoon Escape, a Group Meeting in the wine country, or a Dinner Escape, we'll take care of all the details:

- Arrangements with wineries chosen just for your group
- Comfortable transportation in our much-admired executive vans
- Unparalleled Northwest cuisine matched to wine along the way
- Fun, knowledgeable escape artists to host your entire day

On the day of your escape, we'll greet you at your location. You'll begin to unwind as we take the scenic way to the wine country. Then throughout the day, we'll provide everything you need as you enjoy our wine country in an unhurried, relaxed style.

We provide an array of escapes to suit your budget and needs:

| | | |
|---|---|---|
| Afternoon Escape | Full Day Escape | Grape-r Escape |
| Dinner Escape | Wine Country Safari | Holiday Escape |

New This Year: Our Holiday Escape, a novel way for your company to celebrate the season. We'll visit one or two nearby wineries (in Portland, or the wine country), and end with a festive dinner matched to wine. Yum.

To learn more about what we offer, take a look at our web site or give us a call. We'll guide you through the possibilities. Then once you select your escape, we'll take care of all the details, leaving you with nothing to do but anticipate a day of wine, food and fun.

**Grape Escape Winery Tours**
Don't forget to have a little fun!

# MT. HOOD MEADOWS SKI RESORT

*Marketing and Sales Department*
*1975 S.W. First Avenue, Suite M*
*Portland, Oregon 97201*

*Contact: Karen Lite*
*(503) 287-5438 ext. 182*
*(800) SKI-HOOD*
*Business Hours:*
*Mon–Fri 8am–4:30pm;*
*evenings by appointment*
*E-mail: klite@skihood.com*

*Photography by Steve Wanke*

## Location

Conveniently located just 65 miles east of Portland, Mt. Hood Meadows has the most diverse skiing terrain in Oregon. Our 10 chairlifts (including four high-speed quads), special programs, three base lodges, day care and friendly employees make Meadows the kind of place you will want to visit often.

## Lifts

- **Four high-speed quad chairlifts**
- Six lighted chairlifts
- Six double chairlifts
- One ropetow

## Group Rates

Group rates are available for groups of 25 or more. Meadows offers discounts on lift tickets, rental equipment, group lessons and custom clinics. We can also arrange for luxury coach transportation to the mountain.

## Professional Services

Our staff has extensive experience in corporate events. Our professional banquet and catering staff offers an array of delicious menu items. We can also provide the meeting, conference and banquet amenities to which you are accustomed.

## Race Department

Our race department can arrange a fun or competitive race just for your group on a slope designed for your skill level. **Race course fees: $300 to $500 (2 hours)**

## Lodging at at Cooper Spur Mountain Resort

Owned by Mt. Hood Meadows, Cooper Spur Mountain Resort is a popular destination for overnight guests as well as a truly unique place to hold a company retreat or seminar. Cooper Spur Mountain Resort is located 12 miles from Mt. Hood Meadows Ski Resort.

## EXPERIENCE MT. HOOD MEADOWS

Mt. Hood Meadows has a truly magical ambiance. Majestic Mount Hood, framed by snow-covered trees in the winter and green fields with wild flowers in the summer, provides the perfect alpine atmosphere for your next special event.

**Visit us on the Web:**
**www.skihood.com**
**www.cooperspur.com**

**See page 124 under Banquet, Meeting & Event Sites.**

## WINTER & SUMMER RESORT

*P.O. Box 280*
*Government Camp, Oregon 97028*
*Contact: Karen Norton*
*(503) 222-BOWL (2695) ext. 0*
*Group Sales Office (503) 272-3206 ext. 202*
*Fax (503) 272-3554; Business Hours: Mon–Fri 8am–5pm Web site: www.skibowl.com*

---

**Capacity:** up to 6,000 people (6,000+ with off-mountain shuttle)
**Price Range:** we accommodate a wide variety of budgets
**Catering:** full-service in-house catering or bring your favorite caterer with you
**Types of Events:** company picnics, corporate events, meetings, team building, weddings, private parties and concerts

### Availability and Terms

Reservations are to be made in advance. A deposit of 25% is required upon reservation.

### Description of Facility and Services

**Day lodge:** 2 yurts, 4 day lodges including historic mid-mountain Warming Hut and newly remodeled Multorpor Lodge
**Seating:** tables and chairs provided under six tented picnic areas in addition to the day lodges
**Servers:** professional and friendly staff provided
**Bar facilities:** three full-service host/no-host bars available
**Plates, cups and utensils:** provided with menu at no charge
**Decorations:** theme decorations available for additional charge
**Cleanup:** provided at no additional charge
**Audiovisual and meeting equipment:** available upon request
**Winter activities:** America's Largest Night Ski Area, 65 day runs, 34 night runs, 300 acres of outback gladed terrain, snow tubing and adventure park, tow and rentals, terrain park and horsedrawn sleigh rides. We also specialize in coordinating events, races and obstacle courses.
**Summer activities:** over 20 attractions offering fun for all ages where you're in control: quad sling-shot, 1/2 mile dual alpine slide, two scenic sky chairs servicing nature, interpretive hiking trails, lift-assisted mountain bike park with 40 miles of trails plus rentals and tours, horseback rides, indy karts, disc and miniature golf, space rotation, bungee, automated batting cages, zipline, freefall bungee, rapid riser reverse bungee kiddy jeeps, kiddy canoe ride, indoor super play zone, plus much more.
**Parking:** ample parking available at no charge; free shuttle between east and west locations
**ADA:** complied
**Services:** We can customize any package to meet your needs as well as budget, from no-cost Company Day to renting the facility exclusively for your company. Our professional and friendly staff knows just what it takes to make your event an unforgettable one. Our event coordinator arranges all the details from transportation to catering, simple decorations to custom themes as well as provide promotional support to guarantee a successful event.

## DISCOVER MT. HOOD SKIBOWL…

Discover Mt. Hood SKIBOWL Summer Action Park. Encompassed in over 1,000 acres and less than an hour drive from Portland, SKIBOWL provides the perfect backdrop for any group setting and features 20 hands-on attractions where you're in control. SKIBOWL offers something for all age groups at affordable prices. Everyone will be able to experience unforgettable fun in the unique alpine environment offered only at Mt. Hood SKIBOWL.

# COMPANY PICNICS AT OAKS AMUSEMENT PARK

*Portland, Oregon 97202*
*Contact: Catering*
*(503) 238-6622; Fax (503) 236-9143*
*Web site: www.oakspark.com*
*Business Hours: Mon–Fri 8am–5pm*

---

Oaks Amusement Park, located along the Willamette River, offers a wide variety of options for your company picnic. Thrill rides, skating, garden golf, and green space picnic areas are just a few options your group will enjoy.

Our in-house catering department will work with you in planning this important day. We can individually design your event to meet your expectations, style, and taste.

## NO SURPRISES, JUST FUN AND GOOD TIMES!!!

Join us at our historic riverside park on the Willamette River and let us create a perfect day or evening event for you and your guests. Our facility is ideal for seminars, retreats, corporate dinners, retirement and holiday parties, Children's Christmas parties are a specialty. It is our policy to work with you and offer exemplary step-by-step service all during the event, allowing you to relax and enjoy the party.

**See page 385 under Park Sites**
**and 126 under Banquet, Meeting & Event Sites.**

*1945 S.E. Water Avenue*
*Portland, Oregon 97214*
*(503) 797-4000*
***Science Center Hours:***
***June 15–Labor Day***
*Open daily from 9:30am–7pm*
***After Labor Day***
*Open Tues–Sun from 9:30am–5:30pm*
***Group reservations:*** *(503) 797-4661*

---

## Experience a Day of Adventure at OMSI

Imagine a place where you can journey to the outer reaches of the galaxy, feel the power of an earthquake, uncover a fossil, travel the globe in a five-story high domed theater, dine at the riverside café or shop at the Science Store. Come explore OMSI and receive a discount on groups of 12 or more with 10-day advance reservation. Let OMSI help you plan your next big event from holiday parties to retreats accommodating 25 to 2,500 people with space offering beautiful views of the Willamette River. Ask about our private Omnimax films and planetarium shows. Consider an overnight adventure in the museum where you can have an action packed night of fun and learning or find out what a day in the life of a submariner is like by going on a tour or staying overnight on the U.S.S. Blueback Submarine. For groups, call group registration at 503-797-4661; for event planning, call 503-797-4671.

## OMNIMAX® Theater

Experience the world's most advanced film projection system in the OMNIMAX Theater, where images surround you on a five-story domed screen. See wild animals, far-away places or the depths of the ocean like never before!

## Kendall Planetarium

Travel to the stars in the Kendall Planetarium, now featuring immersive full-dome video that blends science, art and entertainment. Enjoy captivating astronomy shows and laser light productions.

## USS Blueback Submarine

Discover a world known only to a few…the undersea world of the submarine. Take a 40-minute tour on board the 219′ USS Blueback.

## Motion Simulator

Experience OMSI's motion simulator ride, a multi-sensory experience that combines a movie-like audiovisual presentation using a high-definition screen and surround-sound with high-speed motion.

**Visit our Web site:**
**www.omsi.edu**

**See page 127 under Banquet, Meeting & Event Sites.**

# PORTLAND CENTER FOR THE PERFORMING ARTS

*1111 S.W. Broadway • Portland, Oregon 97205*
*(503) 248-4335; Fax (503) 274-7490*
*Performance Schedule: (503) 248-4335*
*Web site: www.pcpa.com*

***Ticket Center—Ticketmaster and TicketsWest***
*PCPA New Theatre Building*
*S.W. Broadway at Main Street • Portland, Oregon 97205*
*Hours: Mon–Sat 10am–5pm*

---

## PCPA's Resident Performing and Cultural Groups

- Oregon Symphony
- Portland Opera
- Oregon Ballet Theatre
- Portland Center Stage
- The Haven Project
- Oregon Children's Theatre
- Portland Arts & Lectures
- Tears of Joy Theatre
- White Bird
- Metro Arts
- One Voice Productions
- Kalakendra
- Portland Youth Philharmonic
- Portland Institute for Contemporary Art
- Metropolitan Youth Symphony

## These groups perform in the following PCPA venues

- **Arlene Schnitzer Concert Hall**
  S.W. Broadway at Main Street
- **Keller Auditorium**
  S.W. Third between Clay and Market streets
- **Newmark Theatre, Dolores Winningstad Theatre, Brunish Hall**
  located in the New Theatre Building
  S.W. Broadway at Main Street

**See page 135 under Banquet, Meeting & Event Sites, and page 336 under Events & Festivals.**

THE HARDEST WORKING TEAM IN PORTLAND

1 US Division Pennant
2002

9 West Division Pennants
'78, '79, '80, '82, '83, '89, '93, '97, '98

8 Western Conference Titles
'79, '82, '83, '87, '89, '93, '98, 2001

2 WHL League Championships
1982 & 1998

2 Memorial Cup Trophies
1983 & 1998

Shipping: 300 N Winning Way Portland, Oregon 97227
Mailing: PO Box 3009 Portland, Oregon 97208

**Tickets: 503.236.HAWK www.winterhawks.com Office: 503.238.6366**

---

Hosting a corporate party or event at a Portland Winter Hawks game saves you money on tickets, meeting rooms and more.

- Great entertainment for the family or business professionals.
- Entertain clients, employees, friends, family and special guests.
- Treat your guests to a game after an exhibition or show.
- Offer a special discount to show or event attendees.
- Corporate and group rate tickets start as low as $9.00, a savings of $5.50 off the regular ticket price.

## Corporate / Group Rates

| | 20+ | 100+ |
|---|---|---|
| **Preferred Level** | $17.00 | $16.00 |
| **Front Row** | $14.50 | $13.50 |
| **Box Level** | $13.50 | $12.50 |
| **Club Level** | $11.50 | $10.50 |
| **Plaza Level** | $10.00 | $9.00 |

**Call: 503.236.HAWK (4295) for more information.**

## 2004 - 2005
## HOME SCHEDULE

**October:**

| | | |
|---|---|---|
| Sat- 2 | Seattle | RG |
| Sun- 3 | Kamloops | MC |
| Wed- 6 | Spokane | MC |
| Sun- 10 | Lethbridge | MC |
| Fri- 15 | Everett | MC |
| Sat- 16 | Prince George | MC |
| Wed-20 | Vancouver | MC |
| Fri- 29 | Kamloops | MC |

**November:**

| | | |
|---|---|---|
| Wed- 3 | Prince George | MC |
| Sat- 6 | Seattle | RG |
| Wed-24 | Medicine Hat | MC |
| Fri- 26 | Tri-Cities | MC |
| Sat- 27 | Calgary | MC |

**December:**

| | | |
|---|---|---|
| Wed- 1 | Kelowna | MC |
| Fri- 3 | Everett | MC |
| Sat- 4 | Kootenay | MC |
| Tue- 7 | Swift Current | MC |
| Fri- 10 | Everett | RG |
| Fri- 17 | Tri-Cities | MC |
| Sat- 18 | Everett | RG |
| Fri- 31 | Seattle | RG |

**January:**

| | | |
|---|---|---|
| Sun- 2 | Vancouver | MC |
| Sun- 23 | Vancouver | RG |
| Sat- 29 | Tri-Cities | RG |

**February:**

| | | |
|---|---|---|
| Tue- 8 | Kootenay | MC |
| Fri- 11 | Spokane | MC |
| Tue- 15 | Red Deer | MC |
| Fri- 18 | Spokane | MC |
| Sat- 19 | Seattle | MC |
| Tue- 22 | Kelowna | MC |

**March:**

| | | |
|---|---|---|
| Sat- 5 | Tri-Cities | RG |
| Sun- 6 | Seattle | RG |
| Fri- 11 | Spokane | RG |
| Sun- 13 | Everett | RG |
| Fri- 18 | Seattle | RG |
| Sun- 20 | Tr-Cities | RG |

MC= Memorial Coliseum All Information is Subject to Change RG= Rose Garden

# *Vista Balloon Adventures, Inc.*

*701 S.E. Sherk Place, Sherwood Oregon 97140*
*503-625-7385 , 800-622-2309*
*Fax: 503-625-3845*
*www.vistaballoon.com*
*E-mail: roger@vistaballoon.com*

---

## Hot Air Ballooning

Imagine floating over Yamhill County's beautiful wine country in one of the greatest adventures of a lifetime. Your hot air balloon adventure happens just 40 minutes south of downtown Portland in a safe, supportive and fun environment. Flying six balloons at dawn, April 1st to October, you will see Oregon from a wonderful and unique perspective!

Flights are about an hour; allow three hours for the experience, concluding with the traditional full catered breakfast and complimentary flight souvenir.

## Capacity

We can accommodate any number from 1 to 50 in six state-of-the-art aircraft. Accommodation for larger groups can also be made.

## Dawn Flights

Dawn flights always include a full catered breakfast after the flight. We fly only at dawn, for safety reasons.

## Season

We fly from April 15th through October, weather permitting. Meeting planners are encouraged to schedule larger groups during July 15th to September 15th only, as the weather is quite reliable between those dates.

## Prices

$179 per person, $160 for groups of four or more. Planners working on larger events, please call our office for rates of groups over 30.

## Location

We are located at Sportsman Airpark off Hwy 219 in Newberg. Flight path is wherever the wind takes us that day. Oftentimes we fly over the Willamette River, the rolling farmlands of the North Willamette Valley, with some of the best vineyards in the world in the near distance.

***Family owned and operated since 1989 with over 20,000 smiling customers!***

P.O. box 1980 • White Salmon, WA 98672
Contact: Jaco Klinkenberg 1.800.306.1673
trip-info@wetplanetrafting.com
www.wetplanetrafting.com

P.O. Box 215 • Husum, WA 98623
Contact: Kris Goodwillie 509.493.2324
kris@windrivercellars.com
www.windrivercellars.com

**An ADVENTUROUS TASTE of the COLUMBIA RIVER GORGE**

*A whitewater rafting trip on the nationally protected 'Wild & Scenic' White Salmon river with Wet Planet Rafting, followed by a Wine Tasting at the Wind River Cellars winery including a gourmet lunch with a fantastic view of Mt Hood and the Columbia River Gorge.*

**Type of Events:** Teambuilding retreats, corporate events, wedding parties, reunions, birthday parties.

**Capacity:** up to 80

**Price Range:** Base rate: $76.50 per person. Group rates available. Minimum group size: 10. Includes a half-day whitewater rafting trip followed by an upscale light summer lunch and wine tasting. Upgraded menu options available upon request tailored to the nature of your event and group needs.

**Bar:** Award winning wines produced by Wind River Cellars. Beer and non-alcoholic beverages available upon request.

**Event Souvenirs**: Rafting trip photos, event t-shirts and personalized wine gifts available.

## Description of Facility and Services:

Nestled in the Columbia River Gorge between the snowy peaks of Mt Hood and Mt Adams, Wet Planet Rafting and Wind River Cellars are uniquely located alongside the White Salmon River, just 1 hour and 15 minutes East of Portland.

Your rafting trip will be conducted by Wet Planet Rafting on the White Salmon River, providing a breathtaking combination of scenery and whitewater. Fed by natural springs and glaciers on Mt. Adams, this class III-IV river tumbles through a narrow cliff-lined basalt canyon before heading out into the warm sunshine of a forested valley. This incredible trip is highlighted by a vertical plunge over the legendary 10' high Husum Falls.

Following your whitewater rafting trip, you will enjoy another taste of the Columbia River Gorge at Wind River Cellars with wine tasting and a catered lunch. Nestled in the terraced hills overlooked by Mt. Hood and just a stones throw away from Wet Planet, Wind River Cellars distributes the majority of their award winning wines right on location in their tasting room. You will enjoy a tasting of Wind River Cellars' hand-crafted wines while relaxing on the winery's decks in front of some of the most beautiful views in the world. Lunch typically includes various types of baguette style sandwiches with pasta salad, fruit salad and desert.

Menu upgrades, transportation options, and lodging recommendations available.

## Availability & Terms:

Schedule your event for any day of the week, between April and October. Reservations can be made with either Wet Planet or Wind River Cellars. A 50% deposit is required upon reservation. Full payment is due 30 days prior to the event. Refunds will be given for cancellations made up to seven days from the scheduled trip date.

# AMUSEMENT CENTERS, RECREATION & SPORTS TEAMS

## AMUSEMENT CENTERS & ATTRACTIONS

**Enchanted Forest**
8462 Enchanted Wy., S.E.
Turner, OR 97392
(503) 363-3060

**Family Fun Center**
29111 S.W. Town center Loop Way.
Wilsonville, OR 97070
(503) 685-5000
www.fun-center.com
*See page 401*

**Oaks Amusement Park**
Foot of S.E. Spokane St.
Portland, OR 97202
(503) 233-5777
www.oakspark.com
*See page 405*

**Wildlife Safari**
P.O. Box 1600
1790 Safari Rd.
Winston, OR 97496
(541) 679-6761
www.wildlifesafari.org

## RECREATION

**Cascade Soaring**
P.O. Box 369
Dayton, OR 97114
(503) 472-8805

**Club Sport**
18120 S.W. Lower Boones Fry Rd.
Tigard, OR 97224
(503) 968-4500
www.clubsportscom

**Ewing's White Water Rafting & Sage Canyon**
P.O. Box 158
502 Deschutes Ave.
Maupin, OR 97037
(800) 538-RAFT
www.sagecanyonriversupply.com

**Flying M Ranch**
23029 N.W. Flying M Rd.
Yamhill, OR 97148
(503) 662-3222
www.flying-m-ranch.com

**H.O.R.S.E.S., Ltd.**
P.O. Box 280
Scotts Mills, OR 97375
(503) 873-3890

**The Hoop**
3575 Fairview Industrial Dr., S.E.
Salem, OR 97302
(503) 361-7706

**Hot Track Indoor Karting**
14010 B, N.E. Third Ct.
Vancouver, WA 98685
(360) 546-5278
www.hottrack.com

**Multnomah Greyhound Park**
944 N.E. 223rd
Wood Village, OR 97024
(503) 667-7700

**North Clackamas Aquatic Park**
7300 S.E. Harmony Rd.
Milwaukie, OR 97222
(503) 557-7873
www.co.clackamas.or.us/ncap/

**LaserPort**
6540 S.W. Fallbrook Place
Beaverton, OR 97008
(503) 526-9501
*See page 365*

**Malibu Grand Prix**
9405 S.W. Cascade Ave.
Beaverton, OR 97005
(503) 641-8122
www.maliburaceway.com

**Oregon Zoo**
4001 S.W. Canyon Rd.
Portland, OR 97221
(503) 226-1561
ww.oregonzoo.com
*See page X*

**Skate Palace**
1860 Fisher Rd.
Salem, OR 97305
(503) 364-8568

**Ultrazone**
16074-10 S.E. McLoughlin Blvd.
Milwaukie, OR 97267
(503) 652-1122
www.ultrazoneportland.com
*See page 369*

*Recreation continued...*

**Uptown Billiards**
120 N.W. 23rd Ave.
Portland, OR 97210
(503) 226-6909
*See page 368*

**Vancouver-Clark Parks & Recreation**
1009 E. McLoughlin Blvd.
Vancouver, WA 98663
(360) 696-8236

**Wet Planet Rafting**
P.O. Box 1980
White Salmon, WA 98672
(800) 306-1673
www.wetplanetrafting.com
*See page 410*

**Willamette Jetboats**
1945 S.E. Water Ave.
Portland, OR 97214
(503) 231-1532
(888) 538-2628
www.willamettejet.com

## SPORTS TEAMS

**Portland Trail Blazers (NBA)**
One Center Court, Suite 200
Portland, OR 97227
(503) 231-8000; Fax (503) 736-2185
www.nba.com/blazers

**Portland Winter Hawks (WHL)**
300 N. Winning Way
Portland, OR 97227
(503) 238-6366; Fax (503) 238-7629
www.winterhawks.com
*See page 408*

**Salem/Keizer Volcanoes (NWLPB)**
P.O. Box 20936
Keizer, OR 97307
(503) 390-2225
www.volcanoesbaseball.com

**Portland Beavers**
PGE Park
1844 S.W. Morrison
Portland, OR 97205
(503) 553-5400
www.portlandbeavers.com

**Portland Timbers**
PGE Park
1844 S.W. Morrison
Portland, OR 97205
(503) 553-5400
www.pgepark.com/timbers

# BREWERIES

**Alameda Brew House**
4765 N.E. Fremont
Portland, OR 97213
(503) 460-9025
www.nowbrewpage.com

**Big Horse Brewery & Pub**
112 State St.
Hood River, OR 97031
(541) 386-4411
www.horsebrass.com

**Big Horn Brewing Co.**
515 12th St., S.E.
Salem, OR 97301
(503) 363-1904
www.theram.com

**Big Horn Brewing Co. & Ram Restaurant**
320 Oswego Point Blvd.
Lake Oswego, OR 97034
(503) 697-8818
www.theram.com

**BridgePort Brewing Co.**
1313 N.W. Marshall St.
Portland, OR 97209
(503) 241-7179
www.bridgeportbrew.com
*See page 81*

**John Barley Corns Brewery**
14610 S.W. Sequoia Pkwy.
Tigard, OR 97223
(503) 684-2688
www.mcmenamins.com

**Lucky Labrador Brewing Co.**
915 S.E. Hawthorne Blvd.
Portland, OR 97214
(503) 236-3555
www.luckylab.com

7675 S.W. Capitol Hwy
Portland, OR 97219
(503) 244-2537

**McMenamins–Cornelius Pass Roadhouse & Brewery**
4045 N.W. Cornelius Pass Rd.
Hillsboro, OR 97124
(503) 640-6174
www.mcmenamins.com

**McMenamins Edgefield Brewery & Power Station**
2126 S.W. Halsey St.
Troutdale, OR 97060
(503) 492-2777
www.mcmenamins.com

**McMenamins–Hotel Oregon**
310 N.E. Evans St.
McMinnville, OR 97128
(503) 472-8427
www.mcmenamins.com

**McMenamins–Kennedy School**
5736 N.E. 33rd Ave.
Portland, OR 97211
(503) 288-3286
www.mcmenamins.com

**Mt. Angel Brewing Co.**
210 Monroe St.
Mt. Angel, OR 97362
(503) 845-9624
www.mtangelbrewing.com

**Old Market Pub & Brewery**
6959 S.W. Multnomah Blvd.
Portland, OR 97223
(503) 244-0450

**Portland Brewing Co.**
2730 N.W. 31st
Portland, OR 97210
(503) 226-7623
www.portlandbrew.com

**Rock Bottom Brewery**
206 S.W. Morrison St.
Portland, OR 97204
(503) 796-2739
www.rockbottom.com
*See page 144*

**Widmer Gasthaus**
955 N. Russel
Portland, OR 97227
(503) 281-3333
www.widmer.com
*See page 159*

# MUSEUMS

**A.C. Gilbert's Discovery Museum**
116 Marion St., N.E.
Salem, OR 97301
(503) 371-3631
www.acgilbert.org

**Clark County Historical Museum**
1511 Main St.
Vancouver, WA 98660
(360) 695-4681
http://www.pacifier.com/~cchm/

**Columbia Gorge Discovery Center**
5000 Discovery Dr.
The Dalles, OR 97058
(541) 296-8600
www.gorgediscovery.org

**End of the Oregon Trail Interpretive Center**
1726 Washington St.
Oregon City, OR 97045
(503) 657-9336

**Evergreen Aviation Museum**
3685 NE Three Mile Lane
McMinnville, OR 97128
(503) 434-4006
www.sprucegoose.org
*See page 94*

**High Desert Museum**
59800 S. Hwy. 97
Bend, OR 97702
(541) 382-4754
www.highdesertmuseum.org

**Marion County Historical Society Museum**
260 12th St., S.E.
Salem, OR 97301
(503) 364-2128

**Maryhill Museum of Art**
35 Maryhill Museum Dr.
Goldendale, WA 98620
(509) 773-3733
www.maryhillmuseum.org

**Mission Mill Museum**
1313 Mill St., S.E.
Salem, OR 97301
(503) 585-7012
www.missionmill.org

**The University of Oregon Museum of Natural & Cultural History**
1680 E. 15th Ave.
Eugene, OR 97403-1224
(541) 346-3024
natural-history.uoregon.edu

**Museum of the Oregon Territory**
211 Tumwater Dr.
Oregon City, OR 97045
(503) 655-5574
www.orcity.com/museum
*See page 125*

**The Museum at Warm Springs**
2189 Hwy. 26
Warm Springs, OR 97761
(541) 553-3331
www.warmsprings.biz/museum

**OMSI–Oregon Museum of Science & Industry**
1945 S.E. Water Ave.
Portland, OR 97214-3354
(503) 797-4000
www.omsi.edu
*See page 127*

**Oregon Electric Railway Museum**
3995 Brooklake Rd. N.E.
Brooks, OR 97303
(503) 888-4014
www.trainweb.org/oerhs/oerm.htm

**Oregon History Center**
1200 S.W Park Ave.
Portland, OR 97205
(503) 222-1741
www.ohs.org

**Oregon Maritime Center & Museum**
113 S.W. Natio Parkway
Boat btwn. Morrison & Burnside Bridges
Portland, OR 97204
(503) 224-7724
www.oregonmaritimemuseum.org

**Oregon Sports Hall of Fame**
321 S.W. Salmon St.
Portland, OR 97204
(503) 227-7466
www.oregonsportshall.com

**Pearson Air Museum**
1115 E. Fifth St.
Vancouver, WA 98661
(360) 694-7026
www.pearsonairmuseum.org

**Portland Art Museum**
1219 S.W. Park Ave.
Portland, OR 97205
(503) 226-2811
www.pam.org

**Portland Children's Museum CM2**
4015 SW Canyon Rd.
Portland, OR 97221
(503) 223-6500
www.portlandcm2.org

**World Forestry Center**
4033 S.W. Canyon Rd.
Portland, OR 97221-2760
(503) 228-1367
www.worldforestry.org
*See page 162*

# SHOPPING

**Beaverton Mall**
3205 S.W. Cedar Hills Blvd.
Beaverton, OR 97005
(503) 643-6563
www.beaverton-or.mallsbycity.com

**Clackamas Town Center**
12000 S.E. 82nd Ave.
Portland, OR 97266
(503) 653-6913
www.clackamastowncenter.com

**Clackamas Promenade**
8974 S.E. Sunnyside Rd.
Clackamas, OR 97015

**Columbia Gorge Factory Stores**
450 N.W. 257th Wy.
Troutdale, OR 97060
(503) 669-8060

**Eastport Plaza**
4000 S.E. 82nd, Ste. 4000
Portland, OR 97266
(503) 771-3817

**Historic Hawthorne District**
S.E. 12th to S.E. 52nd
Portland, OR

**Jantzen Beach Super Center**
1405 Jantzen Beach Center
Portland, OR 97217
(503) 286-9103
www.jantzenbeachsupercenter.com

**Lancaster Mall**
831 Lancaster Dr., N.E.
Salem, OR 97301
(503) 585-1338
www.lancastermall.com

**Lloyd Center**
953 Lloyd Center
Portland, OR 97232-1315
(503) 282-2511
www.lloydcenter.com

**Mall 205**
9900 S.E. Washington St.
Portland, OR 97216
(503) 255-5805

**Multnomah Village**
S.W. 31st to S.W. 37th on Capitol Hwy
Portland, OR
www.multnomahvillage.org

**NIKETOWN**
930 S.W. Sixth Ave.
Portland, OR 97204
(503) 221-6453
www.niketown.com

**Nob Hill/Uptown Shopping District**
Burnside to Vaughn, 15th Ave.
to Portland's Northwest Hills

**Old Sellwood Antique Row**
S.E. 13th North & South of Tacoma St.
8012 S.E. 13th
Portland, OR 97202

**Pioneer Place**
700 S.W. Fifth Ave.
Portland, OR 97204-2033
(503) 228-5800
www.pioneerplace.com

**Pioneer Place II**
385 S.W. Yamhill
Portland, OR 97204
(503) 228-5800

**Portland Saturday Market**
Old Town – *Under the Burnside Bridge*
108 W. Burnside
Portland, OR 97209
(503) 222-6072
www.portlandsaturdaymarket.com

**Salem Center**
401 Center St., N.E.
Salem, OR 97301
www.salemcenter.com

**Washington Square and Square Too**
9585 S.W. Washington Square Rd.
Tigard, OR 97223
(503) 639-8860
www.shopwashingtonsquare.com

**The Water Tower at John's Landing**
5331 S.W. Macadam Ave.
Portland, OR 97201

**Westfield Shopping Center**
8700 N.E. Vancouver Mall Dr.
Vancouver, Washington 98662
(360) 892-6255
www.westfield.com

**Woodburn Company Stores**
1001 Arney Rd. Ste. 508
Woodburn, OR 97071
(503) 981-1900
www.woodburncompanystores.com

# SKI RESORTS & GAMING CENTERS



## SKI RESORTS

**Anthony Lakes**
47500 Anthony Lakes Hwy.
North Powder, OR 97867
(541) 856-3277
www.anthonylakes.com

**Cooper Spur Mountain Resort**
10755 Cooper Spur Road
Mt. Hood, Oregon 97041
(541) 352-6692, (800) ski-hood
www.cooperspur.com
See page 86

**Crystal Mountain Resort**
33914 Crystal Mountain Blvd.
Crystal Mountain, WA 98022
(360) 663-2265
www.crystalmountain.com

**Hoodoo**
Hwy. 20 Box 20
Sisters, OR 97759
(541) 822-3799

**Mt. Ashland Ski Area**
P.O. Box 220
1745 Hwy. 66
Ashland, OR 97520
(541) 482-2897
www.mtashland.com

**Mt. Bachelor Ski Resort**
P.O. Box 1031
Bend, OR 97709
(541) 382-2442
(800) 829-2442
www.mtbachelor.com

**Mt. Hood Meadows**
P.O. Box 470
Mount Hood, OR 97041
*Portland Office:*
1975 S.W. First Ave. Ste. M
Portland, OR 97201
(503) 287-5438
www.skihood.com
*See page 86*

**Mt. Hood Skibowl**
87000 E. Hwy. 26
Government Camp, OR 97028
(503) 222-4158
www.skibowl.com
*See page 404*

**Summit Ski Area**
*East end of Government Camp Loop*
P.O. Box 459
Government Camp, OR 97028
(503) 272-0256

**Timberline Ski Area**
Timberline Lodge, OR 97028
(503) 231-7979
www.timberlinelodge.com
*See page 153*

## GAMING CENTERS

**Chinook Winds**
1777 N.W. 44th St.
Lincoln City, OR 97367
(541) 996-5825, (888) CHINOOK
www.chinookwindscasino.com
*See page 85*

**Kah-Nee-Ta High Desert Resort & Casino**
100 Main St.
Warm Springs, OR 97661
(800) 554-4786
www.kahneeta.com
*See page 445*

**Lucky Eagle Casino**
12888 188th Ave. S.W.
Rochester, WA 98579
(800) 720-1788
www.luckyeagle.com
*See page 197*

**The Mill Gaming Center & Resort**
3201 Tremont Ave.
North Bend, OR 97459
(800) 953-4800

**Seven Feathers Hotel & Gaming Resort**
146 Chief Miwaleta Ln.
Canyonville, OR 97417
(541) 839-1111
www.sevenfeathers.com
*See page 146*

**Spirit Mountain Casino**
27100 Salmon River Hwy.
Grand Ronde, OR 97347
(800) 760-7977
www.spiritmountain.com
*See page 149*

**Wild Horse Gaming Casino & Resort**
72777 Hwy. 331
Pendleton, OR 97801
(541) 278-2274

# SCENIC & HISTORICAL SITES

**Adelman Peony Gardens**
5690 Brooklake Rd., N.E.
Brooks, OR 97305
(503) 393-6185
www.peonyparadise.com

**Bush Pasture Park Gardens**
600 Mission St., S.E.
Salem, OR 97302
(503) 581-2228
www.salemart.org

**Classical Chinese Garden**
Old Town/Chinatown
N.W. Third Ave. & Everett S.
Portland, Oregon 97204
(503) 228-8131
www.portlandchinesegarden.org

**The Columbia Gorge Interpretive Center**
P.O. Box 396
Stevenson, WA 98648
(509) 427-8211
www.columbiagorge.com

**Cooley's Gardens, Inc.**
11553 Silverton Rd., N.E.
Silverton, OR 97381
(503) 873-5463
www.cooleysgardens.com

**Crystal Springs Rhododendron Garden**
S.E. 28th
North of Woodstock St.
Portland, OR 97286
(503) 771-8386
www.rhodies.org

**End of the Oregon Trail Interpretive Center**
1726 Washington St.
Oregon City, OR 97045
(503) 657-9336

**Forest Park**
North of W. Burnside
to N.W. Newberry Rd.,
West of N.W. St. Helens Rd.
to S.W. Skyline Rd.
(503) 823-2525
www.forestparkforever.org

**Fort Vancouver National Historic Site**
612 E.Reserve St.
Vancouver, WA 98661
(800) 832-3599
www.nps.gov/fova

**Frey's Dahlias**
12054 Brick Rd.
Turner, OR 97392
(503) 743-3910
freysdahlias.com

**The Grotto**
8840 N.E. Skidmore
Portland, OR 97294
(503) 254-7371
*See page 100*
*www.grotto.org*

**Historic Deepwood Gardens**
1116 Mission St., S.E.
Salem, OR 97302
(503) 363-1825
www.oregonlink.com/deepwood

**The Historic Elsinore Theatre**
170 High St.
Salem, OR 97321
(503) 375-ELSI (3574)
www.elsinoretheatre.com

**Japanese Garden**
611 S.W. Kingston Ave.
Portland, OR 97201
(503) 223-1321
www.japanesegarden.com

**McLoughlin House National Historical Site**
713 Center St.
Oregon City, OR 97045
(503) 656-5146
www.mcloughlinhouse.org

**Mission Mill Museum**
1313 Mill St., S.E.
Salem, OR 97301
(503) 585-7012
www.missionmill.org

**Mount St. Helens Coldwater Ridge Visitors Center**
3029 Spirit Lake Hwy.
Castle Rock, WA 98611
(43 miles from Castle Rock)
(360) 274-2103

**Oregon Coast Aquarium**
2820 S.E. Ferry Slip Rd.
Newport, OR 97365-5259
(541) 867-3474
www.aquarium.org
*See page 129*

**Oregon State Capitol & Grounds**
**900** Court St., N.E.
Salem, OR 97310
(503) 986-1388

**Oregon Garden**
P.O. Box 155
879 W. Main St.
Silverton, OR 97381
(503) 874-8100
www.oregongarden.org

**Pittock Mansion**
3229 N.W. Pittock Dr.
Portland, OR 97210
(503) 823-3624
www.pittockmansion.com
*See page 133*

**Powell's City of Books**
1005 W. Burnside St.
Portland, OR 97209
(503) 228-4651
www.powells.com

**Schreiner's Iris Gardens**
3625 Quinaby Rd. N.E.
Salem, OR 97303
(503) 393-3232
www.schreinersgardens.com

**Sea Lion Caves**
91560 Hwy. 101
Florence, OR 97439
(541) 547-3111
www.sealioncaves.com

**Silver Falls State Park**
20024 Silver Falls Hwy., S.E.
Sublimity, OR 97385
(503) 873-8681
www.open.org/slvrfall

**Tom McCall Waterfront Park**
Downtown Portland
end of S.W. Salmon St.
Portland, OR 97209
www.parks.ci.portland.or.us

**Washington Park Rose Garden**
400 S.W. Kingston Ave.
Portland, OR 97201
(503) 823-2525

**Willamette University Gardens**
900 State St.
Salem, OR 97301
(503) 370-6300

# Notes

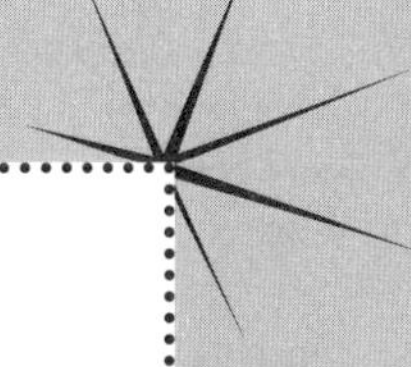

# Rental Services

- *Equipment & Accessories*
- *Tables, Chairs & Linens*
- *Tents & Canopies*
- *Portable Restrooms*

# RENTAL SERVICES

**Rental stores carry almost everything:** You'll find such things as serviceware, portable bars, arches, tents, chairs, tables, and all the tableware, dishes, glassware and flatware you need. Many shops also carry disposable paper products and a variety of decorations. For meetings, seminars and conventions, you will find audio visual, lighting and sound equipment to meet your needs.

**Visit a rental store while planning:** It's smart to visit a showroom for ideas and to see the types and styles of merchandise and equipment available. Rental stores have brochures that describe all the different items available for rent, including style, colors, sizes and prices. Rental stores are also terrific places to get ideas for decorations. Meet with the store's consultants and go through your event plans step-by-step. You'll find they will help you select the right items to meet your needs, as well as help determine the correct quantities. You will work very closely with the rental store you choose–make sure you feel confident in the services its staff will provide you. They will be an important extension of your staff.

**Decide on formality and budget:** Keep in mind the colors and decor of the site. Pick linens or paper products and tableware that will complement the room. Prices will vary depending on the formality you choose.

**Table art has become very popular for many events.** Your event theme is carried through to the tables–the linens, chair covers, dishware and centerpiece all have a purpose. This "table art" is the newest buzz among event planners! Visit a rental, specialty linen, or chair cover company today to get lots of incredible ideas.

**Deposits, delivery and setup:** Reserve your items as far in advance as possible, especially during the summer months when outdoor events (picnics, fairs, etc.) are popular. A deposit will secure the order for your date. Only a certain number of tents and canopies are available, and every item is reserved on a first-come, first-served basis. There is a charge on most items for delivery, setup and pickup. Make sure you ask in advance how much those charges are so you can include them in your budget. You can also make arrangements to pick up and return the items yourself.

**Returning items:** If you don't arrange delivery and pickup services with the rental company, you will want to put someone in charge of picking up and returning the rented items for you. You will be responsible and may forfeit any deposit for items that are damaged, broken, lost, or late.

**Specialty event rentals:** All kinds of equipment, from cellular phones and pagers to computers and specialty staging and lighting, are available for rent. Because of the sophisticated nature of this type of equipment, it is smart to work with specialized rental companies. They have the technicians on staff to maintain, setup and operate this equipment.

**Communications equipment**: Almost every large event, meeting, or convention uses some form of communication equipment. Cellular phones are very popular for on-the-go planners. Most planners and event staff operate with some type of immediate communication system. The pager system is affordable, small, and convenient for carrying around, but requires a telephone to respond. Radio phones allow for immediate communication of the message. The staff at a communications company (located in this section) can explain the benefits of each system and help decide what will be the most appropriate equipment for your function.

**Computer services are also helpful on-site during the event:**

- On-site registration
- Computer signage (last-minute changes)
- Computerized message boards
- Badges
- E-Mail

Computerized accounting systems for meeting and event planners are invaluable and allow the planner to look at the costs by category, function, and income per attendee.

**New specialty linens and chair covers to match your theme**. These custom linens and chair covers are the new decorating sensation. They fill the room with color and are a great enhancement to your theme. The custom linen styles come in a variety of choices: elegant, festive, creative, classic, seasonal, and more. Refer to this section for the companies that specialize in this service. Custom chair covers are a new look for meetings and events. Chair cover styles can be custom-designed with your business logo or matching theme for your event.

**Tent rental:** A tent often serves as an ideal back up location for an outdoor event, in case of unsuitable weather conditions. Many tents feature transparent vinyl siding that can be raised and lowered as needed. A tent supplier can recommend sources for any portable heating or air conditioning that you might need.

**Important note:** Never use canvas tents treated with mineral oil for waterproofing, they are extremely flammable.

**Tent capacities:** The following are estimated capacities for tents of typical sizes under normal conditions:

| | | *Accommodates* | |
|---|---|---|---|
| *Tent Size* | *Reception* | *Buffet w/ seating* | *Sit-down Dinner* |
| 16'x16' | 45 | 32 | 24 |
| 20'x20' | 65 | 56 | 40 |
| 20'x30' | 100 | 86 | 60 |
| 30'x30' | 180 | 124 | 100 |
| 40'x40' | 350 | 280 | 240 |

**Choosing a tent site:** When arranging tents with a single transparent vinyl side, consider the position of the sun during your event; if the clear portion faces due west through an evening event, the sunset may be blinding. Also, be certain that you do not pitch your tent over low or uneven ground that might accumulate water runoff.

**Overlooked, but necessary, rental items**: Portable restrooms are a very important rental item for a large function or event. Portable restrooms today are much improved from years past. They are attractive and function as a normal restroom. Nothing is more annoying than standing in line for a restroom while the awards are being presented or the speaker is beginning the speech.

**Clean Portable Restrooms**

1685 McGilchrist Street S.E.
Salem, Oregon 97301
800-966-2371
***Web site: www.honeybucket.com***

---

Honey Bucket is the most experienced provider of portable sanitation services to Special Events in the Pacific Northwest. From the largest event with hundreds of units and on-site attendants, to a single unit for a wedding or company picnic, Honey Bucket is the right choice.

We take pride in our professional approach to Special Events. Our Honey Bucket name is "on the line" at each event and we expect attendees to have a pleasant experience when they use our units. We are committed to provide you the best planning assistance, equipment, service and value.

We will work with you to ensure a successful event. The ***Event Planning Guide*** on our web site will help you determine the proper number of units, based on attendance, the length of the event and sanitary guidelines.

Our Special Event experts will be happy to help you with your specific needs.

You can go online to get a quote or information on products, event experience, upcoming events, Honey Bucket *"fun stuff"* and much much more at ***www.honeybucket.com***.

Committed to being the best...

## INTERSTATE *Special Events*

*5420 N. Interstate Avenue*
*Portland, Oregon 97217-4597*
*(503) 285-6685; www.ISEvents.com*

At Interstate Special Events, we have everything you need—including the expertise, the attention to detail and the commitment to service—to make your event truly "special." Our inventory contains a wide variety of items needed for every type of event. From casual to formal, we can supply your needs!

### Tables, Chairs and Linens

We offer banquet, round, half-round, umbrella, bistro and stylish serpentine tables. Classic white wood and black wood chairs are available, as well as Gold Chivari's, Silver Chivari's, folding Samsonite, white Bistro and black padded stacking chairs. Our table linens, skirting and napkins are available in a wide array of colors and sizes.

### Tents and Canopies

We have one of the largest canopy inventories in the area. Our tents range from 100 square feet to 18,000 square feet. We also supply elegant tent liners, pole sleeves, lighting and heating. Site inspections are available.

### Tableware, Beverage and Serving Accessories

Our china styles include the classic white, elegant ivory with gold band, white with silver trim, elegant white bone china with gold trim, and clear glass. Whatever the occasion, we have glassware in many styles to meet your needs. Stainless and silver flatware and serving accessories are available. We have many silver plate items such as tea service, punch bowls and chafing dishes as well as vases and bowls in glass, stainless, acrylic and silver. We offer porta-bars, beermeister, beverage fountains, kegtainers, coffeemakers and carafes, pitchers and insulated dispensers.

### Additional Items

We carry a large inventory of concession equipment including briquet and propane BBQs, fryers, grills and griddles, gumbo pots and hot boxes. We specialize in staging and carry a large inventory of dance floors. If games are what you are looking for, we have bingo, volleyball, softball, horseshoes and even a Dunk Tank! And don't forget the helium tank. Also available to rent are overhead and slide projectors, screens, PA systems, TVs, VCRs and bullhorns.

### Retail Merchandise

Our showroom contains an inventory of disposable products in 20 solid colors. It includes paper plates, napkins, table covers and table rolls, hot/cold cups, clear plastic glassware and balloons. You can also find a nice selection of taper candles in assorted sizes, scented floating and pillar candles.

### Ordering and Delivery

Reservations are highly recommended to ensure availability and assistance in meeting your needs. Delivery is available as well as setup and take-down for a reasonable charge. Our Special Events Representatives are eager to assist with your event needs. Please call us today for more information or visit us on the Web at www. ISEvents.com.

# the party place

WEDDINGS EVENTS MEETINGS TRADESHOWS

1211 North Loring Street , (503) 292-8875 and 10101 SE Stark Street, (503) 252-3466

**www.portlandrentall.com**

## TENTS AND CANOPIES

Sizes range from 10'x10' to our 60'x160' New Century Tent. Also available: sidewall, liners, pole covers, lighting, heating, air conditioning and generators. Larger tent sizes available.

## STAGING AND DANCE FLOOR

- Staging, stage skirting and carpet
- Dance floor available in wood parquet or black and white check.

## TABLES AND CHAIRS

- 6′ and 8′ Banquet Tables
- Conference Tables
- 30″, 36″, 48″, 60″, and 72″ Round Tables
- Card and Serpentine Tables
- Childrens Tables
- 60″ square tables
- White, Black and Natural Wood Folding Chairs
- Resin Black and White Bistro Chairs
- Brown or White Samsonite Folding Chairs
- Black Stack Chairs (padded)
- Elegant Chivari Chairs in Gold, Silver or Natural
- Childrens Chairs

## LINENS AND SERVICEWARE

- Solid color and prints available
- Banquet Cloths (60″x120″)
- 90″, 108″, 120″ Rounds
- Square Table Cloths
- Elegant Gathered Skirting or Box Skirts
- Chafers in Plain Stainless, Brass Trim or Silver
- Stainless, Silver or Copper Trays (variety of sizes)
- Serving Bowls in Plastic, Glass or Silver
- Other Silver Pieces and Gold Holloware
- Coffee Makers and Insulated Dispensers

## CHINA, GLASSWARE AND FLATWARE

Our china styles include Clear Glass, White, Ivory with a Gold Band, White with a Silver Band, Black Octagonal, Fiestaware, Square and Triangle china. We also offer a wide variety of glassware options, such as Crystal, Cutglass or Black Stem and our standard glass barware. From Margaritas to Martinis, you'll find the glassware you're looking for. Flatware styles available are plain stainless, hammered stainless, silverplate, bamboo, baguette stainless or gold.

## CONCESSION AND FOOD SERVICE EQUIPMENT

- Barbecues (propane or charcoal)
- Sno-cone and popcorn machines
- Hot dog cookers and cotton candy (supplies also available)
- Cambro insulated food pan carriers
- Electric hot boxes
- Portable oven
- Deep fat fryer

## EVENT MERCHANDISE

We carry a vast selection of decorations, plastic and paper goods such as napkins, plates, cups and flatware, in over 25 colors. Also available, case pricing, and a large selection of catalogs for special orders. Wedding merchandise is available at the Stark Street location only.

**PERSONALIZED SERVICE, QUALITY PRODUCTS AND PROMPT DELIVERY**

# THE PARTY PRO'S

**Visit us at...**
*2460 N.E. Griffin Oaks Street, Suite 1500*
*Hillsboro, Oregon 97124*
*(503) 844-9798; Fax (503) 844-2902*

***FOR DELIVERY AND PICKUP SERVICE TO...***
*Portland, Beaverton, Hillsboro, Tualatin, Tigard, Clackamas, Oregon City, West Linn, Wilsonville and outlying areas*

*Business Hours: Mon–Sat 9am–5:30pm*
*E-mail: PARTYPRO1@juno.com*
*Web site: www.THEPARTYPROS.com*

---

**Company Picnics and Events • BBQs • Graduations and Proms • Weddings**
**Fund Raisers • Church Dinners • Home and Back Yard Parties**

## Rental Items Available

- **Tents and Canopies:** many sizes to fit your needs; elegant tent liners
- **Tables and chairs:** banquet and round, umbrella tables, folding chairs, white wood and white wedding chairs
- **Staging, Dance Floors and Sound Equipment:** staging, stage skirting and carpet; dance floor available in wood parquet or black and white check; sound systems and projectors.
- **Linens:** fine-quality linens available in a variety of colors; banquet for 6' or 8' tables, 90" round, 120" round, skirting and napkins.
- **China:** sophisticated ivory with gold trim and simple clear glass.
- **Glassware:** champagne, punch, coffee, rocks, wine, water or specialty.
- **Serving pieces:** punch bowls, chafing dishes; acrylic, silver or stainless bowls, trays, tongs, spoons and servers; silver tea service; stainless flatware.
- **Beverage service:** champagne fountains, coffee makers, insulated beverage dispensers, carafes, pitchers, keg coolers and beer taps.
- **Centerpieces and decorations:** silk flower bouquets, theme centerpieces, casual or elegant black tie. Many ideas to customize your event.
- **Entertainment and Games:** inflatable bouncers, dunk tank, volleyball, bingo, raffle drums, sack races, tug-of-war, karaoke.
- **Concession Items:** barbeque grills/tools, popcorn, cotton candy and snow cone machines.

***VISIT OUR STORE FOR ALL YOUR PARTY NEEDS!***

## Specialty Retail Items

Decorations, centerpieces and ideas galore. Invitations and imprinted napkins; balloon designs and bouquets; floating and dripless taper candles in a variety of colors. Paper tableware: floral and solid color plates, cups and napkins. Plastic cups, glasses, cutlery, bowls, trays, table covers and skirting.

## Full On-site Decorating Service; Ordering and Delivery

We will come to your event site, design a decorating plan, provide a written proposal and on the day of the event, implement everything. We will handle all setup and takedown.

Reservations are highly recommended so that we can guarantee item availability for your special event. Deliver and pickup service is available. Call our ***PARTY PRO'S*** for an estimate, or set up your free consultation.

## QUALITY & SERVICE IS OUR GOAL!

Our ultimate goal is total customer satisfaction during and after the hustle and bustle of your event planning. Large or small, we can make it happen for you!

# Peter Corvallis Productions

SINCE 1959

*2204 N. Clark Avenue • Portland, Oregon 97227*
*Contact: Athena Paskill*
*(503) 222-1664; Fax (503) 222-1047*
*E-mail: athena@petercorvallis.com*
*Business Hours: Mon-Sat 8am–6pm*

---

## Everything to rent... for every event

Peter Corvallis Productions, Inc. is a northwest pioneer in the event rental industry. Our family business has over 40 years of growth, and event knowledge to invest in your next project.

Our service maintains precise planning, experienced professionals, creative options and an extensive selection of the latest party rental equipment.

Now our clients can share in the process of creating the event by viewing our warehouse of thousands of prop and rental items. Walk the aisles of your favorite themes and choose things that will be the hit of your next party.

Peter Corvallis Productions provides more than just quality products. Here is a list of rental equipment and the many services we offer to make your function run smoothly so you can enjoy your event along with your guests. Having an event will never be easier. We are at our service:

★**Tent and Canopy Rentals:** Tents and canopies in sizes ranging from 10'x10' to 100'x500', including the free span Hoecker, tent accessories: clear sidewall, French window sidewall, pole swags, tent fabric liners, heaters, carpeting, flooring, globe lights and chandeliers.

★**Party Rentals:** Tables, chairs, china, silver, flatware, glassware, catering equipment, stages, dance floors, chair covers, linens and overlays in all colors, patterns and fabrics.

★**Theme Decorations:** Over 100 themes for you to decorate with. Our collection has the most authentic props available to the public. Some of the most well known are Western, Mardi Gras, Fifties, Renaissance, Hollywood, Putting on the Ritz, International, Hawaiian, Mexican, Volcano, Safari, Pirates, Carnival and Circus

★**Audio Visual Services and Rentals:** Event meeting and conference equipment that includes video and television systems, LCD data projectors, screens, microphones, podiums, sound systems, computers, lighting and special effects.

★**Tradeshow Decorating and Rentals:** Pipe, drape and table skirting in all colors. Exhibit booth displays and furnishings, signage, freight, electrical, carpeting, and show design.

★**Additional Services:** Complete Set- Up and Takedown Service. Before and After-Hours, Delivery and Pick up Service to meet your event needs. After- Hours Number for emergency needs.

★**Event Planning Services:** Special Event representatives for ideas and assistance in planning your event. An Event Design Department offering complete planning and event production. Event lay out and design allowing you to visualize your event through computer diagrams. The Event planning guide and rental catalog: a 50-page product catalog including great party planning information.

# SNEAD'S

**Special Events Rentals**

*141st & Tualatin Valley Highway*
*Beaverton, Oregon 97005*
*(503) 641-6778*
*Sneadsrentalneeds.com*
*E-mail: sneadspartytime@aol.com*
*Mon–Sat 7:30am–5pm; Sun 10am–4pm*

## Rental Items Available *(call for free brochure)*

- **Business Meetings:** Formica conference tables in various sizes. Linens and skirting with a corporate look. Padded folding chairs. Coffee makers and servers. China, glassware, and flatware. Coat racks and hangers.
- **Trade Shows:** Plywood tables in various sizes. Linens and skirting. Samsonite folding chairs. Convention pipe and drapery. Staging and skirting and/or drapery background. Stanchions and carpet runners.
- **Audiovisual Equipment:** Portable and professional sound systems. Wireless micophones. Hand-held tour guides and bull horns. TV sets and VCR players. Big screen video projectors with computer interface. Camcorders, Karaokes. Overhead, movie, and opaque projectors. Slide projectors with carts, stands, and screens. Easels, flip charts, and eraser boards.
- **Convention and Serving Equipment:** Hot dog cookers, popcorn poppers, cotton candy, snow cone, ice shaver, milk shake machines and ice cream cart. Drink dispensers, blenders. Meat slicers, deep fat fryers. Propane cookers, griddles, steam tables, holding ovens, hot plates, and warming trays. Chafers in various styles with pans. Coffee makers.
- **Picnics and Parties:** Bars and beer coolers/taps. Barbecues and accessories. Dance floors. Games: volleyball, horseshoes, softball, tug-o-war, croquet and dunk tank. Round tables with umbrellas.
- **Inflatables:** Spacewalk and mini slide.
- **Party Tents:** Free standing from 10'x10' to 20'x40' plus sidewalls, windows, liners, lighting and heaters.
- **Lighting and Special Effects** for parties and shows: beacons, strobe, traffic, black, quartz halogen and color wheel. Mirror ball, bubble and fog machine, waterfalls, fountains. Ground breaking shovel. Artificial flowers, plants, and trees.
- **Tables, Chairs and Linens-Skirting:** Many sizes, styles and colors.
- **China, and Flatware:** Ivory, white, black, and clear. Stainless or silverplate
- **Glassware:** Contemporary, lead crystal or utility, stemware, barware, misc.
- **Plastic, Acrylic and Stainless:** Salad bars, bowls, tubs, serving items.
- **Silver and Gold Holloware:** For elegant entertaining: punch bowls, trays, coffee/tea service, candelabra, wine coolers, champagne or punch fountains, floral pieces.
- **Balloons and Helium:** Large tanks only. Helium tanks in 8 sizes with delivery service and long-term rates.

**Snead's Party Time** welcomes your inquiries and promises top customer service. We are open seven days a week, will take advance reservations and provide delivery service. We offer credit, competitive rates, and a salesperson to come to your location.

***Come in and visit our event photography studios with theme props.***

**(503) 641-6778**

*1400 N.W. 15th Avenue • Portland, Oregon 97209*
*(503) 294-0412; Fax (503) 294-0616*
*Business Hours: Mon–Sat 8:30am–6pm*
*Appointments available any hour*
*www.wcep.com*

## Services

West Coast Event Productions is the Northwest's premier idea center for all events and special occasions. We specialize in the custom planning and design of event staging, lighting, sound, special effects, audiovisual presentations, tabletop décor, and event and theme production. We are able to tailor your event or special occasion to mirror your vision. We are here to help you make all your important event planning decisions. Please feel free to visit our newly designed showroom. Browse for ideas with our Photo Inventory Books. We have many of our specialty props, catering items and equipment displayed to aid in your event planning.

## Rental Items Available

**Tents and canopies:** Sizes range from 10′ x 10′ to 100′ x 200′+ and vary in color from solid white to striped red, green, blue or yellow. Custom tent decorating includes elegant fabric liner, fabric tent pole covers in any color, floral garlands, ambient tent lighting and twinkle lights. French and Cathedral window sidewalls, heaters, air conditioning and flooring are also available.

**Wedding accessories:** Select from several styles of candelabras, brass and silver table candelabras, brass and contemporary full standing candelabras; wedding aisle and carpet runners; custom chuppah; gazebos and arches; wood, ceramic, marble finish and Grecian columns; table accessories include urns, vases, hurricanes, votives, cherubs and table lamps.

**Tables and chairs:** Choose from our complete selection of tables and chairs in a variety of sizes and styles: White wood garden chairs, black wood chairs, gold and silver ballroom chairs, folding and stacking chairs. ***Ask about our new specialty chair covers.***

**Linens and skirting:** The largest selection of linens in numerous patterns, solid colors and types of material. Various skirting colors and sizes are also available for any type of event or theme.

**China, flatware, glassware and serviceware:** Impressive selection of china in 15 different patterns: ivory with gold or silver, white, black octagon and clear octagon. Solid colors in red, yellow, blue and green, formal bone china, contemporary patterns. Stainless, silverplate and goldplate flatware. Glassware for every occasion. Catering items for food service and many other items available.

**Sound system, lighting and audiovisual:** Complete array of sound equipment from amplifiers, microphone and mixing counsels to high-end data projectors. We offer a variety of unique lighting fixtures and special effects for outdoor receptions.

**Stage and dance floor:** An assortment of floors from elegant oak parquet to black and white, all white, or colored checks. Elevated foundations for ceremony, head table riser and entertainment—all attractively carpeted and skirted.

**Props:** We have an extensive inventory of props to support hundreds of themes. Our selection offers a wide range of architectural shapes and elements, building facades, drapery, artificial plants, fiberglass animals, statues, waterfalls, oversize rocks, special effects, hand props, floral supplies, antiques and memorabilia.

# Notes

# Notes

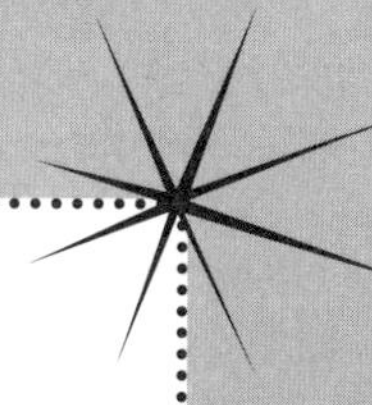

# Resorts & Retreats

**RESORT**

*1555 Hwy 101 • Yachats, Oregon 97498*
*Sales Office: 541-547-5815 or 800-522-3623*
*Reservations: 800-522-3623*
*E-mail: suek@adoberesort.com or adobeinfo@adoberesort.com*
*Web site: www.adoberesort.com*

## LOCATION

The Adobe Resort is located on Pacific Coast Highway 101, one mile from the coastal village of Yachats and is nestled between lush forested mountains of the Coast Range and the crashing waves of the Pacific right on the edge of the Central Oregon Coastline. (Eugene: 86 miles; Salem; 108 miles; Portland: 140 miles) Nearest airport: Newport Airport 25 miles.

## ACCOMMODATIONS

The Adobe Resort, a full service hotel, offers 110 rooms. Most guest rooms have a spectacular ocean view: some have fireplaces and whirlpool tubs. All rooms have refrigerators, microwaves,coffee makers, hair dryers and remote control televisions. Guest room types include hillside view rooms, ocean view rooms, kitchenette suites, pet friendly rooms, whirlpool suites and 1400 sq. foot two bedroom/two bath condos.

## MEETING/BANQUET FACILITIES

The Adobe Resort with almost 5,000 sq. ft of meeting space is the perfect retreat, reunion, and wedding location. Our Executive Board room boasts a table for 12 with a magnificent ocean view and doors that lead out into our landing for those scheduled breaks. Our other three meeting/banquet rooms can comfortably accommodate groups of up to 120. Audio visual equipment is available along with a professional sales and catering staff to make any function a success.

## DINING

The award winning Adobe Resort Restaurant on ocean's edge with one of the most spectacular views on the Central Oregon Coast is open seven days per week serving breakfast, lunch, dinner or a sumptuous Sunday champagne brunch. The restaurant spotlights the best mouth-watering fresh seafood, steak or special dishes prepared for you and/or your group by our Chef. Groups, family or friends, the Adobe Resort Restaurant has what your taste buds have been craving. Our lounge offers three levels of magnificent ocean views and signature drinks. Lunch, appetizers and dinner menus are also served.

## RECREATION

The Adobe Resort features an all-new fitness center with a large indoor pool, a kiddy's pool and whirlpool, sauna and exercise room at no extra charge to our guests. On site massage therapist by appointment only. On site recreation includes whale watching, tide pool exploring, storm watching, agate hunting, watching magnificent sunsets or strolling down the historic 804 trail which leads to 6 miles of sandy beaches. Area attractions include the Sea Lion Caves, Cape Perpetual Visitors Center, Heceta Light house, golf courses, charter boat trips, horseback riding, sand dune rides or 18 miles of trails

*212 E. Main Street • Ashland, OR 97520 • www.ashlandspringshotel.com*
*For Reservations or Information Call (541) 488-1700, Toll free (888) 795-4545*

---

*"An eclectic mix of idyllic small-town living, European taste and the great outdoors."*
—Architectural Digest, June 2002

## Hotel Description

Elegantly restored European style hotel on the National Register of Historic Places offers seventy tastefully appointed, non-smoking guest rooms. All rooms feature hand-painted lamp shades, crisp white linens and French down blankets. Calming colors of apricot, melon and pear evoke an era of relaxed comfort and elegance. Guests are pampered with superb service and luxurious surroundings.

## Location

Situated one block from the Oregon Shakespeare Festival in the heart of downtown Ashland. Within walking distance of the hotel guests enjoy Lithia Park, Oregon Cabaret Theatre, galleries, boutique shopping and numerous restaurants.

## Banquet and Meeting Facilities

Hotel offers 5,700 square feet of meeting space that is ideal for company retreats, lectures, executive and board meetings or social events. Our facility includes two ballrooms, enchanting Elfinwood room available for private events up to 70 people, palm-filled Conservatory, as well as an English Garden filled with exquisite flowers and plants. Two luxurious breakout rooms for smaller meetings complement the meeting facilities. Our banquet staff has been selected and trained to offer every group the finest full service catering.

## Amenities

Spa Service • Afternoon tea served on the Mezzanine • Bulls-Eye Bistro, lounge and sidewalk café featuring live entertainment • High-speed wireless Internet connection • Complimentary continental breakfast served on the Mezzanine • Waffle weave robes, hair dryer, iron, ironing board, modem hookup, refrigerator, television, expanded cable, pay per view movies and Nintendo 64 in every room.

## Area Attractions

Lithia Park • Oregon Shakespeare Festival • Oregon Cabaret Theatre
The Britt Festival in Jacksonville • Crater Lake National Park
Oregon Caves National Monument • Redwoods State Park
Mount Ashland Ski and Snowboard Resort • Local Wineries and Farms
Rafting on Rogue and Klamath Rivers • Historic Trolley Tours

# Best Western Agate Beach Inn

*3019 N. Coast Highway*
*Newport, Oregon 97365*
***Reservations** (800) 547-3310; **Group Sales** (800) 546-5010; **Local** (541) 265-9411*
*E-mail: sales@agatebeachinn.com; Web site: www.agatebeachinn.com*

## Description of Hotel

The Best Western Agate Beach Inn is a 148-room three star full-service hotel offering panoramic views of Agate Beach, the Yaquina Head Lighthouse, and the Pacific Ocean. Our hotel, newly remodeled in a historic turn-of-the-century motif, is clearly the place to stay when visiting Newport. Our tastefully appointed guest rooms feature one king or two queen-sized beds, TV/VCR, microwave, refrigerator, coffee maker, iron, ironing board hair dryer and workspace with telephone and data port.

## Location

The Best Western Agate Beach Inn is located north of downtown Newport, within a few hours of Portland, Salem and Eugene, off Highway 101.

## Meeting Space

The Cove Room and Agate Ballroom total 5,000 square feet of meeting and convention space and accommodate 10 to 500 people. Our professional catering and banquet staff are eager to serve you for your next meeting.

## Other Amenities

- Starfish Grill Restaurant
- Rookies Sports Bar
- Indoor heated swimming pool
- Spa
- Fitness center
- Arcade
- Gift shop
- Movie rentals

## Nearby Attractions

- Oregon Coast Aquarium
- Hatfield Marine Science Center
- Yaquina Bay State Park
- BLM Interpretive Center/Tide pools
- Golf course
- Whale watching
- Fishing and crabbing
- Newport Bay Front attractions and shopping

# BEST WESTERN OCEANVIEW RESORT

*414 N. Prom • Seaside, Oregon 97138*
503.738.3334 or 800.234.8439
*E-mail: sales@oceanviewresort.com*
*Web site: www.oceanviewresort.com*

## MORE THAN A PLACE TO STAY, A GREAT GETAWAY

**Overview:** Best Western Ocean View Resort in Seaside is a AAA three-diamond Resort on Oregon's North Coast. The Ocean View Resort is perfect for group meetings, retreats and conferences for up to 340 people. The ocean front location offers first class accommodations with a "touch of home" with personalized service from our expert staff. New at the Resort is a complete upgrade and remodeling of the ocean front rooms to include the Jacuzzi Suites. The newest addition to the Resort is Salvatore's Cafe, our Italian-American restaurant and Sal's Pub, a quiet conversation Sports Pub offer some of the best cuisine in the area in a lively, colorful atmosphere.

**Location:** Situated beachfront, on the Prom in Seaside, and four blocks north of Broadway (boardwalk with shops, restaurants, arcades, attractions and the End of the Lewis & Clark Trail), we offer guests an unbeatable combination of outstanding scenery and location. Just 75 miles from Portland and a three-hour drive from Seattle and Eugene, we offer an ideal location in the Northwest. The Seaside Civic & Convention Center is only three blocks away; the Factory Outlet Center is eight blocks away; and there are three golf courses within a five mile radius. There are a variety of recreational, historic and tourist attractions in the area.

**Guest Rooms & Suites:** The Resort offers 107 guestrooms and suites, most with a spectacular ocean or coastline views. All of our oceanfront guestrooms and suites were renovated in 2004 to include new pillow top mattresses and bed tops, a second Queen-size bed in each room with sofa, drapes/sheers, and other improvements. A wide variety of guestrooms are available featuring kitchenettes, private balconies, suites, firpelaces and Jacuzzi tubs. All guestrooms at the resort feature a television with video player, coffeemaker, hair dryer, voicemail, and high-speed Internet access. Most guestrooms include a microwave and refrigerator.

**Other Amenities & Services:**

- Over 6,000 square feet of meeting and banquet space accommodating up to 340 theater-style, 300 for receptions, 230 for banquets and 200 classroom style. Small meeting venues are available, as well. Windows in most meeting rooms.
- Wireless High Speed Internet Access in all guestrooms and meeting rooms, as well as most public areas. Hard wire access available in all meeting rooms and some public areas.
- Full Service Catering Department…from custom menus, all-inclusive meal plans to beach functions!
- Group rates available.
- Salvatore's Café, an Italian family-style restaurant and Sal's Pub.
- Indoor pool and spa.
- Gift Certificates are available-perfect for birthdays, anniversaries and weddings.

*1252 E Cascade Drive*
*North Bonneville, Washington 98639*
*Sales Office: 509-427-9702*
*Reservations: (866) 459-1678*
*E-mail: info@bonnevilleresort.com;*
*Web site: www.bonnevilleresort.com*

---

Nestled in the pristine Columbia River Gorge National Scenic area, you will find a soothing and rejuvenating experience at the luxurious new ***BONNEVILLE HOT SPRINGS RESORT.***

## Background

Historical records indicate the waters of the hot springs were used for centuries by Native American tribes living in the area for healing purposes. In 1880 a settler by the name of Mr. Moffet rediscovered the hot springs and offered them to the public. Owner Pete Cam purchased the property in 1991 intent on building a full service resort and natural hot springs spa facility. The new Bonneville Hot Springs Resort opened in October of 2002.

## Accommodations

This magnificent resort features 74 deluxe rooms and four spacious suites each with exterior balconies. Sixteen of the rooms have private hot tubs set out on the balcony filled with the natural mineral springs water. Interior spaces radiate warmth and comfort with the fine craftsmanship of inlaid woods and stonework, all accented with richly woven tapestry fabrics. Rooms offer color television with remote control, Lodge-Net in-house movies and video games, mini-refrigerators, coffee makers, hair dryers, iron and board, terrycloth robes, air conditioners with individual thermostat control. The three-story lobby features a massive river rock fireplace and two walls of floor to ceiling windows overlooking giant Douglas fir and pine trees.

## Dining

The elegant ***Pacific Crest Dining Room*** at *Bonneville Hot Springs Resort* offers a variety of healthful spa entrees and a fine traditional Northwest menu. Enjoy fine dining while overlooking a beautifully landscaped courtyard filled with waterfalls and streams. The Cascade Lounge exudes a sport and leisure type setting with mounted television screens. Lunch, appetizers and a light dinner menu are also served.

## Meeting Space

Two beautifully appointed meeting rooms sit up to 50 people each in conference-style seating or can be combined to accommodate up to 100 for banquet seating.

## Special Services and Recreation

The men's and women's European hot spring spa facility uses the natural hot springs water for all treatments. The spring water comes out of the ground at 97° and is heated as needed. The spa offers soaking baths, body wraps, massages, facials, foot reflexology and numerous other soothing and rejuvenating services. The resort includes an indoor 25 meter lap pool and two soaking pools all filled with the natural mineral hot springs water. Take advantage of numerous outdoor activities including bike trails, horseback riding, hiking, biking, windsurfing, skiing, and fishing are all just a short distance from the comforts of the resort.

DOLCE Conference & Resort Destinations®

*1131 S.W. Skamania Lodge Way*
*Stevenson, Washington 98648*
*Sales Office: (509) 427-2503*
*or (800) 376-9116*
*Reservations: (800) 221-7117*
*Office Hours: Mon–Fri 8am–5pm*
*E-mail: conference@skamania.com;* ***Web site: skamanialodge.dolce.com***

In the Columbia River Gorge National Scenic Area lies a rustic mountain resort and conference center—***DOLCE SKAMANIA LODGE.***

## Accommodations

Just 45 minutes from Portland International Airport, Dolce Skamania Lodge offers 254 cozy guest rooms. The warmth of the lodge is characterized by the Native American-inspired rugs, original stone rubbings, warm Pendleton fabrics and mission-style wood furnishings, along with some of the most spectacular scenic views in the world. Guestroom types include Forest View Rooms, River View Rooms, Fireplace/River View Rooms and One Bedroom Parlor Suites. Rooms feature original artwork, color television with remote control, terrycloth robes, coffee makers, air conditioners with individual thermostat control, hair dryers, honor bars and LodgeNet in-house movies and video games.

## Conference Center

Dolce Skamania Lodge, a member of The International Association of Conference Centers, offers over 22,000 square feet of dedicated meeting space. The conference center contains two large ballrooms totaling 11,500 square feet, and a new 10,000 sq. ft. conference center containing 16 meeting rooms. Breakout options include an open-air courtyard and an outdoor BBQ/Yurt area for special events. The CMP-certified conference services staff is conveniently located adjacent to the conference rooms to provide complete support. On-site audio/visual equipment and technical support is also provided.

## Dining

***The Cascade Room,*** at *Dolce Skamania Lodge*, offers superb Pacific Northwest cuisine in a casually elegant atmosphere. On Friday evenings, experience the *Gorge Harvest Buffet*—featuring all the seafood you can eat, along with regional specialty items. And don't forget our fabulous *Sunday Brunch*. The River Rock Lounge exudes a sport and leisure-type setting with mounted television screens and an outdoor terrace with an incredible view of the Columbia River. Lunch, appetizers and a light dinner menu are served.

## Recreation

Dolce Skamania Lodge also boasts a beautiful 18-hole golf course with driving range, practice bunker, chipping greens and putting greens. The par 70 course is challenging, as well as breathtaking. Beautiful vistas, from elevated greens and towering Douglas firs, make this course a joy to play. Our indoor fitness center features weight systems, as well as free weights, treadmills, exercise bikes and stair climbers, a 20-yard swimming pool, men and women's saunas, massage therapy, hydrotherapy pool, body wraps, and outdoor sun deck and spa. Also featured are two outdoor tennis courts, one sand volleyball court, and over four miles of hiking, fitness and bike trails.

*P.O. Box 1215*
*1522 Cline Falls Highway • Redmond, Oregon 97756*
*Contact: TJ Paskewich (541) 923-9644; (541) 504-1744*
*Web site: www.eagle-crest.com*

---

## Description of Resort

Like a desert oasis, Eagle Crest®Resort beckons from the shadow of Central Oregon's magnificent Cascade Mountains. With nearly 300 days of sunshine and just eight inches of rainfall annually, it's a perfect setting for a world-class meeting or vacation. Our 100 room hotel along the 17th fairway features one bedroom suites. We also offer two, three and four-bedroom condominiums, three year-round and two seasonal pools with hot tubs, tennis, equestrian center, two fitness centers, a day spa with all the treatments to spoil you, three 18-hole golf courses, and a live turf 18-hole putting course.

## Location

Eagle Crest®Resort is just six miles west of Redmond Airport in Central Oregon. Convenient to Bend, Redmond and Sisters.

## Packages and Prices

Year-round golf packages and spa packages. Rack rates range from $76–$151 at the Hotel and $145–$329 in the two, three and four-bedroom condominiums. Group rates are available for 10 or more units.

## Other Amenities

In addition to our two championship golf courses, the Ridge Course and the Resort Course, we offer a par 63 Challenge Course plus the fun and challenging 18-hole putting course. Our Sports Center offers an indoor pool and full basketball court along with a covered picnic area for groups and more. We have a full day spa on-site which provides a variety of massage and skin treatments.

Eagle Crest® also offers over 10,000 square feet of meeting space along with three other meeting rooms in the hotel. Eagle Crest® is a great place to host your next event or retreat.

## Special Services

- Complimentary airport transportation
- Children under 17 play complimentary golf after 3 p.m. when accompanied by a paying adult.
- Complimentary on-site shuttle service

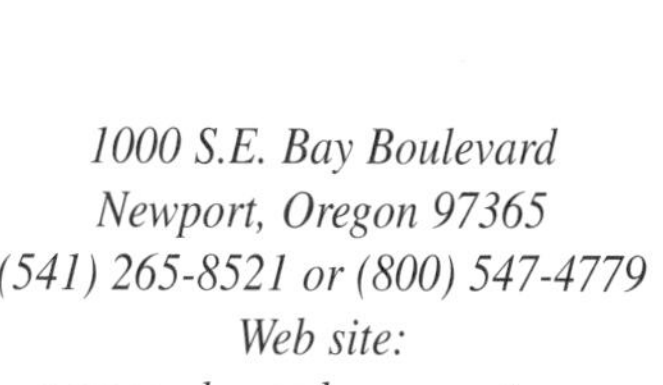

*1000 S.E. Bay Boulevard*
*Newport, Oregon 97365*
*(541) 265-8521 or (800) 547-4779*
*Web site:*
*www.embarcadero-resort.com*

---

## Description of Resort

The Embarcadero Resort Hotel and Marina is located on the central Oregon coast in Newport. Situated on Newport's historic bayfront on the edge of the Yaquina Bay, the Embarcadero offers everything for the vacation traveler and fine facilities for business and group gatherings.

## Conference Facilities

Our six banquet and meeting rooms can accommodate groups of 5 to 200 in a casual or formal atmosphere. We offer professional event coordination, complete food and beverage service and facility setups tailored to your specific needs. Three of our meeting rooms offer spectacular views of Yaquina Bay.

## Accommodations and Dining

Every room has a view of the Bay and a private deck. Choose from a patio guest room, one-bedroom suite with full kitchen and fireplace, or a two-bedroom townhouse. Our award-winning restaurant overlooks Yaquina Bay and Bridge and offers exceptional Northwest cuisine. Guests may crab or fish from our private dock, and sportfishing and whale excursion services are available at the resort. We also have an indoor swimming pool, sauna, two outdoor jacuzzis, crab ring, boat, bike and kayak rentals.

## Newport Activities

There's more to do in Newport than anywhere on the Oregon coast. Directly across the bay from the Embarcadero is the acclaimed Oregon Coast Aquarium. Just down the road is Newport's historic working bayfront where shops, galleries and restaurants coexist with fishing fleets and canneries. Tennis and five golf courses are nearby. And so are miles of gorgeous beach that front the spectacular Pacific Ocean.

**Come see why the Embarcadero is called "The Best of the Coast."**
**Call 1-800-547-4779 for more information or reservations.**

***HALLMARK RESORT NEWPORT***
*744 SW Elizabeth Street • Newport, Oregon 97365*
*Contact: Lucinda Whitacre, Director of Sales*
*541.265.2600; FAX 541.265.9449*
*Website: www.hallmarkinns.com*
*Email: lucinda@hallmarkinns.com*

## Description of Resort

Located on the central Oregon coast, The Hallmark Resort Newport is a full service destination with panoramic oceanfront views from every guestroom. In the world of Hallmark Resort Newport, our goals reach beyond the ordinary. We are dedicated to standards of high quality and excellence. We are determined that you will benefit from our outstanding customer service at a value you can respect. We offer service and comfort in the truest sense of the world. Our warmth, hospitality, and attention to detail will assure your event's success.

## Conference Facilities

- Totaling over 4,000 square feet
- Outstanding on-site catering from theme parties to formal dining
- High-speed Internet in meeting rooms
- Flexible meeting space
- Equipment – audio visual equipment and technical support

## Accommodations and Dining

- Oceanfront balconies
- In-room 2-person spas
- Fireplaces
- Kitchenettes
- Indoor recreation center
- Telephones with data ports
- Free high-speed wireless Internet in select guestrooms
- Oceanfront restaurant and lounge, Georgie's Beachside Grill, featuring "Fresh Northwest Coast Cuisine" and panoramic views of the Pacific Ocean

## Guestrooms Amenities

- 156 oceanfront guestrooms
- Pay-per-view movies and video games
- In-room coffee
- Complimentary daily newspaper delivered to your door

## Special Services

Beach parties with bonfire, Hawaiian Luau, crab feed, traditional Texas barbeque and more!

# HOTEL BELLWETHER
ON BELLINGHAM BAY

One Bellwether Way, Bellingham, WA

**Reservations and Information:** (877) 411-1200

Website: www.hotelbellwether.com

E-mail: reservations@hotelbellwether.com



---

**Capacity:** up to 350 seated, up to 700 reception; includes our Waterfront Terrace and the Bellwether Ballroom with spectacular views of the San Juan Islands and Bellingham Bay.
**Price Range:** varies according to group size and menu selection
**Catering:** full-service in-house catering by Harborside Bistro
**Types of Events:** meetings, retreats, seminars, conferences, receptions, banquets, reunions, Ballroom and Terrace weddings, holiday parties

## Availability and Terms

We recommend reserving your date as soon as possible. Reservations confirmed one year in advance with deposit.

## Description of Services and Facility

- **Seating:** tables and chairs provided
- **Servers:** professional service staff provided
- **Bar facilities:** full service; host or no host; bartenders
- **Dance floor** available; permanent dance floor in ballroom
- **Parking:** private underground parking and public parking
- **Disabled access:** fully accessible, including guest rooms
- **Linens and napkins:** white linens and napkins provided
- **China and glassware:** all provided
- **Cleanup:** handled by our staff
- **Decorations:** please inquire for guidelines

## Special Services

Private 220 sq. ft. dock for guest moorage. Bicycle and kayak rentals, exercise facilities, spa and salon. **Terrace canopy** available. **Audiovisual and other equipment:** in-house screen and microphone; rental service is available; high-speed Internet access in all rooms

## SUBTLE CHARM, CONTEMPORARY COMFORTS

Nestled in a quaint cove on Bellingham Bay, Hotel Bellwether offers the subtle charms of a European Inn along with the contemporary comforts today's guests require. Whether you are planning a corporate brainstorming retreat or a magical waterside wedding, Hotel Bellwether offers unique meeting and event space along with assistance from a talented staff to help you attain your vision of perfection. The unrivaled atmosphere and decadent catering options are sure to please you and your guests. Hotel Bellwether is a 100% smoke free hotel.

**www.hotelbellwether.com**

# The Inn at Otter Crest

***This spectacular resort has long been recognized as one of Oregon's hidden gems.***

*For meetings, banquets and catering: 800-326-5806*
*For accommodations: 800-452-2101*
*www.innatottercrest.com*
*groupsales@innatottercrest.com*
*P.O. Box 50, Otter Rock, Oregon 97369*

---

**A Spectacular Setting!** The Inn at Otter Crest offers the perfect setting for your special event. Conveniently located between Newport and Lincoln City, the resort sits on a bluff above the fabulous Oregon coast—well removed from scenic Highway 101 and steps to the beach.

**Spacious Accommodations.** Studio (1-2 people), Bedroom (1-4 people) and Loft Suite (1-6 people) all have view deck, cable color TV and telephone. Studio and Loft also offer fireplace, full kitchen and separate dining area. Units can be connected to sleep up to 10 people.

**Flexible Meeting Space.** Our 2,900 sq. ft. ballroom can be divided into two or three smaller meeting areas for up to 50 attendees per room. Two additional meeting rooms and an outdoor area offer options for meetings, receptions, banquets and other events. Overall, the resort accommodates groups of up to 200.

**Equipment and Technology.** From audio visual equipment to new sound systems, we are ready to help you make your presentation with all the latest equipment, including high-speed internet access in all our meeting rooms. Let us know what you need, we'll help make it happen.

**Banquet and Catering.** From hors d'oeuvres for a sunset cocktail meeting to a five-course banquet for 150, the cuisine is fresh, imaginative and delicious! You can also count on a top-notch banquet and catering staff for impeccable and friendly service.

**Recreation/Entertainment.** The beach and fascinating tidepools are only steps from the resort. Watch for seals, cormorants and whales. Jog a forest trail to nearby Beverly Beach. Fly a kite. Hit the swimming pool or fitness room. Play basketball, volleyball and horseshoes. Relax in the sauna or whirlpool. Nearby, Lincoln City and Newport offer many activities including the Oregon Coast Aquarium. Otter Crest is a great headquarters for exploring fantastic Central Oregon!

**Price Range.** Please inquire about prices as they vary by season.

**Types of Events.** Business: VIP meetings, corporate gatherings, retirement and award ceremonies. Events: family reunions, retreats, weddings. Food Service: Sit-down dinners, luncheons, indoor buffets, outdoor barbeques, sunset receptions.

*P.O. Box 1240, Warm Springs, Oregon 97761*
*(800) 554-4SUN*
*Web site: www.kahneeta.com*

## Description of Resort

Kah-Nee-Ta High Desert Resort & Casino is situated high among the plateaus of Central Oregon. Guests will enjoy a variety of dining, recreation and lodging choices, as well as the prime, sunny weather found on the east side of the Cascade mountains. With a wide range of flexible meeting space, Kah-Nee-Ta is the perfect destination for your next conference, staff retreat or VIP meeting. Only two hours from Portland, we're just far enough to change your outlook.

## Meeting Facilities

With two ballrooms, we can accommodate up to 540 people in a theater-style setup and 330 in a formal dining atmosphere. We offer nearly 15,000 square feet of adaptable meeting space as well as an elaborate Council Room that can host a small staff retreat or quaint wedding ceremony. This room has been graced with gatherings of the Reservation's three reigning chiefs as well as Fortune 500 company executives. Our professional staff attends to every detail of your event, ensuring its ultimate success.

## Amenities/Recreation

Recreational and nightlife opportunities await around every corner. With an 18-hole golf course, double Olympic-size hot springs pool, horseback riding, kayaking and more, outdoor enthusiasts will never experience a dull moment. If you prefer indoor fun and relaxation, try the European-style Spa Wanapine. Offering every treatment from a cleansing facial to a Vichy shower, you'll relish the healing techniques of ancient tradition. If reviving your senses amidst bells and lights is more your style, try your luck at our 25,000-square-foot casino. Located adjacent to the lodge, the casino offers more than 300 slots, blackjack and poker tables, as well as a major prize drawing each month.

## Surrounding Area

The beautiful vistas and captivating sunsets of this Reservation are not the only visitor attractions. The award-winning Museum at Warm Springs is just minutes away on Highway 26.

## For Additional Group Information

Contact Carlos Smith in Portland at (503)768-9830, toll free at 888-220-9830 or email sales@kahneeta.com. Visit our Web site at www.kahneeta.com or to make an individual reservation call the resort directly at 1-800-554-4SUN.

*19717 Mt. Bachelor Drive • Bend, Oregon 97702*
*Contact: Sales Department*
*(541) 389-5900, (800) 452-9846; Fax (541) 388-7820*
*Web site: www.mtbachelorvillage.com*

---

## Description of Resort

Overlooking the scenic Deschutes River on 170 wooded acres, Mount Bachelor Village Resort provides a distinctly beautiful and tranquil setting where you can truly relax. All of the condominium accommodations are tastefully decorated and include fully equipped kitchens, gas fireplaces, cable TV and daily maid service. River Ridge is our luxury accommodation, which includes indoor and outdoor private spas.

## Location

The Village is located on Century Drive in Bend, Oregon. Just minutes from the shopping and great restaurants of Bend, our resort it ideally situated to take advantage of all Central Oregon has to offer.

## Convention and Meeting Facilities

The state-of-the-art Conference Center has made the commitment to rise above the expected standards of Convention Services. The Village offers 5,700 square feet of flexible meeting space for groups up to 150.

## Other Amenities

Mount Bachelor Village Resort offers 130 guest rooms, six tennis courts, swimming, and a 2.2 mile scenic nature trail overlooking the Deschutes River, as well as complimentary access to Bend's finest athletic club, the Athletic Club of Bend.

## Area Activities

Activities include golf at over 23 local golf courses, hiking, mountain biking, horseback riding, fishing, whitewater rafting, and much more.

# THE RESORT AT THE MOUNTAIN

*68010 East Fairway Avenue*
*Welches, Oregon 97067 (at the western base of Mount Hood, just one hour from downtown Portland)*
*(503) 622-3101; (800) 669-ROOM*
*sales@theresort.com   www.theresort.com*

---

## Description of Resort

The Resort at The Mountain offers the "Spirit of Scotland in the Highlands of Mount Hood." We feature 160 luxury guestrooms including suites and Golf Villas. Our first-class accommodations provide either a scenic forested courtyard, outdoor pool or gorgeous fairway view. Nestled in a spectacular highland valley and bordered by the wild and scenic Salmon River, The Resort features wonderful Scottish décor and artifacts.

## Banquet and Meeting Facilities

We feature 18,000 total square feet of meeting and banquet space, including our 7,040 square foot St. Andrews Ballroom and 3,200 outdoor tented area (seasonal). There are a total of 13 meeting rooms with high speed internet service, on-site audio visual equipment and a business center. Our sales and catering staff are known for their creativity and flexibility, and desire to assist in coordinating a flawless event.

## Amenities / Recreation

The list of possibilities is endless: 27 holes of spectacular golf; croquet and lawn bowling; fitness center; swimming pool, jacuzzi, tennis courts, bike rental, full recreational department specializing in teambuilding activities. Two restaurants and lounges, plus shops. Our Sunday Brunch is a popular choice, with expanded selections on holidays. Available nearby: year-round skiing and snowboarding, fly fishing, hiking, mountain biking.

## Special Events

The Resort hosts many activities throughout the year including:

- Robert Burns Dinner in January
- Portland Youth Philharmonic Concert in May
- The Mountain International Croquet Invitational in June
- Wild About Game culinary adventure in October
- Wine and Arts Festival in November
- Each holiday features a special brunch or dinner

**See page 140 under Banquet, Meeting & Event Sites.**

*5500 Running Y Road*
*Running Y, Oregon 97601*
*(888) 850-0275, (541) 850-5500*
*Web site: www.runningy.com*

---

## THE NEXT GREAT PLACE!

### The Resort

The only destination resort in Southern Oregon, Running Y Ranch has been designed to offer everything you expect of a 3,600-acre residential and recreational development. The resort features a lodge, home sites and townhomes, premier golf course designed by Arnold Palmer, sports center, biking, canoeing, horseback riding, and wildlife viewing.

### The Lodge

Escape, relax, and enjoy the casual elegance of The Lodge at Running Y Ranch. The lodge is built on a ridge overlooking the golf course, wooded hillside, and Caledonia Wetlands. Each of our 81 guestrooms present the north woods theme in their subtle natural hues and art. Our suites feature walkout balconies, romantic fireplaces and family kitchens.

### Area Attractions

There is something here for every taste, mood, whim or desire. Activities include boating, sailing, birdwatching, trout fishing, horseback riding, and golfing.

### Meeting Facilities

Let us host your next conference, retreat, workshop, or golf tournament. Our conference rooms have beautiful views of Klamath Lake, wooded hillside, and the golf course.

### Location

Located seven miles outside of Klamath Falls, along the shores of Upper Klamath Lake in scenic Southern Oregon.

*7760 Highway 101 North*
*Gleneden Beach, Oregon 97388*
*Contact: Group Sales (800) 890-9316 Fax: 541-764-3510 Web site: www.salishan.com*

## Description of Resort

Salishan Lodge & Golf Resort, soon to be "Salishan Spa & Golf Resort," is a four-diamond resort, which offers a unique Northwest setting on the Beautiful Central Oregon Coast. The resort is best described as "Rustic Northwest Elegance," featuring a main lodge, approximately 14,000 sq. ft. of function space, 18-hole championship golf course, fitness center, tennis center, gift shop and the Shops at Salishan. Guestrooms are housed in separate, secluded buildings with covered parking and pathways leading back to the main lodge. The entire resort, including private residential communities, covers 750-forested acres and three miles of secluded beach, while the main lodge, guestrooms and golf course encompass 176 acres.

## Conference Facilities

We have over 14,000 square feet of flexible meeting space. Each room has access to natural lighting and is decorated with original artwork. Our banquet equipment includes our flex-back banquet chairs as well as a variety of banquet tables that can be configured to meet your group's specific needs. The Long House features a 4,500 square foot ballroom that can be divided into three salons. A 325 square foot registration/office space, a 750 square foot foyer, and a terraced patio comprise the rest of the Long house. The Council House Ballroom is 2,600 square feet and can be divided into three salons. Additional meeting space consists of breakout rooms, Sitka, Pine and Lincoln from 650 feet to 1,300 square feet. In spring of 2005 an additional six breakout rooms will be added to the Lodge.

## Dining At Salishan

The Dining Room
The Sun Room
The Grill at the Club House
The Wine Cellar
Attic Lounge

## Location

Salishan is located three miles south of Lincoln City, five miles north of Depoy Bay and sixteen miles north of Newport. Nearby attractions include the Oregon Coast Aquarium, Whale Watching, Oregon's Wine Country, Devils Lake, the Tanger Factory Outlet stores and lots more.

SUITES HOTEL

# BEND

*3105 O.B. Riley Road (N. Hwy 97)*
*Bend, Oregon 97701-7527*
*(541) 389-9600 or (800) 222-2244*
*E-mail: bend@shiloinns.com*
*Web site: www.shiloinns.com*

## Description of Resort

Nestled on the banks of the Deschutes River, the Shilo Inn Suites Hotel – Bend is ideally located near all central Oregon has to offer. This beautiful property offers 151 guestrooms, many with a river view. Experience family dining with Northwest cuisine in our casual restaurant and lounge.Two heated pools (one indoor and one outdoor), a spa, steam room and fitness center delight any guest. Free shuttle to Mt. Bachelor Ski Super Shuttle. Pets are welcome with a fee.

## Guest Room Amenities

Children 12 and under stay free at Shilo Inns with an adult. Enjoy free Showtime. All rooms include microwave, refrigerator, coffeemaker, movies and entertainment.

## Capacity

Meeting and banquet space to accommodate up to 200 people for receptions and 140 for banquets.

## Catering

We have a full service catering department.

## Nearby Attractions

Mt. Bachelor
Petersen Rock Garden
Lava Lands Visitors Center
Newberry Crater tour
Reindeer Ranch
Drake Park Pavilion Concerts
Golf Courses
High Desert Museum
Bend Factory Outlet Store
Cascade Lakes Scenic Byway Tour
Community Theatre
Hiking Trails
Saturday Market-Mirror Pond Park
Les Schwab Amphitheater Performances

## Reservations

Call toll free 1-800-222-2244 or visit our Web site for online pictures, information and reservations at www.shiloinns.com.

"AFFORDABLE EXCELLENCE"

# SHILO INN—NEWPORT OCEANFRONT RESORT

*536 S.W. Elizabeth Street*
*Newport, Oregon 97365-5098*
*(541) 265-7701 or (800) 222-2244*
*E-mail: newport@shiloinns.com;* ***Web site: www.shiloinns.com***

## Description of Resort

This Resort is nestled in the quaint Newport community overlooking the Pacific Ocean. This beautiful resort offers 179 guestrooms, all with an ocean view. Experience fine dining with Northwest cuisine or family-style dining in either of our two restaurants or lounges located on property. Two indoor heated pools are open until 11pm daily. Make Shilo Inns your pet friendly choice.

## Guest Room Amenities

Children under 12 stay free at Shilo Inns with an adult. Enjoy free Showtime. All rooms include microwave, refrigerator, hair dryer, first-run movies and entertainment.

## Capacity

Meeting and banquet space to accommodate up to 600 people.

## Catering

We have a full service catering department.

## Nearby Attractions

Oregon Coast Aquarium
Yaquina Head Lighthouse
Marine Science Center
Golf Courses
Museums
Charter Boat Fishing
Mariners Square
Wildlife Refuge
Whale Watching
Performing Arts Center
Theaters
Hiking Trails

## Reservations

Call toll free 1-800-222-2244 or visit our Web site for online pictures, information and reservations at www.shiloinns.com.

"AFFORDABLE EXCELLENCE"

# SHILO INN—SEASIDE OCEANFRONT RESORT

*30 North Prom • Seaside, Oregon 97138-5823*
*(503) 738-9571 or (800) 222-2244*
*E-mail: seasideoceanfront@shiloinns.com*
***Web site: www.shiloinns.com***

## Description of Resort

Located on the famous Seaside turnaround, overlooking one of the 10 best beaches in the world. This beautiful resort offers all oceanfront rooms featuring fireplaces, kitchens and balconies. Experience fine dining with Northwest cuisine in Seaside's one and only Oceanview Restaurant. Our Sunday brunch is one you should be sure not to miss. Relax in our Oceanfront Lounge with dancing and DJ music nightly. The indoor heated pool, spa, steam room and fitness center are open 24 hours a day.

## Guest Room Amenities

Children under 12 stay free at Shilo Inns with an adult. Enjoy free Showtime. All rooms offer hair dryers, coffee maker, iron and ironing unit, with first run movies and entertainment.

## Capacity

3,916 square feet of meeting and banquet space, which can accommodate up to 350 for receptions; 210 for banquets.

## Catering

We have a full service catering department.

## Nearby Attractions

- Fort Clatsop
- Maritime Museum
- Seaside Aquarium
- Lewis and Clark Salt Cairn
- Seaside Factory Outlet Stores
- Charter Boat Fishing
- Ft. Stevens State Park
- Hiking Trails

## Reservations

Call toll free 1-800-222-2244 or visit our Web site for online pictures, information and reservations at www.shiloinns.com.

*Imagine*

a truly unique setting for your next group meeting or family event, where quality service and attention to detail combine to create great memories.

**WE DID.**

**1.800.797.4666**

cannonbeachmeetings.com

---

**Meeting Space:** 3,000 square foot ballroom that can be divided into three rooms. Two additional breakout rooms available.

**Capacity:** 250 people seated/300 reception style/500 on the beach

**Guest Rooms:** 83 oceanfront and ocean view guest rooms (additional rooms available nearby)

**Rates:** $99–$399

## Location

Nestled between the Coastal Mountain Range and the Pacific Ocean at the foot of Haystack Rock, is the oceanfront Surfsand Resort in Cannon Beach. Just 70 miles from Portland, this ultimate beach resort welcomes guests with warmth and hospitality. Over a dozen different room styles are available, with amenities including panoramic ocean views, jacuzzi, fireplaces and fully equipped kitchens. The Surfsand Resort is 100% non-smoking and pet friendly.

## Facilities and Services

**Seating:** five to 300 people

**Catering:** Full-service catering provided by The Wayfarer Restaurant and Lounge.

**Bar facilities:** Full beverage service provided by The Wayfarer Restaurant and Lounge.

**Dance floor:** Available

**Linens and napkins:** Available in a variety of colors

**Cleanup:** Provided

**Audio/Visual:** On-site AV

**Amenities:** Quality oceanfront accommodations, indoor pool and jacuzzi, guest laundry facilities, high-speed wireless Internet, DVD players, complimentary use of the athletic club, gas fireplaces, premium in-room coffee, fully equipped kitchens, complimentary newspaper, bell and summer cabana service, off-site event planning, the oceanfront Wayfarer Restaurant and Lounge and spa services available.

**Recreation:** Hiking, biking, volleyball, golf, shopping, crabbing, horseback riding and art galleries

*P.O. Box 1158 ~ The Dalles, Oregon 97058*
*Contact: Lorraine or Gene Gravel 1-360-892-7352 or 1-541-298-9942*
*Web site: www.thedallesranch.com*

---

## Description of Ranch

The Dalles Ranch is a rustic elegant wilderness retreat on 75 timbered acres located 16 miles east of Mt. Hood bordering Mt. Hood National Forest. The Ranch has 50 million year old fossils, a solid copper cowboy soaking tub, your own personal theatre, and a gorgeous view of Mt. Hood. Only two hours from Portland, The Dalles Ranch is totally private and waiting for your exclusive use.

**Capacity:** up to 16+ people overnight accommodations; 150 for day use. Conference table for 18. Comfortable 1,000 square foot great room with massive stone fireplace and plasma screen for presentations, plus many areas for smaller group activities. 100 lineal feet of cedar decking with teak tables and chairs for outdoor meetings.

**Price Range:** The Dalles Ranch rents for $1,200 per day.

**Types of Events:** business meetings, religious retreats, holiday parties, trainings, weddings, reunions, getaways.

**Activities:** On site: nature hiking, hot-tubbing, bird watching, barbecues, horseshoes, table tennis, pool, volleyball, badminton, air hockey, foosball, croquet, horses welcome. Local activities: bird hunting, whitewater rafting, fishing, golf, cross country skiing, snowshoeing, hunting.

**Catering:** full service in-house catering can be provided, or you may have your own cookouts and use of gourmet kitchen.

**Equipment:** Internet access, satellite TV, plasma screen, compact disk player, movie theatre, fax, copy machine, satellite, DVD and VCR available in great room and theatre, audio/video connection in great room and theater. Special programs from Direct TV- sports, concerts as available.

**Availability and Terms:** a $500 deposit is required at time of booking. Cancellations made 60 days or more prior to arrival will receive a full refund.

**www.thedallesranch.com**

# Notes

# Notes

Signage, Design & Printing

684-3443 Fax: 684-5058
Business Park 217
12060 SW Garden Place / Tigard, OR 97223
E-mail: graphics@sirspeedytigard.com www.sirspeedy.com/tigard

---

## We'll Make Sure Your Name Is All Over Town

As fellow business owners and neighbors, we know what it takes to operate a business in this area. And in particular, what it takes to get your business noticed. That's because Sir Speedy has been helping businesses just like yours develop successful communications and images for years.

## Here's A Rough Idea Of What We Can Do

We pride ourselves on our ability to help develop your ideas. Whether they're rough ideas on napkins, camera-ready art or computer disks, we'll work with you to make sure you're happy with what you get. And that includes designing, typesetting, printing, collating, trimming, drilling, folding and binding. Because the way we see it, your stationery and other printed materials are more than just office supplies. They're vital links in your business image. And the better they look, the better they make you look—all over town.

## Let Us Handle All Your Paperwork

Now that we've told you what we can do, it's time to give you a bill—or a statement, or even a purchase order. In addition to printing everything to build the right impression of your business, we can print everything to help you stay in business. Including multi-part carbonless forms. So go ahead, bury us in your paperwork—we'll do it right. On time. And at a fair price.

## Here Are A Few More Selling Points

No matter what you're trying to sell, we can develop a look, message and piece to get the job done. From flyers and mailers to pamphlets and brochures. As well as catalogs, manuals, sales kits, price lists, information sheets, and point-of-purchase materials. And all of it will be done with painstaking attention to detail.

## We Can Make You A Company To Watch

Nothing is more important to a business than its appearance. That's why you should trust it to Sir Speedy. We'll print and complete your order with a level of professionalism that will make you the hit of the neighborhood and beyond. Our wide assortment of bindery options will help make your company more presentable than ever before. So give us a call. We'll be right over to pick up the job. Or stop in and let us show you how your neighborhood Sir Speedy can help you spread your name all over town.

408 S.W. Fifth Avenue
Portland, Oregon 97204
Phone 503.222.4229
Fax 503.274.8623
E-mail: info@tisgrafx.com
Web site: www.tisgrafx.com

---

Get your message across with TIS Graphics.

*"As always in planning an event, we had last minute graphic design and sign printing needs. TIS came through with awesome customer service, design ideas and personal delivery. Thanks a ton!"*

– Tracy Martin,
Bravo! Event & Party Show

*"It's nice to know there is a high quality production house I can rely on in near impossible circumstances."*

– Jenn Manly Lee,
ZIBA Design

**TIS delivers the most exhilarating color prints to give your event signage the impact you need, at virtually any size.**

**BIG Color Printing**
- POP Signage
- Posters
- Indoor/Outdoor Banners
- Tradeshow Graphics
- Backlit Displays
- Vehicle and Fleet Graphics

**Small Color Printing**
- Counter Cards
- Flyers
- Brochures
- Marketing Books
- Postcards

As a Full Service Company, we Mount and Laminate right in our shop using a wide variety of mounting substrates and laminates to meet your requirements.

## Scanning Services:

High Resolution Scanning of any original…from 35 mm slide/negs to color prints up to 36" wide.

## Design Services:

Let our experienced Graphic Designers transform your ideas into vivid event signage.

**Satisfied Clients include:** Port of Portland, PGE Park, Fred Meyer Jewelers, Skyline Displays, Wieden & Kennedy, Providence Health Systems, U.S. Bank, The Prop Shop, Banfield the Pet Hospital, McCormick & Schmick's Management Group, Oregon Zoo, McMenamins, Tri-Met, Mt. Hood Meadows, Exhibits Northwest and many others.

**Put the Northwest's most Experienced Graphic Printing Company to work for you!**

*503-736-0111 • 503-736-0930 fax*
*www.withamanddickey.com • info@withamanddickey.com*

---

**Full Service Printing, High Speed Copying, Graphic Design services, Promotional Products, Direct Mail... All under one roof.**

## Full Service Printing

Take advantage of the wide variety of sheetfed offset presses that Witham & Dickey employs to produce virtually any project you may have. From small runs of business cards up to full color catalogs and manuals, we have the equipment and skilled manpower to get your job printed.

## High Speed Copying

Witham & Dickey has recently upgraded our digital end to offer even more capabilities to our customers. Runs of 10,000 – 50,000 high speed black and white copies are produced in a few hours. Also inquire about the different ways in which our digital color copiers can work for your next short run color project.

## Graphic Design Services

Our art department is well equipped to handle all your design and pre-press needs. With the latest in computer equipment for both Macintosh and Windows based computers as well as Adobe and Quark products, we have the tools to create any design you may have envisioned.

## Promotional Products

Get your name out...your message across...your voice heard with apparel and accessories you can easily embellish. We offer hundreds of shirt, sweater and jacket styles in a myriad of hues, plus brief bags, hats, pens, cups, magnets, lapels and so much more. All prominent places to put your logo or message.

## Direct Mail

Witham & Dickey is one of the largest political printers on the West Coast with experience coordinating mailing services all across the country. You can rely on Witham & Dickey when it comes to your direct mail marketing needs. Call us and see just how easy it is to get your name and products out to your customers.

***"Envision the possibilities"***

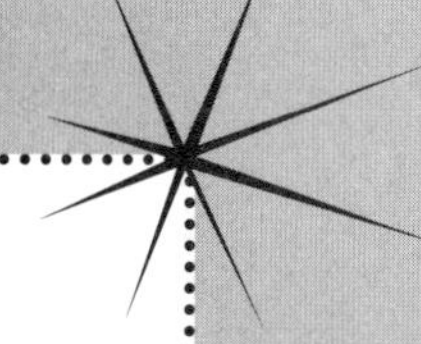

# Speakers & Presentations

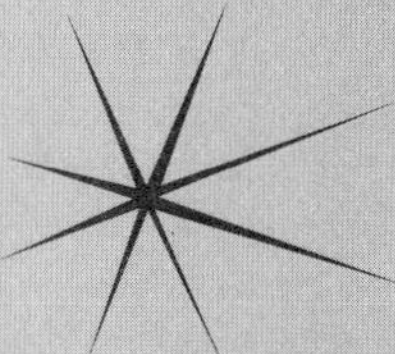

speaker

# *GAIL HAND*

*The Power of Laughter*

**humorist**

*3439 N.E. Sandy Blvd. #104 • Portland, Oregon 97232*
*503-284-2342*
*E-mail:gail@gailhand.com*
*www.gailhand.com • www.thepoweroflaughter.com*

---

**Wouldn't it be great if your program was full of useful content AND was really funny?**

Visit Gail's Interactive Website: **www.thepoweroflaughter.com**

Gail is the author of *The Power of Laughter, Seven Secrets to Living and Laughing in a Stressful World.*

Gail utilizes her years of comedy experience in her program. Audiences rave about her interactive, upbeat style of humor.

## The Power of Laughter Topics

- *Seven Secrets to Living and Laughing Every Day*
- *21 Secrets Guaranteed to Make you Irresistible to Your Prospects*
- *How to Laugh Your Way to More Productivity and Profit*
- *Creative Ways to Honor and Celebrate Differences*
- *How to Put Laughter to Work in the Workplace*
- *Seven Secrets to Living and Laughing in Health Care*

*"Our emergency department loved her interactive program!"*
*— Meeting Planner, OHSU*

**Certified Laughter Leader with the World Laughter Tour**
**Add a Laughter Yoga Program to your next event!!**

**Check www.nsaoregon.net for details on all chapter events.**
**General meetings and hotel events are open to the public.**

---

## Need a Speaker Who Will Really Deliver?

*When you seek both education and entertainment*
*When you need to produce extraordinary results*
*When you must find experts who will thrill your audiences*

**Contact National Speakers Association / Oregon**
**www.nsaoregon.net**

Our members are speaking, training, and consulting professionals who offer experience and expertise, delighting and enlightening audiences internationally.

## Why NSA / Oregon?

★ **Dependability and Quality:** NSA / Oregon members meet the stringent membership requirements of NSA. You can count on their professionalism and commitment.
★ **Responsiveness:** Our speakers deliver material tailored to the needs of your group.
★ **Savings:** Based locally, NSA / Oregon speakers offer national-caliber expertise with minimal – or no -- travel expense.
★ **Accessibility:** Our online directory indexes speakers by name and by topics.

## See our speakers in action at a great NSA / Oregon Showcase Event:

## Speakers Extraordinaire 2005

Premier NSA speakers highlight the resources provided by NSA/Oregon. Topics and styles include business skills, motivation, humor and inspiration!

**When:** February 28, 2005 - 5:30pm Registration and Dinner,
6:30pm Speakers Extraordinaire
**Where:** Sweetbriar Inn, 7125 SW Nyberg Road. Tualatin, Oregon 97062

NSA/Oregon presents bi-monthly programs September through June on topics of interest to professional speakers, trainers and consultants. Open to the public. Check www.nsaoregon.net for calendar and details.

Inquire about the Candidates Fast Track Program for those committed to a career in professional speaking.

**Check www.nsaoregon.net and contact Becky Klotz at 503-655-4775 for reservations.**

# Notes

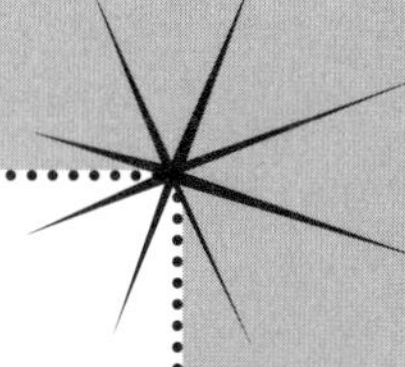

# Staffing & Employment Services

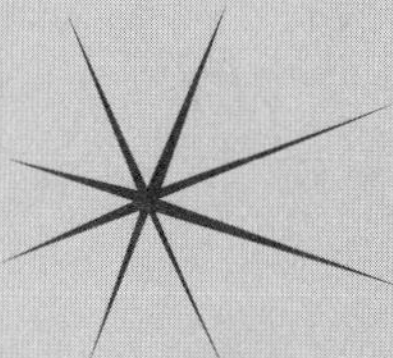

# EMERALD STAFFING

## www.emeraldstaffing.com

Kruse Woods II
5335 Southwest Meadows Road
Suite 210
Lake Oswego, Oregon 97035

Contact: John Burton, Jr., CPC Tel. 503.941.4788 Fax. 503.941.4799

johnjr@emeraldstaffing.com

---

### Emerald Staffing Offers Professional Staffing To Meet All Your Needs…

We specialize in taking the worry out of project management. We have been staffing for temporary, temp to hire and direct placement since 1978. We match your requirements with our employee's abilities. On each new assignment, our friendly staff will call to verify the arrival and progress of our employee assigned to you. In addition to event management, registration and tradeshow services, we also specialize in the following areas:

- Administration
- Clerical/Reception
- Customer Service
- Accounting
- Data Entry
- Insurance
- Mortgage Industry
- Sales
  - Technology Sector
  - Industrial Market
- Medical
  - Front/Back Office
  - Paraprofessional

### Our Commitment:

Our entire staff is committed to total client satisfaction. We listen, we respond, and stand behind you! We value your business and know you will be pleased with our performance. Call today and see for yourself why Top Local and National Companies call Emerald first!

**Staffing Since 1978**

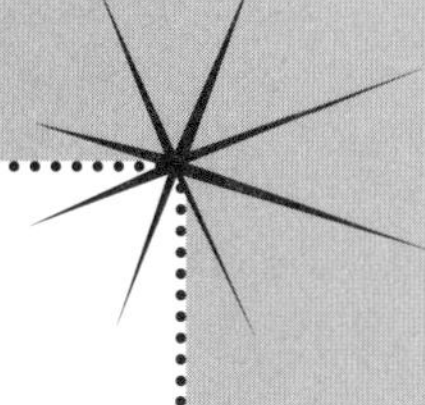

# Themes & Props

# THEMES & PROPS

**Why use a theme?** A theme provides interest and coherence for the attendees. Planning is more efficient with a theme, creating an automatically organized process. In addition, the key to a successful event is audience participation. The more involved people become in the event they are attending, the more likely they are to enjoy themselves and remember the experience. Attendees may not remember the name of the keynote speaker, but they will remember the "Wacky Olympics" special event!

**When is a theme appropriate?** Anytime you have an event. When done properly, themes can be used to enhance a business meeting, client appreciation, awards event, and even reunions.

**How is a theme chosen?** Define the goals of your event first, what you want to accomplish with the event, who is attending, and what you want them to take away with them. Then, you can decide what theme options may work.

**Creative Brainstorming:** Producing a new idea that ties in with the event can be a great challenge. An effective way of coming up with new and innovative ideas is to work with a group of people to draw synergy out of fun, cooperative teamwork to produce ideas and solutions. Find a meeting space free of distraction: phones, foot traffic, etc. A storyboard can be helpful in this meeting so that all ideas can be captured with an open-mind. Some of the smallest ideas can turn into the best campaigns.

**Make sure it is the right theme or concept:** The best ideas can end up a failure unless the details of the theme and campaign are thought out. Ask specific questions like: Does it fit within the organizations' image? Will it offend any of our products, customers or employees? Is it one people will remember? Is the message clear, or lost within the creative? Is it an idea to be proud of and put in the portfolio?

**Are theme events expensive?** They don't have to be. It depends on your budget. Some of your theme ideas can be accomplished with a small budget if you and your committee are willing to spend the time. However, a much better use of your time and money may be to use a meeting planner, prop, or entertainment company.

**Decorating tips for theme events:** Consider three to four main areas of the facility for theme props. Main focus areas can include the entryway to the event, stage, guest tables, beverage and food stations, to name a few.

**Check-out props and displays:** A visit to the prop shop or decorator will allow you the opportunity to see the quality, size and color of the prop. While at the warehouse- browse to see what other props and displays they have. This trip may awaken an idea several months later for a future project.

**Theme ideas for your next event:**

- Casino Night
- M•A•S•H
- Cruise Ship
- Mexican Fiesta
- Western/ Wild West
- International Themes
- Fabulous 50s
- The Jazz Club
- Around the World
- Winter Wonderland
- Tropical Island
- Underwater
- Tropical Rain Forest
- Circus! Circus!
- Hawaiian Luau
- The Great Northwest
- State Fair
- Chinese New Year
- Murder and Mystery
- South of the Border
- African Jungle
- Mardi Gras
- Medieval Castle
- Nautical
- Great Gatsby Party
- Super Bowl
- Beach Party

# PARADYM EVENTS

## EVENTS WITHOUT PRECEDENCE

www.paradymevents.com

611 SE Main Street
Portland, OR 97214
(503) 219-9290
Fax (503) 525-0675
info@paradymevents.com

---

**Paradym Events** makes your company event memorable. An intimate event to a full scale gala, we specialize in originality. We create this experience by…

- **Imagination**… tell us your needs, wants and desires. Let our talented and knowledgeable staff develop an environment that reflects your vision.
- **Expectations**… are what we strive to surpass, whether it's corporate events, conventions, themed events or unique weddings.
- **Designs**… metal to glass, wood to paper, linens to flowers, we bring to life your ideas in an array of mediums.
- **Specialize**… it's your event, unlike you've ever imagined. We customize to meet your needs.
- **Location**… not a problem! East Coast to Hawaii, backyard or the ballroom, we have the experience and ability to go where you need us.

More information? Visit our website, send us an e-mail, or give us a call.

www.paradymevents.com
(503) 219-9290

# THE PROP SHOP

*5406 N. Albina Avenue, Portland, Oregon 97217*
*(503) 283-8828; Fax (503) 283-3651*
*www.propshop.com / info@propshop.com*

---

***Whether it's to surprise, overwhelm, impress or just entertain, surround your guests in beauty and style and you will invoke confidence in your message—confidence in your organization!***

The Prop Shop is a nationally recognized, award-winning creative event design and production company. Our team of expert designers and planners deliver unprecedented results.

We pride ourselves on working closely with our clients guiding them in a direction that will make the most of any budget or venue. The formula is simple—we approach each event as a unique opportunity to showcase your vision using our resources, creativity, team philosophy and most importantly, experience.

## Design

Our signature design services include branding of a corporate image throughout all company functions, from fun-filled employee picnics to synchronized multi-city product launches. The Prop Shop can provide rendering and fabrication of custom props, scenery, staging, backdrops, floral, linens, signage and lighting.

## Decor

Our warehouses hold a plethora of unique sets, backdrops and props, as well as our theatrical designer's workshop and specialty divisions.

## Productions

Our team is equipped with unparalleled national resources and can produce a breadth of events, including corporate meetings, conventions, new product launches, employee appreciations, educational seminars, team building experiences, fundraisers, awards ceremonies, galas, holiday celebrations and picnics.

## Awards

Event Solutions Magazine's Spotlight Award for Designer of the Year 2004
Jack Rosenberg Community Service Award 2003-2004
Bravo! 2002 Best Theme Decor
POVA 2001 Members' Choice Award Most Significant Contribution from a Member

## Memberships

MPI, ISES, POVA, ACEP, CVBWCO & WVDO

*1400 N.W. 15th Avenue • Portland, Oregon 97209*
*(503) 294-0412; Fax (503) 294-0616*
*Business Hours: Mon–Sat 8:30am–6pm*
*Appointments available any hour*
*www.wcep.com*

## Services

West Coast Event Productions is the Northwest's premier idea center for all events and special occasions. We specialize in the concept development, design and coordination of all aspects of your event to make it a success. We also offer design and rental services and custom fabrication of staging, lighting, sound, special effects, audio visual presentations, signage and theme production. We tailor events and trade shows to mirror your corporate identity or direction.

## Custom Themes

West Coast Event Production's dream team are masters in concept development. We work with our clients to construct a concept that mirrors your vision. Our dream team staff at West Coast Event Productions has the experience and creativity to produce events of any size or budget from small gatherings to large corporate and civic events. Visit our showroom, browse for ideas in our photo books, and take a tour of our warehouse. We have many speciality props, catering items and equipment displayed to aid in your event planning.

## Rental Items Available

**Theme Decor:** West Coast designers work in tandem with your project manager to create the perfect environment or individual feature to solve design problems or enhance your theme. Between our Portland, Bend and Las Vegas locations, our collection of sets and props is one of the largest available outside of Hollywood. And what we do not have, we can build to your specifications. The West Coast reputation is one of total commitment to quality work, creativity and thorough professionalism in everything we do.

**Props:** We have an extensive inventory of props to support hundreds of themes. Our selection offers a wide range of architectural shapes and elements, building facades, drapery, artificial plants, fiberglass animals, statues, waterfalls, oversize rocks, special effects, hand props, floral supplies, antiques and memorabilia.

**Scenic Backdrops:** West Coast has added a large collection of custom, professionally painted, high-quality scenic backdrops that are now available for your events.

**Table Top:** West Coast's unique approach to table top design affords you an unusual selection of ideas. Indoors or out, big or small, with fountains and waterfalls, non-floral theme centerpieces, topiaries, statuary, sculptures, garlands, opulent bouquets and leafy accents, our designers will create a magical focal point for your tables and buffets. Choose from the largest selection of table lamps and vases on the west coast. We also have the largest selection of catering equipment, flatware, glassware, and 15 styles of china, including hand-painted elegant bone china and bright ceramics.

**See page 430 under Rental Services.**
**See page 244 under Convention & Exhibition Services.**

# Notes

# Transportation

- *Limousines & Town Cars*
- *Coaches, Buses & Vans*
- *Luxury & Exotic Car Rentals*

BravoPortland.com

# TRANSPORTATION

**Airfare Savings:** Special negotiated airfares are available for groups of ten or more. To qualify, travelers must share a common destination and be traveling in the same time frames. Travelers need not originate from the same city.

**Meeting dates and times for travelers:** Planning your meeting dates and times will enable attendees to take advantage of non-refundable excursion airfares which are discounted up to 70%. Schedule meeting dismissal time so attendees can take the last afternoon/evening flight out to avoid the cost of an additional night stay at the hotel.

**Bus and Coach Transportation:** Buses and coaches come in your basic style of school buses to luxury-Elite Motorcoaches. You'll want to determine your audience and then select the most appropriate transportation.

**Livery Service:** There are taxi cabs, limousines, and livery service. Livery service is a luxury form of transportation without the recognition of a local cab or limousine. The driver is uniformed and highly skilled with exceptional customer service. This is a VIP form of transportation for important attendees, speakers and special guests.

**Valet Service:** For your next event or special occasion valet service adds that special touch. Services include: shuttle vans, lot attendants to park your guests' cars, and parking consulting services to help maximize parking space and to monitor the traffic flow. These companies should be properly insured and licensed.

**Ground Transportation:** Get facts and figures on capacities, capabilities and types of transportation available to and from the meeting site. Talk to planners who have handled groups of your size. Select your transportation on the basis of cost, reputation, degree of service, number, condition and availability of vehicles. Motor-coaches (buses) are the most frequently used vehicle for moving groups. You may need charter buses or shuttle buses. A charter follows a pre-determined route for a specified length of time. A shuttle operates continuously on a regularly established route.

**Common questions that should be asked of various transportation companies:** Are there minimum rental periods? What is the bus capacity? How is dispatch done? Can disabled passengers be accommodated? Are backups available? Are buses air conditioned? What routes will be used? How comprehensive is their insurance liability? Can the price be negotiated?

**VIP Transportation:** Pick up speakers, leaders, and guests at the airport or other locations. These people are critical to the success of your event. They deserve special treatment. Assign staff members as official greeters, select appropriate vehicles, check arrival and departure times and potential customs or immigration problems. Select the best airport location to meet as well as the best drop-off points and the quickest route.

**Don't reserve a vehicle over the phone:** Go to the transportation company and inspect the vehicle you are considering renting. Be sure you are dealing with an established, reputable company. These businesses will display, or readily make available, important information like their business license and their liability insurance certificate. If you have concerns or questions, ask for references.

# ALL STAR LIMOUSINE AND TRANSPORTATION

**Phone: (503) 222-1704** **Fax: (503) 293-2094**

**Email: LIMOUSINE@AOL.COM**

**Web site: WWW.ALLSTARLIMO.BIZ**

*(Online reservations)*

---

## CELEBRATING OUR 12TH SUCCESSFUL YEAR SERVING THE PORTLAND, VANCOUVER AND SALEM AREAS

- Luxury stretch limousines to accommodate four, six, eight, 10 or 12 passengers
- Professionally licensed, insured and airport approved chauffeurs
- Limousines for any event or occasion
- Available 24 hours a day
- Featuring "Air Force One" stretch limousine

***Member or Affiliation with:***

**Oregon Business Network**
**Bravo! Publications and Trade Show**

*Notice: Due to our popularity, advance reservations are highly recommended. All major credit cards accepted*

*SINCE 1977*

*Blue Star Airporters, Charters and Tours Inc.*
*8250 Martin Luther King Jr. Blvd.*
*Portland, Oregon 97211*
*503-249-1837, 360-573-9412, 800-247-2272; Fax 503-493-0165; www.bluestarbus.com*

---

## CHARTERS * TOURS * SHUTTLES

### SERVICES

- CHARTERS & TOURS
- SHUTTLES & CONTRACTS
- AIRPORT TRANSFERS
- CONVENTIONS
- SIGHTSEEING

### EQUIPMENT & PERSONNEL

- FULLY LICENSED AND INSURED
- PROFESSIONAL COURTEOUS DRIVERS
- LIVE 24 HOUR DISPATCH
- G.P.S. EQUIPPED BUSES
- TV/VCR/DVD
- CLIMATE CONTROL
- RESTROOM EQUIPPED

### MANY SIZES AVAILABLE

**Coaches:**

- 55 PASSENGER XLT SUPER COACHES
- 49 PASSENGER XLT SUPER COACHES
- 47 PASSENGER XLT LUXURY COACHES
- 47 PASSENGER DELUXE COACHES
- 36 PASSENGER XLT SUPER COACHES
- 24 PASSENGER MINI COACHES
- 16 PASSENGER MINI COACHES

**Vans:**

- 15 PASSENGER EXECUTIVE VANS

## Our Fleet

Dodge Viper SRT-10 (pictured) – 500 horsepower in a two-seat convertible.
Hummer H2 (pictured) – 316 horsepower in a six-seat SUV.

Coming Soon…
Mini Cooper-S
Corvette convertible
Porsche Boxster

## Celebrate in Style

Anniversaries
Weddings
Birthdays
Weekend getaway

## Arrive in Style

Reunions
Meetings that matter
Employee rewards
Just because

## Complimentary Delivery and Pick-Up

We provide complimentary delivery of our vehicles within a 15 mile radius of downtown Portland (ref: Pioneer Courthouse Square).

## Rates

Evening, Daily and Weekend rates are available.
Gift certificates are also available.

**Please visit our web site for all the latest information as well as on-line reservations.**

**www.DreamCarsNW.com**
info@dreamcarsnw.com

For Reservations and Information
Call **877-803-3001**

*Portland Oregon Visitors Association member*

# LUCKY
## LIMOUSINE AND TOWNCAR SERVICE L.L.C.

*11824 NE Ainsworth Circle, Suite B, Portland, Oregon 97220*
*Phone: 503.254.0010; Fax: 503.257.2800; Toll Free: 1.877.254.0010*
*www.besolucky.com*

---

## Our Fleet includes:
- New Lincoln Towncars & VIP Mercedes Sedans – *for Airport Transfer*
- 6 - 8 - 12 passenger late model stretch limousines - *fully equipped to make **your** special event perfect*
- Three luxury **"LOUNGE CRUIZERS,"** for 14 to 22 passengers fully equipped with a 42" LCD Television, Karaoke machines, XM radio, DirecTV satellite dish and DVD player, and a 31-passenger "CRUIZELINER" – *for corporate meetings, extended excursions, tailgate parties and day trips.*
- Two brand new Executive vans for up to 6 passengers, with a lot of cargo room.

The entire fleet is beautifully appointed, detailed daily, well maintained, smoke free and fully insured.

*Please visit our web site for viewing the entire fleet and services offered!*

## Our Service Includes:
- Experienced, professionally trained and attired chauffeurs
- 24 hour management staffing for all phone inquires, experienced to help you design and coordinate your special event according to your needs
- One way, One hour or All Day rates available

*Our goal is to consistently exceed your highest expectation of what luxury transportation should be, at affordable rates, so every one can...*

***"Be So Lucky!"***

**(503) 254-0010**

Member of:
*National Limousine Association*
*Portland Oregon Visitors Association*
*Parkrose Business Association*
*Oregon Livery and Limousine Association*

*"Where ever you go...go in Style"*

**Deluxe Motorcoaches and LimBusines**

**10350 N. Vancouver Way, #344**
**Portland, Oregon 97217**
**503-737-2222**
**Fax 503-737-1457**
**Toll Free 866-662-4744**

**Web site: www.NACharters.com**

779 Tech Center Drive
Durango, Colorado 81301
888-437-6888

8721 S. 218th Street
Kent, Washington 98032
866-840-0757

---

NA Charters is committed to providing dependable and affordable transportation. With coaches seating from 36-57 passengers, we are able to cater to groups of any size. Our full service centers in Colorado, Oregon and Washington allow us to offer hands-on customer service to you and your guests, wherever you are traveling.

We pride ourselves in being your number one customer service provider. Our friendly, knowledgeable office staff and our experienced, professional drivers are looking forward to providing you an exceptional travel experience.

**NA Charters owns and operates a 2003/2004 fleet of Vanhool and MCI motor coaches and luxury limousines. Each coach is equipped with:**

- Panoramic View Windows
- Reclining Seats
- PA System
- Restroom
- DVD/CD and VHS Players
- Video Screens
- Road Camera
- GPS (viewable on monitors)
- Air Conditioning and Heating
- ADA Coaches (available per request)
- Computer Hook Up (for presentations on monitors)

## Providing Charters For:

- Airport and Cruise Ship Transfers
- Associations and Government Agencies
- Clubs and Organizations
- Corporate Travel
- Special Occasions
- Tour Operators

**For reservations and more info, contact us today.**

NA Charters is a proud member of:
NTA (National Tour Association) • UMA (United Motorcoach Association)
• ABA (American Bus Association) • National Network
POVA (Portland Oregon Visitors Association) • Vancouver Chamber of Commerce

## RAZ TRANSPORTATION CO. / GRAY LINE PORTLAND

*11655 S.W. Pacific Highway*
*Portland, Oregon 97223-8629*
*(503) 684-3322, (888) 684-3322; Fax (503) 968-3223*
***Web site: www.raztrans.com***

---

### Don't charter a bus, charter a bus company…

### WE GO THE EXTRA MILE

**Why deal with *SEVERAL* companies when…**
***RAZ* can service *ALL* your needs?**

Motorcoach Charters • Professionally Guided Sightseeing Tours • Meet & Greet Services

Multilingual Guide Services • Airport Transfers • Shuttle Services • Step-on Guides

**Gray Line Sightseeing Tours,** ***phone 503-243-6789***

- Mount Hood Loop
- Columbia River Gorge
- Mount St. Helens
- Lewis & Clark
- Portland City Tour

- A receptive tour operator able to design itineraries and tour packages specific to your needs
- Serving corporate or group travel: both domestic and international
- Employing only professionally trained step-on guides and tour directors
- Fully experienced convention shuttle operator; all equipment with two-way radios
- On-site dispatch with hand-held radios to accommodate flexibility due to traffic, weather, etc.

**RAZ Transportation Co. / Gray Line Portland**

Providing service since 1937 and offering vehicles for all your ground transportation needs…from ***luxury*** to ***budget***:

**High Liner**
56 passenger

**Luxury Liner**
47 passenger

**Transit Coach**
44 passenger

**Econo Coach**
53 passenger

**Super Liner**
55 passenger

**Deluxe Coach**
47 passenger
36 passenger w/lounge
24 passenger

### Let us *"Go the extra mile"* for YOU!

***Public shuttles to Spirit Mountain Casino EVERY day of the week!***

# PORTLAND STREETCAR AND VINTAGE TROLLEY

*Contact: Sarah Fuller, Director of Fun 503.323.7363; directoroffun@hotmail.com*

## ALL ABOARD!

For a unique gathering, consider hosting a function on board Vintage Trolley or Portland Streetcar. There are many creative ways these cars can be used with large or small groups. Party ideas are limited only by your imagination. We will be happy to work with you to customize your special event. When scheduling, please allow at least 14 days advance notice. Charters are subject to approval by rail operations. The charter price varies based on client specifications.

Catering and entertainment are not included in the charter cost. You may use the caterer of your choice or provide your own refreshments. Arrangements for catering, entertainment or complete event planning are available for an additional fee.

### Vintage Trolley

The fine craftsmanship and elegant styles of the classic trolley cars provide a charming glimpse of Portland's past. Four hand-crafted streetcars, replicas of the Council Crest trolleys from the turn of the century serve as both transportation and an attraction in Portland.

Two specially designed serving tables are available for use in the trolley, however use of these will affect available seating. The trolleys can accommodate up to 70 people, depending on usage. On board is a PA system for your taped music, or to provide an efficient system for your announcements. A conductor rides along and is available to provide a historic perspective on the trolley and sites along the route. Vintage Trolley merchandise may be purchased to use as favors for your guests.

Vintage Trolley charters operate along the MAX route from downtown Portland to Gresham, however we do not operate west of the tunnel. Charters on this route are available on weekdays from 9:30am to midnight (excluding rush hours from 3pm to 6:30pm) and from 6:30am to midnight on weekends. Vintage Trolley charters are also available along the new Portland Streetcar route (see route description below) and are available from 6:30am to midnight on both weekdays and weekends on this route.

### Portland Streetcar

Charters are available on board the modern Czech Republic streetcars along the Portland Streetcar route. This route is a loop from Northwest Portland through the Pearl District to Portland State University. These cars are larger and can accommodate approximately 125 people. Serving tables are available for your use.

Portland Streetcar charters are available weekdays after 6:30pm and from 6:30am to midnight on weekends (excluding Saturday from 3pm to 6pm.)

**To charter either Vintage Trolley or Portland Streetcar, contact**
**Sarah Fuller, Director of Fun**
**503.323.7363 or directoroffun@hotmail.com**

# TRANSPORTATION

## TRAINS

**Amtrak**
800 N.W. Sixth Ave.
Portland, OR 97209
(800) 872-7245
www.amtrak.com

**Mt. Hood Railroad**
110 Railroad Ave.
Hood River, OR 97031
(541) 386-3556
(800) 872-4661

**Oregon Pacific Railroad**
P.O. Box 22548
Milwaukie, OR 97269
(503) 659-5452

## TRANSIT

**Tri-Met**
**MAX Light Rail**
4012 S.E. 17th Ave.
Portland, OR 97202
(503) 238-RIDE (7433)
www.trimet.org

**Salem Area Transit–Cherriots**
555 Court St. N.E. Ste. 5230
Salem, OR 97301-3736
(503) 588-2877

**Portland Streetcar**
(503) 323-7363
*See page 183*

**Vintage Trolley**
115 N.W. First, Ste. 200
Portland, OR 97209
(503) 323-7363
*See page 183*

**Willamette Shore Trolley**
311 N. State St.
Lake Oswego, OR 97034-3111
(503) 697-7436

## BUSES, COACHES & VANS

**Blue Star**
8250 Martin Luther King Jr. Blvd.
Portland, OR 97211
(503) 249-1837, (360) 573-9412,
(800) 247-2272
www.bluestarbus.com
See page 476

**NA Charters**
10350 N. Vancouver Way, #344
Portland, OR 97223
(503) 737-2222, (866) 662-4744
www.NACharters.com
See page 479

**Raz Transportation/ Gray Line of Portland**
11655 S.W. Pacific Hwy.
Portland, OR 97223
(888) 684-3322
www.raztrans.com
*See page 480*

## LIMOUSINE & TOWN CARS

**All-Star Limousine and Transportation**
(503) 222-1704
www.allstarlimo.biz
*See page 475*

**Dream Cars Northwest, Inc.**
(877) 803-3001
www.dreamcarsnw.com
See page 477

**Hut Airport Shuttle**
2990 25th St. S.E.
Salem, OR 97302
(503) 363-8059

**Lucky Limousine and Towncar Service**
11824 N.E. Ainsworth Circle, Suite B,
Portland, Oregon 97220
(503) 254-0010, 1 (866) 844-0010
www.lucky-limousine.com
*See page 478*

## VALET SERVICE

**Premiere Valet Service, LLC**
10175 S.W. Barbur Blvd. Ste. 107B
Portland, OR 97219
(503) 244-7758
www.premierevalet.com

## BOATS & YACHTS

**Sternwheeler "Columbia Gorge" & Marine Park**
P.O. Box 307
Cascade Locks, OR 97014
www.sternwheeler.com
*See page 184*

**Portland Spirit, Willamette Star, & Crystal Dolphin**
110 S.E. Caruthers
Portland, OR 97214
(503) 226-2517
www.portlandspirit.com
*See page 182*

**The Sternwheeler Rose**
6211 N. Ensign
Portland, OR 7217
(503) 286-7673
www.sternwheelerrose.com
*See page 185*

**Willamette Jetboats**
1945 S.E. Water Ave.
Portland, OR 97214
(503) 231-1532
(888) 538-2628
www.willamettejet.com

**Sternwheeler "Willamette Queen"**
P.O. Box 5896
Salem, OR 97304
(503) 371-1103
www.willamettequeen.com

# Notes

Web Design

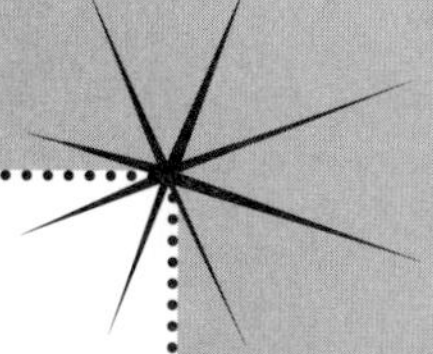

Web Design

BravoPortland.com

## Clean, Professional Design

**SimplyFine Design** believes that Web design does not need to be complicated. It should be a fun, exciting adventure as you launch your small business into cyberspace and make its presence known to all — not a headache from beginning to end.

**SimplyFine Design** caters to small businesses and organizations with a desire for a fresh, creative Web site.

## Web Design

**SimplyFine Design** will design your site from scratch, or revamp an existing site. Because each site is different and unique, **SimplyFine Design** does not offer a "package price." Please call or e-mail for a complimentary estimate.

## The Initial Design of a Site Includes:

- Complimentary consultation
- Creative design of your unique site
- Scanning, sizing and placement of all photos and graphics
- Creation of special graphics for your site
- Formatting, proofing and editing of all text
- Testing in various browsers and platforms
- Creating and checking all hyperlinks on site
- Uploading to your server
- Inserting meta tags

## Payment and Terms

A $200 deposit is required to begin work on your site. After your site becomes live, everything is working properly, and any remaining kinks have been ironed out, payment is due in full. Depending on the size of your site, turnaround time is usually two to six weeks.

www.simplyfinedesign.com

# Winery Tours & Events

# HELVETIA  VINEYARDS

Helvetia Vineyards and Winery
23269 N.W. Yungen Road
Hillsboro, Oregon 97124
503-647-5169
e-mail: info@helvetiawinery.com
Web site: www.helvetiawinery.com

*100 year-old Jakob Yungen Farmhouse on the grounds of Helvetia Winery and Vineyards.*

---

## FINE WILLAMETTE VALLEY WINES

**WINE TOURS AND EVENTS:** Your country farm and winery experience just 25 minutes from downtown Portland and 10 minutes from high-tech Hillsboro. The grounds surrounding our historical farmhouse are available for wine tasting events and picnics with a minimum wine purchase. Take a break from the business at hand and tour the Christmas tree farm, vineyards and winery. A perfect setting to learn about wine and winemaking in a relaxed country atmosphere.

**WINE CATERING:** Helvetia Winery offers a variety of fine vintage wines from our own and neighboring vineyards for wine tasting at your event in your location. Order wines at special case prices and we will assist you and your guests in appreciating the finer points of Oregon wines such as the importance of vintage, winemaking styles and aging.

**CUSTOMIZED LABELS:** A memento for a special event. Business meetings and conventions, presentations, retirement dinners and special thank you's are enhanced by a bottle of fine wine with your message on your own label. Because of federal regulations, please allow six weeks for delivery.

*"The north wind howls here every time it frosts.*
*However, the grapes often ripen full and wonderful."*

– Jakob Yungen writing to his
Swiss relatives in 1917

**www.helvetiawinery.com**

*77 N.E. Holland Street • Portland, Oregon 97211*
*503.283.3380; Fax 503.283.6647*
*E-mail: info@grapeescapetours.com*
*www.GrapeEscapeTours.com*

---

We provide fun, personalized escapes to the Oregon Wine Country for team building events, special group occasions and corporate retreats. Whether you choose an Afternoon Escape, a Group Meeting in the wine country, or a Dinner Escape, we'll take care of all the details:

- Arrangements with wineries chosen just for your group
- Comfortable transportation in our much-admired executive vans
- Unparalleled Northwest cuisine matched to wine along the way
- Fun, knowledgeable escape artists to host your entire day

On the day of your escape, we'll greet you at your location. You'll begin to unwind as we take the scenic way to the wine country. Then throughout the day, we'll provide everything you need as you enjoy our wine country in an unhurried, relaxed style.

We provide an array of escapes to suit your budget and needs:

| | | |
|---|---|---|
| Afternoon Escape | Full Day Escape | Grape-r Escape |
| Dinner Escape | Wine Country Safari | Holiday Escape |

New This Year: Our Holiday Escape, a novel way for your company to celebrate the season. We'll visit one or two nearby wineries (in Portland, or the wine country), and end with a festive dinner matched to wine. Yum.

To learn more about what we offer, take a look at our web site or give us a call. We'll guide you through the possibilities. Then once you select your escape, we'll take care of all the details, leaving you with nothing to do but anticipate a day of wine, food and fun.

**Grape Escape Winery Tours**
Don't forget to have a little fun!

# WINERIES

**BeckenRidge Vineyard**
300 Reuben-Boise Rd.
Dallas, OR 97338
(503) 831-3652
www.bekenridge.com

**Chateau Benoit**
6580 N.E Mineral Springs Rd.
Carlton, OR 97111
(503) 864-2991
www.chateaubenoit.com

**Chateau Lorane**
27415 Siuslaw River Rd.
Lorane, OR 97451
(541) 942-8028
www.chateaulorane.com

**Edgefield Winery**
2126 S.W. Halsey St.
Troutdale, OR 97060
(503) 492-2777
www.mcmenamins.com

**Elk Cove Vineyards**
27751 N.W. Olson Rd.
Gaston, OR 97119
(503) 985-7760
www.elkcove.com

**Eola Hills Wine Cellars**
501 S. Pacific Hwy. 99W
Rickreall, OR 97371
(503) 623-2405
www.eolahillswinery.com

**Erath Vineyards**
9409 N.E. Worden Hill Rd.
Dundee, OR 97115
(800) 539-9463
www.erath.com

**Helvetia Vineyards**
23269 N.W. Yungen Road
Hillsboro, Oregon 97124
(503) 647-5169
www.helvetiawinery.com
*See page 175*

**Kramer Vineyards**
26830 N.W. Olson Rd.
Gaston, OR 97119
(503) 662-4545
www.laurelridgewines.com

**Laurel Ridge Winery**
13301 N.E. Kuene Rd.
P.O. Box 456
Carlton, OR 97111
(503) 852-7050

**Marquam Hill Vineyards**
35803 S. Hwy. 213
Molalla, OR 97038
(503) 829-6677

**Montinore Vineyards**
P.O. Box 490
3663 S.W. Dilley Rd.
Forest Grove, OR 97116
(503) 359-5012

**Rex Hill Vineyards**
30835 N. Hwy. 99W
Newberg, OR 97132
(503) 538-0666
www.rexhill.com

**St. Josef's Wine Cellars**
28836 S. Barlow Rd.
Canby, OR 97013
(503) 651-3190

**Shafer Vineyard Cellars**
6200 N.W. Gales Creek Rd.
Forest Grove, OR 97116
(503) 357-6604
www.shafervineyardcellars.com

**Sokol Blosser Winery**
5000 NE Sokol Blosser Ln.
Dundee, OR 97115
(503) 864-2282

**Torii Mor St. Winery**
909 E. 10th
McMinnville, OR 97128
(503) 434-1439
www.toriimorwinery.com

**Tyee Wine Cellars**
26335 Greenberry Rd.
Corvallis, OR 97333
(541) 753-8754

**Urban Wineworks**
407 N.W. 16th Avenue
Portland, Oregon 97209
(503) 226-9797
www.urbanwineworks.com

**Willamette Valley Vineyard**
8800 Enchanted Wy.
Turner, OR 97392
(800) 344-9463
www.wvv.com

**Wind River Cellars**
196 Spring Creek Rd.
Husum WA 98623
(509) 493-2324
www.windrivercellars.com
*See page 410*

**Wine Country Farm**
6855 Breyman Orchards Rd.
Dayton, OR 97114
(503) 864-3446

# Notes

# Central, Eastern & Southern Oregon Sites

BravoPortland.com

Central, Eastern & Southern Oregon Sites

# CENTRAL OREGON

**Deschutes County Fair & Expo Center** – 3800 S.W. Airport Wy., Redmond, OR 97756
Capacity: up to 1,600
Contact: (866) 800-EXPO *See page 88*

**Eagle Crest Resort** – 1522 Cline Falls Rd., Redmond, OR 97756
Indoor: up to 350; Guest Rooms: 100 – R/B/S/M/C/
Contact: (541) 923-9644, (800) 682-4786 *See page 440*

**Kah-Nee-Ta Resort** – P. O. Box 1240, Warm Springs, OR 97761
Indoor: up to 870; Guest Rooms: 170 – P/R/B/S/M/C/
Contact: Sales Department (503) 768-9830, (800) 554-4786 *See page 445*

**Mount Bachelor Village** – 19717 Mt. Bachelor Drive, Bend, Oregon 97702
Capacity: up to 150; Guest Rooms: 130 – R/B/S/M/C/
Contact: Sales Department (800) 452-9846; Fax (541) 388-7820 *See page 446*

**Shilo Inn – Bend** –3105 O.B. Riley Rd., Bend, OR 97701
Capacity: up to 225; Guest Rooms: 151 – R/B/S/M/C
Contact: (800) 222-2244 *See page 450*

# SOUTHERN OREGON

**The Running Y Ranch Resort** – 5500 Running Y Rd., Running Y, OR 97601
Guest Rooms: 81 – R/B/S/M/
Contact: (888) 850-0275 *See page 448*

**Seven Feathers Casino** – 146 Chief Milwaleta Lane, Canyonville, OR 97417
Capacity: up to 1,500; Guest Rooms: 145 – R/B/S/M/C/
Contact: Sales & Convention Services (800) 548-8461 *See page 146*

*P=Picnic R=Reception B=Banquet S=Seminar M=Meeting C=Convention*

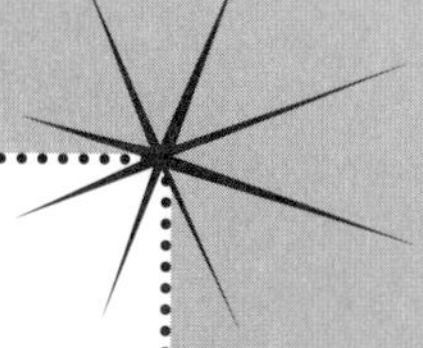



# Coastal Sites

BravoPortland.com

# COASTAL SITES

**Chinook Winds**
**Convention Center** – 1777 N.W. 44th St., Lincoln City, OR 97367
Capacity: up to 2,000– R/B/M/S/C/
Contact: (541) 996-5925, (888) CHINOOK *See page 85*

**Florence Events Center** – 715 Quince, Florence, OR 97439
Capacity: up to 500 – R/B/S/M/C/
Contact: (541) 997-1994; (888) 968-4086- *See page 96*

**Gearhart Golf Resort**– 1157 N. Marion, Gearhart, OR 97138
Capacity: up to 300 – R/B/S/M/
Contact: (800) 547-0115 *See page 98*

**Inn at Spanish Head** – 4009 S.W. Hwy 101, Lincoln City, OR 97367
Reception: up to 200; Sit-down: up to 150; Guest Rooms: 120 – R/B/S/M/
Contact: Betty Nicholson (541) 994-1617, (800) 452-8127 *See page 111*

**Oregon Coast Aquarium** – 2820 S.E. Ferry Slip Rd., Newport, OR 97365
Sit-down: up to 120; Reception: up to 1,000 – R/B/S/M/C/
Contact: Events Office (541) 867-3474 ext. 5216 See page 129

**Salishan Lodge and Golf Resort** – 7760 Hwy 101 N., Gleneden Beach, OR 97388
Capacity: up to 500; Guest Rooms: 205 – R/B/S/M/C/
Contact: Group Sales (800) 890-9316 See page 449

**Seaside Civic and Convention Center** – 415 First Ave., Seaside, OR 97138
Reception: up to 1,950 – R/B/S/M/C/
Contact: (503) 738-8585, (800) 394-3303; Fax (503) 738-0198 *See page 234*

**Surfsand Resort** – P.O. Box 219, Cannon Beach, OR 97110
Capacity: up to 300; Outdoor: unlimited; Guest Rooms: 82 – R/B/S/M/
Contact: Group Sales (800) 797-4666 *See page 453*

**Surftides Inn at the Beach** – 2945 N.W. Jetty Ave., Lincoln City, OR 97367
Capacity: 140; Guest Rooms: 154 – R/B/S/M/
Contact: (541) 994-2191, Toll Free 1-800-452-2159 *See page 150*

*P=Picnic R=Reception B=Banquet S=Seminar M=Meeting C=Convention*

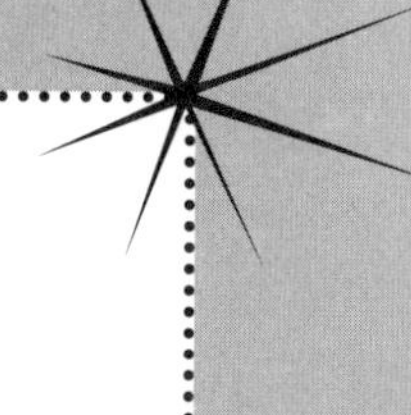

# Park, Boat & Train Listings

# PARK LISTINGS

## CASCADE LOCKS

**Marine Park and Thunder Island** – P.O. Box 307, Cascade Locks, OR 97014
Indoor: up to 175; Outdoor: up to 1,000 – P/R/B/M/
Contact: Sternwheeler Columbia Gorge (541) 374-8427 *See page 386*

## LAKE OSWEGO

**Lake Oswego Parks & Recreation**– P.O. Box 369 Lake Oswego, OR 97034
Contact: Terri Fackrell (503) 675-2546; www.lakeoswegoparks.org – P/

## PORTLAND

**Council Crest Park –** S.W. Council Crest Dr., Portland, OR 97201
Outdoor (no shelter): up to 150 – R/
Contact: Parks Permit Center (503) 823-2525, (503) 823-2514

**Hoyt Arboretum –** 4000 S.W. Fairview Blvd., Portland, OR 97221
Outdoor (shelter): up to 140 – P/R/
Contact: Parks Permit Center (503) 823-2514

**Laurelhurst Park –** S.E. 39th & Oak, Portland, OR 97214
Outdoor (no shelter): 100+ – P/R/
Contact: Parks Permit Center (503) 823-2525

**Oaks Park –** S.E. Portland (Sellwood area), Portland, OR 97202
Capacity: up to 1,000 – P/R/B/S/
Contact: (503) 238-6622 *See page 385*

**The Overlook House –** 3839 N. Melrose Dr., Portland, OR 97227
Indoor: up to 75; Outdoor: up to 150 – P/R/S/M/
Contact: Building Coordinator (503) 823-4524

**Peninsula Park Rose Garden –** N. Albina & Portland Blvd., Portland, OR 97217
Outdoor (shelter):up to 70 – P/R/
Contact: Parks Permit Center (503) 823-2525, Coordinator (503) 823-2514

**Pier Park –** N. Seneca & St. John's, Portland, OR 97203
Outdoor (shelter): 200+ – P/R/
Contact: Parks Permit Center (503) 823-2525

**Washington Park**
**Rose Garden Amphitheater –** 400 S.W. Kingston Blvd., Portland, OR 97201
Outdoor: up to 3,000; P/R/
Contact: Parks Permit Center (503) 823-2525

**Washington Park Rose Garden**
**Gold Medal Garden –** 400 S.W. Kingston Blvd., Portland, OR 97201
Outdoor (small gazebo): up to 100
Contact: Parks Permit Center (503) 823-2525

**Washington Park Rose Garden**
**Shakespearean Garden –** 400 S.W. Kingston Blvd., Portland, OR 97201
Outdoor (no shelter): up to 100
Contact: Parks Permit Center (503) 823-2525

*P=Picnic R=Reception B=Banquet S=Seminar M=Meeting C=Convention*

## ST. PAUL

**Champoeg Park** – 8239 Champoeg Rd. N.E., St. Paul, OR 97137-9709
Indoor: up to 49; Outdoor: up to 200 – P/R/
Reservations Northwest (800) 452-5687; Information Line (503) 678-1251

## TROUTDALE/FAIRVIEW

**Blue Lake Park** – 20500 N.E. Marine Dr., Fairview, OR 97024
Outdoor: up to 7,000; Covered shelters (10): varies: 50-125 people;
Lake House: up to 175 – P/R/B/S/M/
Contact: Metro Regional Parks (503) 797-1834

**Glenn Otto Community Park and Sam Cox Building** –
1120 E. Historical Columbia River Hwy., Troutdale, OR 97060
Indoor: up to 250; Outdoor: up to 1,000 – P/R/B/S/M/
Contact: (503) 665-5175 ext. 238; Fax (503) 665-1137

## WASHINGTON COUNTY

**Cedar Hills Park** – Cedar Hills Blvd. & Walker Rd., Beaverton, OR 97005
Outdoor only: up to 100 – P/R/
Tualatin Hills Park & Recreation (503) 645-3539; Fax (503) 614-9514

**Fanno Farm House** – 8405 SW Creekside Pl., Beaverton, OR 97005
Indoor: up to 35; Outdoor: up to 75 – R/B/S/M
Contact: (503) 642-3855

**Jenkins Estate** – Grabhorn Rd. at S.W. 209th & Farmington, Aloha, OR 97006
Indoor: up to 110; Outdoor: up to 175; Stable: up to 225 – P/R/B/S/M/
Contact: (503) 642-3855; Fax (503) 591-1028

**Metzger Park Hall** – 8400 S.W. Hemlock St., Portland, OR 97223
Indoor Facility Reception: up to 200 – P/R/B/S/M/
Contact: Administrative Assistant. (503) 246-0998

**Raleigh Park** – 3500 S.W. 78th Ave., Portland, OR 97225
Outdoor only: up to 100 – P/R/
Contact: Tualatin Hills Park & Recreation (503) 645-3539

**Scoggins Valley Park/Henry Hagg Lake** –
111 S.E. Washington, Hillsboro, OR 97124
Capacity: "C" Ramp Pavilion: up to 700; Sain Pavilion up to 300;
Two additional sites: up to 125 – P/R/
Contact: Administrative Assistant (503) 846-8715

## WEST LINN

**McLean House and Park** – 5350 River St., West Linn, OR 97068
Indoor & Outdoor: up to 100 – P/R/B/S/M/
Contact: (503) 655-4268

# BOAT & TROLLEY LISTINGS

## BOATS

**Crystal Dolphin** – 110 S.E. Caruthers, Portland, OR 97214
Capacity: up to 120 – P/R/B/S/M/
Contact: (503) 224-3900, (800) 224-3901

*See page 182*

*P=Picnic R=Reception B=Banquet S=Seminar M=Meeting C=Convention*

**Sternwheeler "Columbia Gorge"** – P.O. Box 307, Cascade Locks, OR 97014
Sit-Down: up to 450 – P/R/B/S/M/
Contact: Sales Department (541) 374-8427, (800) 643-1354 *See page 184*

**Portland Spirit** – 110 S.E. Caruthers, Portland, OR 97214
Sit-down: up to 340; Reception: up to 540 – P/R/B/S/M/
Contact: (503) 224-3900, (800) 224-3901 *See page 182*

**Sternwheeler Rose** – 6412 S.W. Vermont Street, Portland, OR 97210
Capacity: up to 130 – P/R/B/S/M/
Contact: (503) 286-7673 *See page 185*

**Willamette Star** – 110 S.E. Caruthers, Portland, OR 97214
Capacity: up to 144 – P/R/B/S/M/
Contact: (503) 224-3900, (800) 224-3901 *See page 182*

## TROLLEYS

**Vintage Trolley & Portland Streetcar** – 115 N.W. First, Ste. 200, Portland, OR 97209
Capacity: up to 70 – R/M/
Contact: (503) 323-7363 *See page 183*

Portland Area Sites

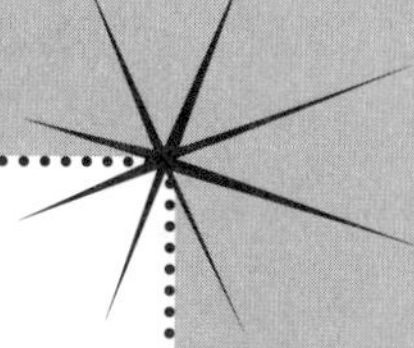

# Portland Area Sites

BravoPortland.com

# DOWNTOWN PORTLAND

**The Adrianna Hill Grand Ballroom** – 918 S.W. Yamhill, 2nd Fl., Portland, OR 97205
Capacity: up to 300 – R/B/S/M/C/
Contact: (503) 227-6285 *See page 74*

**The Benson Hotel** – 309 S.W. Broadway at Oak, Portland, OR 97205
Reception: up to 600; Sit-down: up to 350; Guest Rooms: 286 – R/B/S/M/C/
Contact: Sales (503) 295-4100 *See page 78*

**Days Inn City Center** – 1414 S.W. Sixth Ave., Portland, OR 97201
Capacity: up to 200; Outdoor: up to 400; Guest Rooms: 173 – R/B/S/M/C/
Contact: Catering Sales (503) 221-161, (800) 899-0248 *See page 87*

**Embassy Suites Portland Downtown** – 319 S.W. Pine St., Portland, OR 97204
Sit-down: up to 220; Reception: up to 300; Guest Rooms: 276
Contact: Sales Office (503) 279-9000 ext. 6166 *See page 93*

**The Heathman Restaurant** –
1001 S.W. Broadway at Salmon St., Portland, OR 97205
Sit-down: up to 200; Reception: up to 300 – R/B/S/M/C/
Contact: Catering Office (503) 790-7126 *See page 103*

**Jake's Catering at The Governor Hotel** – 611 S.W. 10th St., Portland, OR 97205
Sit-down: up to 450; Reception: up to 600; Guest Rooms: 100 – R/B/S/M/P/
Contact: Catering Sales (503) 241-2125 *See page 112*

**Jaxs Bar & Restaurant** - 826 S.W. Second Ave., Portland, OR 97205
Sitdown: up to 175; Reception: up to 300 - R/B/M/
Contact: (503) 228-9128 *See page 113*

**Keller Auditorium** – S.W. Third & Clay St., Portland, OR 97201
Sit-down: up to 400; Reception: up to 500; Theatre: up to 3,000 – R/S/M/C/B/
Contact: Booking & Sales (503) 274-6557 or (503) 796-6513 *See page 135*

**Mallory Hotel** – 729 S.W. 15th Ave., Portland, OR 97205
Sit-down: up to 85; Reception: up to 100; Guest Rooms: 130
Contact: (503) 223-6311, (800) 228-8657 *See page 170*

**Pazzo Ristorante Hotel Vintage Plaza** – 627 S.W. Washington, Portland, OR 97205
Sit-down: up to 100 – R/B/S/M/C/
Contact: Private Dining (503) 412-6309 *See page 131*

**Portland Art Museum** – 1219 S.W. Park Ave., Portland, OR 97205
Sit-down: up to 560 in the Grand Ballroom; other rooms vary. – R/B/S/M/C/
Contact: (503) 276-4291 *See page 134*

**Portland Center for the Performing Arts** – 1111 S.W. Broadway, Portland, OR 97205
Newmark Theatre: up to 880; Dolores Winningstad Theatre: up to 292;
Rotunda Lobby: Sit-down: up to 500
Brunish Hall: Sit-down: up to 200 – R/B/S/M/C/
Contact: Booking & Sales (503) 248-4335 *See page 135*

**RiverPlace Hotel** – 1510 S.W. Harbor Way, Portland, OR 97201
Capacity: 200 Guest Rooms: 84 – R/B/S/M/C/
Contact: Sales & Catering (503) 295-6167 *See page 142*

**Rock Bottom Brewery** – 206 S.W. Morrison, Portland, OR 97204
Capacity: up to 100 – R/B/S/M/
Contact: Banquet Coordinator (503) 796-2739 *See page 144*

*P=Picnic R=Reception B=Banquet S=Seminar M=Meeting C=Convention*

**Tiffany Center** – 1410 S.W. Morrison St., Portland, OR 97205
Capacity: up to 1,200 – R/B/S/M/C/
Contact: Events Manager (503) 222-0703 or (503) 248-9305 *See page 152*

**The Treasury** – 326 S.W. Broadway St., Portland, OR 97204
Capacity: up to 300 – R/B/C/M/W
Contact: (503) 226-1240 *See page 154*

**World Trade Center** –
Two World Trade Center; 25 S.W. Salmon St., Portland, OR 97204
Indoor: up to 300; Reception: up to 400
Outdoor: Sit-down: up to 500; Reception: up to 800 – R/B/S/M/C/
Contact: Reservations (503) 464-8688 *See page 163*

## NORTH PORTLAND

**DoubleTree Columbia River** – 1401 N. Hayden Island Dr., Portland, OR 97217
Sit-down: up to 500; Reception: up to 1,400; Guest Rooms: 351 – R/B/S/M/C/
Contact: Sales Office (503) 283-2111 *See page 89*

**DoubleTree Jantzen Beach** – 909 N. Hayden Island Dr., Portland, OR 97217
Sit-down: up to 1,400; Reception: up to 2,000; Guest Rooms: 320 – R/B/S/M/C/
Contact: Sales Office (503) 283-4466 *See page 89*

**Memorial Coliseum** – One Center Court, Ste. 200, Portland, OR 97227
Capacity: up to 12,000 – R/B/S/M/C/
Contact: (503) 235-8771; Fax (503) 736-2192 *See page 233*

**Portland Metropolitan Exposition Center (EXPO)** –
2060 N. Marine Dr., Portland, OR 97217
Capacity: up to 9,000 – P/R/S/M/C/
Contact: Sales Department (503) 736-5200 *See page 228*

**Rose Garden** – One Center Court, Ste. 200, Portland, OR 97227
Arena: up to 21,000; Outdoor: up to 5,000; Reception: up to 300 – P/R/B/S/M/C/
Contact: (503) 235-8771 *See page 233*

**Widmer Gasthaus** – 955 N. Russel, Portland, OR 97227
Capacity: up to 75 – B/P/M/S/
Contact: Manager (503) 281-3333 *See page 159*

## NORTHEAST PORTLAND

**Acadian Ballroom** – 1829 N.E. Alberta St., Portland, OR 97211
Indoor: up to 400; Reception: up to 600 – R/B/
Contact: (503) 546-6800

**Albertina's at the Old Kerr Nursery** – 424 N.E. 22nd Ave., Portland, OR 97232
Capacity: Up to 200 – R/B/
Contact: Event Coordinator (503) 231-3909 *See page 75*

**Ambridge Event Center** – 300 N.E. Multnomah St., Portland, OR 97232
Capacity: Up to 700 – R/B/M/C/S
Contact: (503) 239-9921 *See page 77*

**Bossanova Ballroom** – 722 E. Burnside, Portland, OR 97214
Capacity: 200 seated; up to 600 reception – R/B/
Contact: (503) 233-7855 *See page 80*

**Core Source, The** – 5509 N.E. 30th, Portland, OR 97211
Capacity: Up to 80 – R/B/M/C/S
Contact: (503) 493-9497 *See page 168*

**DoubleTree Lloyd Center** – 1000 N.E. Multnomah, Portland, OR 97232
Capacity: up to 1,100; Guest Rooms: 476 – R/B/S/M/C/
Contact: Catering Department (503) 331-4952 *See page 90*

**The Grotto Conference Center** –
Sandy Blvd. at N.E. 85th Ave., Portland, OR 97294
Capacity: up to 225
Contact: (503) 254-7371 *See page 100*

**Hilton Garden–Airport** – 12048 N.E. Airport Way, Portland, OR 97220
Capacity: up to 100; Guest Rooms: 121 – B/S/M/
Contact: (503) 255-8600 *See page 106*

**Oregon Convention Center** – 777 N.E. MLK Jr. Blvd., Portland, OR 97232
Capacity: up to 2,500 – R/B/S/M/C/
Contact: OCC Sales (503) 235-7575 *See page 230*

**Red Lion Hotel Convention Center** – 1021 N.E. Grand Ave., Portland, OR 97232
Reception: up to 300; Guest Rooms: 174 – R/B/S/M/C/
Contact: Sales & Catering (503) 235-2100 *See page 137*

**Rheinlander German Restaurant** – 5035 N.E. Sandy Blvd., Portland, OR 97213
Capacity: up to 85 seated; 100 reception – R/B/S/M/C/
Contact: Banquet Manager (503) 288-5503 *See page 141*

**Salty's on the Columbia** – 3839 N.E. Marine Dr., Portland, OR 97211
Sit-down: up to 150; Reception: up to 200 – R/B/S/M/
Contact: Sales Department (503) 288-4444 *See page 145*

**Sheraton Portland Airport Hotel** –
8235 N.E. Airport Way, Portland, OR 97220-1398
Sit-down: up to 500; Reception: up to 750; Guest Rooms: 214 – R/B/S/M/
Contact: Sales Department (503) 335-2863 *See page 147*

**Shilo Inn Suites Hotel– Restaurant and Convention Center** –
11707 N.E. Airport Way, Portland, OR 97220
Capacity: up to 400; Guest Rooms: 200 – R/B/S/M/C/
Contact: Catering Office (503) 252-7500 ext. 270 *See page 148*

## NORTHWEST PORTLAND

**BridgePort Brewing Company** – 1313 N.W. Marshall, Portland, OR 97209
Sit-down: up to 150; *Non-smoking – R/B/S/M/
Contact: Event Coordinator (503) 241-7179 ext. 210 *See page 81*

**Ecotrust Conference Center** – 721 N.W. Ninth Ave., Portland, OR 97209
Capacity: up to 130 – R/B/S/M/
Contact: (503) 227-6225 *See page 92*

**Kruger's Farm** – 17100 N.W. Sauvie Island Rd., Portland, OR
Capacity: up to 1,000 – P/R/B/S/M/C/
Contact: (503) 621-3489 *See page 115*

**Montgomery Park** – 2701 N.W. Vaughn St., Portland, OR 97210
Sit-down: up to 400; Reception: up to 800 – R/B/S/M/
Contact: Event Coordinator (503) 224-6958 *See page 123*

*P=Picnic R=Reception B=Banquet S=Seminar M=Meeting C=Convention*

**Pittock Mansion –** 3229 N.W. Pittock Drive, Portland, OR 97210
Sit-down: up to 50; Reception: up to 250 – P/R/B/S/M/
Contact: (503) 823-3623 *See page 133*

**The Uptown Billiard Club –** 120 N.W. 23rd Ave., Portland, OR 97210
Capacity: up to 200 – R/B/M/
Contact: (503) 226-8980 *See page 157*

**Washington County Historical Society and Museum** - 17677 N.W. Springville Rd., Portland, OR 97229
Capacity: up to 100 - R/B/M/S
Contact: (503) 645-5353 *See page 171*

**Wilf's Restaurant and Bar –** N.W. Sixth & Irving, Portland, OR 97209
Sit-down: up to 180; Reception: up to 800– R/B/S/M/
Contact: Manager (503) 223-0070 *See page 160*

## SOUTHEAST PORTLAND

**Chelsea Ballroom, The** – 1510 S.E. 9th., Portland, OR 97214
Capacity: up to 350 – R/B/S/M/
Contact: (503) 236-2759 See page 84

**DeNicola's** – 3520 S.E. Powell Blvd., Portland, OR 97202
Capacity: up to 110 – R/B/
Contact: (503) 239-5220 See page 169

**Eastmoreland Grill at the Eastmoreland Golf Course –**
2425 S.E. Bybee Blvd., Portland, OR 97202
Sit-down: up to 125; Reception: up to 175 – R/B/S/M/
Contact: (503) 775-5910 *See page 91*

**Holocene Lounge** – 1001 S.E. Morrison St., Portland, OR 97214
Capacity: up to 300 – R/B/S/M/
Contact: (503) 239-7639 See page 108

**Melody Ballroom** – 615 S.E. Alder St., Portland, OR 97214
Capacity: up to 1,100 – R/B/S/M/C/
Contact: (503) 232-2759 See page 121

**Molly's Loft on Belmont** – 2236 S.E. Belmont, Porland, OR 97214
Capacity: up to 80 sit-down, 120 reception – R/B/S/M
Contact: (503) 297-9635 ext. 111 See page 122

**Oaks Park Historic Dance Pavilion at Oaks Park (Sellwood)** –
Portland, OR 97202
Indoor: up to 500; Sit-down: up to 275; Reception: up to 500;
Outdoor: up to 1,000 – P/R/B/S/M/
Contact: (503) 238-6622 See page 126

**OMSI–Oregon Museum of Science and Industry** –
1945 S.E. Water Ave., Portland, OR 97214
Capacity: up to 2,500; * after regular museum hours – P/R/B/S/M/C/
Contact: Event Sales Office (503) 797-4671 *See page 127*

## SOUTHWEST PORTLAND

**Chart House Restaurant** - 5700 S.W. Terwilliger Boulevard, Portland, OR 97239
Capacity: up to 200 - R/M/B/S
Contact: (503) 246-696 *See page 83*

*P=Picnic R=Reception B=Banquet S=Seminar M=Meeting C=Convention*

**Rivers at Avalon Hotel & Spa** – 0470 S.W. Hamilton Court, Portland, OR 97201
Capacity: up to 150 – R/B/S/M/
Contact: (503) 802-5814 *See page 143*

**World Forestry Center** – 4033 S.W. Canyon Rd., Portland, OR 97221
Sit-down: up to 250; Reception: up to 300; Outdoor: up to 1,000 – P/R/B/S/M/
Contact: Facilities Coordinator (503) 488-2101 *See page 162*

## AURORA

**Langdon Farms** – 24377 N.E. Airport Rd., Aurora, OR 97002
Capacity: up to 500 – R/B/S/M/
Contact: (503) 678-GOLF *See page 117*

**Willamette Gables** – 10323 Schuler Rd., Aurora, OR 97002
Capacity: up to 200; Sit-down: up to 50 – R/S/M/
Contact: (503) 678-2195 *See page 161*

## BEAVERTON

**The Best Western Greenwood Inn** – 10700 S.W. Allen Blvd., Beaverton, OR 97005
Capacity: up to 800; Guest Rooms: 250 – R/B/S/M/C/
Contact: Catering (503) 643-7444 *See page 79*

**Kingstad Meeting Centers** – 15450 S.W. Millikan Way, Beaverton, OR 97005
Capacity: up to 300 – R/B/S/M/
Contact: (503) 626-6338 *See page 114*

## COLUMBIA GORGE/HOOD RIVER

**Hood River Hotel** – 102 Oak Ave., Hood River, OR 97031
Capacity: up to 200; Guest Rooms: 41 – R/B/S/M/
Contact: Reservations (800) 386-1859; Sales (503) 473-7594 *See page 109*

**Hood River Inn** – 1108 E. Marina Way, Hood River, OR 97031
Sit-down: up to 250; Reception: up to 300; Guest Rooms: 149 – R/B/S/M/
Contact: Sales Office (541) 386-2200; (800) 828-7873 *See page 110*

## FOREST GROVE

**McMenamins–Grand Lodge** – 3505 Pacific Ave., Forest Grove, OR 97116
Capacity: up to 150 Outdoor: up to 1,000; Guest Rooms: 77 – R/B/S/M/
Contact: Group Sales (503) 992-9530 *See page 120*

## GRESHAM

**Persimmon Country Club** – 500 S.E. Butler Rd., Gresham, OR 97080
Capacity: up to 300 – R/B/S/M/
Contact: Catering Department (503) 674-3259 *See page 132*

## HELVETIA

**Garden Vineyards** – Helvetia, OR
Capacity: 500+ – R/B/S/M/
Contact: (503) 547-9046 *See page 97*

**Helvetia Farm & Gardens** – Helvetia, OR
Capacity: 1,000+ – P/R/B/S/M/C
Contact: (503) 789-6221 *See page 104*

*P=Picnic R=Reception B=Banquet S=Seminar M=Meeting C=Convention*

**Helvetia Valley Adventures** – Hillsboro, OR
Capacity: 800 – P/R/B/S/
Contact: (503) 295-7890 *See page 105*

## HILLSBORO/ALOHA

**The Reserve Vineyards & Golf Club** – 4805 S.W. 229th. Ave., Aloha, OR 97007
Capacity: up to 150 – R/B/S/M/
Contact: (503) 259-2010 *See page 139*

**Tuality Health Education Center** – 334 S.E. 8th Ave., Hillsboro, OR 97123
Sit-down: up to 250; Reception: up to 400 – R/B/S/M/
Contact: (503) 681-1700 *See page 155*

**Washington County Fair Complex** – 873 N.E. 34th St., Hillsboro, OR 97124
Capacity: 1,500 – P/R/B/S/M/C/
Contact: (503) 648-1416 *See page 158*

## LAKE OSWEGO

**Clarke's**– 455 Second St., Lake Oswego, OR 97034
Capacity: up to 90
Contact: (503) 636-2667

**Gourmet Stuft Pizza** – 4200 S.W. Mercantile Dr., Lake Oswego, OR 97035
Capacity: up to 80
Contact: General Manager (503) 635-1313 *See page 99*

## MARYLHURST

**Marylhurst University Conference and Retreat Center** –
17600 Pacific Hwy., Marylhurst, OR 97036
Capacity: up to 500; Guest Rooms: 54 – P/R/B/S/M/C/
Contact: Campus Events (503) 697-8730 *See page 119*

## MCMINNVILLE

**Evergreen Aviation Museum** –
500 N.E. Captain Michael King Smith Way, McMinnville, OR 97128
Capacity: up to 3,000 – R/B/S/M/
Contact: (503) 434-4023 *See page 94*

## MILWAUKIE

**Amadeus at the Fernwood** – 2122 S.E. Sparrow St., Milwaukie, OR 97222
Capacity: up to 300 – P/R/B/S/M/
Contact: (503) 659-1735 or (503) 636-6154 *See page 76*

**Paradigm Conference Center** – 3009 S.E. Chestnut, Milwaukie, Oregon 97267
Capacity: up to 290
Contact: (503) 654-6426 *See page 130*

**Ultrazone** – 16074 SE McLoughlin Blvd., Milwaukie, OR 97267
Capacity: up to 150
Contact: (503) 652-1122 *See page 156*

*P=Picnic R=Reception B=Banquet S=Seminar M=Meeting C=Convention*

## MOUNT HOOD/SANDY

**Cooper Spur Mountain Resort** – 10755 Cooper Spur Rd., Mt. Hood, OR 97041
Capacity: up to 70 – R/M/S/C/
Contact: (541) 352-6692 *See page 86*

**Mt. Hood Skibowl – Multorpor Restaurant & Lounge** –
P.O. Box 280, Government Camp, OR 97028
Capacity: up to 250 – P/R/M/S/C/
Contact: (503) 272-3654 *See page 124*

**Mt. Hood Meadows Ski Resort** –
1975 S.W. First Ave, Ste. M, Portland, OR 97201
Capacity: up to 800 – P/R/B/S/M/C/
Contact: Portland Sales Office (503) 287-5438 *See page 124*

**The Resort at The Mountain** – 68010 E. Fairway Ave., Welches, OR 97067
Capacity: up to 700; Guest Rooms: 160 – P/R/B/S/M/
Contact: Director of Sales (503) 622-3101, (800) 669-ROOM *See page 140*

**Timberline Lodge** – Timberline, OR 97028
Sit-down: up to 250; Reception: up to 400; Guest Rooms: 70 – P/R/B/S/M/C/
Contact: (503) 219-3192 *See page 153*

## OREGON CITY

**Abernethy Center and Gardens** – 606 15th St., Oregon City, OR 97045
Indoor: up to 320; Outdoor: up to 500+ – R/B/S/M/
Contact: (503) 722-9400 *See page 73*

**Museum of the Oregon Territory** – 211 Tumwater Dr., Oregon City, OR 97045
Capacity: up to 299 – R/B/S/
Contact: (503) 655-5574 *See page 125*

**Oregon City Golf Club at Lone Oak** – 20124 S. Beavercreek Rd., Oregon City, OR 97045
Sit-down: up to 125; Reception: up to 160 – R/B/S/M/
Contact: Event Coordinator (503) 518-1038 *See page 128*

## TIGARD/TUALATIN/SHERWOOD

**Hayden's Lakefront Grill** – 8187 S.W. Tualatin-Sherwood Rd., Tualatin, OR 97062
Capacity: up to 150 – R/B/
Contact: Sales (503) 691-9111 *See page 101*

**The Sweetbrier Inn** – 7125 S.W. Nyberg Rd., Tualatin, OR 97062
Capacity: up to 400; Guest Rooms: 131 – R/B/S/M/
Contact: Catering Office (503) 692-5800, (800) 551-9167 *See page 151*

## TROUTDALE/FAIRVIEW

**The Lake House at Blue Lake Park** – 21160 N.E. Blue Lake Rd., Fairview, OR 97024
Capacity: up to 150 indoor, 250 outdoor – R/B/S/M/
Contact: (503) 667-3483 *See page 116*

## WILSONVILLE

**Family Fun Center** – 29111 S.W. Town Center Loop W., Wilsonville, OR 97070
Capacity: up to 2,000 in amusement park; 350 in meeting areas– P/R/B/S/M/C/
Contact: Group Sales (503) 685-5000 ext. 21 *See page 95*

*P=Picnic R=Reception B=Banquet S=Seminar M=Meeting C=Convention*

**Holiday Inn Wilsonville Conference Center** – 25425 S.W. 95th Ave., Wilsonville, OR 97070
Sit-down: up to 500; Reception: up to 700; Guest Rooms: 168– R/B/S/M/C/
Contact: Catering Department (503) 682-2211 *See page 107*

# Notes

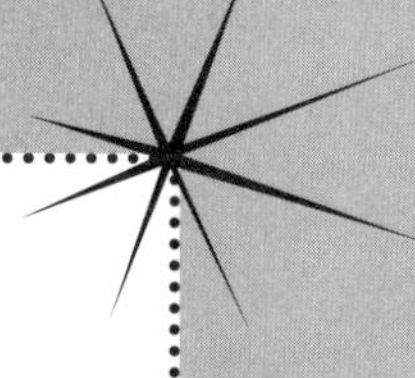

# Salem Area Listings

BravoPortland.com

## ALBANY

**Willamette Events Center at Linn County Fair and Expo –**
3700 Knox Butte Road, Albany, OR
Capacity: up to 6,000 – R/B/S/M/C/
Contact: (541) 926-4314, (800) 858-2005 *See page 237*

## CORVALLIS

**CH2M Hill Alumni Center at OSU –** 204 CH2M Hill, Corvallis, OR 97331
Capacity: please call for details – R/B/S/M/
Contact: (541) 737-2351, (877) 305-3759 *See page 82*

**OSU Conferences and Events –** 100 LaSells Stewart Center, Corvallis, OR 97331
Capacity: up to 1,200 – B/S/M/
Contact: (541) 737-9300, (800) 678-6311 *See page 232*

## GRAND RONDE

**Spirit Mountain Casino** – 27100 Salmon River Hwy., Grand Ronde, OR 97347
Capacity: up to 200; Theatre: up to 250; Guest Rooms: 100 – R/B/S/M/C/
Contact: Group Sales (800) 760-7977 *See page 149*

## SALEM

**Reed Opera House, The –** 189 Liberty St., Salem, OR 97301
Capacity: up to 150 – R/B/S/M/ *See page 138*
Contact: (503) 391-4481

**Salem Conference Center –** 200 Commercial St. SE, Salem, OR 97301
Capacity: up to 1,600 – R/B/S/M/
Contact: (877) 589-1700 *See page 236*

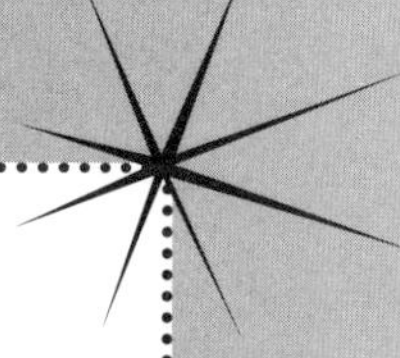

# Vancouver Area Sites

## BELLINGHAM

**Hotel Bellwether** – One Bellwether Way, Bellingham, WA
Sit-down: up to 350; Reception: up to 700 – R/B/S/M/
Contact: (877) 411-1200 *See page 443*

## VANCOUVER

**The Heathman Lodge** – 7801 N.E. Greenwood Dr., Vancouver, WA 98662
Capacity: up to 300; Guest Rooms: 143 – R/B/M/S/
Contact: Catering Office (360) 254-3100, (888) 475-3100 *See page 102*

## WOODLAND

**Lewis River Golf Course** – 3209 Lewis River Rd., Woodland, WA 98674
Capacity: up to 400 – R/B/S/M/
Contact: (360) 225-8566, (800) 341-9426 *See page 118*

# Notes

# Notes

# A



# B

## C



## D

## E



## F



## G

## H



## I



## J



## K



## L

# M



# N

## O



## P

# R



# S

# T



# U



# V



# W

# Y

# Notes

# Notes

# Notes